Always
Elsewhere

THE BLACK ATLANTIC

General Editor: Polly Rewt, The Open University and University of Stirling

Series Advisers: Caryl Phillips, novelist; David Dabydeen, Director, Centre for Caribbean Studies, University of Warwick; Vincent Carretta, Professor of English, University of Maryland; Angus Calder, writer

The cultural and theoretical parameters of the Black Atlantic world are explored and treated critically in this timely series. It offers students, scholars and general readers essential texts which focus on the international black experience. The broad scope of the series is innovative and ambitious, treating literary, historical, biographical, musical and visual arts subjects from an interdisciplinary and cross-cultural perspective.

The books address current debates on what constitutes the Black Atlantic, both geographically and theoretically. They include anthologized primary material and collections of seminal critical value to courses on the African diaspora and related subjects. They will also appeal more widely to a readership interested in biographical and other material that presents scholarship accessibly.

Always Elsewhere

Travels of the Black Atlantic

ALASDAIR PETTINGER

CASSELL
London and New York

For Dorothy and Ted

Cassell

Wellington House, 125 Strand, London WC2R OBB

370 Lexington Avenue, New York, NY 10017–6550

First published 1998

Introduction and editorial apparatus © Alasdair Pettinger 1998
Contributions © as per copyright holders

British Library Cataloguing-in-Publication Data

A catalogue record for this book is available from the British Library.

ISBN 0–304–70084–3 (hardback)
   0–304–70085–1 (paperback)

Library of Congress Cataloging-in-Publication Data

Always elsewhere : travels of the Black Atlantic / Alasdair Pettinger.
       p.   cm. — (The Black Atlantic)
   Includes bibliographical references and index.
   ISBN 0–304–70084–3. — ISBN 0–304–70085–1 (pbk.)
   1. Afro-Americans—Travel.   2. Travellers' writings, American—
Afro-American authors.   I. Pettinger, Alasdair, 1959–   .
   II. Series.
G163.A38   1998
910'. 8996073—dc21   98–8380
                                                                CIP

Designed and typeset by Ben Cracknell Studios

Printed and bound in Great Britain by Biddles Ltd,
Guildford and King's Lynn

Contents

Sources

Nearly all the selections comprise unabridged essays, poems or stories, or whole chapters – or separately identified sections – from larger works. In a few cases, only part of an article or chapter has been reproduced: these are indicated with an asterisk on the source footnote.

The sources are usually the first edition of the work concerned, although – appropriately enough – sometimes the first British edition of a work originally published in the United States was used. Some obvious misprints have been corrected, but spelling and punctuation have not otherwise been changed, except that in some cases double quotation marks have been changed to single, or vice versa. Footnotes and editorial interpolations, where they appear in the original, have generally been retained, although some have been silently omitted.

Introduction

I

In this book, former slaves recall the traumas of the Middle Passage, while African American tourists tell of journeys made in the opposite direction two hundred years later. You can read a famous jazz musician's thoughts on British justice, and the love letters of a revolutionary en route from Vera Cruz to New Orleans. One writer describes the English Lake District for an abolitionist newspaper in the United States; another notes in his diary his impressions of the Great Pyramid of Cheops. Within these pages, a merchant seaman wryly observes the pleasure-seeking passengers on his ship in the Far East; a concert pianist has a narrow escape in the back streets of Santiago, Chile; a child joins her aunt in New York; a nurse surveys the battlefields at the close of the Crimean War, wondering where she will go next. In one extract an American, denied a passport for thirty years, returns to Barcelona. In another, a Cuban exile addresses students in Prague.

Travel writing has enjoyed something of a resurgence in recent years. Classics have been reissued, forgotten works brought to light, and contemporary authors have taken to the genre with renewed enthusiasm. The literature now boasts a considerable body of critical and historical analysis. But who writes about travel and why?

Bill Buford, the former editor of *Granta* magazine, which has done much to rekindle this new interest in travel writing, suggests it is the product of a particular set of circumstances – 'where a traveller goes to a place where we haven't been, is prepared to undergo some sort of adventure, and comes back with something we didn't know'. This is certainly not a neutral definition. It is a defence of travel writing 'in its most traditional and old-fashioned sense', set against 'tourist writing' – the kind of writing which appears in newspapers and colour supplements and 'is fundamentally about place and about places that are pleasant to be in'.[1]

Whether this contrast holds, and how 'traditional and old-fashioned' it actually is, may well be open to question, but it does capture something of the flavour of travel writing as it is commonly construed. It suggests what makes a particular text *count* as 'travel writing', allowing it to be marketed, reviewed and read as such. It is not simply an account of a journey; there are quite strict conditions which the text must meet (even if publishers and bookshops admit exceptions from time to time). Travel books are characterized by a very specific relationship between author, reader and visited place. The authors are most likely to be professional writers who travel at least partly in order to write about it: 'adventure' is the key word here, conjuring up a journey planned to be *interesting*. They typically have no strong link (such as work or family) with the place and do not stay long; their next book will usually be about somewhere else entirely. And the work is aimed at readers who are presumed to be sedentary and ignorant about the destination concerned.

Few, if any, of the selections which appear in this book fully conform to such a model. And yet they are all representations of journeys in one way or another, remarking on an encounter with a culture that is not (or not quite) the author's 'own'. To call them 'travel writings' is perhaps a little provocative – particularly in the case of slave narratives which, some will argue, fit uncomfortably in such a category. But perhaps the conventional definition is too closely tied to the image of a particular kind of travel: it neglects others, or at least forgets that other kinds of travel also find their way into print. Although many of the texts represented here may attract attention – and be profitably read – because they belong to some other category (the *oeuvre* of a famous author, a related genre such as reportage or autobiography or autobiographical fiction), they will also benefit from being read as travel writing, even if it means stretching the concept a little. Grouping them together like this makes it possible to identify certain continuities that might otherwise go unremarked.

II

'Black Atlantic', the term which marks out the historical and geographical parameters of this anthology and the series in which it appears, was coined, or at least put into general circulation, by Paul Gilroy in his 1993 book of the same name.[2] To some extent, 'Black Atlantic' is simply a slogan, a call for a strategic realignment in the study of Black history. It challenges the common tendency to comprehend it in terms of a single trajectory that runs back to pre-colonial Africa (the pull of the ancient homeland, if you like) and forwards to North America (the promise – however distant – of full participation in modernity). The *Atlantic* – precisely because it lies *between* these points of anchorage – offers an alternative model. It encourages us to think of the diaspora not as a river, gathering its tributaries in a relentless voyage to a final destination, but as a vast ocean that touches many shores – Africa, Europe, the Caribbean, the Americas (North, Central and South) – criss-crossed in all directions by people, goods and ideas.

This serves to remind us how varied and extensive the diaspora has become. As Langston Hughes remarked, 'I have learned that there is at least one Negro everywhere'[3] – even in Turkmenistan, which prompted his observation, or the far north of Norway as Caryl Phillips was surprised to discover several decades later (pp. 154–5). Even the least-travelled inhabitant of the remotest village is now touched by transcontinental formal and informal networks – of information, cultural borrowing, mutual aid, emotional solidarity, political collaboration. The Black Atlantic includes, for example, the anti-slavery movements, the various initiatives embraced by the term 'pan-Africanism', syncretic cultural formations such as *vodun*, cricket or jazz; and the travelling, mailing and phoning that keep the members of extended diasporic families in touch with each other.

At bottom, such interconnections rely on modern communication and transport networks: the pages that follow are predictably rich in references to ships, planes, buses, taxis, docks, airports, railway stations, post-offices, cabins, hotels, luggage, maps, timetables and guidebooks. Although the development of these networks on an intercontinental scale was prompted by the imperial expansion of the nineteenth century, they were never simply an instrument of colonial domination; they embody the promise of a global community. In some formulations, Gilroy's 'Black Atlantic' is cohesive enough to be described as a transnational 'counter-culture of modernity', whose leading intellectuals move from one country to another with relative ease and whose rhetoric is appropriately cosmopolitan.

But first and foremost, the 'Black Atlantic' is simply a collective noun embracing the intercontinental movements of Black Africans and their descendants since the late eighteenth century. Historically, of course, the diaspora goes much further back than this. But it was not until the emergence of the anti-slavery movement in Europe and the Americas, and the development of new forms of trading relationships with Africa, that one can speak of a class of Black intellectuals (abolitionists, missionaries, merchants) sufficiently organized to form transatlantic networks of their own. The same processes created markets which enabled accounts of travels they themselves wrote to be published.

Even though Black populations are concentrated in, and travel between, the continents which border the Atlantic, there is – as one critic has recently suggested – a 'Black Pacific' too.[4] This anthology has not interpreted the term so literally, and, since it has not been assembled with the intention of documenting the existence of a single coherent entity, has been happy to include accounts of journeys that begin or end elsewhere. Australia, Japan and India all appear unapologetically in the index.

III

The main title of this book has been taken from a poem by Fred D'Aguiar (p. 280). The phrase 'home is always elsewhere' conveys the attitude of a British immigration official who does not recognize the narrator's unequivocal right to enter the country he was born in. In the context of the poem it has a negative tone, but detached from it, the expression, I hope, captures the sense of permanent displacement and bi-nationality found in many of the writings selected for this volume in a way that does not prejudge its character. Displacement, whether enforced or not, can be a cause for mourning or celebration, neither or both. For different authors respond to it in many different ways.

Diasporic travels are perhaps most characteristically those one-way journeys which lead to extended stays or even permanent settlement. For migrants and exiles, then, there is 'home' and there is 'back home'.[5] But even those with a return ticket, like the conventional travel writer, sometimes have reason, or are expected, to at least consider not going back, as Albert Luthuli found during a lecture tour of the United States (p. 197).[6] In any case it is rarely simply 'adventure' they come looking for: the overseas voyages of Black Atlantic travellers are more likely to be undertaken on behalf of a cause (abolitionism, anti-lynching, the defence of Republican Spain) or to earn a living (as a member of one of those peripatetic professions – missionary, musician, sportsman, soldier, sailor) or to visit relatives (the parents or grandparents who have stayed at home).

Whether this sense of displacement could serve as the differentiating mark of the travels of the Black Atlantic, however, is doubtful. For one thing, even on the basis of the small sample offered by the extracts reprinted here, one could hardly claim that it is an *essential* feature, underlying every one of such a diverse range of cultural experiences. Some writers feel it quite keenly, others don't register it at all. The 'Black Atlantic' does not possess an institutional structure formal enough to enable one to speak of a set of rules or principles to which 'its' practices must conform. And for another, bi- or tri- or even supra-national identity is hardly a uniquely *Black* phenomenon. A comparable anthology of travel writings of the Chinese – or Jewish, Indian, Palestinian, Irish – diaspora would doubtless reveal certain continuities with this collection, suggesting that any common motifs discernible in the work of Black travel writers may well be more widely shared.

Indeed, some critics may claim that we are *all* somehow 'always elsewhere' nowadays. It has become something of a postmodernist cliché to assert that some travelling figure such as the migrant or the tourist is simply a more visible, dramatic embodiment of a universal condition. To some extent, the idea that everyone is a migrant is a useful one: it breaks down the invidious distinction between 'native' and 'foreigner' which underpins a common type of racism. But it becomes unhelpful when it turns into the supposition of a generalized 'nomadism' where distinctions between different forms of displacement are lost – where refugees, conscripts, au pairs, holiday-makers, diplomats and visiting lecturers are grouped together and set on the same footing.[7]

More difficult, but essential, is the need to be alert to certain similarities without losing sight of the differences. John Western, in his oral history of Barbadian Londoners, writes that his own migratory experiences as a white Englishman now living in the United States helped him understand some aspects of the lives of those he interviewed, even though in most cases their reasons for travelling, their social status, their complex sense of 'home', are rather at odds with his own.[8]

IV

This anthology has not been assembled with the intention of making a claim for the special distinctiveness of travel writing by Black authors. While the concept of the 'Black Atlantic' helps to de-centre the diaspora and encourages a move away from a reliance on simple over-arching narratives on which its study has long been dependent, it is less useful when used to promulgate a new general theory – in fact it reproduces the same kind of problems it was designed to overcome.[9]

The case for collecting these texts in one volume must be made on more strategic grounds. In some respects the book forms part of the broader project of 'decolonizing' or 'democratizing' travel literature which has begun to take shape in the last decade or so. Following a pattern already established – in the world of prose fiction, poetry and drama – critics, editors and publishers have been challenging the way the canon of 'great works' of travel writing has tended to automatically privilege white men, and in response they have endeavoured to assert the rights, so to speak, of the unrepresented. Reissues, new critical editions and, of course, anthologies have played an important role in this enterprise. It has led to an increased awareness of women travel writers, for instance, and now there is a sizeable body of critical work devoted to the question of 'gender and travel writing'.[10] A recent collection of writings by disabled travellers may herald renewed interest in this area too.[11]

However, these initiatives, with few exceptions, have focused almost exclusively on *white* authors. If anthologies of 'travel literature' ignore women and Black men, anthologies of 'women's travel literature' ignore Black women. Unfortunately it seems that – if only in the immediate short term – Black travel writers will not be more widely known unless they are explicitly and primarily identified as such, even though this runs the risk – as, in a similar way, do those anthologies organized around the sex of the author – of seeming to make essential claims about 'race'.

This anthology is an attempt to redress the balance. In some ways it departs from, or challenges, more conventional definitions of travel writing – in which the works of relatively privileged Europeans and North Americans are taken as the norm. But those expecting the extracts which follow to offer something completely *different* will be disappointed. In grouping together writings whose only common factor is the fact that their authors are Black, this anthology – unlike those organized around a single subject or theme or point of view – is founded on the principle of divergence rather than convergence. It aims to present as *wide* a range of writings as possible – in terms of both the travelling experience itself (motive, means of transport, destination) and the modes of representation used to convey that experience. The point is not, of course, to demonstrate that 'race' is a meaningless category without effects, but that it would be rash to specify those effects in advance.

I have borne in mind that the extracts chosen should afford plenty of scope to those accustomed to analysing literary or anthropological texts – from their choice of tense or person to their pace and order (or disorder) of exposition. The extracts are complete in themselves, or at least relatively self-contained sections or chapters from larger works. I have given preference to those which convey a strong sense of place, and which therefore include fairly detailed descriptions or lively dialogue.

They should also provide useful primary sources for those coming to the book from a more sociological orientation. The 1990s have seen an outpouring of books with titles or chapters which juggle permutations of words like migration, borders, displacement, nation, location, local, global, diaspora, post-colonial, geography and map. Yet their authors tend to illustrate their arguments with reference to literary fiction rather than travel writing.[12] By including first-person accounts of a wide range of travels, perhaps this anthology will show that there is a wealth of non-fiction rich enough to serve these purposes too.

But above all, the anthology offers the more immediate pleasures – not always comfortable – of recognition and surprise, of fantasy and instruction, that characterize those writings which best evoke the shock of encountering new people and places which travel over long distances usually provokes.

V

If it is not possible – nor perhaps even desirable – to specify the essential, defining characteristics of travel writings of the Black Atlantic, it may nevertheless be helpful to identify some issues which are inevitably raised by this volume and suggest further avenues for research and analysis.

THE RIGHT TO TRAVEL

If the modern world is, as they say, getting smaller, and we are entering an age of globalization, the nation-state continues to play a decisive role. Although it is true that ideas travel more widely than ever before (and nations are increasingly culturally diverse), the infrastructural networks which they use depend on agreements (on anything from copyright to standards of measurement) between states, which in turn ensure that they can be and are adhered to within the territories they govern. When we turn to the movement of *people*, the role of the state is much more obvious. Even in a collection of travel writings, the obstacles put in the way of most travellers of the Black Atlantic are amply documented: the difficulty in obtaining passports, visas and permits; the harassment at national frontiers, being turned away; expulsion. And wherever the rules followed by Western states in regulating the movement of people across their borders are racially discriminatory, those people of colour who live and work in a country quite legitimately will always be potentially illegal aliens in the eyes of public authorities.[13]

Dramas of obtaining visas and crossing frontiers are a regular source of light narrative diversion in much travel writing of the modern period, but for many travellers represented in this book, they often acquire a rather more ominous aspect. If the Black Atlantic began with the trauma of the enforced movement of people, it has become a domain in which even the most mundane forms of travel can become exceedingly difficult.

To some extent, these barriers exist at the level of cultural expectations. In a recent anthology, one writer suggests that the very *idea* that Black people might actually travel for the sake of it is hard for some to accept: 'Are you visiting relatives?' 'Do you work here?'[14] But then, as a contributor to the same collection half-answers, 'former sharecroppers do not teach their children to travel for pleasure'.[15] And even if they learn some other way, their options still appear to be restricted, as a third author discovered when her travel piece was turned down by her editor. 'With pity in his voice he blurted, "Black people don't go to Iceland".'[16]

But it is the more tangible obstructions put in the way by the state that grab the attention. Some travellers tell of the difficulty in obtaining passports because of a lack of documentation of date and place of birth that would satisfy the authorities.[17] The Angolan Eva Carvalho de Chipenda explains that she has to go to Portugal to get her passport before she can take up her scholarship to study in Brazil (p. 68).

Passports are sometimes denied altogether, making foreign travel impossible without paying a heavy penalty. Notoriously, Black South Africans found in the 1960s that the only way they could leave the country was with an 'exit visa' which rendered them stateless.[18] American volunteers hoping to join the International Brigade in 1937 found their passports stamped 'Not Valid for Spain' and had to enter the country secretly from France.[19] Paul Robeson, W. E. B. Du Bois and Richard Wright are simply the best-known of many African Americans whose right to travel was withheld by the State Department. The actions of British and US authorities prevented some delegates from attending the Pan-African Congress in Paris in 1919.[20] The British refused a passport for Marcus Garvey to visit West Africa in 1923; and he was later expelled from the United States. In 1930 Claude McKay was barred from entering British territory (including his native Jamaica).[21] Similarly Miriam Makeba found she could not return to South Africa when she tried to arrange a flight back from New York.[22]

Immigration restrictions of course have impeded the free movement of people, including relatives and spouses. Nicolás Guillén mentions that on one visit to New York he never got further than Ellis Island (p. 118). C. L. R. James, on the other hand, overstayed his welcome and, despite his marriage to an American, was deported in 1953, as was Sidney Bechet from Britain in 1920 (pp. 171–2). Caryl Phillips writes of his less than warm welcome at Oslo's airport (pp. 152–3), and D'Aguiar of his at London Heathrow (p. 280).

WHAT A DIFFERENCE A BORDER MAKES
Once these obstacles are overcome, travellers of the Black Atlantic frequently observe 'what a difference a border makes'.[23] Again, this is something of a commonplace: Claude Lévi-Strauss remarked that 'not only does a journey transport us over enormous distances, it also causes us to move a few degrees up or down in the social scale'.[24] He notes, for instance, how, in Brazil, 'from being poor I had become rich'; while, arriving in New York after the Armistice, the reverse was true. But there are some extra considerations here that the French anthropologist does not contemplate. Consider Langston Hughes:

> In El Paso it was strange to find that just by stepping across an
> invisible line into Mexico, a Negro could buy a beer in any bar, sit
> anywhere in the movies, or eat in any restaurant, so suddenly did Jim
> Crow disappear, and Americans visiting Juarez, who would not drink
> beside a Negro in Texas, did so in Mexico. Funny people,
> Southerners![25]

In the pages that follow, there are numerous examples of foreign travel offering a (temporary) respite from racism, particularly on the part of African Americans in Europe – a theme which echoes from accounts of the Black abolitionists in Britain in the mid-nineteenth century, through to the observations made by late twentieth-century tourists. Though there are also those who argue that this is something of a mirage, travel abroad nevertheless can be instructive, shattering preconceptions of race: a common image is the shock of encountering white manual workers in the 'mother' country (pp. 66–7, 69); another source of enlightenment is the journey from a colony to a now-independent country, as Chipenda is inspired to meet more self-confident Black women in Brazil (pp. 70–1).

Crossing borders involves not only a change of social status, but often a change of *colour* too. As different countries have different systems of racial classification, one may be 'Black' in one country and not in another. This explains why the American Robert Campbell writes of the West Africans he meets that 'they at first regarded me as a white man, until I informed them of my connection with the Negro'.[26] And why the narrator of *An African Savage's Own Story* is puzzled to encounter a 'coloured man' in Philadelphia, 'who, incidentally, was not black, but white. How could they call *him* coloured? What a mix-up!' (p. 175).[27] It is in the contrast between the Manichean either/or of the United States and the complex gradations and tensions between colour and class in the Caribbean that this comes across most vividly. For Belmira Nunes Lopes, daughter of Cape Verdean immigrants who grew up in New England and who spent six years in Puerto Rico – where they 'don't use the same standard for whiteness' – this prompts extended reflections on the constructedness of 'race' in her autobiography, implying that colour is – for some people at least (and the author is assumed by her friends to be one of them) – a matter of *choice*.[28]

SMALL WORLDS

Centred on a protagonist–narrator who rarely stays in one place for long, the conventional travel book tends to assume an irreconcilable gulf between a mobile, singular author and static, plural 'natives'. The overwhelming emphasis is on the unique experiences of the individual traveller, who is the subject rather than object of knowledge – the visitor asking questions to which the host provides answers; rarely, except for comic effect, the other way around.

For many of the travellers represented in this book, this is not the case. Wherever they go, they are constantly bumping into people who are as well-travelled as they are. Of course, the travels are not always comparable. The encounters may give rise to the kind of heavy irony of a scene in Claude McKay's autobiography where he stands before a judge in Pennsylvania who, when he hears where the prisoner is from, comments:

> 'Nice place. I was there a couple of seasons ago.' And, ignoring my case and the audience, the judge began telling me of his trip to Jamaica and how he enjoyed it, the climate, the landscape, and the natives. He mentioned some of the beauty spots and I named those I knew. 'I wish I were there instead of here,' he said. 'I wish I were there too,' I echoed him. I could quite understand how he felt, for who would not like to escape from a winter in steely, smoky, stonefaced Pittsburgh! [29]

And in an echo of McKay, Jamaica Kincaid invokes a similar contrast between the journey which takes a young West Indian to work as a nanny in a North American city and the Caribbean vacations of her employers and their friends: 'somehow it made me ashamed to come from a place where the only thing to be said about it was "I had fun when I was there".'[30]

Black travellers are often the object of curiosity in ways that whites are not. Even in the proverbial jungles, mountains and deserts beloved of the conventional travel author, the Europeans are hardly unknown; if their writings are anything to go by, it is their 'magic' technology that attracts attention rather than themselves. It would be difficult to find a parallel to C. L. R. James's description of the glances cast his way on the London Underground (pp. 113–14) in an Englishman's description of the West Indies. And doubtful if there is anything quite matching up to the 'entrance' of the Togolese, Tété-Michel Kpomassie, onto the quayside in Greenland (p. 138) in the classics of polar exploration.

Their accounts frequently exhibit a sense of racial solidarity which is usually unmarked in travel writing by white authors whose search for an Other is, if anything, threatened by the appearance of someone who looks the Same. Dismissive remarks about fellow-tourists are few and far between. On the other hand, there are numerous examples of diasporic rendezvous: visitors to New York often gravitate to Harlem; members of the expatriate community of African Americans in Ghana feature in each other's writings; Black supporters of the Republican cause find their paths crossing in the Spanish Civil War.

Sometimes the encounters have a 'small world' flavour. Guillén bumps into an old Cuban acquaintance in Harlem (pp. 120–1); Lewis Nkosi recognizes a member of the Pan-Africanist Congress in Paris (p. 82); and in Berlin, Mary Church Terrell is surprised to meet an old friend, the violinist Will Marion Cook (p. 43). On other occasions, the expected fellowship of colour may turn out to be illusory – as in Caryl Phillips's unexpected encounter with a Trinidadian woman and an Eritrean 'brother' in Norway (pp. 154–5). This is so even, or perhaps especially, in the case of those travels to Africa undertaken by those for whom the ancestral bond has become almost meaningless. 'I had understood nothing,' writes Richard Wright about an experience in Accra. 'I was black and they were black, but my blackness did not help me' (p. 232).

DIVIDED LOYALTIES

Finally, the questions of 'home' and of national identity. As Virginia Woolf famously said, 'as a woman I have no country. As a woman I want no country. As a woman my country is the whole world.'[31] It is tempting to argue that patriotism is similarly weak across the Black Atlantic. On the high seas, also in the turbulent late 1930s, Hugh Mulzac comes to the realization that 'my allegiance did not lie with states, kings, or national boundaries *but with people*' (p. 183).

Certainly he had little reason to be grateful to the United States, where his colour meant it was impossible for him to get a job that matched his qualifications and experience. But if this is cosmopolitanism, it is perhaps more apparent than real. Proclaiming a disregard for national schemes is a luxury generally afforded only by those who have never found their right to travel or return home in question. To generalize it across the Black Atlantic would only confirm the suspicions of the American Secret Service agent who tests the loyalty of Addie Hunton and Kathryn Johnson working alongside US troops in World War I. The women pass the test with flying colours. It is true that they rather regret missing 'so splendid an opportunity to share with him certain truths about colored folk at home that he probably had not learned' (pp. 162–3). But this hardly leads them to question their 'longing to serve' those 'virile lads with soul and body steeled for the hour' (pp. 161–6).

Behind the celebration of 'nomadic' identities often lurks a rather patronizing, even contemptuous, attitude towards those 'still' in the grip of nationalist loyalties – replacing the assertion of the superiority of one country over another with a similar assertion of the superiority of cosmopolitans over nationalists. Yet such an attitude is not very helpful for someone fighting a deportation order. It becomes useless when confronted with a real danger such as the threat of foreign invasion or the intensification of colonial rule: sides must be chosen. Fascism was defeated not by déraciné intellectuals but by modern states imposing huge sacrifices on the part of their civilian population. And for all their extended stays in Paris, London and New York, many Black Atlantic exiles returned to play a major part in national liberation movements in Africa and the Caribbean.

There is rarely an unambiguous declaration of allegiance to a single country in this book. But rare too is the romance of world citizenship. More common is a bi- (or perhaps tri-) national identity in which the disappointments of one and the compensations of another coexist, often in creative tension. Writing of her second trip to Europe in 1902, the American Mary Church Terrell declares that:

> Goethe says that everybody was born and reared to have a fatherland
> and a motherland. The country in which I was born and reared and
> lived is my fatherland, of course, and I love it genuinely, but my
> motherland is dear, broadminded France in which people with dark
> complexions are not discriminated against on account of color.[32]

'Home' rarely features in conventional travel writing, for its certainties (safe but boring) can usually be taken for granted. For many authors represented in this collection, it is not always clear where 'home' is. And for that reason it is the subject of a much wider range of emotions – nostalgia, indifference, exasperation, perplexity, embarrassment. In any case, the expected contrast between the familiarity of home and the strangeness of abroad that underpins so much travel literature is often absent.

VI

A word or two about some of the rules of inclusion and exclusion adopted in compiling this anthology, though they have not been adhered to blindly and do admit a few exceptions. Firstly, it is restricted to accounts of journeys between continents – requiring travel by sea or air. It does not, therefore, include narratives of travels from the Southern states of the USA to the north, for instance, or from one part of Africa to another.

Secondly, the extracts are mostly first-person accounts. There are many travels of the Black Atlantic we know about only indirectly – in biographies, reports in newspapers, fleeting references in historical works. Consider, for instance, the case of John Glasgow, a West Indian sailor who set up a farm near Liverpool with his English wife, but when he went back to sea, found himself in 1828 in a Savannah jail and because the captain of his ship refused to pay for his release he was sold at the auction block and ended up on a Georgia plantation.[33] Or that of Nigerian student Robert Nbaraonje, who stowed away in the coal bunker of an England-bound steamer at Freetown in order to get to England and join the RAF.[34] Because neither left an account of his experiences, they could not be represented here.

But I have not applied the rule too strictly. Not all the accounts included are 'direct': apart from the obvious case of translation, there are as-told-to narratives, texts which bear the obvious (and sometimes unwarranted) intrusion of editors, and the invisible revisions that often take place in the publication of oral histories. There are several extracts of a self-evidently *literary* character (fiction, poetry, drama) – the speaking voice here may be deemed autobiographical to a greater or lesser extent – but they are included because they re-create diasporic experiences poorly represented in non-fictional narratives.

The third limitation is the availability of writings in the English language. While translations from the Cuban poet Nicolás Guillén were made specially for this volume, for the most part I had to rely on material already published. As the translation priorities of publishers are heavily geared towards fiction, most travel accounts in French, and especially in Dutch, Spanish and Portuguese, are as yet inaccessible to English-speaking readers. A few of these works are mentioned in the Suggestions for Further Reading at the end of this book.

Finally, the selection tends to favour writings which are out of print (either in the United States or the United Kingdom) over those by authors well-known on both sides of the Atlantic. In general, I have avoided including texts which have appeared in other recent anthologies that overlap at certain points with this one. The chief exceptions are the narratives of the Middle Passage excerpted in Part One – but since the experience forms a major point of reference in accounts of later journeys of migrants, exiles and conscripts (for example, that of Donald Hinds: pp. 57–67) they provide a crucial resource for any study of Black travel writing.

VII

The material in this book is organized into six sections, which are defined not so much geographically or historically, but rather according to a combination of the perspective and subject matter of each text. In most cases, this is a question of emphasis only, as the extracts are too internally complex to fit comfortably into one section or another, especially as they often contain accounts of the travel experiences of people the authors meet as well as those of the authors themselves.

It opens with 'Middle Passages', which includes accounts of enslavement in Africa, the terrifying voyage across the Atlantic and landing on American soil. The sheer problems these texts face in representing such a traumatic experience have led more recent authors to try to capture it more imaginatively, and examples of their approaches are included too.[35]

As a reminder of the importance of Old Testament frames of reference in Black Atlantic cultures, Part Two is entitled 'Stranger in a Strange Land' (Exodus 3:22). This includes writings born of major upheavals such as migration and exile. The extracts convey the sense of displacement experienced by, for instance, passengers on sea voyages or new arrivals in a foreign city – where the tension between 'home' and 'abroad' is perhaps at its most acute.

In Part Three the emphasis is on the description of places and encounters with others, rather than on the more subjective registers foregrounded in Parts Two and Four. The reason for travelling is less prominent here, and the selection includes the work of exiles as well as of more casual travellers, but perhaps the most typical author here is the one who undertakes a voyage in order to write about it. I have called this part 'Ethnography in Reverse', an expression used by the Cameroonian anthropologist Massaër Diallo to describe his research into the white clients of African *marabouts* in Paris – though it also carries echoes of Louise Bennett's famous poem about Caribbean migration to Britain, 'Colonization in Reverse'.[36]

'Tours of Duty' provides a few examples of the short-stay visits undertaken by Black Atlantic travellers – for business more often than for pleasure. The writers here focus on the professional activity which provides the reason for travel – their work as entertainers, delegates, sailors, or on wartime service.

Writings about 'Africa', however, are included in a section of their own. Visits to the continent have assumed a special importance in diasporic Black culture, particularly in the United States. The aim here has been to suggest the range of reasons which have prompted different authors to visit the 'motherland' and of their responses to the encounter.

Finally, Part Six, 'Home', features narratives in which the idea of 'home' plays an important role. They are not all accounts of return journeys – to the land of one's birth or residence or that of one's parents or grandparents – but in each case, where 'home' is – and how easy it is to go there – turns out to be the cause of some confusion or misunderstanding.

NOTES

1. Bill Buford interviewed in Woolnough 1991.
2. Gilroy 1993.
3. Hughes 1993: 104.
4. Lipsitz 1997: 327.
5. Bridglal 1990: 88.
6. See also Douglass 1969: 376; Terrell 1996: 98–9; Anderson 1957: 127.
7. See Woodhull 1993: 88–102.
8. Western 1992: 1–26.
9. See Pettinger 1994, 1998.
10. See, for instance, Jane Robinson 1991, 1995; Morris 1994; Mills 1991; Sharpe 1993; Ware 1992.
11. Walsh 1991.
12. Among those which I have found particularly interesting are: Bammer 1994; Brennan 1997; Chambers and Curti 1995; Clifford 1997; George 1996; Gikandi 1997; Kaplan 1996; and King, Connell and White 1995.
13. Barry 1996; Hirst and Thompson 1996; Clarke 1992.
14. Lazard 1997: 223; see also Kpomassie 1983: 54.
15. Nayo 1997: 232.
16. Bolden 1997: 312.
17. See e.g. Yates 1989: 15, 98–101; Schuyler 1966: 175.
18. See e.g. Nakasa 1995: 167–71; Nkosi 1983: vii–viii.
19. See Kelley 1992: 25; Hughes 1992: 108.
20. Geiss 1974: 237.
21. Langley 1973: 97; Cooper and Reinders 1967: 75.
22. Makeba 1988: 98.
23. Hughes 1993: 399.
24. Lévi-Strauss 1976: 104–5.
25. Hughes 1993: 63.
26. Bell 1969: 171.
27. See also Hughes 1986: 11.
28. Nunes 1982: 121–9.
29. McKay 1995: 8.
30. Kincaid 1994: 65.
31. Woolf 1977: 125.
32. Terrell 1996: 209.
33. Brown 1855: 228–33.
34. Lambo 1994: 133.
35. Others include Dabydeen 1994; Charles Johnson 1991.
36. N'Djehoya and Diallo 1984: 125–30; Bennett 1966: 179–80.

Acknowledgements

For advice and encouragement I wish to thank Vicky Davidson, Polly Rewt, Alan Rice and, especially, Peter Hulme, who also kindly agreed to translate the pieces by Nicolás Guillén. I would also like to thank Frank Faragasso, David Killingray, Phyllis Peres and Pamela Smorkaloff for their helpful suggestions.

This work would not have been possible without a research grant from the Humanities Research Board of the British Academy. I was greatly assisted by the staff of several libraries, including Glasgow University Library, the National Library of Scotland, the British Library, the Commonwealth Institute, the Bibliothèque Nationale de France, the Library of Congress, the Schomberg Center for Research in Black Culture, and the Rare Books Division of Cornell University Library. Special thanks to Jim Murray of the C. L. R. James Institute in New York.

I owe a special debt of gratitude to many friends, especially Rory O'Connell, Claire Nunns and Dom McLoughlin for their generous hospitality, and my colleagues, past and present, at the Scottish Music Information Centre, for their support and unfailing good humour.

Middle
Passages

GEORGE C. WOLFE

'Git on Board'

George C. Wolfe (b. 1954) was born in Kentucky, and studied in California and New York. He has won many awards as director, librettist and playwright, and his work includes the musical Jelly's Last Jam *(1992) and the dance musical* Bring in 'da NOISE, Bring in 'da FUNK *(1996). 'Git on Board' is the first of a series of eleven satirical vignettes or 'exhibits' which make up his play* The Colored Museum *(1987). Wolfe is currently director of the Public Theater / New York Shakespeare Festival.*

(*Blackness. Cut by drums pounding. Then slides, rapidly flashing before us. Images we've all seen before, of African slaves being captured, loaded onto ships, tortured. The images flash, flash, flash. The drums crescendo. Blackout. And then lights reveal* MISS PAT, *frozen. She is black, pert, and cute. She has a flip to her hair and wears a hot pink mini-skirt stewardess uniform.*)

(*She stands in front of a curtain which separates her from an offstage cockpit.*)

(*An electronic bell goes 'ding' and* MISS PAT *comes to life, presenting herself in a friendly but rehearsed manner, smiling and speaking as she has done so many times before.*)

MISS PAT: Welcome aboard Celebrity Slaveship, departing the Gold Coast and making short stops at Bahia, Port Au Prince, and Havana, before our final destination of Savannah.

    Hi. I'm Miss Pat and I'll be serving you here in Cabin A. We will be crossing the Atlantic at an altitude that's pretty high, so you must wear your shackles at all times.

(*She removes a shackle from the overhead compartment and demonstrates.*)

    To put on your shackle, take the right hand and close the metal ring around your left hand like so. Repeat the action using your left hand to secure the right. If you have any trouble bonding yourself, I'd be more than glad to assist.

    Once we reach the desired altitude, the Captain will turn off the 'Fasten Your Shackle' sign . . . (*She efficiently points out the 'FASTEN YOUR SHACKLE' signs on*

George C. Wolfe, *The Colored Museum* (London: Methuen, 1987), pp. 1–6. Copyright © 1985, 1987, 1988 by George C. Wolfe. Used by permission of Grove/Atlantic, Inc.

either side of her, which light up.) . . . allowing you a chance to stretch and dance in the aisles a bit. But otherwise, shackles must be worn at all times.

(*The 'Fasten Your Shackles' signs go off.*)

MISS PAT: Also, we ask that you please refrain from call-and-response singing between cabins as that sort of thing can lead to rebellion. And, of course, no drums are allowed on board. Can you repeat after me, 'No drums.' (*She gets the audience to repeat.*) With a little more enthusiasm, please. 'No drums.' (*After the audience repeats it.*) That was great.

Once we're airborne, I'll be by with magazines, and earphones can be purchased for the price of your first-born male.

If there's anything I can do to make this middle passage more pleasant, press the little button overhead and I'll be with you faster than you can say, 'Go down, Moses.' (*She laughs at her 'little joke.'*) Thanks for flying Celebrity and here's hoping you have a pleasant take off.

(*The engines surge, the 'Fasten Your Shackle' signs go on, and over-articulate Muzak voices are heard singing as MISS PAT pulls down a bucket seat and 'shackles-up' for takeoff.*)

VOICES:
GET ON BOARD CELEBRITY SLAVESHIP
GET ON BOARD CELEBRITY SLAVESHIP
GET ON BOARD CELEBRITY SLAVESHIP
THERE'S ROOM FOR MANY MORE

(*The engines reach an even, steady hum. Just as MISS PAT rises and replaces the shackles in the overhead compartment, the faint sound of African drumming is heard.*)

MISS PAT: Hi. Miss Pat again. I'm sorry to disturb you, but someone is playing drums. And what did we just say . . . 'No drums.' It must be someone in Coach. But we here in Cabin A are not going to respond to those drums. As a matter of fact, we don't even hear them. Repeat after me. 'I don't hear any drums.' (*The audience repeats.*) And 'I will not rebel.'

(*The audience repeats. The drumming grows.*)

MISS PAT: (*Placating*) OK, now I realize some of us are a bit edgy after hearing about the tragedy on board The Laughing Mary, but let me assure you Celebrity has no intention of throwing you overboard and collecting the insurance. We value you!

(*She proceeds to single out individual passengers/audience members.*)

Why the songs *you* are going to sing in the cotton fields, under the burning heat and stinging lash, will metamorphose and give birth to the likes of James

Brown and the Fabulous Flames. And you, yes *you*, are going to come up with some of the best dances. The best dances! The Watusi! The Funky Chicken! And just think of what *you* are going to mean to William Faulkner.

All right, so you're gonna have to suffer for a few hundred years, but from your pain will come a culture so complex. *And*, with this little item here . . . (*She removes a basketball from the overhead compartment.*) . . . you'll become millionaires!

(*There is a roar of thunder. The lights quiver and the 'Fasten Your Shackle' signs begin to flash.* MISS PAT *quickly replaces the basketball in the overhead compartment and speaks very reassuringly.*)

MISS PAT: No, don't panic. I'm here to take care of you. We're just flying through a little thunder storm. Now the only way you're going to make it through this one is if you abandon your God and worship a new one. So, on the count of three, let's all sing. One, two, three . . .
NOBODY KNOWS DE TROUBLE I SEEN
Oh, I forgot to mention, when singing, omit the T-H sound. 'The' becomes 'de.' 'They' becomes 'dey.' Got it? Good!
NOBODY KNOWS . . .
NOBODY KNOWS . . .
Oh, so you don't like that one? Well then let's try another –
SUMMER TIME
AND DE LIVIN' IS EASY
Gershwin. He comes from another oppressed people so he understands.
FISH ARE JUMPIN' . . . come on.
AND DE COTTON IS HIGH.
Sing, damnit!

(*Lights begin to flash, the engines surge, and there is wild drumming.* MISS PAT *sticks her head through the curtain and speaks with an offstage* CAPTAIN.)

MISS PAT: What?
VOICE OF CAPTAIN *(O.S.)*: Time warp!
MISS PAT: Time Warp! (*She turns to the audience and puts on a pleasant face.*) The Captain has assured me everything is fine. We're just caught in a little time warp. (*Trying to fight her growing hysteria.*) On your right you will see the American Revolution, which will give the U.S. of A. exclusive rights to your life. And on your left, the Civil War, which means you will vote Republican until F.D.R. comes along. And now we're passing over the Great Depression, which means everybody gets to live the way you've been living. (*There is a blinding flash of light, and an explosion. She screams.*) Ahhhhhhhhh! That was World War I, which is not to be confused with World War II . . . (*There is a larger flash of light, and another explosion.*) . . . Ahhhhh! Which is not to be confused with the Korean War or the Vietnam War, all of which you will play a major role in.

Oh, look, now we're passing over the sixties. Martha and the Vandellas . . . Malcolm X. (*There is a gun shot.*) . . . 'Julia' with Miss Diahann Carroll . . . and five little girls in Sunday school . . . (*There is an explosion.*) Martin Luther King . . .

(A gun shot). Oh no! The Supremes just broke up! *(The drumming intensifies.)* Stop playing those drums. I said, stop playing those damn drums. You can't stop history! You can't stop time! Those drums will be confiscated once we reach Savannah. Repeat after me. I don't hear any drums and I will not rebel. I will not rebel! I will not re-

(The lights go out, she screams, and the sound of a plane landing and screeching to a halt is heard. After a beat, lights reveal a wasted, disheveled MISS PAT, *but perky nonetheless.)*

MISS PAT: Hi. Miss Pat here. Things got a bit jumpy back there, but the Captain has just informed me we have safely landed in Savannah. Please check the overhead before exiting as any baggage you don't claim, we trash.

It's been fun, and we hope the next time you consider travel, it's with Celebrity.

(Luggage begins to revolve onstage from offstage left, going past MISS PAT *and revolving offstage right. Mixed in with the luggage are two male slaves and a woman slave, complete with luggage and I.D. tags around their necks.)*

MISS PAT: *(With routine, rehearsed pleasantness.)*
Have a nice day. Bye bye.
Button up that coat, it's kind of chilly.
Have a nice day. Bye bye.
You take care now.
See you.
Have a nice day.
Have a nice day.
Have a nice day.

UKAWSAW GRONNIOSAW

from *A Narrative of the Most Remarkable Particulars of the Life of James Albert Ukawsaw Gronniosaw, An African Prince*

Ukawsaw Gronniosaw was born around 1710 in what is now north-eastern Nigeria. Sold into slavery as a teenager, he was introduced to Christianity and taught to read by a Dutch Reformed minister in New York, who freed him on his deathbed in the late 1740s. He subsequently worked as a cook on board a privateer during the Seven Years War (1756–1763), and then enlisted with a British regiment in order to travel to England, where he arrived, after seeing action in the Caribbean, in 1762. He married Betty, an English weaver, the following year, but unemployment forced them to move frequently in search of work, and it was to a 'young lady of the town of Leominster' in the Midlands that he recounted the story of his life, first published around 1770. The Narrative was reprinted numerous times over the next fifty years, but of Gronniosaw's later life nothing is known.

I was born in the city of BOURNOU; my mother was the eldest daughter of the reigning King of ZAARA, of which BOURNOU is the chief city. I was the youngest of six children, and particularly loved by my mother, and my grand-father almost doated on me.

I had, from my infancy, a curious turn of mind, was more grave and reserved in my disposition than either of my brothers and sisters. I often teased them with questions they could not answer; for which reason they disliked me, as they supposed that I was either foolish, or insane. 'Twas certain that I was, at times, very unhappy in myself: it being strongly impressed on my mind that there was some GREAT MAN of power which resided above the sun, moon and stars, the objects of our worship. My dear indulgent mother would bear more with me than any of my friends beside. – I often raised my hands to heaven, and asked her who lived there? was much dissatisfied when she told me the sun, moon and stars, being persuaded, in my own mind, that there must be some SUPERIOR POWER. – I was frequently lost in wonder at the works of the creation: was afraid, uneasy, and restless, but could not tell for what. I wanted to be inform'd of things that no person could tell me; and was always dissatisfied. –

*Ukawsaw Gronniosaw (James Albert), A Narrative of the Most Remarkable Particulars of the Life of James Albert Ukawsaw Gronniosaw, An African Prince (Bath: c. 1770), pp. 7–17.

These wonderful impressions begun in my childhood, and followed me continually 'till I left my parents, which affords me matter of admiration and thankfulness.

To this moment I grew more and more uneasy every day, in so much that one Saturday, (which is the day on which we keep our Sabbath) I laboured under anxieties and fears that cannot be expressed; and, what is more extraordinary, I could not give a reason for it. – I rose, as our custom is, about three o'clock, (as we are obliged to be at our place of worship an hour before sun rise:) We say nothing in our worship, but continue on our knees with our hands held up, observing a strict silence till the sun is at a certain height, which I suppose to be about 10 or 11 o'clock in England: when, at a certain sign made by the priest, we get up (our duty being over), and disperse to our different houses. – Our place of meeting is under a large palm tree; we divide ourselves into many congregations; as it is impossible for the same tree to cover the inhabitants of the whole city, though they are extremely large, high and majestic; the beauty and usefulness of them are not to be described; they supply the inhabitants of the country with meat, drink and cloaths:[1] the body of the palm tree is very large; at a certain season of the year they tap it, and bring vessels to receive the wine, of which they draw great quantities, the quality of which is very delicious; the leaves of this tree are of a silky nature; they are large and soft: when they are dried and pulled to pieces, it has much the same appearance as the English flax, and the inhabitants of BOURNOU manufacture it for cloathing, &c. This tree likewise produces a plant or substance which has the appearance of a cabbage, and very like it, in taste almost the same: it grows between the branches. Also the palm tree produces a nut, something like a cocoa, which contains a kernel, in which is a large quantity of milk, very pleasant to the taste: the shell is of a hard substance, and of a very beautiful appearance, and serves for basons, bowls, &c.

I hope this digression will be forgiven. – I was going to observe, that after the duty of our Sabbath was over (on the day in which I was more distressed and afflicted than ever) we were all on our way home as usual, when a remarkable black cloud arose and covered the sun; then followed very heavy rain and thunder more dreadful than ever I had heard: the heavens roared, and the earth trembled at it: I was highly affected and cast down; in so much that I wept sadly; and could not follow my relations and friends home. I was obliged to stop, and felt as if my legs were tied, they seemed to shake under me: so I stood still, being in great fear of the MAN OF POWER that I was persuaded in myself, lived above. One of my young companions (who entertained a particular friendship for me and I for him) came back to see for me: he asked me why I stood still in such very hard rain? I only said to him that my legs were weak, and I could not come faster: he was much affected to see me cry, and took me by the hand, and said he would lead me home, which he did. My mother was greatly alarmed at my tarrying out in such terrible weather; she asked me many questions, such as what I did so for, and if I was well? My dear mother, says I, pray tell me who is the great MAN OF POWER that makes the thunder? She said, there was no power but the sun, moon and stars;

---

1 It is a generally received opinion, in England, that the natives of Africa go entirely uncloathed; but this supposition is very unjust: they have a kind of dress so as to appear decent, though it is very slight and thin.

that they made all our country. – I then enquired how all our people came? She answered me, from one another; and so carried me to many generations back. – Then says I, who made the *first man?* and who made the first cow, and the first lion, and where does the fly come from, as no one can make him? My mother seemed in great trouble; she was apprehensive that my senses were impaired, or that I was foolish. My father came in, and seeing her in grief asked the cause, but when she related our conversation to him, he was exceedingly angry with me, and told me he would punish me severely, if ever I was so troublesome again; so that I resolved never to say any thing more to him. But I grew very unhappy in myself; my relations and acquaintance endeavoured by all the means they could think on, to divert me, by taking me to ride on goats, (which is much the custom of our country) and to shoot with a bow and arrow; but I experienced no satisfaction at all in any of these things; nor could I be easy by any means whatever; my parents were very unhappy to see me so dejected and melancholy.

About this time there came a merchant from the *Gold Coast* (the third city in GUINEA) he traded with the inhabitants of our country in ivory, &c. He took great notice of my unhappy situation, and enquired into the cause; he expressed vast concern for me, and said, if my parents would part with me for a little while, and let him take me home with him, it would be of more service to me than any thing they could do for me. – He told me that if I would go with him I should see houses with wings to them walk upon the water, and should also see the white folks; and that he had many sons nearly of my age, which should be my companions; and he added to all this that he would bring me safe back again soon. – I was highly pleased with the account of this strange place, and was very desirous of going. – I seemed sensible of a secret impulse upon my mind, which I could not resist, that seemed to tell me I must go. When my dear mother saw I was willing to leave them, she spoke to my father and grandfather, and the rest of my relations, who all agreed that I should accompany the merchant to the Gold Coast. I was the more willing as my brothers and sisters despised me, and looked on me with contempt, on the account of my unhappy disposition; and even my servants slighted me, and disregarded all I said to them. I had one sister who was always exceeding fond of me, and I loved her entirely; her name was LOGWY, she was quite white, and fair, with fine light hair, though my father and mother were black. – I was truly concerned to leave my beloved sister, and she cry'd most sadly to part with me, wringing her hands, and discovered every sign of grief that can be imagined, indeed if I could have known when I left my friends and country that I should never return to them again, my misery on that occasion would have been inexpressible. All my relations were sorry to part with me; my dear mother came with me on a camel more than three hundred miles, the first of our journey lay chiefly through woods: at night we secured ourselves from the wild beasts by making fires all around us; we and our camels kept within the circle, or we must have been tore to pieces by the lions, and other wild creatures that roared terribly as soon as night came on, and continued to do so 'till morning. – There can be little said in favor of the country through which we passed; only a valley of marble that we came through which is unspeakably beautiful. – On each side of this valley are exceedingly high and almost inaccessible mountains. – Some of these pieces of marble are of prodigious length and breadth, but of different sizes and colour, and shaped in a variety of forms, in a wonderful manner. – It is most of it veined with gold mixed with striking and beautiful colours; so that when the sun darts upon it, it is as pleasing a sight as can be imagined. The merchant that brought me from BOURNOU, was in partnership with another gentleman who accompanied us; he was very unwilling that he should take me from home, as, he said, he foresaw many difficulties that would attend my going with them. He endeavoured to prevail on the merchant to throw me into a very deep pit that was in the valley, but he refused to listen to him, and said, he was resolved to take care of me; but the other was greatly dissatisfied; and when we came to a river, which we were obliged to pass through, he purposed throwing me in and drowning me; but the merchant would not consent to it, so that I was preserved.

We travelled 'till about four o'clock every day, and then began to make preparations for night, by cutting down large quantities of wood, to make fires to preserve us from the wild beasts. – I had a very unhappy and discontented journey, being in continual fear that the people I was with would murder me. I often reflected with extreme regret on the kind friends I had left, and the idea of my dear mother frequently drew tears from my eyes. – I cannot recollect how long we were going from BOURNOU to the GOLD COAST; but as there is no shipping nearer BOURNOU than that city, it was tedious in travelling so far by land, being upwards of a thousand miles. I was heartily rejoiced when we arrived at the end of our journey: I now vainly imagined that all my troubles and inquietudes would terminate here; but could I have looked into futurity, I should have perceived that I had much more to suffer than I had before experienced, and that they had as yet barely commenced.

I was now more than a thousand miles from home, without a friend or any means to procure one. Soon after I came to the merchant's house, I heard the drums beat remarkably loud, and the trumpets blow, the persons accustomed to this employ, are obliged to go on a very high structure, appointed for that purpose, that the sound may be heard at a great distance; They are higher than the steeples in England, I was mightily pleased with sounds so entirely new to me, and was very inquisitive to know the cause of this rejoicing, and asked many questions concerning it; I was answered that it was meant as a compliment to me, because I was Grandson to the King of BOURNOU.

This account gave me a secret pleasure; but I was not suffered long to enjoy this satisfaction, for in the evening of the same day, two of the merchant's sons (boys about my own age) came running to me, and told me, that the next day I was to die, for the King intended to behead me. – I replied that I was sure it could not be true, for I came there to play with them, and to see houses walk upon the water with wings to them, and the white folks; but I was soon informed that their King imagined I was sent by my father as a spy, and would make such discoveries at my return home, as would enable them to make war with the greater advantage to ourselves; and for these reasons he had resolved I should never return to my native country. – When I heard this, I suffered misery that cannot be described. – I wished a thousand times that I had never left my friends and country. But still the ALMIGHTY was pleased to work miracles for me.

The morning I was to die, I was washed, and all my gold ornaments made bright and shining, and then carried to the palace, where the King was to behead me himself (as is the custom of the place). He was seated upon a throne at the top of an exceeding large yard, or court, which you must go through to enter the palace; it is as wide and spacious as a large field in England. – I had a lane of life-guards to go through. – I guessed it to be about three hundred paces.

I was conducted by my friend the merchant, about half way up; then he durst proceed no farther: I went up to the KING alone, – I went with an undaunted courage, and it pleased GOD to melt the heart of the KING, who sat with his scymitar in his hand ready to behead me; yet being himself so affected, he dropped it out of his hand, and took me upon his knee and wept over me. I put my right hand round his neck, and pressed him to my heart. – He sat me down and blessed me; and added, that he would not kill me, that I should not go home, but be sold for a slave, so then I was conducted back again to the merchant's house.

The next day he took me on board a French brig; but the captain did not choose to buy me; he said I was too small; so the merchant took me home with him again.

The partner, whom I have spoken of as my enemy, was very angry to see me return, and again proposed putting an end to my life; for he represented to the other, that I should bring them into troubles and difficulties, and that I was so little that no person would buy me.

The merchant's resolution began to waver, and I was indeed afraid that I should be put to death: but however, he said he would try me once more.

A few days after a Dutch ship came into the harbour, and they carried me on board, in hopes that the captain would purchase me. – As they went, I heard them agree, that if they could not sell me *then*, they would throw me overboard. – I was in extreme agonies when I heard this; and as soon as ever I saw the Dutch Captain, I ran to him, and put my arms round him, and said, 'father, save me,' (for I knew that if he did not buy me, I should be treated very ill, or possibly murdered). And though he did not understand my language, yet it pleased the ALMIGHTY to influence him in my behalf, and he bought me *for two yards of check*, which is of more value *there*, than in England.

When I left my dear mother I had a large quantity of gold about me, as is the custom of our country, it was made into rings, and they were linked into one another, and formed into a kind of chain, and so put round my neck, and arms and legs, and a large piece hanging at one ear almost in the shape of a pear. I found all this troublesome, and was glad when my new Master took it from me. – I was now washed, and cloathed in the Dutch or English manner. – My master grew very fond of me, and I loved him exceedingly; I watched every look, was always ready when he wanted me, and endeavoured to convince him, by every action, that my only pleasure was to serve him well. – I have since thought that he must have been a serious man. His actions corresponded very well with such a character. – He used to read prayers in public to the ship's crew every Sabbath day; and when first I saw him read, I was never so surprized in my life, as when I saw the book talk to my master, for I thought it did, as I observed him to look upon it, and move his lips. – I wished it would do so to me. As soon as my master had done reading, I followed him to the place where he put the book, being mightily delighted with it, and when nobody saw me, I opened it and put my ear down close upon it, in great hopes that it would say something to me; but was very sorry, and greatly disappointed when I found it would not speak, this thought immediately presented itself to me, that every body and every thing despised me because I was black.

I was exceedingly sea-sick at first; but when I became more accustomed to the sea, it wore off. – My master's ship was bound for Barbadoes. When we came there, he thought fit to speak of me to several gentlemen of his acquaintance, and one of them expressed a particular desire to see me. He had a great mind to buy me; but the Captain could not immediately be prevailed on to part with me; but however, as the gentleman seemed very solicitous, he at length let me go, and I was sold for fifty dollars (*four and six-penny pieces in English*).

1768

'On being brought from Africa to America'

Phillis Wheatley was born in Africa, possibly in the vicinity of the Gambia River around 1753. She arrived in Boston in 1761 aboard the slave ship Phillis, and was bought by the family of John Wheatley. Taught to read and write, she made astounding progress, and was translating Latin and composing elegant verse by the age of 13. In 1773 she made a short visit to England with Wheatley's son, and it was there that her Poems on Various Subjects, Religious and Moral was published. It was an immediate success, but her fortunes declined following the death of her mistress in 1774. Her marriage to John Peters, a free Black man, was an unhappy one, and she died poor and forgotten in 1786. This poem is one of her earliest surviving works and perhaps her best-known.

'Twas mercy brought me from my *Pagan* land,
Taught my benighted soul to understand
That there's a God, that there's a *Saviour* too:
Once I redemption neither sought nor knew.
Some view our sable race with scornful eye,
'Their colour is a diabolic die.'
Remember, *Christians*, *Negroes*, black as *Cain*,
May be refin'd, and join th'angelic train.

Phillis Wheatley, *Poems on Various Subjects, Religious and Moral* (London: 1773), p. 18.

OTTOBAH CUGOANO

from *Thoughts and Sentiments on the Evil and Wicked Traffic of the Slavery and Commerce of the Human Species...*

Ottobah Cugoano was born in what is now Ghana around 1757. His capture and transportation to the West Indies, described below, took place when he was about 13 years old. In 1772 he was brought to England, where he was baptized and took the name John Steuart. By the late 1780s he was evidently a free man and involved in the campaign against the slave trade, during which time he wrote – possibly with the assistance of his friend Olaudah Equiano – the tract, first published in London in 1787, from which this autobiographical extract is taken.

I was born in the city of Agimaque, on the coast of Fantyn; my father was a companion to the chief in that part of the country of Fantee, and when the old king died I was left in his house with his family; soon after I was sent for by his nephew, Ambro Accasa, who succeeded the old king in the chiefdom of that part of Fantee known by the name of Agimaque and Assinee. I lived with his children, enjoying peace and tranquillity, about twenty moons, which, according to their way of reckoning time, is two years. I was sent for to visit an uncle, who lived at a considerable distance from Agimaque. The first day after we set out we arrived at Assinee, and the third day at my uncle's habitation, where I lived about three months, and was then thinking of returning to my father and young companion at Agimaque; but by this time I had got well acquainted with some of the children of my uncle's hundreds of relations, and we were some days too venturesome in going into the woods to gather fruit and catch birds, and such amusements as pleased us. One day I refused to go with the rest, being rather apprehensive that something might happen to us; till one of my play-fellows said to me, because you belong to the great men, you are afraid to venture your carcase, or else of the *bounsam*, which is the devil. This enraged me so much, that I set a resolution to join the rest, and we went into the woods as usual; but we had not been above two hours before our troubles began, when several great ruffians came upon us suddenly, and said we had committed a fault against their lord, and we must go and answer for it ourselves before him.

Ottobah Cugoano, *Thoughts and Sentiments on the Evil and Wicked Traffic of the Slavery and Commerce of the Human Species* ... (London: 1787), pp. 6–11.

Some of us attempted in vain to run away, but pistols and cutlasses were soon introduced, threatening, that if we offered to stir we should all lie dead on the spot. One of them pretended to be more friendly than the rest, and said, that he would speak to their lord to get us clear, and desired that we should follow him; we were then immediately divided into different parties, and drove after him. We were soon led out of the way which we knew, and towards the evening, as we came in sight of a town, they told us that this great man of theirs lived there, but pretended it was too late to go and see him that night. Next morning there came three other men, whose language differed from ours, and spoke to some of those who watched us all the night, but he that pretended to be our friend with the great man, and some others, were gone away. We asked our keepers what these men had been saying to them, and they answered, that they had been asking them, and us together, to go and feast with them that day, and that we must put off seeing the great man till after; little thinking that our doom was so nigh, or that these villains meant to feast on us as their prey. We went with them again about half a day's journey, and came to a great multitude of people, having different music playing; and all the day after we got there, we were very merry with the music, dancing and singing. Towards the evening, we were again persuaded that we could not get back to where the great man lived till next day; and when bedtime came, we were separated into different houses with different people. When the next morning came, I asked for the men that brought me there, and for the rest of my companions; and I was told that they were gone to the sea side to bring home some rum, guns and powder, and that some of my companions were gone with them, and that some were gone to the fields to do something or other. This gave me strong suspicion that there was some treachery in the case, and I began to think that my hopes of returning home again were all over. I soon became very uneasy, not knowing what to do, and refused to eat or drink for whole days together, till the man of the house told me that he would do all in his power to get me back to my uncle; then I eat a little fruit with him, and had some thoughts that I should be sought after, as I would be then missing at home about five or six days. I enquired every day if the men had come back, and for the rest of my companions, but could get no answer of any satisfaction. I was kept about six days at this man's house, and in the evening there was another man came and talked with him a good while, and I heard the one say to the other he must go, and the other said the sooner the better; that man came out and told me that he knew my relations at Agimaque, and that we must set out to-morrow morning, and he would convey me there. Accordingly we set out next day, and travelled till dark, when we came to a place where we had some supper and slept. He carried a large bag with some gold dust, which he said he had to buy some goods at the sea side to take with him to Agimaque. Next day we travelled on, and in the evening came to a town, where I saw several white people, which made me afraid that they would eat me, according to our notion as children in the inland parts of the country. This made me rest very uneasy all the night, and next morning I had some victuals brought, desiring me to eat and make haste, as my guide and kid-napper told me that he had to go to the castle with some company that were going there, as he had told me before, to get some goods. After I was ordered out, the horrors I soon saw and felt, cannot be well described; I saw many of my miserable countrymen chained two and two, some hand-cuffed, and some with their hands tied behind. We were conducted along by a guard, and when we arrived at the castle, I asked my guide what I was brought there for, he told me to learn the ways of the *browfow*, that is the white faced people. I saw him take a gun, a piece of cloth, and some lead for me, and then he told me that he must now leave me there, and went off. This made me cry bitterly, but I was soon conducted to a prison, for three days, where I heard the groans and cries of many, and saw some of my fellow-captives. But when a vessel arrived to conduct us away to the ship, it was a most horrible scene; there was nothing to be heard but rattling of chains, smacking of whips, and the groans and cries of our fellow men. Some would not stir from the ground, when they were lashed and beat in the most horrible manner. I have forgot the name of this infernal fort; but we were taken in the ship that came for us, to another that was ready to sail from Cape Coast. When we were put into the ship, we saw several black merchants coming on board, but we were all drove into our holes, and not suffered to speak to any of them. In this situation we continued several days in sight of our native land; but I could find no good person to give any information of my situation to Accasa at Agimaque. And when we found ourselves at last taken away, death was more preferable than life, and a plan was concerted amongst us, that we might burn and blow up the ship, and to perish all together in the flames; but we were betrayed by one of our own countrywomen, who slept with some of the head men of the ship, for it was common for the dirty filthy sailors to take the African women and lie upon their bodies; but the men were chained and pent up in holes. It was the women and boys which were to burn the ship, with the approbation and groans of the rest; though that was prevented, the discovery was likewise a cruel bloody scene.

But it would be needless to give a description of all the horrible scenes which we saw, and the base treatment which we met with in this dreadful captive situation, as the similar cases of thousands which suffer by this infernal traffic, are well known. Let it suffice to say, that I was thus lost to my dear indulgent parents and relations, and they to me. All my help was cries and tears, and these could not avail; nor suffered long, till one succeeding woe, and dread, swelled up another. Brought from a state of innocence and freedom, and, in a barbarous and cruel manner, conveyed to a state of horror and slavery: This abandoned situation may be easier conceived than described. From the time that I was kid-napped and conducted to a factory, and from thence in the brutish, base, but fashionable way of traffic, consigned to Grenada, the grievous thoughts which I then felt, still pant in my heart; though my fears and tears have long since subsided. And yet it is still grievous to think that thousands more have suffered in similar and greater distress, under the hands of barbarous robbers, and merciless task-masters; and that many even now are suffering in all the extreme bitterness of grief and woe, that no language can describe. The cries of some, and the sight of their misery, may be seen and heard afar; but the deep sounding groans of thousands, and the great sadness of their misery and woe, under the heavy load of oppressions and calamities inflicted upon them, are such as can only be distinctly known to the ears of Jehovah Sabaoth.

OLAUDAH EQUIANO

from *The Interesting Narrative of the Life of Olaudah Equiano, or Gustavus Vassa, the African. Written by Himself*

Olaudah Equiano (c.1745–1797) was born in what is now south-eastern Nigeria. At the age of 10 he was kidnapped and taken on a long journey by foot to the coast, where he was put on board a slave ship bound for Barbados. Shortly afterwards he was taken to Virginia where he was set to work on a plantation. Later he was sold to a British naval officer who renamed him Gustavus Vassa, and the boy served with the Navy in the Seven Years War (1756–1763) during which time he learnt to read and write; he was baptized in 1759. After the war, he was sold again, and returned to the West Indies, but was able to engage in trade of his own and save enough to buy his freedom in 1766.

He spent most of the following ten years at sea – he even took part in an expedition to the Arctic in 1773 – and did not settle in England until the late 1770s. A deeply religious man, he was active in the campaign to abolish the slave trade and in defending the rights of fellow Africans in Britain. His autobiography, The Interesting Narrative of the Life of Olaudah Equiano, or Gustavus Vassa, the African, *first appeared in 1789, but went through many editions in several languages over the next fifty years. It was rediscovered in the 1960s, and its literary and historical importance is now widely recognized.*

The first object which saluted my eyes when I arrived on the coast was the sea, and a slave-ship, which was then riding at anchor, and waiting for its cargo. These filled me with astonishment, which was soon converted into terror when I was carried on board. I was immediately handled and tossed up to see if I were sound by some of the crew; and I was now persuaded that I had gotten into a world of bad spirits, and that they were going to kill me. Their complexions too differing so much from ours, their long hair, and the language they spoke, (which was very different from any I had ever heard) united to confirm me in this belief. Indeed such were the horrors of my views and fears at the moment, that, if ten thousand worlds had been my own, I would have freely parted with them all to have exchanged my condition with that of the meanest slave in my own country. When I looked round the ship too and saw a large furnace or copper boiling, and a

---

*Olaudah Equiano, *The Interesting Narrative of the Life of Olaudah Equiano, or Gustavus Vassa, the African. Written by Himself* (London: 1789), pp. 70–88.

multitude of black people of every description chained together, every one of their countenances expressing dejection and sorrow, I no longer doubted of my fate; and, quite overpowered with horror and anguish, I fell motionless on the deck and fainted. When I recovered a little I found some black people about me, who I believed were some of those who brought me on board, and had been receiving their pay; they talked to me in order to cheer me, but all in vain. I asked them if we were not to be eaten by those white men with horrible looks, red faces, and loose hair. They told me I was not; and one of the crew brought me a small portion of spirituous liquor in a wine glass; but, being afraid of him, I would not take it out of his hand. One of the blacks therefore took it from him and gave it to me, and I took a little down my palate, which, instead of reviving me, as they thought it would, threw me into the greatest consternation at the strange feeling it produced, having never tasted any such liquor before. Soon after this the blacks who brought me on board went off, and left me abandoned to despair. I now saw myself deprived of all chance of returning to my native country, or even the least glimpse of hope of gaining the shore, which I now considered as friendly; and I even wished for my former slavery in preference to my present situation, which was filled with horrors of every kind, still heightened by my ignorance of what I was to undergo. I was not long suffered to indulge my grief; I was soon put down under the decks, and there I received such a salutation in my nostrils as I had never experienced in my life: so that, with the loathsomeness of the stench, and crying together, I became so sick and low that I was not able to eat, nor had I the least desire to taste any thing. I now wished for the last friend, death, to relieve me; but soon, to my grief, two of the white men offered me eatables; and, on my refusing to eat, one of them held me fast by the hands, and laid me across I think the windlass, and tied my feet, while the other flogged me severely. I had never experienced any thing of this kind before; and although, not being used to the water, I naturally feared that element the first time I saw it, yet, nevertheless, could I have got over the nettings, I would have jumped over the side, but I could not; and, besides, the crew used to watch us very closely who were not chained down to the decks, lest we should leap into the water; and I have seen some of these poor African prisoners most severely cut for attempting to do so, and hourly whipped for not eating. This indeed was often the case with myself. In a little time after, amongst the poor chained men, I found some of my own nation, which in a small degree gave ease to my mind. I inquired of these what was to be done with us; they gave me to understand we were to be carried to these white people's country to work for them. I then was a little revived, and thought, if it were no worse than working, my situation was not so desperate: but still I feared I should be put to death, the white people looked and acted, as I thought, in so savage a manner; for I had never seen among any people such instances of brutal cruelty; and this not only shewn towards us blacks, but also to some of the whites themselves. One white man in particular I saw, when we were permitted to be on deck, flogged so unmercifully with a large rope near the foremast, that he died in consequence of it; and they tossed him over the side as they would have done a brute. This made me fear these people the more; and I expected nothing less than to be treated in the same manner. I could not help expressing my fears and apprehensions to some of my countrymen: I asked them if these people had no country, but lived in this hollow place (the ship): they told me they did not, but came from a distant one. 'Then,' said I, 'how comes it in all our country we never heard of them?' They told me because they lived so very far off. I then asked where were their women? had they any like themselves? I was told they had: 'and why,' said I, 'do we not see them?' they answered, because they were left behind. I asked how the vessel could go? they told me they could not tell; but that there were cloths put upon the masts by the help of the ropes I saw, and then the vessel went on; and the white men had some spell or magic they put in the water when they liked in order to stop the vessel. I was exceedingly amazed at this account, and really thought they were spirits. I therefore wished much to be from amongst them, for I expected they would sacrifice me: but my wishes were vain; for we were so quartered that it was impossible for any of us to make our escape. While we stayed on the coast I was mostly on deck; and one day, to my great astonishment, I saw one of these vessels coming in with the sails up. As soon as the whites saw it, they gave a great shout, at which we were amazed; and the more so as the vessel appeared larger by approaching nearer. At last she came to an anchor in my sight, and when the anchor was let go I and my countrymen who saw it were lost in astonishment to observe the vessel stop; and were now convinced it was done by magic. Soon after this the other ship got her boats out, and they came on board of us, and the people of both ships seemed very glad to see each other. Several of the strangers also shook hands with us black people, and made motions with their hands, signifying I suppose we were to go to their country; but we did not understand them. At last, when the ship we were in had got in all her cargo, they made ready with many fearful noises, and we were all put under deck, so that we could not see how they managed the vessel. But this disappointment was the least of my sorrow. The stench of the hold while we were on the coast was so intolerably loathsome, that it was dangerous to remain there for any time, and some of us had been permitted to stay on the deck for the fresh air; but now that the whole ship's cargo were confined together, it became absolutely pestilential. The closeness of the place, and the heat of the climate, added to the number in the ship, which was so crowded that each had scarcely room to turn himself, almost suffocated us. This produced copious perspirations, so that the air soon became unfit for respiration, from a variety of loathsome smells, and brought on a sickness among the slaves, of which many died, thus falling victims to the improvident avarice, as I may call it, of their purchasers. This wretched situation was again aggravated by the galling of the chains, now become insupportable; and the filth of the necessary tubs into which the children often fell, and were almost suffocated. The shrieks of the women, and the groans of the dying, rendered the whole a scene of horror almost inconceiveable. Happily perhaps for myself I was soon reduced so low here that it was thought necessary to keep me almost always on deck; and from my extreme youth I was not put in fetters. In this situation I expected every hour to share the fate of my companions, some of whom were almost daily brought upon deck at the point of death, which I began to hope would soon put an end to my miseries. Often did I think many of the inhabitants of the deep much more happy than myself. I envied them the freedom they enjoyed, and as often wished I could change my condition for theirs. Every circumstance I met with served only to render my state more painful, and heighten my apprehensions, and my opinion of the cruelty of the whites. One day they had taken a number of fishes; and when they had killed and satisfied themselves with as many as they thought fit, to our astonishment who were on the deck, rather than give any of them to us to eat as we expected, they tossed the remaining fish into the sea again, although we begged and prayed for some as well as we could, but in vain; and some of my countrymen, being pressed by hunger, took an opportunity, when they thought no one saw them, of trying to get a little privately; but they were discovered, and the attempt procured them some very severe floggings. One day, when we had a smooth sea, and moderate wind, two of my wearied countrymen, who were chained together (I was near them at the time), preferring death to such a life of misery, somehow made through the nettings, and jumped into the sea: immediately another quite dejected fellow, who, on account of his illness, was suffered to be out of irons, also followed their example; and I believe many more would very soon have done the same, if they had not been prevented by the ship's crew, who were instantly alarmed. Those of us that were the most active were, in a moment, put down under the deck, and there was such a noise and confusion amongst the people of the ship as I never heard before, to stop her, and get the boat out to go after the slaves. However two of the wretches were drowned, but they got the other, and afterwards flogged him unmercifully for thus attempting to prefer death to slavery. In this manner we continued to undergo more hardships than I can now relate, hardships which are inseparable from this accursed trade. Many a time we were near suffocation from the want of fresh air, which we were often without for whole days together. This, and the stench of the necessary tubs, carried off many. During our passage I first saw flying fishes, which surprised me very much: they used frequently to fly across the ship, and many of them fell on the deck. I also now first saw the use of the quadrant; I had often with astonishment seen the mariners make observations with it, and I could not think what it meant. They at last took notice of my surprise; and one of them, willing to increase it, as well as to gratify my curiosity, made me one day look through it. The clouds appeared to me to be land, which disappeared as they passed along. This heightened my wonder; and I was now more persuaded than ever that I was in another world, and that every thing about me was magic. At last we came in sight of the island of Barbadoes, at which the whites on board gave a great shout, and made many signs of joy to us. We did not know what to think of this; but as the vessel drew nearer we plainly saw the harbour, and other ships of different kinds and sizes: and we soon anchored amongst them off Bridge Town. Many merchants and planters now came on board, though it was in the evening. They put us in separate parcels, and examined us attentively. They also made us jump, and pointed to the land, signifying we were to go there. We thought by this we should be eaten by these ugly men, as they appeared to us; and, when soon after we were all put down under the deck again, there was much dread and trembling among us, and nothing but bitter cries to be heard all the night from these apprehensions, insomuch that at last the white people got some old slaves from the land to pacify us. They told us we were not to be eaten, but to work, and were soon to go on land, where we should see many of our country people. This report eased us much; and sure enough, soon after we were landed, there came to us Africans of all languages. We were conducted immediately to the merchant's yard, where we were all pent up together like so many sheep in a fold, without regard to sex or age. As every object was new to me every thing I saw filled me with surprise. What struck me first was that the houses were built with stories, and in every other respect different from those in Africa: but I was still more astonished on seeing people on horseback. I did not know what this could mean; and indeed I thought these people were full of nothing but magical arts. While I was in this astonishment, one of my fellow prisoners spoke to a countryman of his about the horses, who said they were the same kind they had in their country. I understood them, though they were from a distant part of Africa, and I thought it odd I had not seen any horses there; but afterwards, when I came to converse with different Africans, I found they had many horses amongst them, and much larger than those I then saw. We were not many days in the merchant's custody before we were sold after their usual manner, which is this:– On a signal given, (as the beat of a drum) the buyers rush at once into the yard where the slaves are confined, and make choice of that parcel they like best. The noise and clamour with which this is attended, and the eagerness visible in the countenances of the buyers, serve not a little to increase the apprehensions of the terrified Africans, who may well be supposed to consider them as the ministers of that destruction to which they think themselves devoted. In this manner, without scruple, are relations and friends separated, most of them never to see each other again. I remember in the vessel in which I was brought over, in the men's apartment, there were several brothers, who, in the sale, were sold in different lots; and it was very moving on this occasion to see and hear their cries at parting. O, ye nominal Christians! might not an African ask you, learned you this from your God, who says unto you, Do unto all men as you would men should do unto you? Is it not enough that we are torn from our country and friends to toil for your luxury and lust of gain? Must every tender feeling be likewise sacrificed to your avarice? Are the dearest friends and relations, now rendered more dear by their separation from their kindred, still to be parted from each other, and thus prevented from cheering the gloom of slavery with the small comfort of being together and mingling their sufferings and sorrows? Why are parents to lose their children, brothers their sisters, or husbands their wives? Surely this is a new refinement in cruelty, which, while it has no advantage to atone for it, thus aggravates distress, and adds fresh horrors even to the wretchedness of slavery.

1854

from *Biography of Mahommah G. Baquaqua*

In his Biography, 'written and revised from his own words' by an author and publisher, Samuel Moore, we learn that Mahommah Gardo Baquaqua was born in the early 1830s, 'in the peninsula formed by the great bend of the river Niger'. Moore begins with an extended description of his Muslim upbringing, and the manners and customs of the country. The text then shifts into the first person as Baquaqua, 'in nearly his own words', tells of his capture, enslavement and transportation to Pernambuco in Brazil – reproduced below. He was subsequently sold to the captain of a cargo ship plying the coast, until one trip took him to New York, where he succeeded in escaping his master's clutches.

Baquaqua later sailed to Haiti, where he was taken in by a Baptist missionary who helped him to return to New York 'in order to educate me preparatory to going to my own people in Africa, to preach the Gospel of glad tidings of great joy to the ignorant and benighted of my fellow countrymen who are now believers in the false prophet of Mahomed'. At the time of the book's publication, he was a British subject, living in Canada.

It has already been stated, that when any person gives evidence of gaining an eminent position in the country, he is immediately envied, and means are taken to put him out of the way; thus when it was seen that my situation was one of trust and confidence with the king, I was of course soon singled out as a fit object of vengeance by an envious class of my countrymen, decoyed away and sold into slavery. I went to the city one day to see my mother, when I was followed by music (the drum) and called to by name, the drum beating to the measure of a song which had been composed apparently in honor of me, on account of, as I supposed, my elevated position with the king. This pleased me mightily, and I felt highly flattered, and was very liberal, and gave the people money and wine, they singing and gesturing the time. About a mile from my mother's house, where a strong drink called Bah-gee, was made out of the grain Har-nee; thither we repaired; and when I had drank plentifully of Bah-gee, I was quite intoxicated, and they persuaded me to go with them to Zar-ach-o, about one mile from Zoogoo, to visit a strange king that I had never seen before. When we arrived there, the king made much of us all, and a great feast was prepared, and plenty of drink was given to me, indeed all appeared to drink very freely.

*Mahommah G. Baquaqua, *Biography of Mahommah G. Baquaqua, A Native of Zoogoo, in the Interior of Africa* . . . Edited by Samuel Moore (Detroit: Geo. E. Pomeroy & Co., 1854), pp. 34–44. Reprinted with the permission of the Division of Rare and Manuscript Collections, Cornell University Library.

In the morning when I arose, I found that I was a prisoner, and my companions were all gone. Oh, horror! I then discovered that I had been betrayed into the hands of my enemies, and sold for a slave. Never shall I forget my feelings on that occasion; the thoughts of my poor mother harrassed me very much and the loss of my liberty and honorable position with the king, grieved me very sorely. I lamented bitterly my folly in being so easily deceived, and was led to drown all caution in the bowl. Had it not been that my senses had been taken from me, the chance was that I should have escaped their snares, at least for that time.

The man, in whose company I found myself left by my cruel companions, was one, whose employment was to rid the country of all such as myself. The way he secured me, was after the following manner: – He took a limb of a tree that had two prongs, and shaped it so that it would cross the back of my neck, it was then fastened in front with an iron bolt; the stick was about six feet long.

Confined thus, I was marched forward towards the coast, to a place called Ar-oo-zo, which was a large village; there I found some friends, who felt very much about my position, but had no means of helping me. We only stayed there one night as my master wanted to hurry on, as I had told him I would get away from him and go home. He then took me to a place called Chir-a-chur-ee, there I also had friends, but could not see them, as he kept very close watch over me, and he always stayed at places prepared for the purpose of keeping the slaves in security; there were holes in the walls in which my feet were placed (a kind of stocks.) He then took me on to a place called Cham-mah, (after passing through many strange places, the names of which I do not recollect) where he sold me. We had then been about four days from home and had traveled very rapidly. I remained only one day, when I was again sold to a woman, who took me to E-fau; she had along with her some young men, into whose charge I was given, but she journeyed with us; we were several days going there; I suffered very much traveling through the woods, and never saw a human being all the journey. There was no regular road, but we had to make our passage as well as we could.

The inhabitants about Cham-mah live chiefly by hunting wild animals, which are there very numerous; I saw many during the two days, but do not know their names in English; the people go nearly naked and are of the rudest description. The country through which we passed after leaving Chir-a-chir-ee, was quite hilly, water abundant and of good quality, the trees are very large; we did not suffer anything from heat on the journey, as the weather was quite cool and pleasant; it would be a healthy and delightful country, were it inhabited by civilized people, and cultivated; the flowers are various and beautiful, the trees, full of birds, large and small, some sing very delightfully. We crossed several large streams of water, which had it not been the dry season, would have been very deep, as it was they were easily forded, being no more than three feet of water in some places. There were great quantities of aquatic birds sporting about; we saw swans in abundance, we tried to kill some, but found it very difficult, as their movements are very quick upon the water; they have a most beautiful appearance when on the wing, the necks and wings extended in the air, they are perfectly white, never fly very high nor far away; their flesh is sweet and good, and considered a great dish. After passing through the woods, we came to a small place, where the woman who had purchased me, had some friends; here I was treated very well, indeed, during the day, but at night I was closely confined, as they were afraid I would make my escape; I could not sleep all night, I was so tightly kept.

After remaining there for the space of two days, we started on our journey again, traveling day after day; the country through which we passed continued quite hilly and mountainous; we passed some very high mountains, which I believed were called the mountains of Kong. The weather all the time continued cool and pleasant, water was found in great abundance, of very excellent quality, the roads, in some places, where the land was level, was quite sandy, but only for short distances, together. – The country was very thinly settled all the way from Cham-mah, the woods along the route are not very extensive, but large tracts of land, covered with a very tall grass. We passed some places where fire had consumed the grass, something after the manner of the prairies of South and South-western North America.

I will here describe the manner of firing grass in Africa. The grass when it has attained a large growth, is a refuge or haunt for the wild animals, abounding in that part of the country, and when it is decided to fire the grass, notice is sent to all people for miles round about, and the hunters come prepared with bows and arrows, who station themselves all around for several miles, and form a large circle; when the fire is applied at one point, it is soon discovered by the party on the opposite, who immediately fires his portion, and so on, all round about until the whole is fired; the fire strikes inward, toward the centre, never spreading outside the circle; the hunters follow up the flames, and being prepared with branches of trees, bearing large leaves, throw them down before them to stand upon, so as to let fly their arrows upon the terrified animals, who flee before the devouring element into the centre of the fire; the hunters of course following up their game around the outside of the burning mass, slaying all before them as they proceed; they are excellent marksmen, and the poor affrighted creatures have very little chance for their lives, at such times; immense numbers are killed, as well as serpents in great quantities.

But to return: – Whilst passing over those places which had been recently burned, our travel was much quicker, not having much of anything to impede our progress, but where the grass stood as a wall on either side of us, we had to travel very cautiously, fearing the wild animals would spring out and fall upon us. The people of America do not know anything about tall grass, such as in Africa; the tall grass of the American prairies is as a child beside a giant, in comparison with the grass of the torrid zone. It grows generally twelve feet high, but sometimes much higher, and nothing can be seen that is ever so near you, it being so thick and stout; closer even than the small groves of timber in this country. At length we arrived at Efau, where I was again sold; the woman seemed sorry to part with me, and gave me a small present on my leaving them. Efau is quite a large place, the houses were of different construction to those in Zoogoo, and had not so good an appearance.

The man to whom I was again sold, was very rich, and had a great number of wives and slaves. I was placed in charge of an old slave; whilst there a great dance was held and I was fearful they were going to kill me, as I had heard they did so in some places, and I fancied the dance was only a preliminary part of the ceremony; at any rate I did not feel at all comfortable about the matter. I was at

Efau several weeks and was very well treated during that time; but as I did not like the work assigned me, they saw that I was uneasy, and as they were fearful of losing me, I was locked up every night.

The country around Efau was very mountainous, and from the city the mountains in the distance had a noble appearance.

After leaving Efau, we had no stopping place until we reached Dohama; we remained in the woods by night and traveled during the day, as there were wild beasts in great abundance, and we were compelled to build up large fires at night to keep away the ferocious animals, which otherwise would have fallen upon us and torn us to pieces, we could hear them howling round about during the night; there was one around in particular, the people most dreaded; it was of the form of a cat with a long body, some were all of a color, others spotted very beautifully; the eyes of which shone like lustrous orbs of fire by night; it is there called the Goo-noo. I presume from the description, it must be what is here known as the Leopard, as from what I understand, the description is about the same.

Dohama is about three days journey from Efau, and is quite a large city; the houses being built differently to any I had previously seen. The surrounding country is level and the roads are good; it is more thickly settled than any other part I had passed through, though not so well as Zoogoo, the manners of the people too, were altogether different to anything I had ever before seen.

I was being conducted through the city, and as we passed along, we were met by a woman, and my keeper who was with me immediately took to his heels and ran back as hard as he could. I stood stock still, not knowing the meaning of it; he saw I did not attempt to follow him, or to move one way or another, and he called to me in the Efau language to follow him, which I did, he then told me, after we rested, that the woman we had met was the king's wife, and it is a mark of respect to run whenever she is in sight of any of her subjects. There were gates to this city, and a toll was demanded on passing through. I remained there but a short time, but I learned that it was a great place for whisky, and the people were very fond of dancing. At this place I saw oranges for the first time in my life. I was told, whilst there, that the king's house was ornamented on the outside with human skulls, but did not see it. When we arrived here I began to give up all hopes of ever getting back to my home again, but had entertained hopes until this time of being able to make my escape, and by some means or other of once more seeing my native place, but at last, hope gave way; the last ray seemed fading away, and my heart felt sad and weary within me, as I thought of my home, my mother! whom I loved most tenderly, and the thought of never more beholding her, added very much to my perplexities. I felt sad and lonely, wherever I did roam, and my heart sank within me, when I thought of the 'old folks at home.' Some persons suppose that the African has none of the finer feelings of humanity within his breast, and that the milk of human kindness runs not through his composition; this is an error, an error of the grossest kind; the feelings which animated the whole human race, lives within the sable creatures of the torrid zone, as well as the inhabitants of the temperate and frigid; the same impulses drive them to action, the same feeling of love move within their bosom, the same maternal and paternal affections are there, the same hopes and fears, griefs and joys, indeed all is there as in the rest of mankind; the only difference is their color, and that has been arranged by him who made the world and all that therein is, the heavens, the waters of the mighty deep, the moon, the sun and stars, the firmament and all that has been made from the beginning until now, therefore why should any despise the works of his hands which has been made and fashioned according to his Almighty power, in the plenitude of his goodness and mercy.

O ye despisers of his works, look ye to yourselves, and take heed; let him who thinks he stands, take heed lest he fall. We then proceeded to Gra-fe, about a day and half's journey; the land we passed was pretty thickly settled and generally well cultivated; but I do not recollect that we passed any streams of water after entering upon this level country. At Gra-fe, I saw the first white man, which you may be sure took my attention very much; the windows in the houses also looked strange, as this was the first time in my life that I had ever seen houses having windows. They took me to a white man's house, where we remained until the morning, when my breakfast was brought in to me, and judge my astonishment to find that the person who brought in my breakfast was an old acquaintance, who came from the same place. He did not exactly know me at first, but when he asked me if my name was Gardo, and I told him it was, the poor fellow was overjoyed and took me by the hands and shook me violently he was so glad to see me; his name was Woo-roo, and had come from Zoogoo, having been enslaved about two years; his friends could never tell what had become of him. He inquired after his friends at Zoogoo, asked me if I had lately come from there, looked at my head and observed that I had the same shave that I had when we were in Zoogoo together; I told him that I had. It may be as well to remark in this place, that in Africa, the nations of the different parts of the country have their different modes of shaving the head and are known from that mark to what part of the country they belong. In Zoogoo, the hair is shaven off each side of the head, and on the top of the head from the forehead to the back part, it is left to grow in three round spots, which is allowed to grow quite long; the spaces between being shaven very close; there is no difficulty to a person acquainted with the different shaves, to know what part any man belongs to.

Woo-roo seemed very anxious that I should remain at Gra-fe, but I was destined for other parts; this town is situated on a large river. After breakfast I was taken down to the river and placed on board a boat; the river was very large and branched off in two different directions, previous to emptying itself into the sea. The boat in which the slaves were placed was large and propelled by oars, although it had sails as well, but the wind not being strong enough, oars were used as well. We were two nights and one day on this river, when we came to a very beautiful place; the name of which I do not remember; we did not remain here very long, but as soon as the slaves were all collected together, and the ship ready to sail, we lost no time in putting to sea. Whilst at this place, the slaves were all put into a pen, and placed with our backs to the fire, and ordered not to look about us, and to insure obedience, a man was placed in front with a whip in his hand ready to strike the first who should dare to disobey orders; another man then went round with a hot iron, and branded us the same as they would the heads of barrels or any other inanimate goods or merchandize.

When all were ready to go aboard, we were chained together, and tied with ropes round about our necks, and were thus drawn down to the sea shore. The ship was lying some distance off. I had never seen a ship before, and my idea of it was, that it was some object of worship of the white man. I imagined that we were all to be slaughtered, and were being led there for that purpose. I felt alarmed for my safety, and despondency had almost taken sole possession of me.

A kind of feast was made ashore that day, and those who rowed the boats were plentifully regaled with whiskey, and the slaves were given rice and other good things in abundance. I was not aware that it was to be my last feast in Africa. I did not know my destiny. Happy for me, that I did not. All I knew was, that I was a slave, chained by the neck, and that I must readily and willingly submit, come what would, which I considered was as much as I had any right to know.

At length, when we reached the beach, and stood on the sand, oh! how I wished that the sand would open and swallow me up. My wretchedness I cannot describe. It was beyond description. The reader may imagine, but anything like an outline of my feelings would fall very short of the mark, indeed. There were slaves brought hither from all parts of the country, and taken on board the ship. The first boat had reached the vessel in safety, notwithstanding the high wind and rough sea; but the last boat that ventured was upset, and all in her but one man were drowned. The number who were lost was about thirty. The man that was saved was very stout, and stood at the head of the boat with a chain in his hand, which he grasped very tightly in order to steady the boat; and when the boat turned over, he was thrown with the rest into the sea, but on rising, by some means under the boat, managed to turn it over, and thus saved himself by springing into her, when she righted. This required great strength, and being a powerful man, gave him the advantage over the rest. The next boat that was put to sea, I was placed in; but God saw fit to spare me, perhaps for some good purpose. I was then placed in that most horrible of all places,

THE SLAVE SHIP

Its horrors, ah! who can describe? None can so truly depict its horrors as the poor unfortunate, miserable wretch that has been confined within its portals. Oh! friends of humanity, pity the poor African, who has been trepanned and sold away from friends and home, and consigned to the hold of a slave ship, to await even more horrors and miseries in a distant land, amongst the religious and benevolent. Yes, even in their very midst; but to the ship! We were thrust into the hold of the vessel in a state of nudity, the males being crammed on one side and the females on the other; the hold was so low that we could not stand up, but were obliged to crouch upon the floor or sit down; day and night were the same to us, sleep being denied us from the confined position of our bodies, and we became desperate through suffering and fatigue.

Oh! the loathsomeness and filth of that horrible place will never be effaced from my memory; nay, as long as memory holds her seat in this distracted brain, will I remember that. My heart even at this day, sickens at the thought of it.

Let those *humane individuals*, who are in favor of slavery, only allow themselves to take the slave's position in the noisome hold of a slave ship, just for one trip from Africa to America, and without going into the horrors of slavery further than this, if they do not come out thorough-going abolitionists, then I have no more to say in favor of abolition. But I think their views and feelings regarding slavery will be changed in some degree, however; if not, let them continue in the course of slavery, and work out their term in a cotton or rice field, or other plantation, and then if they do not say hold, enough! I think they must be of iron frames, possessing neither hearts nor souls. I imagine there can be but one place more horrible in all creation than the hold of a slave ship, and that place is where slaveholders and their myrmidons are the most likely to find themselves some day, when alas, 'twill be too late, too late, alas!

The only food we had during the voyage was corn soaked and boiled. I cannot tell how long we were thus confined, but it seemed a very long while. We suffered very much for want of water, but was denied all we needed. A pint a day was all that was allowed, and no more; and a great many slaves died upon the passage. There was one poor fellow became so very desperate for want of water, that he attempted to snatch a knife from the white man who brought in the water, when he was taken up on deck and I never knew what became of him. I supposed he was thrown overboard.

When any one of us became refractory, his flesh was cut with a knife, and pepper or vinegar was rubbed in to make him peaceable (!) I suffered, and so did the rest of us, very much from sea sickness at first, but that did not cause our brutal owners any trouble. Our sufferings were our own, we had no one to share our troubles, none to care for us, or even to speak a word of comfort to us. Some were thrown overboard before breath was out of their bodies; when it was thought any would not live, they were got rid of in that way. Only twice during the voyage were we allowed to go on deck to wash ourselves – once whilst at sea, and again just before going into port.

We arrived at Pernambuco, South America, early in the morning, and the vessel played about during the day, without coming to anchor. All that day we neither ate or drank anything, and we were given to understand that we were to remain perfectly silent, and not make any out-cry, otherwise our lives were in danger. But when 'night threw her sable mantle on the earth and sea,' the anchor dropped, and we were permitted to go on deck to be viewed and handled by our future masters, who had come aboard from the city. We landed a few miles from the city, at a farmer's house, which was used as a kind of slave market. The farmer had a great many slaves, and I had not been there very long before I saw him use the lash pretty freely on a boy, which made a deep impression on my mind, as of course I imagined that would be my fate ere long, and oh! too soon, alas! were my fears realized.

'Middle Passage Anancy'

Andrew Salkey (1928–1994) was born in Panama of Jamaican parents, was educated in Jamaica and as a young man went to London where he was based from 1952 to 1976. He then moved to the United States to take up a teaching post in Amherst, Massachusetts. Alongside his work as broadcaster, editor, teacher and reviewer, he is well-known as a poet, novelist and author of short stories. This story is taken from his second collection, Anancy, Traveller *(1992), which, like its predecessor* Anancy's Score *(1973), draws on the celebrated spider trickster figure of Afro-Caribbean folklore.*

The voices of the ancestors was bubbling up out of the Atlantic like peas. Memory time, yes? All the souls who lose life when them bodies get throw way overboard, centuries, calling out in nough under ocean pain. The total Atlantic full up of froth and waves and voices and plenty back time slave ship tormentation.

Anancy, as a restless sort of traveller, find one giant rock in the midst of the water, and he sitting down on it as witness to the time of year when the Dance of the Souls of the Dead Slaves taking place inside the world of the Atlantic. As a traveller, he got this best privilege, you see. It don't come to those who stay handcuff on the land, all the time, at all. Is only those who take chance with land and water, who go way far from home and roam world views, who stretch distance with foot, who for ever making home out of homelessness and drift, no matter what, that can see what Anancy seeing, here, right now. And one more something else nobody must forget, never, no time, is that the Atlantic is a rass of a history ocean. History lick up plenty dust over it, and plenty more history lay down under it, ever since the big time continents them say goodbye to one another and gone out into the world them different ways. Is one ocean that see plenty, know plenty and hold secret tight as magnet.

So, is what the voices saying? Some of them calling out tribe names. Some of them calling out how them get capture in the bush on the homeland. Some of them calling out the names of long time ancestors, manners, ways, people sayings, dreams and gods in trees, earth, mountains, rivers and caves.

Anancy listening on the rock and witnessing history walking and trampling up and down on the surface of the water of the Atlantic.

Sudden so, one of the souls, a woman of family wisdom, break the foam surface and touch Anancy wrist and feel him pulse and wink satisfy, when she hear

Andrew Salkey, *Anancy, Traveller* (London: Bogle L'Ouverture Press, 1992), pp. 11–15. Reprinted with the permission of the publisher.

through her fingers Anancy life beat answer back. The soul dip down into the bubbling water and gone.

Sudden so, again, a next soul, a man of land work wisdom, jump up on the rock with Anancy, and say, 'Is mongst all the weeds and dead ship and dead airplane down a bottom we living, you know, and we bring down plenty of them weself, especial when we come to understand what them mission is, and especial when them passing over we and taking sins and bad moves and crooked buy-and-sell-and-snatch-and-grab and profit wickedness to where poor people living on the land.'

The soul touch Anancy shoulder, and say, 'We dead but we not dead. We don't know a thing but we know all. The triangle trade don't stop. It still happening in different shape and form. It dress up and walking and talking in another style, according to how the nowadays parangles go. Watch yourself, Anancy!'

Anancy go to say something to the soul of land work wisdom but the soul dip down back into the Atlantic and gone.

The bubbling going on. The voices going on. And the Atlantic looking like hurricane. Some parts of the surface wrinkling into fountain spurts. Other parts into jets make out of chains and neck irons and foot braces. And still other parts of the moving, jerking, spewing surface sending up deep throat belly groans and heart tearing moans and cries.

Anancy just sitting there swallowing everything with him eye. He know that when history bubble up, no control can grab it and play the ass with it, no how. Besides that, this history have teeth fasten into people memory, all across the land, two side of the Atlantic. But now, what really shaking Anancy is the voices of the souls. After all the centuries, them loud and clear tone and solid as bedrock.

Sudden, yet again and again, ups come a torrent of names of countries that buried ages at the bottom of the Atlantic. Anancy hearing Portugal and Spain. He hearing England, France and Holland. And more. And he hearing America. Anancy stand upon the rock, and watch all the names of countries spurting up as if them was dry, yellow palm trees. He notice that when them spurt up, them stay in the air for a while and then them crack up, splinter and blow way over the bubbling surface of the Atlantic.

The next thing Anancy see is some whips and guns shooting up out of the water. Every one of them fly up straight into the hurricane bubbling and all of a sudden start to crackle like fireworks and burn out into black powder.

Anancy reach out him hand and catch some of the powder. He finger thin it out, and he smell it. Nothing.

A soul with a Fanti smile on her face bubble up behind Anancy, and say quiet, 'Don't expect anything to have substance. Everything is pure memory. And every single memory into history.'

Anancy nod at the soul and turn back to look at the bubbling Atlantic. In the seconds it take Anancy to listen to the soul with the Fanti smile on her face and turn back to the surface of the water, the Dance of the Souls of the Dead Slaves start to happen.

Glory heaps of thousands and thousands of slave souls standing up tall, all over the Atlantic. Drums beating true old time messages of Middle Passage life and death. Thousand more dancers dancing processions of tribal community and capture lamentation.

Spears and shields meeting up against one another and clashing a whole civilization tattoo in mid-air.

All on them own, chains, manacles, whips, ropes and wire slicing and beating the surface of the water.

Neck irons with fan out spikes spinning like wheels everywhere. Them going so fast that most shining star light.

Then, the thousands and thousands of slave souls forming up into separate groups: those with faces mark up with flux vomit and pox pus; those with breasts with rat bite and gangrene; those with bodies with break neck and gun shot; those with sores running river from head to foot; those with sargasso twine up all over them; those who get throw way alive into the Atlantic for insurance; those with baby pickney crying and clinging to them; and those who fighting back strong as iron times.

As that going on, a swarm of cracking cat-o-nine tails and clicking speculum oris in force open mouth and jaw flying all about the place. The cat-o-nine tails lashing lightning. The speculum oris them breaking teeth and gums, loud as wrench tree limb.

As all that happening round him, Anancy turning slow on the rock, and hearing some different voices calling out. These have a proper power tone from Portugal, Spain, England, France, Holland and the rest of the Europe slavery systems, and America own, and them saying phrases like: 'Property, not people, not real human beings!' and 'Cargo jettisoned, not lives thrown overboard!'

Then, Anancy turning slow on the rock, one more time, and hearing a turn up lip England voice saying, sharp as lime: 'A nursery for our seamen, the slave trade!'

A bad chuckle with a curly top wig surrounding it swing before Anancy, as the echo of the England voice dying out across the waves. The wig circle two time and follow the voice into the water. Anancy feel like laughing but a soul appear up and touch her lips to stop him from doing it. And Anancy just smile a cute smile, and the soul do the same, plus a wink, and drift way into the Dance of the Souls of Dead Slaves.

Anancy staring and wondering at the spectacle of memory and history exploding out of the waves and all over the bubbling Atlantic and high up above it. It was like say the ocean boiling up and bursting and letting go all the stories of pain and suffering and brutality and horrors it been hiding quiet mongst the stillness of shipwreck and planewreck and sargasso grass and submerge mountain and earthquake whispers.

Same time, Anancy know that he reaching a roots change deep down inside him spiderman self. All the living dead he facing causing him to calm the Anancy nature in the world, especial about the last sting. But he still against the murder of the ancestors and today murder.

Yet and all, when he see himself dead and gone, he not frighten; he just calm and peaceful in him head. Living is catching up with the sting that flying a little way up front, he saying to himself, as he sitting down on the rock.

Well, that come to that. But now, even though Anancy certain that the Dance of the Souls of Dead Slaves happening in broad daylight, he certain as well that the daylight changing, now and then, into dawn light, middle morning light, midday light, afternoon light, twilight and midnight blackness.

The light change flicking, in and out, back and front, as if some sort of giant plan hand playing with a giant switch that controlling day and night across the Atlantic.

The voices wailing and tumbling sorrows. The souls walking and floating, slow and fast. The black instruments of raw torture flying loops like john crow. Sizzling history words and phrases splashing themself with foam, water and air. And in one typhoon whirlpool, it look to Anancy that every single liana of sargasso grass coming together from where the Caribbean Sea join up with the Atlantic Ocean, and forming miles and miles of leaping, circling lasso ropes; and these same out-and-out shapes taking them time and snaking into plenty masks of knife slash, whip lash, wire gash and bullet hole.

The masks have deep cut eyes and mouths that crying out with gut pain. As the bodies get rip open wide, Anancy seeing how them falling in the stinking quarters below and on the slippery mucous deck on top.

One body that bleeding not falling. That body staggering and going after a wicked, grinning whiphand mask. Bullet shower catch him, again. Still, he moving up to the whiphand mask. A next shower. But he moving. Final thing is a knife slash in him neck from another whiphand mask, and he make a last move with him hands spread with claw vengeance, but is only salt air the hands holding.

Without any sort of warning or even pretty please, the rock that Anancy sitting on beginning to shift sideways. Anancy losing balance and sliding off into the water.

The first soul that talk to Anancy, the woman of family wisdom, drop out of the commotion in the sky and raise him up and put him back on the rock.

She say to him, 'Nothing on the land and nothing under the water ever stay steady, too long, you know. Everything moving up and down and sideways, according as to how life and death always going. So, hold on tight and watch yourself, Anancy! A travelling spiderman got to read the natural moves he living with, light and dark, or else he going turn into desert pickney, just circling round on himself, sun and moon making fool out of him, constant. And try member one thing: the world spinning, and all the sunlight and all the shadows staying on it like skin and coming on and on a next time and a next time, on and on, as long as ball rolling.'

And Anancy say to her, 'Ball is one thing I know. But what happening with change condition?'

She laugh little bit, and say, 'That never, never just happen by itself, Anancy. You youself must cause it. Is so it come to all who spinning through sunlight and shadows.'

But Anancy soon come to find out that the rock moving swift stream. It pulling out of the dread scene of the Dance of the Souls of the Dead Slaves. It backing out towards north east Atlantic.

Anancy, born traveller from way back, understand the movement of the rock, and the most he finding himself doing is waving to the ancestors, to the souls who know capture and murder and no peace on earth or under water.

2

Strangers in a Strange Land

W. E. B. DU BOIS

1892

'Harvard in Berlin'

*The long life of W. E. B. Du Bois (1868–1963) defies summary. A historian,
sociologist, editor, journalist, novelist and poet, he was one of the founders of
the National Association for the Advancement of Colored People, and edited
its magazine* The Crisis *for many years. He played a leading role in the Pan-
African movement, travelling widely, but in the 1950s his radical ideas fell foul
of McCarthyism and he was not allowed to leave the country for six years. In
1961 he renounced his US citizenship and took up residence in newly
independent Ghana at the invitation of its President, Kwame Nkrumah.*

*Born in rural Massachusetts, he was left orphaned and penniless at the age
of 17, but, with the aid of scholarships, worked his way through Fisk University
and Harvard College, and in 1892 made his first trip abroad after securing a
grant to study at Friedrich Wilhelm University in Berlin. In* The Dusk of Dawn
*(1940) he remarked how 'Europe modified profoundly my outlook on life and
my thought and feeling toward it, even though I was there but two short years
with my contacts limited and my friends few'. He found time to make several
trips across Central Europe, venturing as far as Naples, and returned via Paris.
In this essay, published for the first time in 1985, he describes the intricacies of
student enrolment.*

The American contingent of student exiles, two hundred strong, have scarcely
settled down to their year's work although Christmas, and a German Christmas
at that, is in sight. Our vocabulary is yet a most delightful conglomeration of
unintelligible 'Deutsch,' and unintelligent English. Nevertheless light is gradually
breaking in dark places, intricate jungles of sounds become passable, and strings
of gutturals [are] resolving themselves into clear ideas. Our Berlin academic halls,
too, are getting hard and solid, losing that sort of ethereal sheen which, to the
fresh American, envelops everything European.

German universities used to have a way of opening whenever the various
students and professors thought best. These delightful days are now past and by
the law of the land lectures begin somewhat more promptly, generally about the
last week in October.

To be a bit chronological, the first ordeal of the student is to matriculate – a
ceremony of no mean proportions in Berlin. I remember we used to make certain

W. E. B. Du Bois, *Against Racism: Unpublished Essays, Papers, Addresses, 1887–1961*, edited by
Herbert Aptheker (Amherst: University of Massachusetts Press, 1985), pp. 29–33. Copyright © 1985
by The University of Massachusetts Press.

sarcastic remarks over Harvard 'red tape,' but it was because we had not seen the deeper crimson of the Berlin quality. I consumed three mortal hours (one of which was my lunch hour) in the process of getting my name on the official rolls of the university. There we shivered and waited, outside the mystic room 33, the Americans spending their time in discovering each other, talking shop, and – football. Here I learned my one infallible rule for picking out an American in a German crowd. Look at his feet – the two styles of shoes have absolutely nothing in common.

Finally about 12 o'clock (my entrance card said 10) there came a rush, and a hundred or more students sallied out of the holy of holies, and a like number crowded in, myself among them. It was a large room, with high ceiling, and a row of four windows on one side in the deep recesses of which stood busts of Berlin's famous professors. The center of the room was occupied by chairs, in which the students seated themselves; at the upper end was a long table about which perhaps a dozen officials were grouped. Near the left end was the present year's *rector magnificus*, the widely famous Rudolf Virchow, doctor of medicine, laws and philosophy, city councillor and member of the Reichstag. He is a meek and calm looking man, white haired and white-bearded, with a kindly face and pleasant voice. At smaller tables ranged before the windows, were the deans of various faculties.

The method of procedure was thoroughly and, I think I may say, painfully, German. First the chief secretary at the side of the magnificent rector was invested with the pile of gymnasium diplomas and passports we had surrendered in the ante-room. Then he slowly read out the names, and as a student heard his name he disentangled himself and approached the table. Recognizing with some difficulty my Germanicized name I presented myself with some trepidation at the bar. The stiff secretary (it's quite the thing to be stiff in the new Germany) with my help more clearly deciphered my name, ascertained under which faculty I wished to study, firmly declined to examine any of my sheepskins, and passed me over to the rector: rector Virchow smiled benignantly, made some remark as to my faculty, and after filling out the blanks with some remarkably poor writing, presented me with a large 24 × 18 inch sheet of paper: this stated that a certain . . . [1] had in the general goodness of his heart endowed the present Mr. Virchow with various powers; among these was that of making me (who was described with some infelicity of phrase as a 'most ornamented young man') a legalized and licensed Berlin student. This was well printed, on fair paper, and I shall, eventually, have it framed. Armed with this I was introduced to magnificent No. 3, who wrote my name in a ponderous and sinister looking volume, together with an unnecessarily large amount of elicited information as to my previous history and the personnel of my ancestors. I was then shoved on to secretary after secretary: this one furnished me with another diploma for my particular faculty; that one with a card.

The next filled this out with my name and number. Meantime I was getting weary of this prolonged ceremony and very full of suggestions for improvement; also hungry. I was still gently urged on – a bit more willingly now as I had almost completely encircled the table and felt morally certain that much further progress

---

1 Illegible word in the original; probably a reference to some title for the kaiser.

would necessitate architectural changes in the room. The last official after prolonged calculation relieved me of fifteen marks, and added to my load of sorrow a rich and varied assortment of literature, comprising among other things, rules and regulations (O, world-book!), library commands and demands, blanks for the questor, recipes against moral turpitude, etc., etc. Before and behind me the line of students continued the dead march, in a manner that strongly reminded me of Mr. Armour's Chicago hog parlors. Nor was the end yet; with the easy German contempt of time I was now piloted to the dean of the Philosophical faculty, to whom I laid siege being armed with enough signed and sealed printed matter to have enabled me to achieve brilliant social success anywhere west of Buffalo. Down my name went again, and down went another autograph on my diplomas. Well, he was the last man: I gave a polite little sigh of relief, and – was informed that I must now resume my seat, wait till the whole line behind me were through, when the rector would hold a hand-shaking. Being peaceful and law-abiding I sat down; if I had the ability to have told a straight lie, I don't know what I might not have attempted. I am quite certain that many of the German students disappeared and escaped with honor. As it was I lingered, and, finally, all being duly labelled and ladened, the rector arose and addressed a few words of fatherly advice – something about being good and studying, etc., – and then we all filed past him, bowed, shook his hand, and departed to give room to the next hundred lambs. So great was the labor necessary to becoming a full-fledged Berlin student.

The next business before me was that of finding a room – a work of more than ordinary difficulty in an unknown tongue. There are numbers of American students who come to Germany and go into American boarding-houses, talk and walk with Americans, and leave having missed the true poetry of student life. Imagine a Harvard student boarding at Young's and spending his leisure in Newton!

The correct Berlin method is to hire a nook in a flat, from three to five stories up. There with pipe and beer, coffee and black bread, he lives not like a king, but as a free and easy viking bound to the student world by his kneipes (drinking bouts), his societies, and – possibly – his lectures. The student quarter of Berlin – so far as a distinctive quarter can be assigned them – is the old Latin quarter. In an ordinary city this would be the slums, but Berlin being an extraordinary city with no visible proletariat, this quarter is merely narrower and darker than the rest of the Berlin world. Here you can hire a comfortable room for $5 to $10 a month. Morning coffee costs perhaps $1.30 per month extra, and heat 7 or 8 cents a day. O yes, I must not forget to say that boot-blacking is thrown in and the most impecunious student may always have a faultless polish.

My room is roomy and four flights up, with books, papers, and *her* picture – of course! There is the wardrobe and bureau with mirror to match, lounge and table, screened bed and commode, and a ponderous institution called a stove. I am devoutly awaiting the advent of a domestic Bismarck, who shall make some compromise and transfer the wild and seething heat of the German feather-bed covering to the coldly placid and beautiful tile stove. My floor is uncarpeted, my walls are but scantily adorned – in fact this is not the shadow of a Harvard dormitory room, and yet I live in remarkable freedom and contentment and feel somewhat disposed to sneer at the effeminate luxuries beyond the sea.

My coffee with two fat rolls and butter, I take at eight. About ten I follow the example of my fellow Germans, I stalk through the academic halls reflectively munching a sandwich to ward off starvation. I find the custom much better for study than [word illegible]; ah! how often have I groaned in a nine o'clock recitation under the weighty exuberance of a Memorial breakfast! Germans are compelled to dine at 12, because their language calls the meal 'mittags-essen' while 'dinner,' which could come at six is – *ach weh!* – French. We all dine in restaurants; I generally pay about 21 cents including beer and tip. Coffee comes again at 3, and my *abendbrot*, I take in my room from my private larder – my landlady warming the tea. Thus my total expenses, including theater once or twice a week, a symphony now and then, and other good music galore, together with various other recreations, cost me about $200 a term or $400 for the year. If more economically minded, I might make this $300.

MARY CHURCH TERRELL

'I Study in Germany'

*Mary Church Terrell (1863–1954) was born in Memphis, Tennessee, and
educated at Oberlin College. In 1887 she moved to Washington, DC, to take
up a teaching post, and then studied in Europe for two years. Following her
return, she became the first President of the National Association of Colored
Women (1896–1901) and a founder member of the National Association for
the Advancement of Colored People. A leading public speaker, she
campaigned for improved education, welfare and health care, votes for
women, and anti-lynching legislation. She travelled widely in the United
States and addressed conferences in Berlin (1904), Zurich (1919) and London
(1937). In this extract from her autobiography,* A Colored Woman in a White
World *(1940), she recalls episodes from her first trip abroad.*

On the way to Berlin I stopped in Munich and Dresden. In Munich I employed a
guide to show me the city. I had spoken nothing but French for a year, and,
although I had spoken German fairly well before I left home, both my tongue and
my ear were somewhat out of practice. As soon as I reached Germany, however,
I was delighted to see that I could understand what was said to me and could
express everything I wanted to say.

My guide, a blond German, suggested that he could carry my Baedeker's
guidebook more conveniently than I could. I had bought it before I left Lausanne,
so that I could read up on the journey I was about to take and decide what I wanted
to see, before I reached the places. It always amused me a bit to see Americans
with their heads buried in their guidebooks and their eyes glued to the printed
page instead of looking at the works of art or at the structures they had come so
far to see.

I forthwith entrusted my Baedeker to the guide's watchful care. As we boarded
a street car on our way to a church, a man standing on the rear platform looked
at me very seriously and said something to me in German which I did not quite
understand, but which sounded like a warning of some kind, as he nodded toward
the guide. In thinking about the words spoken rapidly I was sure I heard
'Geldbeutel,' and I knew it meant 'purse.' I observed also that the guide looked
daggers at this man, who was speaking directly to me as though he were trying
to tell me something for my own good. It finally dawned on me that the stranger
was warning me against the guide and telling me to watch my purse.

Mary Church Terrell, *A Colored Woman in a White World* (Washington, DC: Ransdell, 1940),
pp. 72–80.

When I settled with my guide that evening I understood perfectly what the man on the trolley car was trying to tell me. After paying him for the time he had given me, I asked him for my book. At first he denied having taken it from me at all. He could not remember doing so, he said. But when I insisted he had, he began to search carefully through the many pockets in his trousers and sweater, as though he were trying to find it. After looking for it in vain, he opined that he must have lost it somewhere during the day. But when I told him in German that if he did not find my Baedeker I would call the police, he fished it from the depths of his sweater, being obliged to insert his hand so far down in his clothing I feared he could never bring it up again. But when his hand did finally heave in sight, so did my Baedeker's guidebook. That was one of the very few cases in which an effort was made to steal from me while I was abroad. Sometimes the cabmen or the small tradesmen would try to withhold a few centimes in making change, but they did it so cleverly and had reduced their manipulations and explanations and gesticulations to such a work of art that it was almost a pleasure to be cheated by those skillful gentlemen. No woman of any nationality ever tried to cheat me out of a sou from the time I left the United States till I returned.

When I reached Dresden I was glad I had decided to study in Berlin. The city was full of Americans and English. Wherever I turned on the streets, I heard my mother tongue. I knew that a foreign city full of my white countrymen was no place for a colored girl. I was trying to flee from the evils of race prejudice, so depressing in my own country, and it seemed very stupid indeed for me to place myself in a position to encounter it abroad.

In Dresden I received my first taste of German opera, for there the most noted singers were appearing at that time. I went alone, for it was never unpleasant for me to go anywhere unaccompanied. From the time I first began to travel, I preferred to go by myself, so that I might see just what interested me and stop to look at it as long as I pleased without feeling I was annoying somebody else who was not so eager to gaze on it as I was. On several occasions I have had the pleasure of traveling with people who were interested in the same things that I was, and then 'I had the time of my life.'

When I reached Berlin I decided to remain temporarily at a pension on Markgrafen Strasse which was kept by a neat, pleasant little Jewess. She had only one vacant room, which was so small I did not see how I could be comfortable in it. There was no place to hang my clothes and no way to heat the room except by a gas stove, and I had always heard that heat from a gas stove was injurious to the health. For that reason I looked at a room in another pension and talked with the proprietor about it, discussed the price, and told him I would notify him at a certain time whether I would take it or not. In the meantime, the guests in the Markgrafen Strasse pension were so agreeable and so eager to have me stay, and the clever landlady made the little room so comfortable and attractive, I decided to remain there. The fact that there were no Americans in the pension to tempt me to speak English was an added inducement for me to stay where I was.

According to promise, therefore, I communicated my decision to the proprietor of the pension who had shown me a room several days before. He claimed that I had definitely engaged the room and that he had saved it for me, and insisted upon having me pay the rent for a month. As the less of two evils, I acceded to his demand. Some American women who had seen me pass through the hall told the proprietor I was quite swarthy and it was barely possible I represented a race which was socially ostracized in the United States by all white people who had any self-respect. I learned afterward on good authority that my countrywomen would have made it decidedly unpleasant for me if I had gone to that pension to live.

When I reached Berlin I had not heard from home for three weeks. Before leaving Lausanne I had instructed Father to send my letters *poste restante* to Berlin. As soon as I reached Berlin, therefore, and decided on the pension at which I would remain temporarily, I started for the city post-office, eager to get the mail which I knew was awaiting me. I received many letters, and when I had finished reading them, I started to return to my boarding house. It was the first week in December, the afternoons were short, and I observed that it was growing dark rapidly. When I looked for the paper containing my new address, it was nowhere to be found. While joyously reading my letters from home, I had undoubtedly lost that slip of paper of such great value to me. So there I was in the great city of Berlin with night coming on, actually lost, acquainted with no one, while practically everything I possessed was in my luggage deposited in an apartment house which I could not locate to save my life.

After cudgeling my brain a long time I thought I remembered the name of the street on which my pension was located. I was also able to tell the policeman to whom I related my troubles the name of the car I had boarded to reach the post-office, and I described pretty accurately the corner on which I had taken it. So systematically is everything conducted in Germany that it is quite easy to secure quickly practically any information one needs. The names of people who keep boarding houses are on file, and a stranger may remain in the city only a short while before he is required to register his name and tell everything about himself the authorities want to know, and they want to know EVERYTHING.

And so, after several processes of induction and deduction plus consultations with a certain office, I discovered where I had deposited my belongings. When I finally reached the pension, it was quite dark, and I found that both my landlady and all her boarders were very much alarmed about the inexplicably long absence of the young American girl who had just reached the big city. After such an experience I carefully guarded my addresses in the future and was never lost in a strange city again.

Our family included two brothers, Hebrews, one of whom was a bank official, very learned, very sedate, and mature. The other was much younger and was connected with the stock exchange. He was an entertaining, witty Lothario. Then there was a tall young German with a magnificent physique who was studying something or other which was a dead secret and who was always talking about a girl to whom he was engaged back home. 'Meine Braut' was a subject which he never tired of discussing and regaled us with, in season and out. He had been an officer in the army, since he was living in the heyday of German militarism, and he told us over and over again how his fiancée used to come to his house every day, so that she and his mother might look out of the window as he proudly marched by. No human being could possibly be more conceited than he was, and no human being, not even excepting Bismarck himself, could have believed more implicitly in brute force than he did. Not only did he believe in war and all the horrors incident thereto, but he smacked his lips with relish when he told how he intended to whip his children and boss his wife.

There was also an interesting little clerk who was heels-over-head in love with the landlady, who had no idea of marrying a man as poor as he was. Being of a romantic turn of mind, I did everything in my power to soften Fräulein's heart, but she always silenced me by saying that she herself had long outgrown the romantic age, when women marry for love alone. It was the first time I had ever heard a woman declare openly and above-board that she did not intend to marry for love, and I marveled at her frankness.

The two Hebrew brothers helped me greatly in learning German and becoming thoroughly acquainted with Berlin as well as its interesting suburbs. They advised me with reference to the books it was best to read, and directed me to various objects of interest which are not generally mentioned in a traveler's guide and which I should not have seen but for them. On several occasions these two brothers and a cousin took me to see the castles in the environs of Berlin. I especially enjoyed visiting the one at which Frederick the Second and Queen Victoria's daughter, his consort, spent their honeymoon.

This Englishwoman was the first person to establish a school in Germany for the higher education of girls. But the German idea of the higher education of girls differed materially from that entertained in the United States. Some of the professors from the University of Berlin delivered lectures at this girls' school which might easily have been digested by children of twelve. But the facilities for the so-called higher education offered women at this institution were greater than those which could be found anywhere else in Germany at that time and they were, therefore, gratefully accepted by many.

I attended this school, and one day when the Empress Frederick, who had founded it, visited it, I curtsied to her in true German fashion like the other girls. Twice and sometimes three times a week I attended the opera while I remained in Berlin. I often attended the theater also, for there is no better way of educating the ear and acquiring the correct pronunciation in studying a foreign language than by listening to good actors. I had a dear little Russian friend who was one of the most remarkable linguists I have ever met. She spoke at least seven languages fluently. We usually attended the opera together and sat in the peanut gallery, which was frequented by students, from whose comments I learned much more about the operas and music on general principles than I could have acquired in any other way.

Thus I became acquainted with the youth of many lands, some of whom were rated as geniuses and expected sooner or later to startle the world with their achievements. Many of them were poor in this world's goods, however rich in talent and great expectations they were. To me it was pathetic to see the desperate struggle to get along and keep soul and body together which many of them made. The schemes which some of them hatched to make life a bit easier than it was were also amusing.

One day my landlady knocked at my door and told me some callers wished to see me. When they were ushered into my room, one of my Belgian friends introduced me to a blind musician from Austria. He had come to propose marriage to me. He had probably heard from some American student that I had African blood in my veins, was very fond of music, and might be glad to marry a promising musician. Since I hailed from the United States, he took it for granted that I had a respectable bank account. He was perfectly willing, therefore, to link his destiny with mine, assuring me that what he lacked in money he more than made up in talent. I learned from a reliable source that this was true. He begged me to marry him and he promised to become a great artist. Several of the friends he brought with him gave glowing accounts of the laurels he had already won as a pianist. He would surely be heard from some day, they declared. There was no doubt about that, and then, they said, I would be proud to be the wife of one of the greatest virtuosos in Europe.

The blind musician explained that he had heard me talk on several occasions, liked my point of view about some of the questions discussed, and thought I had a beautiful voice. He said he had dared to come to propose because one of his friends had pursued a similar course and had succeeded in marrying an American girl with a lot of money.

Although I was greatly amused, and could scarcely conceal my disgust, I felt sorry for the afflicted man and tried not to say anything which would wound his feelings. I declined his offer, however, in no uncertain terms, saying that I had been reared to believe that marrying for anything but love was a sin, and that his cold-blooded proposition shocked me beyond expression.

While I was in Berlin, I was greatly indebted to a young man of my own race for several musical treats I enjoyed and for information concerning musical people which I could have secured from no other source. And the way I happened upon this friend was very romantic indeed. Shortly after reaching Berlin I walked out with an American girl whom I had known in Oberlin to see the beautiful shops so brilliantly lighted and artistically decorated for Christmas. We had stopped several times to admire the wonderful display. I felt that somebody was following me, and I turned around several times to see if I could discover anyone. Once I thought I saw a man stop suddenly quite a little distance behind me, but I was not sure, so I said nothing to my companion. We continued our stroll, stopping every now and then to discuss the beautiful objects displayed. Just as we drew up to a window I turned around suddenly and saw standing behind us Will Marion Cook, a young man with whom I had been well acquainted for years and who was then studying music in Berlin.

He said he had suddenly spied me, as he turned the corner, and although he felt sure he recognized me, he could not believe the evidence of his eyes, because he had not heard I had left the United States to travel and study in Europe. He was so impressed with the resemblance I bore to the girl he knew at home, however, he decided to follow my companion and me until he could catch a glimpse of my face, and he was just coming up to greet me when I recognized him. This young man had remarkable talent for the violin. At that time Joachim, one of the greatest teachers of the violin of modern times, taught nobody who was not unmistakably talented in that instrument. Neither wealth, power, nor high social position could tempt this great master to teach anybody who was not a presumptive genius. It was rumored in Berlin that more than one member of the aristocracy had implored Joachim in vain to teach his son. But the great Joachim taught this young colored man from the United States, so impressed was he with his superior talent. Instead of confining himself to the violin, however, this young musician has become a renowned composer of popular music characteristic of his race.

I talked with a young colored man who was studying in Europe because he possessed exceptional talent. He seemed listless rather than lazy, and it pained me to hear from some of his friends that he was wasting his time. When I urged this young man to avail himself of the marvelous opportunities and advantages he enjoyed, he replied, 'What's the use of my trying to do anything extraordinary and worth while? A man must have some kind of racial background to amount to anything. He must have a firm racial foundation on which to build. What have we accomplished as a race? Almost nothing. We are descended from slaves. How can you expect a people with such a background as that to compete successfully with white people?'

I confessed to him that I myself had once become very much depressed and discouraged when, as a young girl, I realized for the first time I had descended from slaves. But I told the young man that I had recovered my equilibrium immediately, when I learned from the study of history that with a single exception practically every race of the earth had at some time in the past been the subject of a stronger, so that when colored people in this country passed through a period of bondage, they were simply suffering a fate common to other groups. And then I called his attention to the marvelous progress which the colored people in the United States had made in less than forty years.

I could not convert him to my point of view. But no young colored person in the United States today can truthfully offer as an excuse for lack of ambition or aspiration that members of his race have accomplished so little, he is discouraged from attempting anything himself. For there is scarcely a field of human endeavor which colored people have been allowed to enter in which there is not at least one worthy representative.

During the first winter I was in Berlin my mother wrote that she and my brother were coming abroad in the spring to spend the summer with me in Europe, that they would land in Liverpool and she wanted me to meet them.

Just before I left Berlin I was the recipient of a unique gift which I have always highly prized. 'Fräulein, what is your coat of arms?' the elder Mannheimer asked me one day. 'You know full well I have no coat of arms,' I replied. 'Well, you deserve one and you shall have one,' he said. A few days after that he and his brother brought me an elegant leather portfolio on which a quaint little church had been embossed in an American flag. So I think I have the distinction of being the only person of African descent in the United States who has a coat of arms.

While I was preparing to leave Berlin, I broke a small hand mirror. How wretched I was after that! I did not know till then how superstitious I was. I feared that broken mirror was an omen that some terrible disaster would overtake my loved ones at sea. I reached Liverpool at least ten days before the steamer arrived, and, in spite of strenuous efforts to control myself, I was very apprehensive indeed. I dreaded to read the newspapers, lest I might learn that the steamer had gone down and everybody on board had been lost. The afternoon that I saw the speck far out on the ocean that I knew was the steamer bearing my mother and brother to me was a happy one indeed. I waved my umbrella so vigorously that I broke it into pieces, before I realized what I had done. Never since Mother and Brother arrived safely in Liverpool in spite of the broken mirror have I allowed myself to worry much about any superstition.

C. L. R. JAMES

1939

Letters to Constance Webb

*C. L. R. James (1901–1989) grew up in Trinidad and moved to England in
1932. Originally harbouring ambitions as a writer of fiction (a novel, Minty
Alley, was published in 1936), he discovered Marxism and quickly made a
name for himself as a radical journalist and public speaker. His still-classic
study of the San Domingo revolution, The Black Jacobins, appeared in 1938.
The same year, he took up an invitation from James Cannon of the American
Socialist Workers' Party to address audiences in the United States.*

*Towards the end of his speaking tour he met Constance Webb, a young
woman who was in the audience in a Los Angeles church for his talk. He was
on his way to Mexico and a meeting with Trotsky, and it was from the exiled
revolutionary's headquarters that he began a correspondence with her that
lasted nearly ten years. Although they married and she bore him a son, the
relationship was strained by the factionalism and surveillance that went with
James's undercover political activities. They separated, and James, after being
interned on Ellis Island as an illegal alien, was forced to leave the United States
in 1953.*

*The two letters reprinted here were written on board ship as he returned to
the United States from Mexico in 1939, signing himself N (for Nello, a name
used only by family and close friends).*

S.S. Terrible Spanish-Mexican-Indian Name
I'll find it out afterwards

Sunday 3 p.m.

Sunday afternoon, sweetheart, 3 o'clock. The boat is small but riding as in a bath.
The sun is as hot as fire, bluish-green, blue and white sky. It has been lovely . . .

What have you [been] doing on Sunday? You would have been happier here, I
hope. It has been a wonderful trip. Two of us alone travelling – the other is a Mexican
tenor – a real honest to God tenor – going to fill an engagement in Rio de Janeiro,
30, his first big chance I think, he was enquiring about buying 'tails' in New Orleans.
He has a splendid voice – sings popular Songs – but with a passion worthy of the
revolution. He and I sang at one another all during breakfast. I know the lines of
many operatic arias, and he sang Mexican songs. I know 11 words of Spanish and
he 12 words of English but 'love will find out a way' and he and I said it in music.

C. L. R. James, *Special Delivery: The Letters of C. L. R. James to Constance Webb, 1939–1948*, edited
by Anna Grimshaw (Oxford: Blackwell, 1996), pp. 40–9. Reprinted with the permission of
Constance Webb Pearlstien and Anna Grimshaw.

End of Act I

Act II brings a further surprise. There is a steward here, a little Englishman, who has sailed the seas for twenty years. He too is a musician. He sings Spanish songs and plays them on his guitar. So now he and the tenor and I sang during lunch – and after lunch Mr. Steward brings out his guitar and – Mr. James chiefly audience – the two of them sing and play till 5 to 3. As I write, the steward is trying some of the chords the tenor has taught him, the tenor is looking at a book and all the time singing away, chiefly snatches, and I am scribbling away. We are in the little stateroom, six tables only and if I wore a top-hat and stood up suddenly it would get crushed. Through the door and the port-holes is the sun on the sea, and the ship taking everything in its stride. You know how it is on a ship. You are sick, well, happy, miserable, tired or fit, the ship does not care. It just goes on.

I stopped to find out a train to N.Y. for the tenor. Meanwhile, he sang from Pagliaca and I stopped to sing from Martha. And the steward who was washing dishes came back and is now guitaring away. Meanwhile steward No. 2 is making tea in the little room next door. Am I right in thinking that you would love it here? Or am I just being masculine and egoistic and saying: I would like her to be here and therefore naturally she would like it too. You will have to tell me.

Au Voir for the present. Truth compels me to add that it is getting very hot, and there is no shower, only those terrible English tubs – but still, I think it would be lovely.

Now I am alone here and the guitar is lying on a seat, yellow-faced guitar, brown seat, white table-cloth. You know those pictures by Picasso, though, alas, the pictures are always so much more beautiful than the actual still-life. But it has been lovely . . . monotonous but true.

8 p.m.

The ship just keeps going on. Dinner was early, 6; it wasn't so hot after all – I haven't had to change my shirt. And after dinner I sat on the upper deck while the tenor walked up and down, practising his songs very quietly with a little note-book in which he has the words typed. I spend a great deal of my spare hours doing the same – I have now four speeches [I am] working at – one to whites on Negro question, one to Negroes on same, one on war – which may come at any minute – and one specially to Negroes on war. One gets ideas and works them up and jots them down; bit by bit they take shape. It isn't bad fun really . . .

But I sat on the deck and watched the sun go down – a glorious evening, so still, and nobody about, only a member of the crew now and then, and our tenor strolling up and down.

It went dark and I came in here, intending to make some notes on something; instead here I am.

Monday tomorrow; then Tuesday – and Wednesday a.m. New Orleans and once more the world of men again. But these three days, with practically nobody on the ship mean a lot and would have meant so much more if you were here, i.e., if you would like to be here. We are now all four of us listening to Lawrence Tibbett – the guitar player, another steward, tenor and me. L. T. has just sung Largo al Factotum from the Barber of Seville a bravura aria, which half-an-hour ago I was singing to myself on the deck – he sang magnificently – but before and after, i.e., now he is talking a lot of stuff, the silliest patter imaginable. It is an odd combination. For he really sang well. Who cares anyway? Do you? I don't.

I came in here to write lots and lots of things to you. But I have changed my mind. I could say them, but not write them. I wonder if you could imagine what it is like to be on this boat – under these circumstances (there hasn't been a ripple yet); and to sit and dream how lovely it would be if you were here. The stupid chatter on the radio continues . . . Not so stupid though.

A man asks a girl to go to his old childhood slum-home and she turns up her nose; he goes in and she meets a little boy who tells her she is not the girl he wants to marry – she is so cruel. He has a cut on his finger. Suddenly he disappears, and her husband comes back. He has seen no little boy but she asks him to show her his finger. There is the same scar. She begs to be allowed to go in, all will be different, etc. Not bad. But it reminds me of something else – a superb story, superbly told by an East Indian girl, wife of an old old friend of mine, a clergyman, also E. Indian in the W. Indies. Here it is.

One bitter night a man was driving a car and missed the road. He went searching and searching and at last saw a light far in. He turned into a drive, with superb gates, and drove in. A liveried footman met him at the door and led himself (and his wife) into the house. They were entertained by an old-fashioned couple and early next morning they left. The last thing the man did was to give the footman a half-crown.

Later they found that a bridge had been broken by the storm and if they had gone on they would have lost their lives.

But next day when they told their friends nobody knew the house. Rather puzzled, they drove out again, found the road, followed it, and finally came to a drive. But the gates though familiar in outline were old and dilapidated. They drove up the drive – full of weeds – the place had not been lived in for scores of years. They came to the house at last, broken down ruins – they couldn't possibly have stayed there the night before. It must have been all a dream. They got out and walked up the steps and there – there my dear Connie on the top step was the half-crown he had put in the hand of the footman the night before.

Do you thrill at that sort of thing? I hope so. I do. I know some superb tales of that kind, Gautier, the Frenchman, Poe, and Pushkin, and Ambrose Bierce. They belong to a non-industrial age, and they appeal to that healthy fear of the supernatural and mysterious which even in this age of electric light and no forests just behind our houses, still appeal to many of us. And how beautifully written most of them are! They are a memory of my pre-MARX days.

The funny thing is that this one is supposed to be true – some English paper asked for true mystery stories and this one was sent in and my friend read it there and told it to us one evening just before I left for England in 1932. She is the ablest woman I know and it is a tragedy that she is buried in the W. Indies – clergyman's wife – 6 children. But she has a marvellous gift of speech and a great sense of the dramatic. (The tenor has just turned on another tenor from Havana, his 'companero' he tells me; the man sings well, this radio fellow and has just sung 'Mi amor' with great feeling. Why, oh why, my dearest Connie, aren't you here? There it is again 'Mi Amor;' the song is silly, I can feel that, I mean by that cheap, but still for the time it is good to hear.)

I absolutely must stop, or I shall write forever and ever and then my hand will hurt me tomorrow. (The guitar is still on the brown seat.)

I have just looked outside – one star and then a million miles away another, and then two million miles away, a third. But there are dim lights on the deck, and if you were here, we would now clear out of the dining-saloon and go and sit on the deck and we would talk . . . Good-night (*No. 1*) and I hope you have had a lovely day, and remembered me at odd moments; and not thought too much of your past troubles. Sweetheart, I must write one more scrap. 'Guitar' fumbled at the radio and behold the Seventh Symphony of Beethoven. The slow movement; one of the loveliest of all the works before the last ones. Now the slow movement is over, and they are playing the quick one – the middle part – one day I may listen to it with . . . Once more, good-night.

Darling a tragedy. This pair of Philistines have cut off the symphony. 'Guitar' suddenly discovered in a Mexican magazine the fingering of the guitar-accompaniment to a song the tenor knows. So they got very excited and are now hard at it. (Listen and you can hear them.) 'Guitar' is a typical cockney, with a little sharp face; how English he looks, but Spanish-America has captured him and he loves these Spanish rhythms and his guitar. So for the last time (I swear) Good N.

Monday
Here we are, sweetheart, 7:45, and I am writing to you already. True devotion, and (for truth must be told) I am 10 minutes too early for breakfast.

I have something to relate. This a.m. I rose at 7 and looked out of the port-hole till 7:20 waiting for the steward. There is no shower and he has to put water into the bath. I got up and went into the bathroom for my own purposes and there was water in the bath, towels, etc. My dear, had you been there you would have been proud of your Nello. I did not hesitate. For about two minutes I pondered. Was this bath mine or not? I weighed up both sides and then decided that I didn't know . . .

Then I remembered I was a Bolshevik. Would I be deterred and impeded in my progress towards the World Revolution (the radio is playing: I love you truly, old-fashioned and trite but it always brings memories of a rose-garden in Trinidad and the friends of my youth, Cuesa D, playing the piano and Eric Roach the violin). But to return. As I was saying, I came to a decision. And once having decided, nothing stopped me. Without a trace of Menshevism with nothing that might even be construed as Lovestonism (centrism) this hero (darling, it is the *only,* word; forgive me if I sound boastful, but I *must* be true to myself), this HERO took the bath. Calmly I poured the water over my shoulders, etc. Did my heart beat at the thought that at any moment I would hear the tenor's voice running up and down the scale outside and calling imprecations on the head of this intruder? Truth to tell sweetheart (I must tell you the truth) it did. But it would have been invisible to the mortal eye. I concluded, not hastily, with dignity, though I did not linger. It would have been foolhardy to do so.

It is now some 20 minutes and I have heard nothing. Audacity has conquered again. The tenor has come in. He smiles, I smile. Either the bath was mine or he is a man of deep deception. Obviously the latter. But will he catch me late at night on the quarter-deck when no one is looking. Oh, no, my dear, 1000 times no; I shall avoid these obscure places and shall arrive safe in N. Orleans to post this letter.

But before we leave the subject, I have to say that I did not show myself inferior. The best observers agree that my demeanor hitherto has showed not the slightest resemblance to that of the traditional countenance usually assumed by stealers of baths. Enough, I must not boast, though it would be lovely if you were here to share my triumph. As it is, the only man I can tell is the tenor, and that would show a lack of proportion.

Afternoon: 2:30

If you were here you would have been out of this. Though I would have been able to tell you after, which I cannot do now. The little Englishman has been telling me tales of his adventures with girls in Vera Cruz, N. Orleans, Jamaica, Rio, etc. Never was an Englishman so transformed. He has the typical Latin's attitude to women; and has accumulated an enormous amount of knowledge. Being a bit of an artist, he of course is happy to hold forth and I have one great virtue my dear: I can listen, for hours and hours . . . To all sorts of people, especially strangers. And my greatest weakness? Impatience at party meetings and committees. One of my best friends, an experienced Ceylonese, checked me 3 or 4 times at a little meeting we held just before I left – asked questions, wanted to know what X thought or Y – and told me afterwards that it didn't matter what they thought but that I was giving an impression of railroading the meeting – and that was bad. He was right; but I find it terribly hard to be patient with party 'leaders' who waste a great deal of time displaying 'ego' under cover of revolutionary zeal. For long I have made the best resolutions but failed. And yet on the other hand I have sat for hours in America listening to people, all sorts of poor working people, telling me all about themselves. It is indispensable for any understanding of anything. It must go side by side with the books. Well I couldn't help thinking how differently I would have listened to him 6 years ago. He told me many things which interested me as a man. But he told me also some grand tales. Now 6 years ago I was all set for being a novelist. I had written a novel (it was published. Do you want to read it?) and many short stories. And I would have taken down all these tales – and very very revealing some of them were – and worked them up into a good story. But those days are over. Though I still listen to stories with the same interest. One of them, told with rich and intimate detail, was of his relations with a prostitute in Vera Cruz. She could do what she liked until he came into port, but when he came, nothing doing with any other man. They used to fight, knives, etc. One day he nearly killed her and the next day he told her 'You know I am married. If you stay here I am going to kill you one day. So I don't want to see you in this port again. Go to Mexico City.' She begged but he said No. And she went. Packed her traps and went and left a letter to tell him she had gone. I could see on his face how miserable he was. It happened only a few weeks ago. Says when the ship comes in now, he doesn't know what to do with himself; thinks of her all the time! It is a funny world. He is a most interesting man – not one atom of class-consciousness but a man of the world, with a spirit of adventure and intelligence above the average. Quite a personality in his way. He is a fine talker and that is one sure sign of a capability to dominate men. He is the kind who would join the revolution, afterwards, and do very well.

Tonight I shall try to meet the Negro cooks for a talk. I had a long talk yesterday with another steward – married to a Mexican woman. Another Englishman. A very serious, capable fellow, told me all about his wages, the ship's profits, wages of women in New Orleans, etc. Does not think of changing society, but instinctively feels that such and such wages are a damned shame – sees through the profiteering, etc., – this ship flies the Honduras flag to escape taxes. But I'll keep politics out of this letter for the time being. But the little man did say a lot of very interesting things. He explained in great detail the physiology and psychology of the prostitute. I could write a good and startling story especially as I have spent a day in Vera Cruz and have some idea of the locale. But my days for fiction are over. The day? Perfect, a cloudless if somewhat sullen-looking sky, sullen by implication as it were; blazing sunshine, a shimmering sea, and the ship ploughing steadily on. The tenor has disappeared. Perhaps he is having a bath.

The boatswain is the man in charge of the crew, and is a Negro. I was astonished for he has whites under him. The secret? The captain knows the boatswain for years, likes him, and says 'As long as you do your work no one will trouble you.' But the chief mate is a Norwegian who hates Negroes and if he got the chance he would not only have a white boatswain, but he wouldn't have a Negro on the ship. But the old captain says 'No.' The illuminating thing is that they all get on very well together. There is never any trouble. They know the captain will stand no nonsense.

Red, the second steward, tells me that he and the captain's steward, a Negro, go out sometimes in N.O. 'But when we get into the car,' says Red, 'I have to go to the front and he has to go to the back.' Now Red is a practical man and does not seem to probe too deeply into the why or wherefore of things.

So what annoys him is that 'when I go to the back with him to continue our investigation, then the conductor comes after me.' Truly, man is an irrational animal.

(The stretches of green island are getting larger and larger . . .) There are taxis for white and taxis for black, and as few blacks travel by this boat there will be no taxis for them and I shall have to telephone for one. So that is my introduction to the South. People have been warning me and I have said 'Oh, I'll manage,' perhaps with too much confidence. If I were an American citizen I wouldn't care, but if I get into any trouble with the police bang go my hopes for a further extension of my visa and re-entry after a little trip abroad. Strange, as I near the actual contact, I begin to feel a slight nervousness. I shall get through of course, unless someone goes out of his way to annoy me, but the feeling of uncertainty shows me how terribly the minds and characters of Negroes must be affected, especially those who have no experience or political or historical background to help them, or no consciousness of a way out.

When I see you sometime I shall tell you some things about Negroes, things which I have experienced in my own person, and give you some idea of what goes on in a Negro's mind. (Guitar has been laying the table, singing accompaniments to the radio-tunes. He is a most lively man and he harmonises and displays really unusual musical gifts.)

So now to dinner. And if I do not get a letter from you at N.O. P.O. I shall not forgive you. No, it is no use asking for forgiveness. NO, I said. But as it's you and for a bribe (guess what that will be) I shall magnanimously forgive you. Not guilty but don't do it again. Now, am I not a nice man? I forgive you (with bribe) for a sin you have not committed. Any fool can forgive for an actual transgression, but it takes a man above the average to rise to the heights I have just attained. But, sweetheart, if there isn't a letter I'll swear and it will be lucky that you will not be there to hear what I shall say.

Sweetheart, a funny thing. It is 7 and we have just taken on board the second pilot for the river trip and it seems he brings letters. He brought one for Guitar – from his wife it seems. He was jumping round as usual, but he grinned. Then he fumbled around and at last sat down and read it eagerly; but he looked at me with a knowing grin as if to excuse himself. 'I am not one of those soft chaps you know.' I was surprised. And the silly goat, ashamed of being happy at receiving a letter from his wife a day before he reaches home, after being away less than a fortnight. You see he has boasted so much about his knowledge of women that he feels he is letting himself down by being so eager to receive a letter from his own wife. He is a happy man, although he does miss his little Vera Cruz prostitute. I shall not forget this little man. There he is again, chattering away to the other steward, but he has his letter in his pocket and sweetheart, I *know* that as soon as he gets away from us, he will pull it out and start reading again.

And now, sweetheart, it is nearly over. We land at 7 tomorrow. We have just had a rollicking 1 radio 'grammes Pepsodent Linoleum something, Walter Raleigh tobacco, and lots more. How I laughed. Such vigour and wit and rollicking humour, and chiefly vigour. You know, England and France, and Germany haven't got it in them. The whole bunch of us sat round and laughed except tenor, who was away, but came late. He couldn't understand the language.

In a few minutes I go in to pack and then look out the port-hole until I drop asleep. I will think of you last before I go to sleep and first thing when I get up in the morning.

It will have taken you a terrible long time to read this letter. Has it surprised you? It would be very strange if it didn't. But all unknown to yourself you have been my dear companion on this journey. I saw you that afternoon in the church, then that impudent Carlo said at your house 'Isn't she lovely?' and I had to rebuke him. You remember? When we came back you were in a red dressing gown and all sleepy and exciting. I was sorry I didn't see you on the last Saturday. I intended to write but very soberly all about politics; and then came your first letter, written very honestly and with a generosity of aspiration and confidence that startled me; then the second – you were so excited about your Sunday trip that you wanted to write and wrote off to me at once. And now I have replied. You see I am a dangerous man to write to. Write him 3 pages and he writes back 23. I have been crazy on this trip I believe, but you are worth being crazy about. It is your fault. You must not write such eager letters and at the same time appear suddenly before lonely men, wearing red dressing gowns and rubbing your eyes like a big baby who needs to be put to bed. It isn't fair, my dearest Connie, if you write such letters then you must wear spectacles, have your hair brushed back and wear plain clothes; or if you must look as you do (Phoebus calls you zoftig – a Jewish word), then you must ask me if I don't just *love* Clark Gable. Not the two together. The result is 23 pages. Till I don't know when; soon I hope. And now good-bye. Is it a hand only you extend to me? No, the initiative is mine, now. So out on to the deck we go and (if I don't write it you will still know, so why shouldn't I) I take you into my arms and kiss you, as we would kiss if we had really spent these days together and it were our last night.

Good night – once more – and yet again, good night.

Sincerely,

N

Suppose I sat and read this over. It might go into the Mississippi in lots of little pieces. Would you have been sorry? But I am not going to re-read it. You opened your heart to me (though a woman always keeps back a little; have you?). I have done the same. You have confidence in me. I have in you also.

S.S. Tegucigalpa (Got it at last)

Night 7:50

I have just listened to a radio-drama. Absolutely priceless, my dear C, absolutely priceless.

Apple Annie was an old hag who had a daughter in a convent in Spain. Annie sold apples but used to write the daughter as a Mrs. Socialite from a swell hotel. Now the daughter is coming and bringing her lover, a Count's son and his father. Annie is in the soup but a tough guy promises to help. He'll set her up as the Socialite for a few weeks. An old stage-trick but it always gives good fun; that's why it lasts.

They have to get a husband and they get one, an old rascal with a gorgeous voice and a choice gift of phrase; but they have to give a reception and the tough guy scours the town to get all the criminals of the town to be Sec'y of the Interior, Attorney General of U.S.A., etc. The rehearsal is rich. But they are all arrested by the police. However the tough guy in chief who can help the police in a case tells the tale to the Mayor and the Governor. They are moved, they come over, there is a small reception, and, wedding bells.

But that was only half the fun. Guitar found it and settled down to listen with me. (Tenor couldn't understand a word so sat on the deck and admired the seascape.) Now Guitar as would be expected from a man of his temperament enjoyed it from the start (though he knew the story). Twice he told me what was coming and I had to sit on him and tell him not to. But suddenly at a most exciting part, the reception went bad, and we couldn't hear a word. My God, you should have seen Guitar. He raged, jumped up, twisted the knobs, called the radio names, among which son of bitch was the mildest; swore that he knew it would do that. This, the unrehearsed part of the show, pleased me vastly. Luckily, things improved but once more it happened again and once more he got mad.

I haven't enjoyed a radio play as much for a long time. It is years since I heard one . . .

I am going in early to-night. I'll write you to-morrow, something serious. For the time being, good-night. One kiss only on your forehead. Shut your eyes. Can you feel it? That's all – for the present.

9:50 Here I am again. I have to. For you are concerned. We sat on the deck and sang and played the guitar. Sweetheart, imagine. The moon was up, the sea still and we sat out there singing away and the tenor playing and singing as if on the stage at Rio – those charming rhythmic Mexican Songs. I have almost learnt one. It says in parts 'Help me to live again,' and 'Life of my life,' i.e., Vida de mi vida. Old stuff, and rather commonplace. But, sweetheart very very moving in these circumstances.

An old man who is a watchman is quite a character here. He has a handsome old face, and he says 'good-morning,' but he is very old and they say that he is very shaky on his feet for the first hour or so every morning. But he is not musically inclined – not to-night at least. He came and listened for a minute and then shuffled away.

And another big sailor in an armless singlet, the dirtiest I have seen for many years, with all his huge arms out, came and sat on a bale. Then he put his elbows on his knees, propped his head on his hands and beat time with his fist for two or three minutes. Music hath charms.

And you? You were here. Sitting next to me, I had an arm around you, just sitting close, no more. To-morrow is the last day. We begin to go up the river in the afternoon – the wonderful Mississippi. We shall have a last night – they and I and you too, sitting on the deck, watching the lights, and singing, the tenor playing the guitar. Could you be happy that way, just sitting, with an arm around you, and a hand holding yours. I'll never forget this journey. Not only has it been lovely in itself but you have been here with me every hour. You should hear me sing 'Vida de mi vida.' Good-night, my dearest Connie.

Tuesday 9
A great change in the weather, darling; no rain but the sea no longer ripples, it heaves, very slightly – the ship scarcely feels it – but different it is; and there is no sun. When you look up into the height of the sky there are clouds of blue and white but they look tired and dull as if they have been out too late last night; around the horizon the sky is dull grey, so is the sea, and they merge one into the other so that this a.m. I saw something in the distance, took it for a plane and it turned out to be a ship.

For all the others it means merely a change in the weather. But for me, darling, it means that my holiday is approaching its end – to-morrow I begin to experience in my own person the rural discrimination of the South. I hope to heaven I do not lose my temper. It would be very stupid to do so.

I am sitting on the deck. Guitar has just done a tap-dance and won the applause of Tenor and me. How happy he was to have given us another pleasant shock! He is now polishing the brass of the windows; and hates it. He tells me so but ironically. 'How I love this job!' He says 'To-day is a field-day.' He has the defects of his temperament, a dislike of sustained labour and drudgery. That is the difference between the artist and the artistic temperament. The temperament can feel, but not strongly enough, or somehow else, lacks the capacity to sit and work and work and work. The artist can. Don't believe, my precious, in any short-cuts. It is work that does it. Patient determined sustained labour. 'Red,' the other steward, complained without bitterness that Guitar does not do his work but stays talking with the passengers all the time. I know the type well. Do you know where? In the revolutionary movement. Quite right, my dear, quite right. Your observation is acute . . .

Guitar is clever. He suspects that I am writing about him. He sees me writing and writing, he knows I write and he would laugh long at the idea that it is a letter. Men of his type, who have lived so much with prostitutes, lose something . . .

So he guesses at any rate – and correctly. Worried? Not he. He is happy and to encourage me, he tells me of a woman passenger who wrote a book about a cruise and put him and 'all his stuff' into it. No wonder he, tenor, and I get on well together – I understand them both and play a modest third violin – I encourage tenor to sing and encourage Guitar to talk. They compliment me on my knowledge of music, and I am suitably modest. I know more about music than they will know in 50 years and I am merely an amateur (Sol Babitz is a real musician: 100%). But I lie low, sing the songs with them, as if I had spent all my life singing popular songs, and we are very happy. Guitar, however, is a remarkable person, on a small scale, despite his cheap little face. And he is no fool in other ways either. I asked him if he would go to England to fight. He said 'Am I a damned fool? My brothers went and what the hell they got? The dole.' 'Would you fight for America?' I said. 'Ah, that's different,' said G. 'For 15 years they gave me work and food and clothes. I would fight for America.' 'But,' I said, 'They didn't *give* you food and clothes. You worked for it. They didn't give it to you because they loved you. They wanted service and you gave it.'

He was serving and he stopped. He had never seen it that way before. He considered it for quite a while, then went on with his chatter. But obviously he was a man who could grasp a new idea quickly, think it over and see its force. His job in the revolution would be as an agitator, to go round and sell the idea. He would pick it up quickly and go around among his friends, having drinks and talking by the yard. They would listen, too. But while he could be used, he should *never never* be a member of the party. The revolution will use all sorts, but not in the party. I am quite sure of that.

And so, sweetheart, I shall be up to my neck soon. I shall write to you of course, but not little treatises like this. I want you to do two things for me. One is to send me a picture – a large one, no little snaps. The second is harder. It is to write to me a long letter telling me how you are getting on, what you are doing and *what you are thinking*. I am not prying into your secrets. But I would like to know much more about you. I shall have to decide on my plans soon. I may get a holiday of a month or two; I will come to Los Angeles during that time for one reason only – to spend it near to you. Otherwise I shall stay near to N. York. *You will of course not mention the slightest hint of this to anyone.* Macbeth, whom I met in Mexico City, tells me about his house in the country – there may be others. I don't know. If I were coming I would ask you to make the arrangements for me, I would give the secretary of the organisation my address in a sealed envelope, and I would bring my books and come in like a thief and live like one. Sweetheart, I have been thinking over the Negro question. I have got hold of a book (in ms.) on statistics of the Negro. And I have been reading as best I could on the way. Also I have talked much with L. T., and have been thinking over all that he said. I am now certain that no one in America, none in the party, has ever seen the Negro question for the gigantic thing it is, and will increasingly be. L. T. sees it, I was groping towards it. I begin to see it now, every day more clearly. The American Negroes touch on one side the American proletariat, on whom so much depends in the present period; on the other they and *not* the British or French proletariat, form the link with the African revolution; and they can form a link with the millions of Indians and Negroes and half-castes who form so much of the population of Spanish-America. And not only before but after the revolution. The American Negro will have to do most of the actual contact between Western civilization and the millions of Africans.

Now I shall have to do a few months of intensive study, before we launch the organisation. How long I shall be able to stay here I do not know. I may have to go to Mexico or Haiti for a few months and then seek to come in again. I want the war to find me in America. I shall probably have to go to Africa some time. All these things have to be worked out. I want to be quiet for a few months, perhaps it will be only weeks; and I would like to come your way. May I? *Do not write until you hear from me.* If you are going to work on the Negro question, sweetheart, you are tackling an almost Virgin field, and one that will amply repay any serious work that you do on it. I would like, in fact I terribly want to tell you all about it; but for that I shall have to come to L.A. Voila.

from *Journey to an Illusion*

Donald Hinds (b. 1934) was born in Jamaica, emigrated to Britain in 1955 and worked for London Transport as a bus conductor. He wrote for the West Indian Gazette, and after publishing an article on young West Indians in the Observer, he was offered a book contract with Heinemann which enabled him to become a full-time writer. Journey to an Illusion: The West Indian in Britain (1966) is a classic study of the migration experience, drawing on conversations with fellow immigrants.

In a 'Prefatory Letter to Kastard Isaac-Henry', the author recalls their last meeting in Cabin 94 on the SS Auriga in 1955 which took them from Kingston to Plymouth. The early sections of the book examine the reasons for migration, focusing on the lives of several individuals in the Caribbean before they leave for England, among them 'Devon Herne', whose subsequent account of his sea voyage is reprinted here. Hinds introduces it with the comment that 'it is typical and yet personal in a way that allows several conclusions to be drawn from it'.

When the S.S. *Auriga* pulled away from the Number One Pier in Kingston Harbour, on Tuesday, 2 August 1955, the news went around that there were eleven hundred of us Jamaicans on board ship. That number was a record for any one trip. The S.S. *Castel Verde*, the sister vessel, was to sail in a day or two with perhaps the same number. Emigration was at that time a life-belt thrown out to a drowning generation. I was twenty-one and had not worked in any kind of employment. I had a certificate for the Third Year Jamaica Local Examination, which should at least have qualified me for a junior teaching post. Most schools could boast three or more passes in the Third Year Examination each year, so if a job could not be found at your own school, it was hopeless trying elsewhere. Even if a job could be found at another school, the salary was so low that it would have been impossible to exist outside your native village. At that time too, there were no Employment Exchanges where someone could register for a job, though there were several privately run Employment Bureaux, whose main functions were to find jobs for domestics, yard-boys, handymen and chauffeurs to the well-to-do residents of Lower St Andrew and Kingston.

Earlier that year I was one of the estimated two thousand who tried to get a place at the Jamaica School of Agriculture. There were only twenty-five vacancies. My

*Donald Hinds, *Journey to an Illusion* (London: Heinemann, 1966), pp. 35–51. Reprinted with the permission of the author.

mother, who at the time had remarried and was living in London, decided that it was about time I fended for myself, so she paid my passage, and I was on my way.

The dock at the Number One Pier was a seething mass of humanity. At least seven of my relations had turned out to see me off, and if an average of three had turned out to see other migrants off that would give a fair idea of what the scene looked like from the deck of the ship. I did not feel sad about emigrating. It was more in the line of something I had to do. Some of the friends and relations I had met during my last days of preparation adopted the view that it was just a matter of time before they too would be journeying to Spanish Town to get their birth certificates and lining up outside the Passport Office. It was a relief to be finished with queues in the boiling sun and waiting around in offices. It was wonderful to be finished with uncertainties. We migrants knew what we wanted from Britain. That was why we were trekking there. We were going to make good the second chance though most of us were unaware of having missed the first!

There were six of us to a cabin for a passage costing eighty-five pounds, but another friend who had only paid seventy-five pounds was sharing a cabin with twenty-three others. The thought of this recalled to us the horrors of the Middle Passage which brought our ancestors from the African coast to the Caribbean and slavery. However, the voyage from the Caribbean was the final leg of the triangle of sea routes which made the wealth of London, Marseilles, Bristol, Bordeaux, Cadiz, Seville and Lisbon. Europe's chickens were coming home to roost!

Of the five who shared Cabin 94 with me, one was Ralph Martin, ex-R.A.F., who was demobbed in 1949 after he had injured his knee in an accident. He returned to Jamaica in 1950, but could not settle down. What money he had received for his service had been squandered before he finally decided to farm the land which the Government had given all ex-servicemen. So now with his land leased out he was going back to Britain. During the year he had spent after his demob he had lived with an English couple in Sutton Coldfield. He was going back to them. His friend was a foreman at an engineering works and Ralph was certain of getting a job. Not many people on board had such a clear idea of what they were going to.

Congreve Williams was nearly seventeen. He was going to his parents who were living in West Bromwich. He hoped to go to university and eventually become a doctor.

Busta was only eleven. He was going to join his parents in Liverpool. He was being looked after by Johnson, who was a very mysterious character. Sometimes we would not see him for several days. We heard that there was a cabin where some of the boys gambled, and decided that Johnson was a gambler. Busta said Johnson would only be keeping an eye on him until the ship reached Plymouth. After that he would continue on alone to Liverpool by train, where his parents would meet him. He made it sound as simple as going by lorry from Cedar Valley to Kingston, and then by bus to Mandeville. Busta wanted to be an engineer, and planned to be back in Jamaica by the time he was twenty-five.

Murray, the last of our cabinmates, had been a poorly paid cabinet maker from Kingston. He had two addresses, one in Stamford Hill and the other in Brixton. He wanted to save enough money to buy machinery for a cabinet workshop he intended setting up when he returned to Jamaica. He did not know how long it would take him to save the money required, but ten years seemed more than enough.

Two days after leaving Jamaica we sailed up the estuary of the Ozama to the city of Ciudad Trujillo (now once again known as Santo Domingo). We were now in the third-nearest country to Jamaica. This is the oldest cathedral city in the Americas and the body of Christopher Columbus is supposed to be at rest in its vault. Ciudad Trujillo seemed to lack the crowd and the noise of Kingston, and that perhaps gave it breathing space. Ruddy, my friend who was in the cabin of twenty-four, almost got picked up by a white prostitute. He was embarrassed and confused that a white woman should want to take him off to a brothel. When we got back on board ship, Ralph told him that was a preface to the English story.

After the Dominican Republic we sailed down the archipelago to Barbados. By this time the boundaries of the West Indies were being pushed steadily back. The ship anchored in Carlisle Bay and launches took some people to the pier at Bridgetown. Next we called at Dominica, Montserrat and St Kitts. The Jamaicans nicknamed migrants from Montserrat – Monster-rats, and the Kitticians – Kittens. Life for us was never to be the same. Before the islands were merely sister colonies sharing a common heritage. Now we were meeting the natives. Our dialects and accents were different, we could be told one from another. We knew then that there would be rivalry! By the time the Caribbean was at last behind us, there were thirteen hundred migrants from the British West Indies bound for the 'mother country'.

Congreve Williams and I reflected on the fate which made our 'mother country' Britain instead of Spain, to which most of our islands once belonged; or France who fought Britain for the West Indies. Indeed had not Sir George Rodney defeated Count de Grasse at the Battle of the Saints in 1802 – a battle in which the British Negro slaves 'behaved with undaunted courage in some desperate service' – we would certainly not be now bound for Sutton Coldfield, London and West Bromwich.

After a week's sea voyage, it dawned on me that emigration was not merely a romance. Names, places and faces would soon be blurred by events. I had to learn to make friends. It was not easy to begin with the 'other West Indians'. They had become suspicious of all Jamaicans. They resented being called 'small island people', and wrote off Jamaicans as bullies. Congreve, who had written a good essay for his last term at school on 'The Prospect of a Caribbean Federation', was worried about the insularity separating one island from the other. In his prize-winning essay he had discussed the possibility of the independent Caribbean States of Cuba, Haiti and the Dominican Republic joining the Federation, also Puerto Rico, the American Virgin Islands, and the French and Dutch West Indies, making his Caribbean nation over a hundred thousand square miles with a population of just over sixteen millions, and speaking French, Spanish and Dutch besides English. It was a boy's dream, but within the bounds of possibility. Evidently when he wrote his essay, Congreve was not aware of the Caribbean insularity. He had often seen the crowds at Sabina Park cricket ground cheering Weekes and Walcott and believed that everything was as easy as cricket. Now not even cricket was easy. We listened to a big Jamaican describe Barbadians as a nation of liars.

'When ah was up the States' – the big Jamaican wanted to make it plain that he had travelled before – 'a Bajan man tell me one big lie, you see! The Bajan said that back in 1942 him see Frank Worrell bat and play some pretty strokes, that a man who was watching drop off him seat and dead like nit . . .'

'That ain't no lie,' a Barbadian, who must have been a spy, shouted. 'No lie, man! The man had a weak heart and all the excitement bring on a heart failure. And what is more, if the Bajan did tell you that a man rushed out on the field and gave Frankie a turkey fowl, that would be true, too.'

'Gu'way, you Bajan too damn lie. You stick up fer you one another too much.'

But all that did not save the day for Jamaica. Another day Congreve overheard the same man complain that: 'These small island people is no-good people. Them min' small like the place them from. You could stay 'pon the mountain top and piss all round the island. Ah been to 'Merica so ah know what I talking 'bout. Them goin' to make a whole rarse heap of trouble for we Jamaicans in England.'

There were numerous gossips going around the ship. There was a splendidly built Jamaican girl who was always elegantly dressed. The gossips said that the sailors took turns in sleeping with her. There was a girl with ugly projecting teeth who had defied her parents and was going to London to marry a man who was her family's handyman. She had been sick ever since she boarded the ship at Bridgetown. Rumour had it that she was pregnant. There was another girl who was plainly an expectant mother. Murray discovered that she was going to her husband in Birmingham. The interesting thing was that her husband had been away for more than a year.

There was, too, a matronly saint in long sleeves. She had been a deaconess or 'mother' at her church. She had not heard from her husband for more than two years, and had undertaken the journey to find him and perhaps save his soul. There were more of her religious sect on board and they usually held meetings in the second-class dining-room when it was not in use. Once when Congreve and Busta stayed behind in our cabin to play draughts I went to one of the prayer meetings. The meeting was presided over by the 'mother' assisted by an orange-coloured girl who had an attractive face, but whose shapeless clothes made her unimpressive. The 'mother' warned the meeting that the journey to Britain was like that of the children of Israel going into the land of Moab until the famine was over. She warned all those who thought they would make good without divine help of the Lord, to beware that they did not meet the fate of Naomi, who came back from the land of Moab desolate. The assistant compared Britain to Sodom. She promised that she would be 'in constant prayer for those who are weak and will be tempted by the flesh. Remember Sodom was a flourishing city, even as London and Birmingham and Brixton is today! Many are going to be cut down by the wrath of God for their wickedness. Take heed. Be one of the precious ones who were saved from the calamity of Sodom and Gomorrah . . .'

'Mark my word,' said an unbeliever, 'I give her two months to forget Jamaica and three months to forget religion. You ever see white people jumping up in the Spirit? Then how you going to England to jump up in the Spirit. Is the white man who print the Bible. How come you going to England to teach him religion?'

'You foolish man! You never hear that the white man take the Bible to the black man and tell him about the kingdom of gold after death; that earthly gold only breed corruption. So today the black man have the Bible and the white man have the gold. But don't you think that no black man is going to fool, fool the white man out of his gold . . .'

When we had finished reading all the paperback novels we could get, Congreve began to be homesick for Jamaica. He confessed he had fallen in love during his last term at school. He walked around with a dog-eared photograph of a girl whose racial origin seemed to be a panorama of Jamaica. She was at that exciting age when a girl's body seemed to be adjusting to the mould of maturing womanhood. Congreve knew that there was not a good chance of his ever seeing Joyce again in ten years. He knew the chance of his falling in love again was quite good, but he could not reconcile himself to the thought of his ever forgetting the girl he kissed during matinées in the Carib cinema. He wanted to know whether I was ever in love and was surprised to know that I had deliberately broken off an affair with a girl I met when I was about his age. I tried to make him understand that at twenty I became convinced that to prolong the affair was to invite a responsibility I was totally unprepared for. So I went to live in Mandeville and refused to answer all her letters until I knew it was too late for reconciliation. He hoped that when I reached London I would go to Birmingham and try to win her back. I told him that though I would like to see my Mavis again, I did not think that reconciliation was possible.

We agreed that the women on board the *Auriga* were not the type we could love. There would be no ship romance. We wondered if there was a dearth of 'our type' of girl in England. We called in Ralph who told us that when he left Britain in 1950 there were not many coloured women to be found. Because of that the coloured men had started going out with white women and fights had taken place. He said that in 1949 there was a fight between Polish refugees and West Indians which started on a Friday night and went on to Sunday morning. They were competing for the few white women they could find in the jazz clubs. He said that if my Mavis was as attractive as I made her out to be, there was not the slightest chance of her remaining single in Birmingham until I found her. I experienced a slight pain of jealousy that night.

Sometimes we would watch the first-class passengers gambolling in the swimming pool. There were two Spanish girls, a blonde in a yellow swimming suit and a dark haired, slimmer girl in a striped costume. They interested us. Congreve claimed the blonde and named her 'Marilyn' and I named the other 'Jane'. One day we were discussing the girls when we heard a voice close to our ears say:

'God's only mistake!'

Despite the softness of the man's voice, the sentence exploded in our ears like a meteorite. I looked furtively about me to see whether the 'mother' was near enough to have heard the terrible blasphemy.

'God made man and rest,' the speaker said, 'then He made woman and no one has had a rest since.'

The man had a distinguished ebony face. His head was bald except for the fringe of cotton and ink hair around his ears. We had seen him before, once speaking to a sailor in Spanish. The old man, who was immaculately dressed, motioned us to a seat and then lowered himself carefully between us. He must have known that we were a little afraid of him, for he smiled from one to the other tapping our knees reassuringly. The smile, though it calmed us, also had a paralytic effect on us. The old man knew that, and he took his time about lighting his pipe. We knew that when he relaxed the bellows of his cheeks he was going to talk to us.

'There never was brought about the ruin of man, by nought else but by a woman,' he said at last. He went on to name a few Biblical and historical characters. Then he seemed to have been lost in the maze of his memories. 'Yes,' he said more to himself than us, 'yes there was Brakra Clarke, God rest his soul . . . not to think of Busha Clifford, hope no more again to be seen in this land of the living. Then there was Cyril, Bulla and Boardhand, they all died without a cent to their names in Bocas del Toro. All these were men brought low by the wiles of women. When the angels saw that women were populating this earth, they cried out, 'Woe unto man!' That was how they got their name 'woe-man'!' He wiped his lips with a soggy handkerchief.

'¿Habla vd. español, señor?'

'Si niño. ¿Y vd?' the old man smiled and a minute later when Congreve had tied himself up in knots, the old man laughed.

'¿Como años tiene vd?' the old man asked Congreve.

'Yo tengo años dieciseis, señor,' Congreve replied.

'¿Y vd?' he asked me.

'I do not speak Spanish.' I understood what he asked me, but I was not enjoying the conversation.

'Where are you from?' he asked me.

'St Thomas.'

'Your name?'

'Devon Herne.'

'Herne . . . Herne . . . ugh. Don't know no Herne from St Thomas. And you,' he turned to Congreve, 'where you from?'

'St Catherine. Congreve Williams from St Catherine.'

'Tcho, the name Williams is as common like cow grass on the hillside. I know some Williams from Linstead. Relation of yours?'

'No,' Congreve said firmly.

Silence fell again, and the old man once more worked the bellows of his cheeks until the bowl of his pipe again glowed like the last red star in the morning sky.

'I am an old man,' he said. Suddenly he held the stem of his pipe firmly between his teeth and twisted around in his seat until he was able to get his hand into his fob pocket without his elbow putting out Congreve's eyes. He pulled out his watch, pressed the catch so that the face came up. He then consulted the sun, then the watch. He nodded to the ageless timekeeper, then proceeded to wind his old watch. 'Panamá, 1912!' he said swinging the watch by its chain, first at me, then at Congreve. We marvelled, and he beamed with pride and replaced it in his fob pocket. We must have passed the age test for whatever story he was going to tell us, but he was not going to be hurried. We had more than a week to go before Plymouth. He closed his eyes as if to break the lock off the door of his memory. 'I am an old man,' he said once more. 'That don't mean that my brain is gathering water. I was about your age when it happened,' he nodded at me. 'I going to tell you boys a story – a parable. A parable is an earthly story with a heavenly meaning,' he said. 'Women! this story got everything to do with women. When I was a growing lad, the craze of the day was tea meeting. Ever been to a tea meeting, boys? Well I guess not,' he answered himself. 'In those years when I was growing up, it was for the tea meetings the young girls usually bought that pretty, new dress, and patent leather shoes. Weeks before the tea meeting everybody would prepare for it. The musicians would practise their new tunes and the girls with good voices would practise day and night. The men of the district would build booths from coconut boughs, and the tables would be laden with fruits and cakes. Everything would soon be set for three nights and three days of jollification. It was a pagan ceremony with religious overtones. Right now I am thinking back on the last one I 'tended in nineteen-eleven. There was not a man who could not get a woman at a tea meeting! I am thinking back on nice girls, you know! No what-left or job-lot! The parable concern a young man I met at that tea meeting. That young man had one pound in his pocket! For three days of jollification, only one blessed pound. Nowadays, I guess you young chappies would have fanned away thirty pounds just like that. Well, those days you could get all the pretty girls for a pound. And I tell you that young man was a fellow with an eye for the ladies. They called him Parish. That is parish ram! Just before the tea meeting Parish's cousin had left for Cuba and the first night of the tea meeting the musicians put Parish and his cousin's woman in song.' He broke off, took his pipe from his mouth, cleared his throat and started stomping. He found his voice:

> Busha Wright gone, his cousin take over,
> timber lae-lae, Busha Wright gone!
> Busha Wright gone a Panya man country,
> timber lae-lae his cousin take over.

'I guess I forget the rest of the song. It was a long, long time ago. Part of the song went that cousin and cousin boil sweet soup! You would think that after a man was scandalized like that all women would avoid him. You wrong boys. Women like men like that. Show the timidest maiden a man who is innocent and another with his pants down, jumping out of a woman's bedroom, and I bet you everything you got that quiet virgin will go for the man with his pants off! To get back to the parable-story, girls flocked after Parish all through that tea meeting like ants going after sugar. A couple months later when we heard the shouting and the bawling, six women in the family way for Parish.' The old man paused for it to soak in.

'Six?' Congreve asked.

'Six!' the old man said to me.

I avoided the man's hawk-like eyes, and grinned foolishly. I could not understand my own embarrassment. Though this story was new to me, I had known few men who did not have children with more than one woman. On my part, I had no reason to believe that my father, whom I have never met, did not have six children born to him the same year I arrived.

'I said six,' the old man continued. 'Oldtime people in Jamaica usually say that what sweet nanny goat gwine to run 'er belly. Well, all the pleasure gone now and the young man had to face the problem of looking after six pregnant women. How could he? I telling you lads this parable so it may help you just as how monkey see and learn and then declare that him never swing on the same dry vine twice! You know boys it takes another woman to get a man out of the trouble that other women put him into. Well, Parish's mother run here and run there and before anybody could guess what that little woman was about she raise the fifteen pounds she was after and carried Parish to Kingston and put him on a boat for Panamá. When all the girls finish scratching them-one-another eyes out, not a Parish could be found. Boy, in those days a man could buy a passage to Cuba and Panamá just like he was buying a bus ticket to Grange Hill. Parish find himself working for ten cents an hour for a Chinese man who had a restaurant in La Boca in the Panamá Canal Zone. That was about the year 1912. He stay off women for a while. But a man who love women is like a rummer. Few ever get cured. How a man could ever stay off women in the Canal Zone those days? Parish had a Spanish lady who ran a whoring house. She was a big, hard woman in her forties, and she like' the young black man. They lived together for about two years. Then one night when they were in bed, there was a sudden knock! Bam bam! Know what that was? Well, make me tell you. It was the woman's husband come back. Can you imagine a man living with a woman for two years and never hear chick nor chack about any husband? Well she had one all right. The Spaniard burst into the bedroom with a bullwhip and started to drop blows on the black man's skin like him was knocking down a house. That black man just grab' a chair and one lick boof and the husband drop dead. Dead like nit, I tell you. You know what that woman did? She grab' a gun and start' shooting after the black man, crying out that he killed her beloved husband. Lucky thing that she couldn't shoot straight. Parish jumped out of the window, and later manage' to find his way to Bocas del Toro. That was out of frying-pan into fire, because it was Bocas that the woman and her husband was living when they had just got married. It seemed that the husband had killed his wife's lover a month after they were married and they had thrown him into prison for life, but he was released when the authorities found out that he was dying anyway. Parish managed to find his way again to Port Limon and from there to Harlem where he settled down for some thirty years gone March. Recently the prodigal returned to Jamaica.' The old man paused for the first time since he started his narrative he seemed to have been overcome with emotion. 'It was just like war and desolation had descended on the district that Parish come from. The entire district of Grass Piece has disappeared from the face of the earth. What happened to Granny Mathews and the host that used to live in her yard? Tata Joe and his multitude? Young fellows like Governor, Kingdom and Flute? They have now left without a trace, they dead and gone. Parish's mother's grave cannot be found. Overgrown by bush long time ago and cows, donkeys and goats trampled it out of sight. When I was a growing lad, you could call out thirty men between the age of twenty and fifty any time of the day. What happen to them all? You mean that your generation will disappear when you return from England in thirty years' time, too?'

'Thirty years?' Congreve asked.

'There must be somebody left somewhere, sir,' I said.

'Yes, Jemima Walters, old and blind; Dandy Jones, deaf and crippled, living off the pauper's roll. Where did they all go?'

'Surely he must have had a lead on one of the six children born in 1912. After all they would be more than forty-three years old.'

This part of the story was evidently painful for the old man. He tried to tell us the rest of the story but broke off. He had lost his composure.

'Birmingham,' he said as if we were not there, 'Birmingham, England, one of them is living there . . . Somebody has got to listen.' He broke off and staggered to his feet, looking older and very humble. He did not even say good-bye. He walked away desperately trying to look dignified. The wind had suddenly become stiffer and there was a little moisture in it.

'Parish was quite a guy in his days,' Congreve said.

'I don't know why he singled us out, but it must have been hell living with that story for forty-three years.'

'You probably reminded him of himself in 1911. I had the feeling that he was speaking to you all the time. Listen, Buddy, you have not left the same situation behind you in Jamaica, have you?'

'Don't be ridiculous.' Yet I suddenly felt fear. I was afraid for my country. I wanted to know if when the search for an identity ended I would want to return to Jamaica; and if I did, would she be something I could love? For the first time in the months during which I was busy preparing myself for the journey to Britain, I questioned the decision to make the voyage. It did not matter whether I saw Parish again, or if the loose ends of the story were to remain untidy for ever. He had succeeded in unnerving me. We did in fact see him again, but he never spoke to us. He even pretended that he did not know us. It was his generation which inspired this song:

> One, two, three, four Colon man ah come
> ask him what the time
> and him look upon the sun,
> with brass chain a knock him belly
> bam! bam! bam!

We saw him several times take out his old watch with its splendid chain sparkling in the sun. We hoped that his daughter in Birmingham would receive him, as the others never did.

Towards the end of the journey the ship stank. The stairs smelt of vomit and urine, and each day reminded us of the horrors our forbears must have suffered during that terrible Middle Passage; but this leg of the journey of the slavers was the best of the three. It was the one of great profit, the sea routes which gave Europe the financial resources to be great. Perhaps we were on the right track after all. Almost everyone had wilted somewhat. The deputy leader of the saints had not appeared in the second-class dining-room for prayer meetings for days. She was not a good sailor. Others appeared on deck with their heads wrapped in brightly-coloured bath towels looking like bedouin and reeking of bay rum and other spirits. There were several solemn vows that the return journey would be by 'plane. Once Congreve and I went without food for a whole day. As we sat at table watching a sailor who was stripped to his waist serving diners, we saw a bead of sweat break away from the sailor's forehead and run down his face and take a header from the man's nose into the bowl of fish he was serving. No one else seemed to have seen it, and the sailor brushed his palm across his face and continued dishing out. The whole thing had now become something completely without dignity. Yet because it was a sea voyage it was romantic, and also it was adventure because there was an element of challenge in it. We were jaded, but not beaten. On the twentieth morning of the voyage I awoke to the sound of bells and came to the conclusion that we were in Plymouth Harbour. I was too much of a good colonial not to have been excited. I thumbed the pages of history on my mind. This was Plymouth! From here Drake sailed ravaging the Spanish colonies as he completed his voyage around the world. From here the English fleet sailed to repel the Armada, and later the Pilgrim Fathers set sail in the *Mayflower* towards new horizons. To Plymouth thirteen hundred of us had come towards a future. It was important to me that I knew these things. I had passed my colonial eleven plus! I was convinced that this would stand me in good stead with those who could make my stay in Britain a happy and successful one. I thought I had more right to come to Britain than the others who did not know of these things.

From the deck could be seen knots of white people staring back at us. I had hardly ever seen more than twelve white people together before. I had always been a member of the majority race. That vast multitude which thronged the docks at the Number One Pier at Kingston twenty days ago was black. Now white people were loitering below. During this fortnight I had undergone a metamorphosis. My images of white people were of a race which had all the good jobs and therefore lots of money. A people whose menfolk work while their women stay at home or play tennis. Now down there white people were waiting like the black people of the docklands back home, waiting for some gullible tourist to fall into their hands. Our conversation had already such adjectives as 'Bajan' and 'Small Island', now it seemed that people would be even more factionalized as we divided them into 'whites', and 'blacks' and sub-divided the latter into Jamaicans, Bajans, Trinidadians, Africans and Small Islanders. An interior skirmish had just taken place.

The occupants of Cabin 94 said good-bye without much ceremony. Only Congreve gave me his address, the others expressed a weak hope of our meeting again and left it at that. The London passengers were the first to disembark. Buses were provided to take us to the railway station. There we found that our cases were smashed almost beyond recognition. After some delay we boarded the boat train for Paddington. Yet another blow to romance: at the London end of the line I saw white porters asking for our bags. They actually said, 'Thank you, sir,' and accepted tips. That was a turning of the tables! For some years now I had been fighting the image of Negro menials that Hollywood turns out. As I intensified my fight against the 'Negro image' it was necessary for me to distrust everything in the movies except the excitement. It was easier for me to believe that there were no white porters because I had never seen one. On the other hand my fight against the black man saying 'Yus sah' was a tough battle because I knew a great many people who have said it like that. I was fighting because I have never said it that way, and was determined not to. The Negro image I wanted to see was my own reflexion. Now as I mingled with the crowd in the London station I knew that, in spite of everything, I was totally unprepared for the sudden change that had taken possession of me since I arrived at Plymouth. I began to dread the coming of the next morning when I would look from my window and see a white man sweeping the streets, and fear that, in the shop nearest where I should live, a white girl would sell me cigarettes. Now I was seeing my colonial society in a terrible light. I had never hoped to challenge the whites in Jamaica for a job. I realized in the confusion of the crowded station that I was starting on a desperate phase of life. If the white man was sweeping the streets, then any job I asked for would mean a challenge to him. I was not one of the 'mother country's' children. I was one of her black children. That was to be my first lesson on arriving in Britain.

'Brazil: Go and Learn'

Eva de Carvalho Chipenda was brought up by her brother Julio, a Methodist pastor, and his wife, at a mission station in rural Angola. Moving to Luanda during World War II, she continued her school education and, following the offer of a scholarship to study abroad, spent three years in Brazil. It is her account of this first trip overseas in her autobiography The Visitor *(1996) which is reprinted below.*

Back in Angola, she married the Jose Chipenda mentioned in the text, and later, as the armed struggle against the Portuguese intensified, followed him to New York with their two children, after a clandestine escape from Lisbon in a fishing boat. As her husband's career in the international Christian movement progressed, her subsequent travels took her to London, Paris, Geneva and Nairobi – where she began a long-standing involvement in local training and development projects. Not until several years after independence did they return 'home' – but the end of the book finds them back in Nairobi, where she is honoured to oversee a major construction project.

Before leaving for Brazil, I went to visit my father in the village. He was very happy for me but some of my relatives were worried about whether I would come back the same person or different – as a white person, a non-virgin, or perhaps married to some stranger. Many people who had not been interested in me before were now jealous of my opportunity. My father said: 'Why are you worried about her now, when you never have been before? Let her go.'

I had to travel by boat to Lisbon to obtain a passport. Angola was still a Portuguese colony, and except for identity cards and birth, marriage and death certificates, all official documents had to be applied for and obtained in Lisbon.

The trip seemed long, although it took only fifteen days. I could not believe that I was out of Angola, out of my parents' and brother's home. I was seasick and uneasy about being the only black passenger on the boat, and so I stayed in my cabin most of the time. Even so I was afraid. I recalled seeing a young black Angolan woman intercepted and abused by two white men as she walked on the street in Luanda. Only with great effort did she manage to get away from them. It was common knowledge that Portuguese men liked black women a lot, but did not respect them. I feared that one of them might come to my room at night when I was alone and try to violate me.

I was met at the port in Lisbon by a man named Mr Silva. He was a short Portuguese man, efficient and friendly, with a soft voice and polite manners. As public relations officer for missionaries en route from Canada and the USA to Angola and Mozambique, he looked after legal matters such as passports and permits. He took me to the student hostel at the Carcavelos seminary, where I would stay for nine days while my passport was being processed.

Lisbon was a beautiful city – the architecture, trams, trains, streets, especially the Avenida da Liberdade, the main downtown area, full of shops and cinemas and fancy restaurants. I spent hours there, sitting on the benches, watching all of the different people: market women selling fish and vegetables and fruit, gypsies reading palms, elegantly dressed women on shopping sprees.

All Angolan school children learned about Portugal in geography class, but I had never imagined it would be like this. When I was shown the Tejo River, I could not believe I was seeing the real thing. In Angola, if we did not know about the Tejo River, our teachers would twist our ears.

One thing that shocked me was to see how many Portuguese women lived such difficult lives. The Portuguese women in Angola were very chic and always stylishly dressed and never touched anything dirty. Angolans were the nannies, the laundrywomen, the cooks, the servants. I had simply assumed that the women in Portugal would be the same or even better off. Now in Lisbon I was seeing Portuguese market women wearing rough and dirty blankets, thick socks and heavy shoes, women with hard hands and blistered lips, carrying huge baskets on their heads, yelling 'fresh fish!' Many of them were illiterate, while I was striving to learn to speak the way the Portuguese do. There were of course upper-class Portuguese women in Lisbon, but it was very rare to see them. The women seen every day were the cleaning women. I wondered to myself incredulously, 'Are these the people that oppressed us?'

I spent my mornings seeing the sights of Lisbon, and the afternoons and evenings at the seminary, where a number of other Angolan students, some of whom I knew from childhood, others whom I met for the first time, were studying medicine, theology, social sciences, law. It was their first time out of Angola also, and being with them helped to make me feel at home in a strange place.

The academic year had already begun, and to pass the time in the afternoons I helped out in the seminary kitchen or laundry room. The Portuguese staff were amazed because I showed no complexes, either of inferiority or superiority. None of the other Angolan students spent any time in the laundry room or the kitchen – they were too busy with their studies. The staff found it interesting and amusing to have me around. I was interested in their lives – how they lived, their families. the places that they came from. They talked to me about how hard their lives were, how hard they worked and how expensive it was to live. Like many Portuguese, they dreamed of going to Brazil where they believed they could earn much more money and perhaps even become rich.

On my last day at the seminary before sailing to Rio de Janeiro, I cooked an Angolan meal of cassava flour porridge accompanied by stew, fish and cooked vegetables. My sister-in-law would have been amazed. In Angola I had not cooked much, because we had no stove. We had to cook over an open fire, with the pot resting on three stones, and I was afraid of burning my feet and hands. My sister-in-law was convinced that I would never learn to cook.

That evening we all went to the beach. It was a beautiful sight: bright sun on the calm waters of the Atlantic ocean, soft sand and the sound of the waves that took me to an unknown world, a world of my imagination.

When the immigration official in Rio de Janeiro saw my name in my passport, he smiled and asked, 'Eva . . . so where is Adam?' That was my official welcome to Brazil.

Julio, who had left Angola to do further studies at the seminary and visit churches in Brazil some four months earlier, met me in Rio. We were very happy to see each other, and it was a special time for both of us. We had time to get to know each other and discuss many things that we had never had time to talk about at home. He confided more of his feelings about his life and gave me advice: to study hard, to work towards living independently and to be myself, personally, professionally and in every other way.

The next day we boarded a bus for the 15-hour journey to my final destination, the Methodist Institute at St Amaro, where I would spend the next three years of my life studying.

The Institute, funded by United Methodists from the U.S. and headed by teachers from the U.S. and Brazil, prepared women to do development and social work in both urban and rural settings. From 20 to 25 students, all women, lived and studied there. Each of us had a small plot of land on which we grew vegetables; and part of our work was to encourage people in the villages around to start their own gardens. The only drawback to the Institute was that the diploma it gave was not recognized by the state, only by the churches.

As the Institute's first black African student, I was quite a novelty with my dark complexion, kinky hair and strange accent. The others in turn were a novelty to me: blonde, brown and black people. Brazilians, very much a mixed people, had a good sense of humour and seemed more open than Angolans. They questioned and argued and were curious. At first I was a bit sensitive about their jokes and their teasing me about my accent. But soon I began teasing them back, because their accent was just as strange to me.

I felt very much at home in Brazil. I was free. I became myself. It was as though I had been carrying a heavy load on my back and when I got to Brazil I just dropped it and forgot about it. It was such a different world. The level of understanding – people's statements, minds and attitudes – everything was so clear. In Angola I was blind; in Brazil I began seeing. In Angola I was hesitant and timid, afraid of saying what I felt. My life seemed artificial, trying to be invisible and to avoid problems, fearful of being reported to an adult for what I was or did. It was not that I was doing bad things, but that I was afraid of doing them and being caught or seen. Now, because I did not have to be preoccupied by these inhibitions and fears, I was able to concentrate on my studies and my new life.

One thing I really enjoyed was that the Brazilian young women were as outspoken as the young men. At youth meetings in Angola usually only men would get up and talk. At the youth meetings and seminars I attended in Brazil,

I found that the young women also had strong opinions about social, political and educational issues, and did not hesitate to make them known. At first I was astonished, but before long I was joining in with the rest of them. I would even argue sometimes with our Bible teacher, something I would never have thought of doing in Angola.

Many of our discussions centred on colonization and the political system in Angola. I explained about assimilation and enculturation – the whole process of trying to transform us from Africans to Portuguese. At this time in Brazil it was the Portuguese immigrants who were treated as second-class citizens; and it was hard for my fellow students to imagine them as all-powerful colonizers. We also spoke about slavery in Brazil, and they admitted that black people, Angolan slaves, had made a great contribution to Brazil.

I enjoyed my programme of study, particularly working with children in slums and teaching Sunday School. Our supervisor would pay us surprise visits to assess our work. I recall that my turn came on Easter Sunday. All week I had been pondering over how to explain the resurrection to a group of children. In the end, I used an egg, comparing the shell to the cold and lifeless grave, and the egg to the essence of life that could be shared by all. While the illustration was somewhat simplistic, the children understood, and my supervisor was pleased by it.

From time to time, a group of students would go to Sao Paulo to shop or to watch a movie. Sao Paulo was much bigger and more exciting than Luanda, with beautiful shops. On one occasion we sent to see *Exodus*. I had read the book and was looking forward to seeing the movie. Just as we were about to enter the theatre, a policeman stopped me and asked, 'How old are you?' Attendance was restricted to those 18 or older, and although I was 21, I was small and looked much younger. Unfortunately, the policeman did not believe me, and I had left my identity card at the school. He refused to let me enter. Two of my school friends felt sorry for me, and the three of us found another movie, *Four Brothers and Four Sisters*, which I enjoyed. But I still regretted not to be able to see *Exodus*.

The school had a strict visitor's code. We received guests once a month, and only on special request. I received just one visitor during my entire three-year stay, my nephew who later got a scholarship from the seminary in Sao Paulo where Julio had studied. On one of his visits, he brought me a letter from one of the students I had met in Portugal. His name was Jose Chipenda. He had been studying theology in Lisbon and finishing university entrance qualifications. At the time I had taken no special notice of him. I assumed that because he was from southern Angola, he was with the Evangelical Lutheran Church of Central Angola. The letter was rather short, enquiring how I was enjoying my time in Brazil and encouraging me to reply, which I did – and promptly forgot all about him. I received very few other letters during my time in Brazil – none from Julio or my family or any of the missionaries.

The three years I spent in Brazil were particularly enriching for me. I discovered not only a new country, but also a new home, new people and a different way of living. Even more important than the diploma at the end of the course were the practical skills and techniques I learned for dealing with the day-to-day situations and problems I would encounter back in Angola, especially the better perspective I gained on the condition of rural women at home.

I realized that sometimes we are what we are not because we have chosen it, but because we are conditioned to be that way. People in villages in Africa have few choices and try to survive with what exists in the village. They do things the way they have always been done, even though it might not be the best way, because they do not see other options. If you do not move from the place you live, how can you see how others live on the other side of the river? Being exposed to other people's lives and experiences gives one a new perspective on one's own situations. It is then possible to say, for example, 'We are spending hours every day cutting down trees for firewood and carrying it home. Those people across the river use cow dung for fuel. Why don't we try that?'

Why is it that development in Angola stayed in the cities? Was this the villagers' choice? No. I became convinced that if rural women were given new perspectives on their situations, and if their perceptions were changed, then they themselves would discover different methods of living and developing and improving their situations. There is a saying in Portuguese: 'It is not difficult to live. What is difficult is to know how to live.' That is what development means. We do not need big development projects; indeed, many Western development projects have been a headache for us. Machinery breaks down and cannot be fixed because there are no parts. Many projects, imposed by others, are inappropriate to begin with.

Knowing how to live is the key to life. For example, rural women spend hours every day carrying water. Why not build a tank and fill it with water that would last a week, rather than going to the river four times a day? If a community gets together and decides to help each other, they can rent a water tank, buy a pump or dig a borehole. People do not need to have these things done for them, but they do need to know what it is possible to do.

It was also an eye-opening experience to discover that the lessons the missionaries taught us in Angola were not necessarily applied elsewhere. The missionaries had intended to build a system in which Christians lived separately from non-Christians. They advocated the idea of not mixing with 'pagans.' Christianity in Angola was based on too many don't's: don't drink, don't dance, don't watch football on Sundays, don't go to the movies. This strict message found fertile soil among the local leaders of the church, for pre-colonial Angolan culture had its own very rigid code of conduct. A son-in-law was not allowed to talk to his mother-in-law face-to-face. A daughter-in-law could not hug her father-in-law, for this would show a lack of respect. In some societies, women could not eat chicken: it was only for the men. During the menstrual period, a wife could not prepare food for her husband. If a woman became a widow, she had to stay in a dark room for a week, dressed in black from head to toe. A woman was not allowed to make any decisions. Boys could not interact with girls before circumcision. It was unheard of for someone to contradict the elders or to speak to them disrespectfully. To go against these rules was to bring disgrace on your self and your family.

With the whole new set of 'don'ts' that the missionaries came with, I assumed that everyone in their countries always acted in an exemplary manner and no one went against the Christian code of behaviour. So it was a surprise to visit other countries and discover that not everyone acted in the way the missionaries had advocated. I was unable to distinguish Christians from non-Christians. They looked alike and in many ways behaved alike. All of the things that we were told not to do were a part of their lives, and no one seemed worried about burning in hell. Swimming was seen as an enjoyable sport, movies as harmless entertainment, sipping a drink a normal social activity. None of it was regarded as sin.

It would have been quite different if things had been put in a scientific or healthy way; for instance, that excessive drinking will harm your health. But we had been lied to and threatened with hell to keep us controlled, to keep us obedient, in a cage.

Even before leaving Angola, I had struggled within myself over questions about all the distinctions made between Christians and non-Christians. For instance, we had been told that all non-Christians would go to hell. I had relatives who were animists, but they were good people, and I could see no reason why they should suffer in hell. Many church leaders looked down on traditional marriages. My own parents had been married traditionally before they became Christians; yet they were happy and believed that they were blessed before God in traditional marriage. At the same time, I wondered if some of the Christians I knew did not in fact deserve to go to hell.

In Angola we were encouraged to avoid and look down on non-Christians, as though we were superior. Once again, it was a surprise to find that in other places, people both Christian and non-Christian were equally capable of wonderful and horrible things.

My time in Brazil gave me new insights, inspiration and confidence. I had not forgotten what my father said when I was leaving Angola: 'Go and learn. Come back and help your people.' I was determined to do as he said, and after receiving my diploma I started preparing for the trip home.

ARTHUR NORTJE

'London Impressions'

Arthur Nortje (1942–1970) was born in Oudtshoorn, South Africa, and educated at the University of the Western Cape. He went to England in 1966 after winning a scholarship to Oxford University. Following a spell of teaching in Canada, he returned to Oxford to pursue further studies, but died a few months later, probably of a drug overdose. His collected poems, Dead Roots, *were published posthumously in 1973.*

I

Out of the Whitehall shadows I pass
into a blaze of sun as sudden as fountains.
Between the bronze paws of a lion
a beatnik stretches his slack indifferent muscles.

Nelson's patina of pigeon shit
hardly oppresses that plucky sailor. Cloudbanks
lazily roll in the blue heavens beyond.
The birds home in on seas of seed.

Foil tins float on the dusty water.
The walls are full of faces and thighs.
I smoke a Gold Leaf close to the filter,
viewing dimly the circles of traffic.

The isle is full of Foreign Noises
that jangle in trafalgar square,
England expects every tourist
to do his duty now the Pound is sickly.

Arthur Nortje, *Dead Roots* (Oxford: Heinemann, 1973), pp. 56–7. Reprinted with the permission of the Unisa Library, Pretoria.

II

A girl plays games with mirrors
in Hyde Park while I'm half-suggestive
with the dolly scanning a volume idly.
In the flare of an instant it takes to light
a cigarette:
against her treetrunk comes to lean
the ugliest bloke that you have ever seen.
Predictably they disappear
through the distance of August green.

The nymph on the grass behind
proves her point by blinding my return look.
She picks her black bag up and drifts on further,
not helpful as to whether I should follow.
Meanwhile a huge Alsatian sniffs my loose boots,
the gentleman with the leash exchanges gossip.

Sun, you are all I have:
the grass already welcomes the brown leaves.
I do not want to cross the road again,
having learnt the value of other faces,
acquired the pace and tone of other voices.

And big red buses; I thought I would never catch
sight of the gentle monsters
when I was young and shackled for my sharpness
in the Union of South Africa.

LEWIS NKOSI

'Doing Paris with Breyten'

*Lewis Nkosi (b. 1936) was born in Durban, Natal, and worked as a journalist
on* Drum *magazine in the 1950s before leaving South Africa in 1961 on a one-
way exit permit to take up a Niemann Fellowship at Harvard University. He
pursued further studies in England, and went on to teach in Zambia, Poland
and the United States. He is the author of a play,* The Rhythms of Violence
(1964), and Tasks and Masks: Themes and Styles of African Literature
(1981); Mating Birds *(1986) was his first novel. This account of his experiences
in Paris in the early 1960s is taken from the revised edition of his first collection
of essays,* Home and Exile *(1983).*

*In the introduction to that volume, he writes that 'the reader will probably
realise after reading my impressions of New York, Paris and Los Angeles, that
exile is not all pain. There are unexpected bonuses, not the least of which is
the distance from the lunacies of South Africa; for this distance necessarily
means the ability – perhaps 'opportunity' is a better word – to purchase,
however temporarily and regionally, the private freedoms which are very early
taken away from someone like myself in South Africa. These freedoms include
the ability to buy books, to enter a restaurant of one's choice, a bar, a night
club, indeed to enter into relationships which would have been both
unthinkable and strictly forbidden in South Africa.'*

---

*Her white dress in the sun was an unbearable shimmer sloping to her
body's motion and she passed from sunlight to shadow mounting the
steps . . . Then her white dress faded beyond a fanlight of muted colour
dim with age and lovely with lack of washing, leaving George to stare at
the empty maw of the house in hope and despair and baffled youthful
lust.*

WILLIAM FAULKNER, *SOLDIER'S PAY*

*I watched a good-looking girl walk past the table and watched her go
up the street and lost sight of her, and watched another and then saw
the first one coming back again. She went by once more and I caught
her eye, and she came over and sat at the table.*

ERNEST HEMINGWAY, *THE SUN ALSO RISES*

Lewis Nkosi, *Home and Exile* (Harlow: Longman, 1983), pp. 80–7. Reprinted by permission of
Addison Wesley Longman Ltd.

1

Paris in Summer! In the white light of August we grew dim with heat. We sat at Café Le Select on Boulevard Montparnasse watching the girls arrive and depart. At the end of the first week it seemed to me that we had done nothing but watch girls arrive and depart from the cafes. They bore themselves gravely against the wild light of August, against the very motionless stillness of summer, their elegantly French bodies hallowed in a nimbus of startlingly white brightness, sometimes arriving delicately at the crowded cafe, pausing briefly near the entrance to survey the perpetually shifting scene, then in a carefree moment of sudden, inscrutable decision, stepping firmly toward an empty seat; and silhouetted men who had hoped against hope that this 'careless, unemphatic' body would deposit itself in the empty, adjacent seat would watch it go by, growing lax with despair.

Though they pretended otherwise in their cultivated French ennui the girls' departures seemed to me even more spectacular! They would get up from the tables with an air of utmost gravity, pushing back their chairs with little scraping sounds; then carefully weighing their bodies against the concentrated vision of lascivious males, they would pick their way adroitly among tables and chairs, all the time cajoling the eye with an amazing hip-rolling motion that instantly informed the cafe with an atmosphere of an absurdly desolate regret for some thing we all felt to have been within reach but which we had failed to notice or possess.

It seems to me that French girls do not walk at all. Their movement is a perpetual dance, a subtle abandonment of the body to the gay crowded activity of the street. In no other city have I seen girls walk like that. As days went by it seemed somehow that every walk away from a cafe was a wealthy event to be solemnly witnessed and marvelled at. The swaying hips, the quivering quick narrow breasts inadequately sheltered behind low-necked sweaters, the sly subtle mutilation of air by bare arms and bronzed legs which shocked by their eager surrender to the bawdy, fatal, joy of sensual movement – Sex: however, unconscious and reluctant these momentous motions and casual pausings, they brought the slumbering sexual images naturally to mind. Something dark and ancient was being celebrated every time a French girl walked away from a cafe. In my mind these girls awakened memories of Zulu women balancing incredible cargo on their sturdy, beautiful necks and the effortless manner in which they negotiated their way up the incline of a hill. To walk like that a girl has to lose all fear of the body and be on terms of absolute trust with it.

Paris is of course a city hopelessly obscured by history, and yet forever accessible, even to those who have never seen it, through its history. It is obscured because so much has been written about Paris that it is no longer possible for anyone to arrive in the city for the first time without looking at it through glasses coloured by a wealth of fiction and literary romance. For Africans who neither had the literary technique nor much use for documented history, it is awesomely astounding to see how much of eighteenth and nineteenth century Paris still abides to intrude into the twentieth century. It is an intimation of a past forever engraved in stone, secreted in darkened ageless building and weather-bitten statuary.

My first encounter with Paris was in my early boyhood in Durban, South Africa, even before I had raised any hopes of ever walking her streets in some distant future.

Having discovered at an early age that I wanted to write I began a systematic raid of the libraries during which I was continuously but graciously rebuffed by embarrassed English lady librarians, until, one day, in angry desperation, I cornered a mobile library for non-whites in (of all places) Red Square, that scene of many stormy political meetings, during which my rights to read were hotly demanded and unjustly disputed. In those first books I borrowed I was introduced for the first time to the literary embodiment of European history by the works of Dumas, Flaubert, Balzac and Hugo, and I began my first journey to France and to Paris. I grasped at the Collins classics primarily because for any slum boy the neat leather-bound books looked invaluably posh and expensive; the vocabulary gave me as much pleasure as it gave me trouble; but such is the power of adventure and romance on a boy's imagination that I struggled through the novels with an array of dictionaries until I had garnered a formidable word-list that astonished my essay master. It is to the credit of Dumas' compulsive readability that I pursued his three musketeers through their daily assignations until, many books later, they were no longer sufficiently young or agile to carry them out; whereupon I turned my attention to the rising fortunes of their offspring till the day I ran out of Dumas' novels. Hugo's *Les Miserables* reduced me to tears and for years I was haunted by the spectre of poor starving wretches in dark narrow streets. It was a picture of Paris that was only counterbalanced by that other Paris of Louis XIV and his powdered, coiffured, glittering courtiers.

My Paris is therefore stubbornly eighteenth and nineteenth century – a city of horses and cobble streets, a city of revelry, intrigue, romance, violent revolution and desperate sexual liaisons; a city of duels and dark assignations. For me Dumas and Hugo have ruined forever the actual city; I can't possess the Paris of 1965 without possessing the literary ruins of another Paris irrecoverably lost in the shadow of dream and romance. Asleep in the Paris hotel room of 1965 I can still hear the horses of Porthos and D'Artagnan cantering in the midnight streets outside and the dark narrow lanes of Victor Hugo's Paris are still there, fearful with the squandered secrets of yesterday. In fact so possessed is my imagination that when I see a French lady pouring out tea I stare instinctively and apprehensively at the large stone on her finger, for the nineteenth century novelist taught me to expect a thimbleful of poison to be stored up inside that gleaming stone, the contents of which might be emptied into somebody's cup at the flicker of the modest eyelashes.

It is perhaps understandable that when I encountered my real Paris for the first time in 1963 I felt that I had been inexcusably let down. It seemed to me that the beautiful city of my dreams had fallen before advancing hordes of American tourists whose pockets bulged with dollars. Each time or nearly each time I put my hand under the cafe tables in St Germain-des-Près it came into contact with lumps of chewing gum left there by American coeds from Louisville Kentucky or wherever they are supposed to come from! French people on the other hand were skinning everyone within range of the cash register. One night in Montmartre we had to protest loudly that we were no American tourists though we spoke English before a third had to be taken off the price of the drinks! That – the meanness and the bad weather – finally proved too much for me and I was glad to leave for the quiet of Normandy. It was only during the subsequent visits that I saw the Paris which I had not permitted myself to see during that first encounter. I suppose for everyone there is still enough of the old Paris to cherish the city – there is the air of informality and freedom, the much storied Parisian indifference to what people do with their lives, the inimitable style of the French woman and the much enduring beauty of the city's architecture.

2

> *I learned to know Paris and French affairs much better than before – I*
> *got a certain familiarity with Paris.*
>
> THE NOTEBOOKS OF HENRY JAMES

The first time I saw Paris was in the summer of 1963 when I was on my way back to Africa. An American television company had signed me on as an interviewer for a series of programmes on African writers. In the hope of tracking down M. Leopold Senghor, the poet-president of the Senegalese Republic, M. Leon Damas, the Martinique poet, and French critics specialising in the field of African literature, we flew into Paris on a Thursday in the evening of August 1, 1963. It was a trying time for me; after the hustle and bustle of London interviews my nerves were shot; I was feeling – well, yes – feeling very black, very irritable, demanding of Paris that it should be everything it was rumoured to be – and more! I find that the entry I made in my ill-kept diary on that occasion tells a grim story of nerves, dark depression and disappointment:

> *The drive to the air terminus (Invalides) was disappointing. Paris is so*
> *bleak and drab, it reminds me of Ronnie Segal's description of it: 'an*
> *old whore in a dirty shabby corset.' It started to rain while we were on*
> *our way to the terminus. Then we had to wait for a taxi while it*
> *poured down on us. Saw my first French policeman wearing a black*
> *cape over his dark uniform. Certainly not as tall and forbidding as*
> *policemen look elsewhere. Looks rather like an actor impersonating the*
> *police . . .*

On that first, dark rainy drive into the city the outer edges of Paris had seemed to me no more than a 'vast post-war slum' and it took me somewhat longer to discover that soft, rose-hued Paris of imperishable beauty and ineluctable romance. It was during the four days I spent in the city in the April of 1964 which confirmed the grievous error I had made on that first dark encounter with Paris. Then this year, through the kindness of a friend, my wife and I were left in possession of a three-roomed apartment on Rue Brezin, very near Montparnasse, from which we made daily sorties into the Quarter. The apartment we occupied was up on the fifth floor, with balconies overlooking a small park and square. Climbing up the narrow winding staircase every day was an arduous task, but one which we soon grew to appreciate after the French police who had been called out one night to suppress a party that had become too boisterous left without firing a shot. It seemed to them a long way to travel to the fifth floor on that winding old-fashioned stairway; so they contented themselves with shouting warnings and threats from the street below.

It was a beautiful apartment and we slept with the windows open. Lying in bed at night it was possible to gaze across the empty square at the buildings opposite, which were then shrouded in darkness save for the lighted windows that looked like rectangular shapes of muted, coloured lights against the darkened night sky. Watching Paris from the balcony at night always made me feel as though we were suspended in a void of darkness over the city. In the morning, before we were fully awake, French voices were already assailing the peace in the shopping street below; and in the park, across the street, white and Negro children frolicked in outbursts of energy and noise which were not dissimilar to random explosions of cannon fire. Indeed, the children captured the quarter early in the morning and did not break their seige until late forenoon when they were completely dazed by the sun. The adults, on the other hand, sat contentedly on benches, placed inside the park, their faces uplifted to the sun in a dutiful pose of worshipful adoration. By nine o'clock in the rear balcony the sun was already hot enough to sunbathe; occasionally, I came out in pyjamas to see a young woman, nude as a spear, standing at the balcony window of the apartment across the courtyard, her glossy, shadowless, white skin yellowed to dull gold by the rising sun; her form, so casual, so seemingly free, was always too stark not to be startling; and yet there was nothing erotic about it; I am perhaps making too much of a small incident; but it seemed to me that despite the rapid embourgeoisement of much that is radical and independent in Parisian life, that nude woman symbolised what is still the essence of Paris – a certain worldliness and freedom which attract new waves of exiles to this city every year, young people in flight from the inhibiting provincialism of their own native cities.

3

'What do you do night, Jake?' asked Krum. 'I never see you around'.
'I'm coming over some night. The "Dingo".That's the great place, isn't it?'
'Yes. That or this new dive, "The Select".'

ERNEST HEMINGWAY, *THE SUN ALSO RISES*

All day long at the Café Select, on Boulevard Montparnasse, people arrived, mostly young men and women, to sit at the tables, sunning themselves like lizards. A number of them came to stare and be stared at, and for this purpose dark glasses were worn like armour. When the sun dipped down behind the buildings on the western fringe the migration began to the Coupole across the street. The Dome, the Coupole, and the Select are just three of the Montparnasse cafes which used to be frequented by some of the leading figures of the so-called Lost Generation;

and it was surprising to me to find that after two successive generations, writers and artists who now find it unthinkable to be seen at places like Deux Magots, still haunted these cafes in Montparnasse; and the impression they conveyed was always that of beleagured artists manning the last front against the creeping inroads of the French bourgeoisie and dollar-laden tourists.

The Coupole, which is full almost every day round about midnight, looks like a large medieval banqueting hall with murals which were painted by famous artists before they became too famous to paint for nothing. We found Giacometti, the internationally famous sculptor, there one night, brooding over a piece of white paper upon which he had been doodling. 'In this quarter,' a young painter told me, 'it is still a shock to hear anyone introduced as a businessman.' Like many historic places the Coupole is now threatened with demolition and there are rumours that an American-owned business establishment is to be set up in its place.

At the Select across the street announcements are made at intervals through the loudspeaker system, summoning famous personalities to the telephone. At one time it is a well-known French theatre critic; the next moment it is the small, doll-like, blonde actress of the *nouvelle vague* films: blue eyes, skin like honey and white-fringed conical breasts visible for all the world to see under the plunging neckline of her mustard sweater and scanty bra.

What immediately shocks someone coming from London is to find this casual acceptance of the proximity of glamour and fame and the complete lack of hostility toward the artist. For ages the artist has been part of the community and no one reacts any more. In London any confession that one writes, paints or sculpts is treated as cause either for mirth, pity or as reason for the profoundest distrust. It is also generally assumed that any famous artist who visits a popular pub – except the obscure country places – is either not serious or is shamelessly cadging for publicity. For a sculptor of Henry Moore's stature to be seen frequenting a pub in Soho would stimulate so much doubt about his sense of propriety as to be actually damaging to his reputation. That is because the relationship between the artist and his society in England is still essentially one of suspicion and distrust. Yet in Paris, there was Giacometti, to be seen almost every night either at the Coupole or the Dome, and his presence there was treated by the cafe crowd with respectful but most casual interest.

Our own guide into the Latin Quarter of 1965 was Breyten Breytenbach, a South African painter and poet who has lived in Paris for five years and speaks fluent French. Breyten is something rare among Afrikaners: he has pushed his rebellion against the Afrikaner's narrow parochialism to a point where, without making any political gestures, he has been able to mix and be accepted by some very left-wing artists in Paris. His estrangement from his own Afrikaner people was perhaps sealed when he married a Vietnamese girl, the daughter of a former Vice-President of South Vietnam. On one score at least the decision could not have been very difficult to make, for Yolande Breytenbach is a ravishing beauty; and being Paris-born she combines naturally and gracefully the occidental and the oriental sides of her upbringing.

Each day then we carried to the cafe our neat stack of notebooks, papers and pens which we heroically supposed were mightier than swords and each day we suffered cruel defeat in the face of other more numerous, diversionary interests. How any writer has been able to work in a Paris cafe is the kind of mystery that I cannot hope to unravel. Yet it seems that the lonely and the homeless, the dwellers in cold-water flats, the romantic searchers and the predatory, have, each in his own season, sometimes found it necessary to annex a Paris cafe as a place in which to work, to rendezvous, or simply to become part of the daily drift to nowhere. I know of no other city where it is so easy to drift and more difficult to work.

For an African in Europe the Paris cafe is what gives street life its tang, sharpness and point. At the Coupole one night a young Dutch painter told me: 'I've visited London from time to time; I'm afraid I cannot live there. For a painter there is no community, no place to meet other painters, and everything closes so early!' He shrugged his shoulders and surveyed the boulevard which at the hour of midnight was swirling with September crowds. It is true, of course, that we have the English pub in London; but the business hours are so restrictive that they only compel the sleepless, neurotic artist as well as the potential sexual offender to roam the street aimlessly after hours. 'Time gentlemen, please,' a cry in which the English take such secret pride, is a cruel mindless surrender to self-inflicted pain and discomfort. After 11 p.m. in London you really have no place in which to meet your friends except in some noisy discotheque or dreary expensive night club or some sad, indescribably pretentious restaurant.

Perhaps the observation is no longer fresh, but after spending two months in Paris it was possible to discover anew just how effectively the cafe has served Parisian society as the focus of the city's social life. The rich may have Maxim's but the poor have the cafe in which it is possible to lunch on a sandwich and cheap red wine while calmly enduring the withering scornful gaze of the *garçon*. I am also certain that not only are the sins of murder, adultery and theft conceived mostly at the cafe table, but important books, plans for revolutionary warfare and the assassination of national figures thousands of miles away from French soil continue to be plotted at the cafe table.

In the space of one morning at the Café Select we had spoken to an African student from Kenya, a Negro musician from Martinique, a coloured painter from the United States. Walking by to buy English newspapers from a kiosk I caught a glimpse of a member of the Pan-Africanist Congress (South Africa) concealed behind his dark glasses; then sat down with a French girl who was a member of the Liberatory Committee of Portuguese Guinea and then chatted with a London representative of the African National Congress recently flown in to collect some paintings for his London exhibition. Indeed, I would not have been surprised to find a member of Dr. Verwoerd's government similarly anchored in a nearby seat. Paris is truly a city of exiles and the cafe is its window to the world. Here it is well-nigh impossible for any young woman to nourish her dreams of solitude or to indulge small private griefs and disappointments without being offered a shoulder to cry on. And any Frenchman, however puny, imagines that his shoulder is broad enough to offer to any young woman in distress.

In London I have often been appalled by the depth of loneliness to which single girls from the provinces are condemned, especially if they are shy and retiring by nature. There is no way whatever to meet boys in an atmosphere of freedom, without feeling a sense of commitment, save by attending numerous, insupportably dull, parties from which any girl is lucky to emerge with a bumbling oaf who is capable of defending the cause of human reason in tolerably good English. As a consequence, any 'decent' English girl who finds herself approached by a strange man in the street feels it her moral obligation to reach under her tweed skirt for a former Girl Guide whistle. Talk about 'sexual revolution'; it would be more accurate to describe it as 'sexual panic'!

One can understand, of course, why it is now generally believed that because French girls are friendly they are just as ready for a tumble. In Paris, especially in a cafe, there is no opprobrium which attaches to a girl for speaking to a complete stranger, an attitude which appeals enormously to a great many Africans like myself, brought up to feel that it is failing in one's social obligation to sit next to a young woman without paying her some gallant attention, however unprepossessing she looks. I was therefore happily surprised by the freedom of Paris! Here at the crowded or almost empty cafe, dreams are finally harvested or nullified: the golden woman in your troubled feverish dreams arrives mercifully on the appointed hour to sit in full view at the table across from yours. Naturally, it may take a certain amount of ingenuity and hard talk to convince her that you are indeed the Prince destined to sweep her off her feet; but at least the woman of your fantasies is not forever imprisoned in some obscure dream of a super Mayfair night club or country estate, forever fleshless and inaccessible to your sweaty, tobacco-stained fingers!

4

In the corner a huge American Negro with his arms around a lovely French tart, roared a song to her in a rich beautiful voice and suddenly . . .

F. SCOTT FITZGERALD, *THE CRACK UP*

When evening came and the dense heat of a summer day had changed into a bracing sensual coolness of a Paris evening, we rode a cab from St Michel to Rue Brezin, collecting liquor bottles as we went along. The old woman hauled the bottles down from the shelves as we pointed them out at the shop; then as we seized them, ready to leave, she held our attention with a fretful insistent desire to talk. 'You're lovers?' she said. 'Young love is a beautiful thing, no?' The French girl and I laughed, but did not explain that we were not lovers because it seemed a good thing to give flesh to the old woman's nostalgia for a departed youth. After the damp fog of England's racism it was also refreshing to find an old woman who was able to take inter-racial love so much for granted; indeed, this was a prelude to a bright, orgiastic night of dance, talk and drinking which went on for two days. The police came, shouted their threats, then left, and the party went on, a little quieter but still wanton enough, sharpened at times by intellectual contention. After a long evening of theoretical debate with someone a French girl gave up on the English language: 'I'm too tired to think in English!' Raymond Kunene, the Zulu poet, shuttled between the bookshelves and the dance floor, was seen at one time executing a spectacular war dance which brought a passionate exaltation to the face of an old Negro painter, Beauford Delaney, for twelve years self-exiled from the United States. 'I came to Paris for a weekend and stayed for twelve years!' Now drawn to the madcap frolic of that Zulu dance Beauford Delaney looked both sombre and fervid, sad and ecstatic, already beginning to ask himself what Africa meant to him, which is to say he had already started on that long journey into the dark night of the Negro psyche where every question leads to the nightmare of slave ships. But if there is anything that Paris teaches it is that exile is the modern condition; and yet for the Negro and the African this is also the century of reunion; here in the warm intimate hour of midnight; with the city slumbering in the darkness, exile spoke to exile, the South African to the doubly exiled American Negro, and out there at the cafe tables one knew there were others just as exiled, just as quick, just as reckless, just as driven, each knowing the truth of his loneliness only in the private cells of his body, or in the illuminated faces of those who had similarly suffered. Dancing, jumping up and down, fierce in dispute, gaiety and sadness was finally their portion. 'Aren't they jus' beautiful people!' Delaney enthused.

EDWIGE DANTICAT

from *Breath, Eyes, Memory*

Edwige Danticat (b. 1969) was born in Haiti, went to the United States at the age of 12 and published her first writings in English two years later. She studied at Barnard College and Brown University and now lives in Brooklyn. She has published Krik? Krak! (1995), a collection of short stories, and a novel. Breath, Eyes, Memory (1994) tells the story of Sophie, who at the age of 12 leaves her aunt and grandmother in Haiti to join her mother in New York. Their troubled relationship haunts the subsequent narrative, and is evident even in the description of her first day in the city, reprinted here.

The streets along Flatbush Avenue reminded me of home. My mother took me to Haiti Express, so I could see the place where she sent our money orders and cassettes from.

It was a small room packed with Haitians. People stood on line patiently waiting their turn. My mother slipped Tante Atie's cassette into a padded envelope. As we waited on line, an old fan circled a spider's web above our heads.

A chubby lady greeted my mother politely when we got to the window.

'This is Sophie,' my mother said through the holes in the thick glass. 'She is the one who has given you so much business over the years.'

The lady smiled as she took my mother's money and the package. I kept feeling like there was more I wanted to send to Tante Atie. If I had the power then to shrink myself and slip into the envelope, I would have done it.

I watched as the lady stamped our package and dropped it on top of a larger pile. Around us were dozens of other people trying to squeeze all their love into small packets to send back home.

After we left, my mother stopped at a Haitian beauty salon to buy some castor oil for her hair. Then we went to a small boutique and bought some long skirts and blouses for me to wear to school. My mother said it was important that I learn English quickly. Otherwise, the American students would make fun of me or, even worse, beat me. A lot of other mothers from the nursing home where she worked had told her that their children were getting into fights in school because they were accused of having HBO – Haitian Body Odor. Many of the American kids even accused Haitians of having AIDS because they had heard on television that only the 'Four Hs' got AIDS – Heroin addicts, Hemophiliacs, Homosexuals, and Haitians.

Edwige Danticat, *Breath, Eyes, Memory* (London: Abacus, 1995), pp. 50–6. Reproduced by permission of Soho Press, New York and Abacus, London.

I wanted to tell my mother that I didn't want to go to school. Frankly, I was afraid. I tried to think of something to keep me from having to go. Sickness or death were probably the only two things that my mother would accept as excuses.

A car nearly knocked me out of my reverie. My mother grabbed my hand and pulled me across the street. She stopped in front of a pudgy woman selling rice powder and other cosmetics on the street.

'*Sak passé*, Jacqueline?' said my mother.

'You know,' answered Jacqueline in Creole. 'I'm doing what I can.'

Jacqueline was wearing large sponge rollers under a hair net on her head. My mother brought some face cream that promised to make her skin lighter.

All along the avenue were people who seemed displaced among the speeding cars and very tall buildings. They walked and talked and argued in Creole and even played dominoes on their stoops. We found Tante Atie's lemon perfume in a botanica shop. On the walls were earthen jars, tin can lamps, and small statues of the beautiful *mulâtresse*, the goddess and loa Erzulie.

We strolled through long stretches of streets where merengue blared from car windows and children addressed one another in curses.

The outdoor subway tracks seemed to lead to the sky. Pebbles trickled down on us as we crossed under the tracks into another more peaceful neighborhood.

My mother held my hand as we walked through those quiet streets, where the houses had large yards and little children danced around sprinklers on the grass. We stopped in front of a building where the breeze was shaking a sign: MARC CHEVALIER, ESQUIRE.

When my mother rang the bell, a stocky Haitian man came to the door. He was a deep bronze color and very well dressed.

My mother kissed him on the cheek and followed him down a long hallway. On either side of us were bookshelves stacked with large books. My mother let go of my hand as we walked down the corridor. He spoke to her in Creole as he opened the door and let us into his office.

He leaned over and shook my hand.

'Marc Jolibois Francis Legrand Moravien Chevalier.'

'*Enchanté*,' I said.

I took a deep breath and looked around. On his desk was a picture of him and my mother, posed against a blue background.

'Are you working late?' my mother asked him.

'Where are you going?' he asked.

'We are just walking around,' my mother said. 'I am showing her what is where.'

'Later, we'll go someplace,' he said, patting a folder on his desk.

My mother and I took a bus back to our house. We were crowded and pressed against complete strangers. When we got home, we went through my suitcase and picked out a loose-fitting, high-collared dress Tante Atie had bought me for Sunday Masses. She held it out for me to wear to dinner.

'This is what a proper young lady should wear,' she said.

That night, Marc drove us to a restaurant called Miracin's in Asbury Park, New Jersey. The restaurant was at the back of an alley, squeezed between a motel and a dry cleaner.

'Miracin's has the best Haitian food in America,' Marc told me as we parked under the motel sign.

'Marc is one of those men who will never recover from not eating his *manman*'s cooking,' said my mother. 'If he could get her out of her grave to make him dinner, he would do it.'

'My mother was the best,' Marc said as he opened the car door for us.

There was a tiny lace curtain on the inside of the door. A bell rang as we entered. My mother and I squeezed ourselves between the wall and the table, our bodies wiping the greasy wallpaper clean.

Marc waved to a group of men sitting in a corner loudly talking politics. The room was packed with other customers who shouted back and forth adding their views to the discussion.

'Never the Americans in Haiti again,' shouted one man. 'Remember what they did in the twenties. They treated our people like animals. They abused the *konbit* system and they made us work like slaves.'

'Roads, we need roads,' said another man. 'At least they gave us roads. My mother was killed in a ferry accident. If we had roads, we would not need to put crowded boats into the sea, just to go from one small village to another. A lot of you, when you go home, you have to walk from the village to your house, because there are no roads for cars.'

'What about the boat people?' added a man from a table near the door. 'Because of them, people can't respect us in this country. They lump us all with them.'

'All the brains leave the country,' Marc said, adding his voice to the mêlée.

'You are insulting the people back home by saying there's no brains there,' replied a woman from a table near the back. 'There are brains who stay.'

'But they are crooks,' Marc said, adding some spice to the argument.

'My sister is a nurse there with the Red Cross,' said the woman, standing up. 'You call that a crook? What have *you* done for your people?'

For some of us, arguing is a sport. In the marketplace in Haiti, whenever people were arguing, others would gather around them to watch and laugh at the colorful language. People rarely hit each other. They didn't need to. They could wound just as brutally by cursing your mother, calling you a sexual misfit, or accusing you of being from the hills. If you couldn't match them with even stronger accusations, then you would concede the argument by keeping your mouth shut.

Marc decided to stay out of the discussion. The woman continued attacking him, shouting that she was tired of cowardly men speaking against women who were proving themselves, women as brave as stars out at dawn.

My mother smiled at the woman's colorful words. It was her turn to stand up and defend her man, but she said nothing. Marc kept looking at her, as if waiting for my mother to argue on his behalf, but my mother picked up the menu, and ran her fingers down the list of dishes.

My mother introduced me to the waiter when he came by to take her order. He looked at us for a long time. First me, then my mother. I wanted to tell him to stop it. There was no resemblance between us. I knew it.

It was an eternity before we were served. Marc complained about his *boudin* when it came.

'I can still taste the animal,' he said.

'What do you expect?' my mother asked. 'It is a pig's blood after all.'

'It's not well done,' he said, while raising the fork to his mouth. 'It is an art to make *boudin*. There is a balance. At best it is a very tight kind of sausage and you would never dream of where it comes from.'

'Who taught you to eat this way?' my mother asked.

'Food is a luxury,' he said, 'but we can not allow ourselves to become gluttons or get fat. Do you hear that, Sophie?'

I shook my head yes, as though I was really very interested. I ate like I had been on a hunger strike, filling myself with the coconut milk they served us in real green coconuts.

When they looked up from their plates, my mother and Marc eyed each other like there were things they couldn't say because of my presence. I tried to stuff myself and keep quiet, pretending that I couldn't even see them. My mother now had two lives: Marc belonged to her present life, I was a living memory from the past.

'What do you want to be when you grow up?' Marc asked me. He spoke to me in a tone of voice that was used with very young children or very old animals.

'I want to do *dactylo*,' I said, 'be a secretary.'

He didn't seem impressed.

'There are a lot of opportunities in this country,' he said. 'You should reconsider, unless of course this is the passion of your life.'

'She is too young now to know,' my mother said. 'You are going to be a doctor,' she told me.

'She still has some time to think,' Marc said. 'Do you have a boyfriend, Sophie?'

'She is not going to be running wild like those American girls,' my mother said. 'She will have a boyfriend when she is eighteen.'

'And what if she falls in love sooner?' Marc pushed.

'She will put it off until she is eighteen.'

We washed down our meal with watermelon juice. Tante Atie always said that eating beets and watermelon would put more red in my blood and give me more strength for hard times.

3

Ethnography in Reverse

WILLIAM WELLS BROWN

from *Three Years in Europe*

William Wells Brown (1814–1884) was a slave in Kentucky and the Missouri Territory. In 1834 he fled north and reached Cleveland, later moving to Buffalo, and took advantage of his work on Lake Erie steamboats to help other fugitive slaves reach Canada. In the early 1840s he became a lecturer in the anti-slavery movement, and moved to Boston in 1847. In 1849 he travelled to Britain on behalf of the American Peace Society to counter the propaganda of the American Colonization Society, which for thirty years had been promoting the resettlement of emancipated slaves in Liberia. The passage of the Fugitive Slave Law (1850) delayed his return to the United States until 1854, when his freedom was purchased by supporters.

He published an account of his time abroad in Three Years in Europe: or Places I Have Seen and People I Have Met *(1852), consisting of letters written to the abolitionist newspaper, the* North Star. *The letter concerning his visit – in the company of fellow fugitive, Ellen Craft – to the home of Harriet Martineau in the English Lake District is reproduced below. His other publications include the* Narrative of William Wells Brown, A Fugitive Slave *(1847);* Clotel; or, The President's Daughter *(1853) – the first novel by an African American; and the pioneering historical work,* The Rising Son; or, The Antecedents and Advancement of the Colored Race *(1873).*

A series of public meetings, one pressing close upon the heel of another, must be an apology for my six or eight weeks' silence. But I hope that no temporary suspense on my part will be construed into a want of interest in our cause, or a wish to desist from giving occasionally a scrap (such as it is) to the *North Star*.

My last letter left me under the hospitable roof of Harriet Martineau. I had long had an invitation to visit this distinguished friend of our race, and as the invitation was renewed during my tour through the North, I did not feel disposed to decline it, and thereby lose so favourable an opportunity of meeting with one who had written so much in behalf of the oppressed of our land. About a mile from the head of Lake Windermere, and immediately under Wonsfell, and encircled by mountains on all sides, except the south-west, lies the picturesque little town of Ambleside, and the brightest spot in the place is 'The Knoll,' the residence of Miss Martineau.

William Wells Brown, 'Letter XVI', from *Three Years in Europe; or, Places I Have Seen and People I Have Met* (London: Charles Gilpin, 1852), pp. 196–207.

We reached 'The Knoll' a little after nightfall, and a cordial shake of the hand by Miss M., who was waiting for us, soon assured us that we had met with a warm friend.

It is not my intention to lay open the scenes of domestic life at 'The Knoll,' nor to describe the social parties of which my friends and I were partakers during our sojourn within the hospitable walls of this distinguished writer; but the name of Miss M. is so intimately connected with the Anti-slavery movement, by her early writings, and those have been so much admired by the friends of the slave in the United States, that I deem it not at all out of place for me to give the readers of the *North Star* some idea of the authoress of 'Political Economy,' 'Travels in the East,' 'The Hour and the Man,' &c.

The dwelling is a cottage of moderate size, built after Miss M.'s own plan, upon a rise of land from which it derives the name of 'The Knoll.' The Library is the largest room in the building, and upon the walls of it were hung some beautiful engravings and a continental map. On a long table which occupied the centre of the room, were the busts of Shakspere, Newton, Milton, and a few other literary characters of the past. One side of the room was taken up with a large case, filled with a choice collection of books, and everything indicated that it was the home of genius and of taste.

The room was usually occupied by Miss M., and where we found her on the evening of our arrival, is rather small and lighted by two large windows. The walls of this room were also decorated with prints and pictures, and on the mantle-shelf were some models in *terra cottia* of Italian groups. On a circular table lay casts, medallions, and some very choice water-colour drawings. Under the south window stood a small table covered with newly opened letters, a portfolio and several new books, with here and there a page turned down, and one with a paper knife between its leaves as if it had only been half read. I took up the last mentioned, and it proved to be the 'Life and Poetry of Hartley Coleridge,' son of S. T. Coleridge. It was just from the press, and had, a day or two before, been forwarded to her by the publisher. Miss M. is very deaf and always carries in her left hand a trumpet; and I was not a little surprised on learning from her that she had never enjoyed the sense of smell, and only on one occasion the sense of taste, and that for a single moment. Miss M. is loved with a sort of idolatry by the people of Ambleside, and especially the poor, to whom she gives a course of lectures every winter gratuitously. She finished her last course the day before our arrival. She was much pleased with Ellen Craft, and appeared delighted with the story of herself and husband's escape from slavery, as related by the latter – during the recital of which I several times saw the silent tear stealing down her cheek, and which she tried in vain to hide from us.

When Craft had finished, she exclaimed, 'I would that every woman in the British Empire, could hear that tale as I have, so that they might know how their own sex was treated in that boasted land of liberty.' It seems strange to the people of this county, that one so white and so lady-like as Mrs. Craft, should have been a slave and forced to leave the land of her nativity and seek an asylum in a foreign country. The morning after our arrival, I took a stroll by a circuitous pathway to the top of Loughrigg Fell. At the foot of the mount I met a peasant, who very kindly offered to lend me his donkey, upon which to ascend the mountain. Never having been upon the back of one of these long eared animals, I felt some hesitation about trusting myself upon so diminutive a looking creature. But being assured that if I would only resign myself to his care and let him have his own way, I would be perfectly safe, I mounted, and off we set. We had, however, scarcely gone fifty rods, when, in passing over a narrow part of the path and overlooking a deep chasm, one of the hind feet of the donkey slipped, and with an involuntary shudder, I shut my eyes to meet my expected doom; but fortunately the little fellow gained his foothold, and in all probability saved us both from a premature death. After we had passed over this dangerous place, I dismounted, and as soon as my feet had once more gained *terra firma*, I resolved that I would never again yield my own judgment to that of any one, not even to a donkey.

It seems as if Nature has amused herself in throwing these mountains together. From the top of the Loughrigg Fell, the eye loses its power in gazing upon the objects below. On our left, lay Rydal Mount, the beautiful seat of the late poet Wordsworth. While to the right, and away in the dim distance, almost hidden by the native trees, was the cottage where once resided Mrs. Hemans. And below us lay Windermere, looking more like a river than a lake, and which, if placed by the side of our own Ontario, Erie or Huron, would be lost in the fog. But here it looks beautiful in the extreme, surrounded as it is by a range of mountains that have no parallel in the United States for beauty. Amid a sun of uncommon splendour, dazzling the eye with the reflection upon the water below, we descended into the valley, and I was soon again seated by the fireside of our hospitable hostess. In the afternoon of the same day, we took a drive to the 'Dove's Nest,' the home of the late Mrs. Hemans.

We did not see the inside of the house, on account of its being occupied by a very eccentric man, who will not permit a woman to enter the house, and it is said that he has been known to run when a female had unconsciously intruded herself upon his premises. And as our company was in part composed of ladies, we had to share their fate, and therefore were prevented from seeing the interior of the Dove's Nest. The exhibitor of such a man would be almost sure of a prize at the great Exhibition.

At the head of Grassmere Lake, and surrounded by a few cottages, stands an old gray, antique-looking Parish Church, venerable with the lapse of centuries, and the walls partly covered with ivy, and in the rear of which is the parish burial-ground. After leaving the Dove's Nest, and having a pleasant ride over the hills and between the mountains, and just as the sun was disappearing behind them, we arrived at the gate of Grassmere Church; and alighting and following Miss M., we soon found ourselves standing over a grave, marked by a single stone, and that, too, very plain, with a name deeply cut. This announced to us that we were standing over the grave of William Wordsworth. He chose his own grave, and often visited the spot before his death. He lies in the most sequestered spot in the whole grounds, and the simplicity and beauty of the place was enough to make one in love with it, to be laid so far from the bustle of the world, and in so sweet a place. The more one becomes acquainted with the literature of the old world, the more he must love her poets. Among the teachers of men, none are more worthy of study than the poets; and, as teachers, they should receive far more credit than is yielded to them. No one can look back upon the lives of Dante,

Shakspere, Milton, Goethe, Cowper, and many others that we might name, without being reminded of the sacrifices which they made for mankind, and which were not appreciated until long after their deaths. We need look no farther than our own country to find men and women wielding the pen practically and powerfully for the right. It is acknowledged on all hands in this country, that England has the greatest dead poets, and America the greatest living ones. The poet and the true Christian have alike a hidden life. Worship is the vital element of each. Poetry has in it that kind of utility which good men find in their Bible, rather than such convenience as bad men often profess to draw from it. It ennobles the sentiments, enlarges the affections, kindles the imagination, and gives to us the enjoyment of a life in the past, and in the future, as well as in the present. Under its light and warmth, we wake from our torpidity and coldness, to a sense of our capabilities. This impulse once given, a great object is gained. Schiller has truly said, 'Poetry can be to a man, what love is to a hero. It can neither counsel him nor smite him, nor perform any labour for him, but it can bring him up to be a hero, can summon him to deeds, and arm him with strength for all he ought to be.' I have often read with pleasure the sweet poetry of our own Whitfield of Buffalo, which has appeared from time to time in the columns of the *North Star*. I have always felt ashamed of the fact that he should be compelled to wield the razor instead of the pen for a living. Meaner poets than James M. Whitfield, are now living by their compositions; and were he a white man he could occupy a different position.

After remaining a short time, and reading the epitaphs of the departed, we again returned to 'The Knoll.' Nothing can be more imposing than the beauty of English park scenery, and especially in the vicinity of the lakes. Magnificent towns [downs?] that extend like sheets of vivid green, with here and there a sprinkling of fine trees, heaping up rich piles of foliage, and then the forests with the hare, the deer, and the rabbit, bounding away to the covert, or the pheasant suddenly bursting upon the wing – the artificial stream, the brook taught to wind in natural meanderings, or expand into the glassy lake, with the yellow leaf sleeping upon its bright waters, and occasionally a rustic temple or sylvan statue grown green and dark with age, give an air of sanctity and picturesque beauty to English scenery that is unknown in the United States. The very labourer with his thatched cottage and narrow slip of ground-plot before the door, the little flower-bed, the woodbine trimmed against the wall, and hanging its blossoms about the windows, and the peasant seen trudging home at nightfall with the avails of the toil of the day upon his back – all this tells us of the happiness both rich and poor in this country. And yet there are those who would have the world believe that the labourer of England is in a far worse condition than the slaves of America. Such persons know nothing of the real condition of the working classes of this country. At any rate, the poor here, as well as the rich, are upon a level, as far as the laws of the country are concerned. The more one becomes acquainted with the English people, the more one has to admire them. They are so different from the people of our own country. Hospitality, frankness, and good humour, are always to be found in an Englishman. After a ramble of three days about the lakes, we mounted the coach, bidding Miss Martineau farewell, and quitted the lake district.

FREDERICK DOUGLASS

1846

Letter from Scotland

Frederick Douglass (c.1817–1892) was born Frederick Bailey, a slave in Maryland, but in 1838 escaped to the North. Already literate, he became active as an abolitionist lecturer in Massachusetts and in 1845 published an autobiography under his new name, chosen after the hero of Walter Scott's poem, The Lady of the Lake. *The book was an enormous success, but as a fugitive Douglass was still in danger of being recaptured, and he spent most of the following two years in the relative safety of Great Britain, addressing audiences from Exeter to Dundee, from East Anglia to the West of Ireland. In Scotland, the main issue was the decision of the Free Church of Scotland to accept donations it had recently received from Presbyterian churches in the American South, and the cry of 'send back the money' dominated his speeches north of the border. Douglass's love of Scotland did not end with Scott, however, as this letter to an unidentified recipient, first published in the* New York Tribune, *shows.*

I am now in the town of Ayr. It is famous for being the birth-place of Robert Burns, the poet, by whose brilliant genius every stream, hill, glen and valley in the neighborhood have been made classic. I have felt more interest in visiting this place than any other in Scotland, for as you are aware, (painfully perhaps) I am an enthusiastic admirer of Robt. Burns. Immediately on our arrival, Friend Buffum and myself were joined by Rev. Mr. Renwick, the minister in whose meeting house we are to lecture during our stay, and proceeded forthwith to see Burns's Monument. It is about three miles from town, and situated on the South bank of the river 'Doon,' and within hearing of its gentle steps as it winds its way over its pebbled path to the Ocean. The place of the Monument is well chosen, being in full view of all the places mentioned and referred to in the Poet's famous poem called 'Tam o' Shanter,' as well as several others of his most popular poems. From the Monument (which I have not time to describe,) may be seen the Cottage where Burns was born – the old and new bridge across the Doon – 'Kirk Alloway,' called by Burns the 'Haunted Kirk.' The banks of 'Doon' rising majestically from the sea toward the sky, and the Clyde stretching off to the highlands of Arran, whose dim outline is scarcely discernible through the fog by which it is almost constantly overhung, makes the spot admirably and beautifully adapted to the Monument of Scotland's noble bard. In the Monument there is a finely executed marble bust of Burns – the finest thing

Frederick Douglass, 'A Fugitive Slave Visiting the Birth-place of Robert Burns', extract from a letter, dated 23 April 1846, *New York Tribune*, 9 July 1846, p. 4.

of the kind I ever saw. I never before, looking upon it, realized the power of man to make the marble speak. The expression is so fine, and the face is so lit up, as to cause one to forget the form in gazing upon the spirit.

In another room, there are two statues carved out of free stone – the one of Souter Johnny and the other of Tam O'Shanter, two characters named in his most famous poem. These were also finely executed and shared my attention, but I was drawn to Burns. In a glass case near his bust there was a Bible, given by Burns to his 'sweet Highland Mary' – there is also in the same case a lock of her hair neatly fastened to a cord. As I gazed on the hair of her he so dearly loved, and who by death was snatched from his bosom, and up to his bust glowing with expression, I received a vivid impression, and shared with him the deep melancholy portrayed in the following lines:

> Ye banks and braes o' bonnie Doon,
>> How can ye bloom sae fresh and fair;
> How can ye chant, ye little birds,
>> And I sae weary, fu' o' care?
> Thou'lt break my heart, thou warbling bird,
>> That wantons thro' the flowering thorn:
> Thou 'minds me of departed joys,
>> Departed, never to return!
>
> Oft hae I rov'd by bonnie Doon,
>> To see the rose and woodbine twine,
> And ilka bird sang o' its luve,
>> And fondly sae did I o' mine;
> Wi' lightsome heart I pu'd a rose
>> Fu' sweet upon its thorny tree;
> And my fause lover stole my rose,
>> But, ah! he left the thorn wi' me.

On our way to the Monument we enjoyed a pleasure and privilege I shall never forget. It was that of seeing and conversing with Mrs. Beggs, an own sister of Robert Burns, and also seeing and talking with the Poet's two nieces, daughters of Mrs. Beggs. They live by the road side in a small thatched cottage, humble but comfortable. When Mr. Renwick made them acquainted with the fact that we were from America they received us warmly. One of the nieces said her uncle was more highly esteemed in America than in Scotland. – Mrs. Beggs is the youngest sister of Robert Burns, and though now approaching 80, she does not look to be more than sixty. She enjoys good health, is a spirited looking woman, and bids fair to live yet many days. The two daughters are truly fine looking women. Coal black hair, full, high foreheads, and yet black eyes, sparkling with the poetic fire which illumined the breast of their brilliant uncle. Their deportment was warm and free, yet dignified and lady-like. They did every thing to make our call agreeable, and they were not ignorant as to the means of putting us freely at ease. Two letters in their uncle's own hand writing was early put into our hands. An original portrait, said to be excellent, was discoursed upon; I thought it much like those we usually see in his works.

We sat fifteen or twenty minutes. It might have been longer, as happy moments pass rapidly. Took leave – bade farewell. I saw in them so much of what I love in every body else, I felt as if leaving old and dear friends. I have ever esteemed Robert Burns a true soul but never could I have had the high opinion of the man or his genius, which I now entertain, without my present knowledge of the country, to which he belonged – the times in which he lived, and the broad Scotch tongue in which he wrote. Burns lived in the midst of a bigoted and besotted clergy – a pious, but corrupt generation – a proud, ambitious, and contemptuous aristocracy, who, esteemed a little more than a man, and looked upon the plowman, such as was the noble Burns, as being little better than a brute. He became disgusted with the pious frauds, indignant at the bigotry, filled with contempt for the hollow pretensions set up by the shallow-brained aristocracy. He broke loose from the moorings which society had thrown around him. Spurning all restraint, he sought a path for his feet, and, like all bold pioneers, he made crooked paths. We may lament it, we may weep over it, but in the language of another, we shall lament and weep with him. The elements of character which urged him on are in us all, and influencing our conduct every day of our lives. We may pity him, but we can't despise him. We may condemn his faults, but only as we condemn our own. His very weakness was an index of his strength. Full of faults of a grievous nature, yet far more faultless than many who have come down to us in the pages of history as saints. He was a brilliant genius, and like all of his class, did much good and much evil. Let us take the good and leave the evil – let us adopt his virtues but avoid his vices – let us pursue his wisdom but shun his folly; and as death has separated his noble spirit from the corrupt and contemptible dust with which it was encumbered, so let us separate his good from his evil deeds – thus may we make him a blessing rather than a curse to the world.

Read his 'Tam O'Shanter,' 'Cotter's Saturday Night,' 'Man was made to Mourn,' 'To my Mary in Heaven.' Indeed, dear A., read his poems, and as I know you are no admirer of Burns, read it to gratify your friend Frederick. So much for Burns.

Ida B. Wells

from 'Memories of London'

Ida B. Wells (1862–1931) was born in Mississippi, and educated at a local freedmen's school. She worked as a teacher, and later, after moving in 1884 to Memphis, Tennessee, as an investigative journalist. She was a tireless campaigner against discrimination, segregation and racial violence, and her speaking tours took her across the United States, and – in 1893 and 1894 – to Great Britain, where she alerted audiences to the horrors of lynching. On her return, she settled in Chicago, and continued to be involved in local and national civil rights struggles, founding the first Black women's suffrage organization, the Alpha Suffrage Club. She was an active member of many organizations including the National Association of Colored Women. This is an extract from a series of articles entitled 'Ida B Wells Abroad' that she wrote for the Chicago Inter-Ocean during her second British tour in 1894. It was later incorporated in her autobiography, edited and published posthumously by her daughter Alfreda Duster in 1970.

LONDON, JUNE 6 – SPECIAL CORRESPONDENCE. The thermometer has been at freezing point several times the past week in town and there has been frost in the country. Last May when I was here, everybody said there had not been such a mild and lovely spring for twenty years; this time it is said there has not been a time within memory of the oldest inhabitant when May was so cold and rainy as now. I fully agree with the American tourist who, when asked about the English climate, remarked that 'they had no climate – only samples.' The only other English thing I do not like is the railway carriage. They can change the one if they cannot the other. To me, the narrow railway compartments, with seats facing each other, knees rubbing against those of entire strangers, and being forced to stare into each other's faces for hours, are almost intolerable and would be quite so, were the English not uniformly so courteous as they are, and the journeys comparatively short. But primitive as are these railway carriages, I as a Negro can ride in them free from insult or discrimination on account of color, and that's what I cannot do in many States of my own free (?) America. One other thing about English railways must strike the American traveler, the carefulness with which human life is guarded. The lines of railway are carefully inclosed on both sides by stone wall or hedge the entire length, and never cross a roadway as they invariably do in America. The railway always goes under the roadway through a tunnel or over it on a bridge. Passengers are never allowed to cross the track from one side of the station to the other – there is always a bridge or subway. As a consequence, accidents to human life are most rare occurrences, and I begin to understand how aghast the Britisher was to see our railway and streetcar tracks laid through the heart of our towns and cities and steam engines and cable cars dashing along at the rate of thirty miles per hour. Even in London the only rapid steam or cable locomotion is under ground.

They call the streetcars here tramways, or tram-cars, and I puzzled over it very much until I learned that a man named Outram first hit upon the experiment of rolling cars or trucks on tracks – this was before the invention of the steam engine – and all cars so propelled without the aid of steam were called Outram cars. This has since been shortened. The first syllable of the name of the inventor has been dropped, and they are known as trams. I have found many Englishmen who do not know the origin of the word, yet are surprised that the green American does not at first know what he means by trams.

London has been in the throes of a cab strike for two weeks, but beyond making it safe for pedestrians there seems little notice taken of it. The hansom is the only rapid means of general locomotion in London, save the Underground Railway, and there were thousands plying every hour of the day and night. They never slacken the pace when crossing the street, because there are so many streets they would always be stopping. So that between the omnibuses and cabs, persons took almost as much risk in crossing a street as they do in Chicago from the cable cars. The strike has taken more than half the usual number of cabs off the street, and the pedestrian is enjoying the result; for this two-wheeled friend of the weary – the hansom – has rubber tires and as it rolls along the asphalt pavement, there is only the sound of the horses' hoofs, and the cab is upon you before you know it.

London is a wonderful city, built, as everybody knows, in squares – the residence portion of it. The houses are erected generally on the four sides of a hollow square, in which are the trees, seats, grass and walks of the typical English garden. Only the residents of the square have the entree to this railed in garden. They have a key to this park in miniature, and walk, play tennis, etc., with their children, or sit under the trees enjoying the fresh air. The passerby has to content himself with the refreshing glimpse of the green grass and inviting shade of these trees which make such a break in the monotony of long rows of brick and stone houses and pavements. The houses are generally ugly, oblong structures of mud-colored brick, perfectly plain and straight the entire height of the three or four stories. This exterior is broken only by the space for windows. The Englishman cares little for outside adornment – it is the interior of his home which he beautifies.

There is also the charm of antiquity and historic association about every part of the city. For instance, I am the guest of P. W. Clayden, Esq., editor of the *London Daily News*. His house is near Bloomsbury Square, in the shadow of St. Pancras Church, an old landmark, and from where I am now writing, I look out the windows of the breakfast-room across to Charles Dickens' London home. We are also only a few squares – five minutes' walk – from the British Museum.

I have been too engrossed in the work which brought me here to visit the British Museum (although I pass it every day), the Royal Academy or Westminster Abbey, which every American tourist does visit. I have been to the Houses of Parliament twice, and also to Cambridge University. My first visit to the British Parliament was under the escort of Mr. J. Keir Hardie, M.P. Mr. Hardie is a labor member and he outrages all the propriety by wearing a workman's cap, a dark flannel shirt and sack coat – the usual workingman's garb – to all the sittings. He is quite a marked contrast to the silk-hatted, frock-coated members by whom he is surrounded. The M.P.'s sit in Parliament with their hats on, and the sessions are held at night A great deal of ceremony must be gone through to get a glimpse of the British lawmaking body at work. A card of permit must be issued by a member for admission to the galleries, and it is a mark of honor to be conducted over the building by one. Mr. Hardie himself had to secure a card to permit me to enter the House of Lords and look upon a lot of real live lords, who, according to the trend of public opinion, should no longer be permitted to sit upon their red-feathered sofas and obstruct legislation. There is a special gallery for women, and the night I stood outside the door and peered into the House of Commons I noticed about the speaker's chair a wire netting which extended to the ceiling. Behind this there were what I took to be gayly dressed wax figures, presumably of historic personages. Imagine my surprise when I was told that was the ladies' gallery, and it was only behind this cage that they were allowed to appear at all in the sacred precincts hitherto devoted to men.

The question of removing the grille was again brought up in Parliament this year, as it has been for several years past, but nothing came of it. An amusing incident happened two weeks ago when two ladies, strangers, had applied for permission to visit the House. A member of Parliament left them, as he thought, at the door while he went into the chamber for the necessary card. Unaware that women were never permitted to enter, and the doorkeeper being for the moment off guard, they followed the member of Parliament up the aisle nearly halfway to the speaker's chair, when they were discovered and hurriedly taken out. They are said to be the first ladies who were ever on the floor of the House during a sitting.

Mr. Hardie interviewed me for his paper, the *Labor Leader*, and explained much that was strange while we had tea on the beautiful terrace overlooking the Thames at 6 o'clock that evening. British M.P.'s are not paid to legislate and unless they are gentlemen of means they pursue their different avocations meanwhile. An M.P. does not necessarily reside in the district he represents; he may be, and most always is, an entire stranger to his constituents until he 'stands' for election. M.P. Naoriji, a native of India, is representing a London constituency. He is the gentleman about whom Lord Salisbury said: 'The time has not come yet for a British constituency to be represented in Parliament by a black man.' The English people resented this attempt to draw a color line and promptly returned Naoriji to Parliament, and Lord Rosebery, the present Prime Minister, gave him a dinner on the eve of his election.

A. B. C. Merriman-Labor

'The Visible Spirit of the Britons'

Britons Through Negro Spectacles; or, A Negro on Britons (1909) had its origin in 'entertainment-lectures' delivered during the author's recent tour of Africa. The book takes the form of a narrative of a single day's journey across London, as the author guides 'Africanus' east to west, beginning in the City at 9 o'clock in the morning. This chapter on the 'visible spirit of the Britons' is later balanced by one on the 'invisible spirit of the Britons': Christianity. 'The invisible and the visible are coexistent in the Briton, but not coequal.'

Referring to what people have called his 'humorous style', Merriman-Labor comments: 'I shall indeed be sorry to be regarded solely as a humorist, for one of my aims in writing is not so much to be humorous, as to reveal truths as may be best spoken in jest. Considering my racial connection, and the flippant character of literature which, at the present time, finds ready circulation among the general public, I am of the opinon that the world will be better prepared to hear me if I come in the guise of a jester.'

Of course it would be impossible for you to see these different parts of London during the few hours at our disposal. We shall therefore confine our walk to Central London where people meet on business during the day, and to West London where they meet for pleasure at night. If you will walk about the first City in the British Empire arm in arm with Merriman-Labor, you are sure to see Britons in *merriment* and at *labour*, by night and by day, in West and Central London.

The most prominent position in Central London, a position whence we shall start westwards, is the area opposite the Mansion House, the official residence of the Lord Mayor, the Chief Magistrate of the City.

If we visit the Lord Mayor, history will, in a way, repeat itself. You would remember that an ancient Chief Magistrate, Solomon, was visited by a number of persons who, according to several commentators, were Africans. I mean the Queen of Sheba and retinue. They presented Solomon, on the occasion of their visit, with 'much gold and precious stones.' Should we visit London's Chief Magistrate, we need not present him with gold and precious stones. None whatever of such precious presents for him; for, I daresay, the Lord Mayor – if not himself, then, his relatives – have subtracted, extracted, or abstracted (whichever it may be) for themselves enough gold and diamonds from West and South Africa already.

A. B. C. Merriman-Labor, *Britons Through Negro Spectacles; or, A Negro on Britons. With a Description of London* (London: Imperial and Foreign Company, 1909), pp. 25–8.

In any case, his official residence is in the very heart and centre of British wealth and finance. Nearly all the leading commercial houses, some of which can boast, each, of a turnover of a hundred thousand pounds in one day, besides all the most important financial institutions in the United Kingdom, are in the immediate neighbourhood of the Mansion House.

Conspicuous among these institutions is the famous Bank of England. I was once allowed to visit its gold-weighing room. That visit revealed hundreds of thousands of loose sovereigns on the counters. I merely saw the sovereigns 'through a glass darkly.' I did not touch them, not because I would not, but because I could not. I had been warned by the writing on the wall within merely to 'look but touch not.' I heard then that, at any time, there would be within the vaults of the Bank about fifty million pounds of solid cash. I was also told that the Old Lady does an annual business which runs into billions of pounds sterling.

I now think of all I saw and heard, and I am convinced that the Bank of England, situated as it is, in front of the Mansion House, and surrounded as they are by the great financial institutions before mentioned, renders our proposed starting point the richest spot on earth.

Hence the expression, 'All roads lead to the Bank.' But the roads leading to the Bank of England are so zig-zag, for London was formed hundreds of years ago when there was no surveyor, and when everyone made out for himself short cuts and narrow paths through commons and waste land. Zig-zag or not, Africanus, let us hurry to the Bank. That is the place I long for. Away we go! From West Africa we are flying thither with the wings of thought. It is now nine o'clock of a morning. The Bank of England is in sight.

Wonderful! Wonderful!! What mighty jostling crowds, huge waves upon huge waves of living humanity! See how 'multitudes upon multitudes' rush hither and thither, helter-skelter-like, with so much motion and commotion, verging and converging in all directions, in and out and through themselves, some on foot, others on horse, others besides on wheel. What moves so mightily these innumerable caravans of men, women, and children? What energises these moving pyramids of human ants?

I answer. The keen necessity to live, the consequent struggle for existence, the means for such existence, gold – the means, gold – the god of this world, *gold* – '*the visible spirit of the Britons.*'

BOOKER T. WASHINGTON

1912

'The Man at the Bottom in London'

Booker T. Washington (1856–1916) was by the end of the nineteenth century perhaps the most influential Black leader in the United States, best known for his advocacy of 'industrial education', pioneered by the Tuskegee Institute, Alabama, which he founded. Though he described a visit to Europe in his autobiography Up from Slavery *(1901), where he associated with high society (including the Duchess of Sutherland), his second trip in 1910 was quite different. Accompanied by his private secretary, Robert Ezra Park (later to become well-known as a sociologist), he planned to acquaint himself with 'the condition of the poorer and working classes of Europe, particularly in those regions from which an ever-increasing number of immigrants are coming to our country each year'. The resulting book,* The Man Farthest Down *(1912) – which Park effectively co-wrote – shows how much they crammed into eight weeks, and includes descriptions of the slums of Naples, child labour in Sicily, the Cracow Ghetto, and – as in this chapter – the homeless of London.*

The *Carmania*, the ship in which I had sailed, disembarked its passengers late Saturday at Fishguard, off the coast of Wales. The special train which sped us on to London reached the city early Sunday morning, August 28.

As I drove from the railway station in the gray of the early morning my attention was attracted by a strange, shapeless and disreputable figure which slunk out of the shadow of a building and moved slowly and dejectedly down the silent and empty street. In that quarter of the city, and in comparison with the solid respectability and comfort represented by the houses around him, the figure of this man seemed grotesquely wretched. In fact, he struck me as the most lonely object I had ever laid my eyes on. I watched him down the street as far as I could see. He turned neither to the left nor to the right, but moved slowly on, his head bent toward the ground, apparently looking for something he did not hope to find. In the course of my journey across Europe I saw much poverty, but I do not think I saw anything quite so hopeless and wretched.

I had not been long in London before I learned that this man was a type. It is said that there are ten thousand of these homeless and houseless men and women in East London alone. They are, however, not confined to any part of the city. They may be found in the fashionable West End, lounging on the benches of St James's Park, as well as in the East End, where the masses of the labouring people live.

Booker T. Washington, *The Man Farthest Down: A Record of Observation and Study in Europe* (Garden City, NY: Doubleday, Page & Co., 1912), pp. 21–36.

The Salvation Army has erected shelters for them in many of the poorer parts of the city, where, for anything from two to eight cents, they may get a room for the night, and sometimes a piece of bread and a bowl of soup. Thousands of them are not able to compass the small sum necessary to obtain even this minimum of food and comfort. These are the outcasts and the rejected, the human waste of a great city. They represent the man at the bottom in London.

Later, in the course of my wanderings about the city, I met many of these hopeless and broken men. I saw them sitting, on sunshiny days, not only men but women also, crumpled up on benches or stretched out on the grass of the parks. I discovered them on rainy nights crouching in doorways or huddled away in dark corners where an arch or a wall protected them from the cold. I met them in the early morning hours, before the city was awake, creeping along the Strand and digging with their hands in the garbage-boxes; and again, late at night, on the Thames Embankment, where hundreds of them sleep – when the night watchman permits – on the benches or stretched out on the stone pavements. After a time I learned to distinguish the same type under the disguise of those street venders who stand on street corners and sell collar-buttons, matches, and other trifles, stretching out their hands in a pitiful sort of supplication to passers-by to buy their wares.

Whenever I found an opportunity to do so, I talked with some of these outcasts. Gradually, partly from themselves and partly from others, I learned something of their histories. I found that it was usually drink that had been the immediate cause of their downfall. But there were always other and deeper causes. Most of them, it seemed to me, had simply been borne down by the temptations and the fierce competition of life in a great city. There comes a time when trade is dull; men who had been accustomed to spend much money begin to spend less, and there is no work to be had. At these times it is 'the less efficient, the less energetic, the less strong, the less young, the less regular, the less temperate, or the less docile' who are crowded out. In this way these men have lost their hold and sunk to the bottom.

I remember meeting one of these men late at night wandering along the Thames Embankment. In the course of my conversation with him I asked him, among other things, if he voted, and, if so, to what political party he belonged.

He looked at me in amazement, and then he said he had never voted in his life. It was his expression rather than his words that impressed me. This expression told me how out of touch he was with the world about him. He had, in fact, as I learned, no family, no home, friends, trade; he belonged to no society; he had, so far as I could learn, no views on life. In the very midst of this great city he was as solitary as a hermit.

A few weeks later, in a little village in Galicia, I asked the same question of a Polish peasant. 'Oh, yes,' he eagerly replied; 'every one votes here now.'

Sixty years ago most of the peasants in this village to which I have referred were serfs, and it was not until two years ago that the Government gave them all the right to vote. Nevertheless, at the present time the people in this village are represented by one of their own number in the Imperial Parliament at Vienna. I stopped on my way through the village at the little store kept by this man. I found two young girls tending the store, his daughters, but the representative himself was not at home.

I do not know why I should mention this circumstance here, except that I was impressed by the contrast in the reply of these two men, the one coming from a peasant in Poland and the other from an Englishman in London.

It is generally said that the Negro represents in America the man farthest down. In going to Europe I had in mind to compare the masses of the Negro people of the Southern States with the masses in Europe in something like the same stage of civilization. It would not be difficult to compare the Negro in the South with the Polish peasant, for example, because the masses of the Poles are, like the masses of the Negroes, an agricultural people.

I know no class among the Negroes in America, however, with whom I could compare the man at the bottom in England. Whatever one may say of the Negro in America, he is not, as a rule, a beggar. It is very rarely that any one sees a black hand stretched out for alms. One does see, to be sure, too many idle and loafing Negroes standing on the street corners and around the railway stations in the South, but the Negro is not, as a rule, a degenerate. If he is at the bottom in America, it is not because he has gone backward and sunk down, but because he has never risen.

Another thing in regard to the Negro: although he is frequently poor, he is never without hope and a certain joy in living. No hardship he has yet encountered, either in slavery or in freedom, has robbed the Negro of the desire to live. The race constantly grew and increased in slavery, and it has considerably more than doubled in freedom. There are some people among the members of my race who complain about the hardships which the Negro suffers, but none of them yet, so far as I know, has ever recommended 'race suicide' as a solution of the race problem.

I mention this because I found just the contrary to be the case in England. I do not think that anything I saw or heard while I was in England gave me a more poignant impression of the hardships of the labouring man in England than the discovery that one of the most widely read weekly papers in England, under the caption of 'The White Slaves of Morality,' was making a public campaign in favour of reducing the size of the families among the working classes.

The articles I refer to, which were written by a woman, were a protest, on the one hand, against the clergy because they taught that it would be immoral for women to refuse to have children, and, on the other hand, against the physicians who withheld from these women the knowledge by which they might be able to limit the size of their families. These articles were followed from week to week by letters purporting to come from working men and women telling of the heartbreaking struggle they were making to support their children on the wages they were able to earn.

What made these articles the more startling was the fact that, at the very time when they were proposing to the English labourer what ex-President Roosevelt has defined as 'race suicide,' thousands of immigrants from the south of Europe were pouring into London every year to take the places left vacant by the recession of the native Anglo-Saxon.

On my previous visit to England I had been struck by what seemed to me the cold and formal character of the English newspapers. It seemed to me that they were wholly lacking in human interest. Upon my last visit my opinion in regard to the London newspapers was considerably altered. A careful study of the daily newspaper, I found, will repay any one who wants to get an insight into social conditions in England.

I had not been in London more than a day or two, for example, when my attention was attracted to the following item in one of the morning papers:

STARVING FAMILY

CORONER'S APPEAL TO THE PUBLIC FOR AID

> Telling of a terrible case of starvation in the Stoke Newington Coroner's Court, Dr. Wynn Westcott, the coroner, asked the press to bring a deserving case before the notice of the charitable public.
>
> He said that he had held an inquest upon a three-weeks-old baby which had died of starvation. Its father had had no regular work for three years, and only a little casual work in that time. There was so little money that the mother, Mrs Attewell, of White Hart Street, Stoke Newington, was half starved too. She had only had a crust of bread to sustain her on the day her child died, although she had done nine and a half hours' washing to assist the home.
>
> The home was perfectly clean, although practically destitute of furniture. It was a most deserving case.

After reading this item I began studying the papers more closely, and I was surprised at the frequency with which items of this kind occurred. I learned that the Local Government Board, which is represented in the English Cabinet by Mr. John Burns, has issued since 1871 an annual report, or return as it is called, of the cases in which, upon formal investigation by a coroner's jury, it appears that the persons came to their death in London as a result of starvation. I obtained a copy of the return for 1908, in which are included the statistics on starvation not merely for London but for the rest of England and Wales.

The forms issued to coroners were explicit. They provided that the return should include only cases in which the jury found that death was brought about by starvation or privation due to destitution. Cases in which death was caused by cold, starvation, exposure, etc., unconnected with destitution, were not entered in this return. Of the one hundred and twenty-five cases of starvation reported, fifty-two occurred in London. In eleven cases death was described as due to starvation in conjunction with some other cause – that is to say, disease, drink, exposure, or self-neglect. In eight of the one hundred and twenty-five cases no application was made for poor relief, or application was made only when the deceased had been in a dying condition.

A few days after I had succeeded in getting this report my attention was attracted one morning by the heading of a newspaper article: 'How the Poor Die.' The article was an account of the finding of the body of an unknown woman in a cellar in the basement of a house not very far from where I was stopping.

'It appears,' the article said, 'that during the earlier part of the morning a tenant of the building observed a woman sleeping in the cellar, but no particular notice was taken of this because of the fact that strangers frequently utilized the cellar for such purposes. Mr. Oliver, one of the occupants of the building, had occasion to go downstairs, and saw the woman. She was crouched in a corner and her head was lying back. The police were called in and the services of Doctor Barton were requisitioned . . . Although the cause of death will not be known until a post-mortem examination of the body has been made, death, it is thought, was due to starvation. The woman was about six feet in height, between forty and fifty years of age, and was in a very emaciated condition and clad in a very scanty attire.'

Not infrequently, when in my public speeches I have made some reference to the condition of the Negro in the South, certain members of my own race in the North have objected because, they said, I did not paint conditions in the South black enough. During my stay in England I had the unusual experience of being criticised in the London newspapers for the same reason, this time by an American white man. At the very moment that this man attacked me because in my public interviews I emphasized the opportunities rather than the wrongs of the Negro in the South I had in my possession the document to which I have referred, which gives the official history of fifty-two persons, one for every week in the year, who had died in the city of London alone for want of food.

I have never denied that the Negro in the South frequently meets with wrong and injustice; but he does not starve. I do not think a single case was ever heard of, in the South, where a Negro died from want of food. In fact, unless because of sickness or some other reason he has been unable to find work, it is comparatively rare to find a Negro in an almshouse.

It has not been my purpose in anything I have written to pass judgment upon the people or the conditions that I have found in the countries which I have visited. Criticism is an ungrateful task at best, and one for which I am not well fitted. Neither shall I attempt to offer any suggestions as to how conditions may be improved; in fact, I am convinced from what I learned that the people on the ground understand conditions much better than I possibly could, and in a later chapter I hope to tell something of the great work that has been done in England and elsewhere to raise the level of life and comfort among the people who are at the bottom in the countries which I visited. What I am anxious to do here is to emphasize some of the advantages which it seems the members of my own race, and particularly those living in the Southern States, have at the present time. It is not difficult to discover the disadvantages under which the Negroes in the South labour. Every traveller who passes through the South sees the conditions existing, and frequently returns to write books about them. There is danger, however, that the opportunities to which I have referred will be overlooked or not fully appreciated by the members of my race until it is too late.

One direction in which the Negro in the South has an advantage is in the matter of labour. One of the most pitiful things I saw in London, Liverpool, and other English cities was the groups of idle men standing about on the street corners, especially around the bar-rooms, because they were not able to get work.

One day, as I was going along one of the main avenues of the city, I noticed an unusually large crowd standing in front of a street organ which was drawn up at the side of the pavement. Pausing to see what there was about this organ that attracted so much attention and interest, I found that the man who owned this instrument was using it as a method of advertising his poverty.

All over the front of the organ were plastered papers and documents of various kinds. On one side there was a list of advertisements cut from the 'Want' columns of the daily newspapers. Attached to this was a statement that these were some of the places that the man had visited the day before in search of work, which he was not able to find. On the other side of the organ were attached six or seven pawn tickets, with the statement that 'these are some of the articles which my dear wife pawned to get food for our children.' This was followed by a pitiful appeal for help. The pathetic thing about it was that the only persons who stopped to look at these exhibits besides myself were a group of hungry and disreputable-looking men who were evidently in just as great want as the man who ground the organ. I watched those men. After reading the signs they would look inquiringly at the other members of the group and then relapse into the same stolid silence which I had noticed so many times in the forlorn figures that filled the benches of the parks.

It seemed to me that they both pitied and admired the man who had conceived this novel way of advertising his misfortune. I have noticed these same people in other cases where it seemed to me they looked with something like envy upon a beggar who was blind or lame or had some other interesting misfortune which enabled him to win the sympathy of the public.

Of course the persons that I have attempted to describe do not represent the labouring classes. They represent the man at the bottom, who lives by begging or casual labour. It shows, nevertheless, how bitter is the struggle for existence among the labouring class higher up, that the class below, the class which lives in actual poverty, is so large and so much in evidence.

While I was in London I received letters from a great many persons of all classes and conditions. One of these was from a coloured man who was born and raised in the South and was anxious to get back home. I am tempted to quote some passages of his letter here, because they show how conditions impressed a coloured man from the South who got closer to them than I was able to. He had been living, he said, in London for fourteen months without work.

'I have tried to apply for work,' he continued. 'They said they want Englishmen. It seems to me that all Britain are against the Negro race. Some say, "Go back to your own country," knowing if I had the means I would fly to-morrow.'

Perhaps I would do better to quote some passages from his letter verbatim. He says:

> I cannot get a passage; to be alone in London without any help or
> funds, like a pin in a haystack, nothing but sorrow and distress.
> Hearing Mr. B. T. Washington were in London I appeal to him in the
> name of God Almighty if he can possibly help me with a ticket to get
> across, because the lady that was kind enough to give me a shelter is
> without fund herself; being a Christian woman she gave me food for
> what she can afford. At night I have to sleep in a house with a widow
> which has two children which has to make her living by chopping
> wood, whom some day, does not earn enough to buy a loaf of bread for

her children. The winter is coming on and I like to get home to shuck
corn or to get to Maryland for a oyster draggin. It is a long time since I
had watermelon, pig's feet and corn. Say, Mr. Washington, is you ever
knew what's a man in a hole is I guess I am in a hole and the cover
over. I can see the pork chops and the corn bread and the hot biscuits
calling me to come over and get some and many a time I have tried but
failed. I can't reach them; the great Atlantic Ocean stop me and I
remain

Your Obedient Servant, _____

This letter from which I have given a few extracts is but one of many which I received during my stay in London, not only from coloured but from white Americans who had come to England to better their condition or seek their fortune.

These letters served still further to impress me with the fact that the masses of my own people in the South do not fully appreciate the advantages which they have in living in a country where there is a constant demand for labour of all kinds and where even poor people do not starve.

If I were asked what I believed would be the greatest boon that could be conferred upon the English labourer, I should say that it would be for him to have the same opportunities for constant and steady work that the Negro now has in the South. If I were asked what would be the next greatest benefit that could be conferred on the English labourer, I should say that it would be to have schools in which every class could learn to do some one thing well – to have, in other words, the benefit of the kind of industrial education that we are seeking, in some measure, to give to the Negro at the present time in the Southern states.

C. L. R. JAMES

1932

'The Men'

*James travelled to England from his native Trinidad for the first time in 1932,
armed with a manuscript of his first novel and a draft of* The Case for West
Indian Self-Government. *His 'First Impressions' of London were published as
a series of five articles in the* Port-of-Spain Gazette. *The first (in two parts)
provided an hour-by-hour narrative of 48 hours in Bloomsbury, the second
described terraced housing (inside and out) in meticulous detail, and was
followed by observations on 'The Men' (reprinted below) and its companion
piece, 'The Women'. The final article offered more general reflections on 'the
particular quality of the English people' – which are not particularly flattering,
although he finds some signs of better qualities once he leaves London for
Nelson, Lancashire, and hears of a successful community struggle against
unscrupulous cinema-owners.*

I shall begin first by relating what I have been assured and have every reason to
believe is a perfectly true story. Two Englishmen took the train from a suburb
every morning and sat opposite one another in the same compartment. When
they got in they arranged overcoats or rather blew their noses, arranged overcoats,
blew their noses again, lit up and read the newspaper. This they did for six years,
but never having been introduced, never spoke to one another. After six years, it
happened that they took their holiday, the same week. Unknown to each other,
they both decided to go to France. One day they met in Paris, face to face. They
looked at each other. Then each I suppose, remembered that he was an
Englishman. Each turned aside and went his way.

> *Speak when you are spoken to*
> *And answer when you are called.*

That by way of preliminary.

I am going to give a few isolated shots. The reader will be able to build up his
general impressions. I say his general impressions, advisedly. In forming
judgments on so wide a subject, one has to go slowly.

One day I walked into a bookshop to buy a couple of French Magazines. A girl,
a pretty girl, with her hair most delightfully done, and her finger nails most
abominably black, a not unusual combination, spread them out before me, heaps

C. L. R. James, 'London: First Impressions. No. 3 – The Men', *Port-of-Spain Gazette*, 4 August
1932, p. 8.

and heaps – in fact, all except the particular two I wanted. I was speaking English and if I may say so, quite good English. A woman of about forty, dressed in black came into the shop. She stood looking at some Magazines for a while and then when the shop assistant turned her back, she came up to me and spoke in French. Did I read French a lot? As much as I could. Where did I come from? La Trinité – Les Antilles Britanniques. Was I staying in London a long time? Yes. For some years, I thought. Did I hope to visit France someday? Yes, I very much hoped to. That was very nice. I smiled appreciatively. Goodbye. Goodbye. A slight but quite charming episode. But please note that she was a Frenchwoman.

Now see what happened on another day. I stood in the Strand with a map in my hand, trying to find out exactly how certain streets went. It may have looked strange. I didn't care. London is a blessed place where you need not care. I knew where I was, and I knew where I was going, but I wished to place myself well in my own mind with a view to future wanderings in the same quarter. So I stood at the corner and with map and pencil did a little astronomy or whatever is the proper name for it. Then I became aware of a man about twelve feet away who was peeping at me out the corner of his eye. He was over fifty, a short fellow, clean shaven, with a healthy red face and a very pleasant well-meaning look. He was obviously peeping at me so while I busied myself with my map, I had a peep at him. His behaviour was most curious. He had a peep and then he looked round, then he sidled towards me about a foot or so. Then he looked at the roadway, he looked at me and he sidled towards me another foot. When he had done that twice I put the map away and looked at him rather suspiciously. By this time he had decided to do what he wanted to do. He came up to me. Was there anywhere I wanted to find?

The poor man had wanted all the time to offer his services. But whether he thought I could not understand English, or whether he thought I would bark at him and bite him if he spoke to me, I do not know. I believe that he behaved as he did for the same reason that those two who travelled in the train for six years would not speak to each other, even when they met in Paris. I had nowhere to go in particular, but I gave him some fictitious address, and we walked along together. He pointed out one or two places to me on the way, directed me carefully to the post-office I asked him for, and then told me goodbye. He was not a rogue, pickpocket or anything of the kind. He behaved as he did, because he was an Englishman. The contrast between his discomfort and the easy, pleasant manner of the Frenchwoman, was vast.

Let me give another isolated shot.

I used to frequent a cafe, the Russell Street Tube cafe, and I do not want to start to talk about that cafe at all, because I would never stop. I sat usually right down at the back with my back to the wall, so that I could see all that was happening in front. One night, I noticed a man sitting just opposite to me. He looked at me and I looked at him. The next night, I had a rather long discussion about Colonial Administration with a West African and an Abyssinian. My friend was in the corner again. He had his paper before him, but I could see that he was listening closely. The next night, we got into conversation. He offered me matches or something. I used to meet him fairly often after that and we used to talk. He was a man in business, rather an important business too, a firm with a very well-known name, and his name was on their note paper. He was a young fellow, in the middle thirties I would say, with a delicate, refined, very handsome face. I used to tell him about the West Indies. He used to tell me about business in England. He was not very well educated, at least in the academic sense of the term. He had come from below, but he had made the best use of his opportunities, and though I have met some clever men here, I have met few men who spoke so well. It was nothing for us to talk for an hour or two, and he put me wise about many many things in the business world of London. Well, then, one night, he told me that he was taking a mid-night train to one of the biggest towns in England to meet the representatives of a certain firm. He was going to put through a deal which might mean thirty thousand pounds to his firm and may be a thousand pounds for himself. He had been to the Continent some six or seven times to make sure of all his facts. He put them before me. I asked him lots of questions. Then he drew from his pocket the prospectus which he was going to use as the basis of his attack the next day, and asked me to look it over, and point out to him anything which I noticed out of place or ill-sounding. I was taken a bit by surprise. But I looked through and pointed out a few things. From that we went on to discuss literature and writing which we had discussed now and then before. It got late, we became more intimate, and at last I gathered that my friend was not too confident about his interview of the morrow. He confessed to me that he was always a bit uncertain of himself when he had to meet and speak to groups of people. His education – I told him that I didn't see what he had to be nervous about, he spoke as well as most people whom I had met, and if he spoke to boards or directors or to people of any kind as he spoke to me, I didn't see that he had anything to be afraid of. I told him that in these matters I was rather critical and a bit of a judge myself. But I must confess, that his attitude had me a bit surprised. We talked on, but he still harped on his uncertainty for the next day, and at last he blurted out the truth:

'You see a good many of those fellows whom I am going to meet tomorrow are titled men, Lord so-and-so, Sir so-and-so O.B.E., and lots of them have been to Oxford and Cambridge –'

The thing came as a violent shock to me.

The man was master of his subject. He had taken an enormous amount of trouble to be quite sure of all his facts. He spoke admirably, not only on this particular business, but on all sorts of subjects that cropped up. And yet, here he was nervous and shaking because the men he would have to speak to were Lords and had titles, and had been to Oxford and Cambridge. The reader need not accept it from me. But I believe that is a particularly English characteristic. You meet it all over the place and in the most unexpected quarters. I remember one day talking to a man, a West Indian, a magnificent pianist, well-known in the musical world of London. He was talking of how sometimes you meet people who would help you on towards the realisation of your aims. And he mentioned so-and-so, who was the cousin of Lord so-and-so. Not Sir Henry Wood, mark you, nor Sir Landon Ronald, nor Mr. Ernest Newman, nor Mr. Frederick Lamond, nor anybody big in the musical world, but Mr. so-and-so, who was a cousin of Lord so-and-so. And I dare say the man who said it was quite right in his point of view. It is a thing I have noticed also in Trinidad with English people. More than any creole, white or black, they lose their heads at the prospect of contact with the great. I remember one of the finest Englishmen I have ever known, Mr. William Burslem, getting so excited one morning, that I don't think he knew his right hand from his left, and simply because the Governor had sent to say, that on his way down to work he would pass in for a visit of a few minutes. I was a small boy at the time, but I saw it and remembered distinctly being puzzled over it for quite a while. The Governor was coming. You had to give orders that everything was to be ship-shape. You would meet him at the gate and bow and say that it was an honour and a pleasure, and carry him round and introduce him, and tell all the boys that it was an honour and a pleasure. And thank him graciously for the half holiday and say that it was an honour and a pleasure, and then bid him goodbye, bowing in the proper way, while assuring him that his visit was indeed an honour and a pleasure. But why there should have been all this running up and down the stairs, and putting on the gown, and putting on the cap, and taking the cap off again, and running to class-rooms, and giving orders, and conferring with masters, and standing in the passage with hand to eyes gazing into the distance to see if the carriage with the policemen out riding was coming, with almost the same intentness that the sailors of Columbus looked for land, all this I could not understand then and I must say, cannot understand now. But if they do a lot of it in the Colonies, English do quite a lot of it at home. You see it everywhere.

I cannot make this article too long. But there is one subject which I must refer to. And that is colour prejudice. The average Englishman in London is on the surface, quite polite. Furthermore you will make friends with certain people or even certain families and they will stick by the average coloured man and even quarrel with some of their friends who treat him in any out of the way manner, and generally prove themselves staunch with a staunchness that is particularly English. But nevertheless the average man in London is eaten up with colour prejudice. This is a big subject and I am going to tackle it someday in the way it deserves. Meanwhile, here are three more shots.

I have been to two dances here. There were heaps of nice girls, really nice people, well educated, good manners, and some of them quite beautifully dressed. Who thinks that the average coloured student has to associate with barmaids, shabby waitresses and that type is very much mistaken. He associates with them only if he wants to, or if he carries himself in such a way that only persons of that type will take any notice of him. But there were very few English men there. Those present were either connected with the giving of the dance, or friends of those who had given it. At one dance in particular, there were no more than about five men under thirty, one might almost say under fifty. And these five sat in corners and glowered, and looked as unpleasant and as dissatisfied as possible. That tells its own tale.

For another, even more significant.

One night, I got into the last tube at a crowded station. The train was waiting for a while and I sat in a corner reading. I lifted my eyes quite by chance and through the glass door caught the eye of a girl who was standing on the platform waiting for another train. She was not particularly good looking, but she was tall with a good figure and had a very healthy red face. So man-like, I began to read my paper, but took a slight squint over the top of it. I noticed that the young lady was engaged in the same game, but woman-like in a way not quite as discreet as mine. Two people cannot peep at one another for any length of time without bouncing, so to speak. Our eyes met fairly and she smiled a bit. I dropped my paper and we looked at one another in a friendly sort of way. A friend of hers was near, reading a paper. She gave the friend a dig in the ribs with an elbow. The friend looked up. They both had a look. And started to giggle. They were not common women. I dare say they were only having a little fun with a strange looking man and enjoying themselves in their own way. It didn't worry me. The train started to move out. They smiled more and more and I gave them a grave bow and a faint smile by way of goodbye, at which they laughed more than ever. But before I got back to my paper, I was attracted by the strange antics of an Englishman sitting next to me. This fellow, it seemed, had seen all that had taken place. What business it was of his, I do not know. But as the train moved off, he glared at me and glared at the girls and shuffled his feet, and glared at me, and looked me up from head to foot, and squirmed and twisted like a man suffering from an acute attack of dysentery or colitis. Friends of mine had warned me, and I could recognise his symptoms. He was a chronic sufferer from colour prejudice. The idea that an English girl would smile at a negro almost drove him mad. And it is a characteristic of large numbers of Englishmen. On the other hand men who have been to France say that the average Frenchman no more looks at you than he would look at a very tall or a very short man.

This man I could afford to ignore. Sometimes, however, these interfering wretches cannot be so easily dismissed, and can make life very unpleasant.

I brought a letter of introduction to a girl in London from a friend at home. I carried it to her and none of my own people could have given me a warmer welcome. Any friend of _____ she was only too glad to see. How was he? How was his wife? Anyway, more of that later. One night, we went out and coming home together stood up in a lift. In the lift with us was an Englishman, an ordinary, middle class, commonplace Englishman. There are millions like him all round you in London every day, the kind of person I would not walk five yards out of my way to meet, except for the same of curiosity and to find out what was in his 'Daily Express', cinema-fed mind. But he, this Anglo-Saxon member of a ruling race, despised me to such an extent that he could not contain his wrath at seeing me with a girl who was not from the street. He chewed at his cigarette and looked round and stared at the girl as if to say, 'You ought to be ashamed of yourself for going about with this fellow.' There was another woman in the lift whose eyes and general demeanour said much the same thing. And they were not the only two, although they were the most obstreperous. The girl told me afterwards that she saw quite well, but it is a thing that girls who go out with coloured men have to be prepared for. Someday, as I have said, I am going to strip this question raw of all the cant and hypocrisy with which it is covered to-day. The fault, by the way, is not all on the English side. Not by any means. But when every allowance is made, there remains something in the average Englishman, which can only be called sheer, blind prejudice. It is a commonplace among students. Often you meet people who are quite cordial. India, West India, East Indies, West Indies, they are for the most part very hazy about. Often curiosity makes them anxious to know you. An Englishman is always willing to add a few facts to his store. It is ideas that beat him. He makes your acquaintance. He is agreeably surprised. Come to lunch. Come to tea. This is my wife, my daughter. This is Miss X. This is Miss Y. Charmed. Delighted. So happy. Very very pleased. But let him see you sitting in the park talking with Miss X. That is another story. An Englishman can cause any scandal. German, Frenchman, South African, Canadian. 'What a pity! Rascal,' they say and leave it at that. But let Mr. black man beware. Go to France, to Spain, to Italy, I am told. Carry yourself like a gentleman, you'll be treated as one. But in England watch your step and however much at home you feel, watch it in this particular direction.

So much for the present. The next article will be on the girls.

RICHARD WRIGHT

from *Pagan Spain*

Richard Wright (1908–1960) grew up in the Deep South. Moving to Chicago, he soon built a reputation as a radical social critic, and remains best known for his essays and fiction of the late 1930s, particularly the novel Native Son *(1940). After World War II he moved to Paris, where he was based until his death. His writings of the period have unfortunately attracted comparatively little attention from critics. Among them is an ambitious work (much longer than the final, published, version) describing his visits to Franco's Spain in 1954 and 1955. Much more than a travel narrative, it is a searching attempt to account for the appeal of fascism in a country whose primeval religious culture has – he believes – more in common with those of Africa and Asia than the rest of Europe. This extract is taken from Part IV of* Pagan Spain, *entitled 'Sex, Flamenco and Prostitution'.*

Have I sounded harsh in my speaking of the women of Spain? It has not been my intention to slur or slight them.

The Spanish women are undoubtedly the most electrically beautiful of all the women in all the world. Stalwart, they bear the burdens of their poor nation and with but few complaints. They bind up their men's wounds, cater night and day to their childish passions and needs. Against impossible odds, they administer the routine of millions of bleak, hungry, and ignorant families; indeed, it is but for the dutiful presence of Spanish women alone that the hovels that shelter those families can be called home – in short, the women of Spain make her a nation.

The daily striving and suffering of Spanish women make what little structure there is to Spanish society, knitting together in a web of care and love what would otherwise be a landscape of senseless anarchy. They are proud women, sweet women, forgiving women, compassionate women, women of easy laughter and easy tears. The mighty maternal instinct of the Spanish woman is the anchor of responsibility that holds the ship of Spanish life steady while the Spanish man babbles abstract nonsense in the countless smoky coffee-houses.

They are lithe-limbed women who whirl and clack their castanets and stamp their heels and make of an otherwise dull nation an exciting and human spectacle; women who plough the fields; who wash clothes in country streams; who drive the oxen-drawn carts; who satisfy their men and nurse their babies; and who, at the beginning and the end of the day, creep forward and kneel humbly before the weeping and jewelled virgins in the dim and draughty cathedrals; long-suffering and enduring women who follow their hot-eyed men into war and peace when they understand nothing of the causes of war and peace; desperately practical women who sleep with strange men for food while their babies coo or cry in nearby cribs; undernourished, skinny women who flee the chill of their concrete houses to sit on curbstones and mend tattered clothing in the sun's wan light; despairing women who send lunch boxes to their daughters who work in the whore-houses; old lonely women who weep at the memory of their sons and daughters who have gone off to seek their destinies in the cold, strange world; silly women who sleep half the day and pay their maids five dollars a month and who primp themselves long and lovingly before their mirrors so that they can walk arm in arm with five other women down the Ramblas and not impair their respectability; Lesbian women living their quiet, secluded lives within the shadows of cathedrals where they go to confess and make their atonements; undaunted women who fight the régime for their right to marry the men they love; blind women who sit on street corners in rain or sun and sell lottery tickets; bold-eyed women who begin staring at you ten feet away and whose eyes hold yours until you are abreast of them; women who ask men to their beds without a flicker of shame; shy little women who swab the tile floors on their knees and whose frightened eyes beseech you not to soil the floor that they have so meticulously cleaned; beautiful, rouged, jeweled women drinking cognac in bars and who will tell you with a sweet, sad smile that they cannot read or write; ugly women with black and blue marks on their arms from the embrace of drunken sailors; hard-faced women who are willing to escape loneliness by cooking, working, whoring, and dying for a man; frail, dry little women who sell candies and sunflower seed and almonds and who some-times die while sitting in their little wooden stalls; fat and frightened women who, when they see the black hearse drawn by two magnificent black horses with purple plumes on their heads, cross themselves and throw a kiss from their index fingers to the Virgin of their devotion; tall, long-limbed women who stride down the street, lifting up their big feet and planting them down with the assurance of men; solemn vindictive women who stand gossiping in the middle of the street with elbows akimbo; young, devout women who have husbands who are hopelessly ill and who stifle their deepest physical needs while their hair whitens before they are thirty; yes, all of these and more are the women of Spain, the heart of Spain. Spanish men have built a State, but they have never built a society, and the only society that there is in Spain is in the hearts and minds and habits and love and devotion of its women.

NICOLÁS GUILLÉN

'From New York to Moscow, via Paris'

Nicolás Guillén (1902–1989) was born in Camagüey, Cuba, and in 1920 went to Havana to study law, but he soon abandoned a legal career and worked as a typographer and journalist. His poetry was published in various magazines from the early 1920s and his first collection, Motivos de son, *appeared in 1930. The Machado regime was overthrown in 1933, but political repression intensified. In 1936, with other editors of* Mediodía, *Guillén was arrested on trumped-up charges, and spent some time in jail. The following year he made his first trip abroad, to attend a Congress of Writers and Artists in Mexico; and he travelled to Spain and reported on the Civil War.*

Guillén returned to Cuba – via Guadeloupe – and in 1940 stood as a Communist candidate in local elections. The following year he was refused a visa to enter the United States, but he travelled widely over the following twenty years – in South America, China and Europe. Prevented by the Batista government from entering Cuba, he did not return until after the Revolution in 1959. This travel account and many others were included in Prosa de Prisa *(1962), a collection of newspaper and magazine articles. Although best-known as a poet, he has said that 'I am a journalist and then a poet . . . For me journalism is an outlet and through practising it I free myself of many things which I cannot express by means of verse.'*

A flight that starts in the United States and ends in the Soviet Union is fairly complicated, not just geographically, but also politically.

At the beginning of this year, in March, I was in New York. A month later I was back in the big city. Despite the short time that separated them, the two visits were as different as could be with respect to reception, stay, and departure, since on the second occasion I couldn't get beyond Ellis Island.

This wasn't, in any case, the first time I'd stepped on North American soil. In 1937 I passed rapidly across en route for Canada, on a train journey from Mexico. My final destination was Spain, then ablaze with the struggle against Franco, its embers still glowing today. It was a slow and monotonous journey, involving a change of trains at the border and searches that were ostentatious rather than thorough. All through the north of Mexico, with its burning deserts; all through

Translation of 'De Nueva York a Moscú, pasando por París', from Nicolás Guillén, *Prosa de Prisa* (Havana: Editorial Arte y Literatura, 1975), vol. 2, pp. 23–44. English translation copyright © 1998 Peter Hulme.

the south of the States, by the side of the dramatic Mississippi, along the banks of which stretch black townships sunk in misery.

But that was no more than a too brief encounter. I could hardly have spent more than ten or twelve hours swept up in the colossal whirlwind of the city, whose staggering silhouette was etched on my memory as a rocky mass, shrouded in smoke and criss-crossed with metal. Now I had more time, perhaps two weeks. Not much, no doubt, in which to write a three-hundred-page book, as some foreign journalists do in Cuba after a fortnight spent with 'highballs' or in the bars of the capital; but long enough to get a settled impression in my mind from those sensations that had been floating there since that first visit.

Besides, how can you forget Harlem? The famous black district was familiar to me not just from numerous books, but also from American and Cuban friends who gave me in person lots of news about what was going on in that vast New York neighbourhood. In some ways it was an almost morbid impulse that propelled me to get to know that black city crammed into a white city. I wanted to see 'with my own eyes' half a million people separated from the rest of the population as if they were suffering from some terrible contagious disease. I'd heard so often about Lenox Avenue and 145th Street!

So it was that Harlem produced in me a slow-burning anguish that won't easily be wiped from my memory even if it's a long time before I return to New York. Yes, I know very well that there is the Apollo, the most important black theatre in the United States, and that Small Paradise and the Savoy are luxury cabarets only for people with dark skin. I'm not forgetting that from 145th Street to 161st there live elegant blacks who, in places like Edgecombe and Convent Avenue, achieve the heavenly delight of being tolerated by their white neighbours. But along 111th, 113th, 115th, 138th, thousands of blacks drag themselves in misery, alongside the opulence and happiness of the richest city in the world.

In any case, the story is different. It consists precisely in Harlem itself, with blacks who are happy or sad, rich or poor, stupid or intelligent, ignorant or educated. Harlem isn't a *quartier* in the European fashion, that is to say a voluntary grouping of people related through ethnic origin, economic standing, or simply nationality. What big city, including New York, doesn't have its Chinatown or Jewish quarter, its artists' district or millionaires' row? The serious point is that the blacks have no option but to remain in 'their' district, to study in 'their' university, to pray to God in 'their' church, and even to sleep eternally in 'their' cemetery.

Of course I am not a militant anti-American (as many may think), and I know that among that vast population living across the water from us there are many people who look on saddened at the fatal destiny that has befallen their dark-skinned brother. And not only 'look on', but who also work passionately to overcome such injustice, if not at a stroke, then at least in the slow and gradual fashion that circumstances allow.

For the rest, and to speak in less strict terms, I must say I have the impression that in North America Cuba is known – or at least knowledge is circulated – by adopting superficial and picturesque points of view, rather than looking for those profound traits that give universal meaning to a people. Many North Americans think that our most serious occupation consists in singing *El manisero* in the stark shade of tall palm trees, whilst a dense, burnished, and high-powered sun shines forth from a blue sky. We usually pay back in the same coin, because for many Cubans being a yankee is just another way of being a tourist, or vice versa. The stereotype is quite simple: a cap, a pipe, a check sports-suit, a comical shape with a long bottom and a red and angular face with two little blue eyes . . .

Nobody denies – nor should they – that many Cubans dance the rumba. A plain domestic rumba, without the affectations with which Señor Cugat has disfigured it.[1] But there are others, not a few, who faced with this rhythm would hardly be able to move their feet, without this endangering their status as Cuban citizens. Perhaps all the men and women born in the North like to buy maracas at the port and frequent the brothels in the *barrio de Colón*? Even though we may find it hard to believe, we have to recognize that there are poor Americans who don't have a dime and who are capable of smiling sweetly at a black person.

But, one way and another, these ideas are acquired very slowly indeed. Havana and New York are separated not by five hours' flying time, as the airline companies suggest, but rather by imperceptible but real frontiers which come about through different mentalities, diverse origins, and distinct languages. 'Can you speak English?', they asked a friend of mine. 'Naturally not,' she replied with innocent bravery. 'Naturally', as well, millions of Americans do not know Spanish and don't think it would be useful to learn it.

The same mutual ignorance that exists between the yankees and the white Cubans – speaking *grosso modo* – prevails between the respective black populations. One night, in Harlem, I talked to an educated girl who was generally *au fait* with Cuba. But when she mentioned Antonio Maceo, it was by referring to him as the man 'who had led the black troops in Cuba's wars against Spain'. It was as surprising for me to hear this as it was for her to find out that the truth was different. That is to say, that Maceo was a mulatto, true enough, but that he exercised his command over all the insurrectionary forces, made up of white and black soldiers, because racial prejudice (with some well-known exceptions) was always hidden in the patriot army, just as now, in the same way, in the Republic, it is shamefaced. Specialists on our world? But of course! Just as here we have students of over there, who know North American life better than many yankees.

As far as I could, I walked through New York in the flesh, with Mirta Aguirre as guide. What on earth could we achieve shut up within the four walls of the hotel, learning from guide books and leaflets what life could give us directly, hot to the touch? And there I met friends – met them again – in a quite unpredictable way, almost inconceivable in a city heaving with eight million people.

One afternoon I was strolling along a certain street in the Latin quarter, when thirst stopped me at a small restaurant where they served iced beer. The atmosphere was just like that of any bar in Havana, especially in the old city: blacks with guitars, whites with blacks, and 'everyone' with black and mulatto girls . . . I had my *bock* in front of me, when I heard a woman's voice shouting my name from behind my stool. I turned round, with the surprise and speed that the reader

1. Xavier Cugat, director of a band based in the USA, who has taken up and falsified much Cuban music.

can imagine, and found myself unexpectedly facing a girl I hadn't seen for five or six years. The apron she was wearing, the sweat on her face, the potato-peeler she wielded with indubitable professionalism, very soon convinced me that my friend had conscientiously dedicated herself to the honest art of cooking. To make a long story short, she had married a quick-witted compatriot and the two of them were running this establishment which, to judge by the clientele, free-spending and very numerous, gave them a good living. There appeared . . . can you guess what? Only chicken and rice. I soon met up with the rest of the colony, spread out through the *barrio*. I could even bet in a fellow-countryman's barber's shop, on my favourite lottery number, 'the knife thrust', which didn't win!

But just as in this case I met up with many friends I hadn't thought I would see, how difficult it turned out to be to find others that I'd intended to meet! Eusebia Cosme, for example, I came across almost as I was due to leave, and only with the help of Bola de Nieve, who was over there moving from piano to piano and triumph to triumph. One memorable night, the three of us met up together in the house of the poet, Langston Hughes. The people dealing with Eusebia say that the genial black story-teller has become very mysterious since she got married. I found her just the same as ever: the same age, the same beautiful hands, the same Oriente tone of voice, just like the students from Santiago saying: 'My father has a coffee plantation', the same shy and modest charm, that helped her get so far. She also told me that she was getting ready to go back to Havana: and that she'd been doing so for ten years.

Meanwhile, the reader will be asking me with a malicious smile just what I definitively think of New York. Well . . . I'll offer up a raw New York, based on the two weeks I had there. It seems to me a cruel but instructive city. The portentous development of North American technology would make life there very simple, if the city weren't so complicated. What I mean is that New York achieves the miraculous effect of making it seem normal to have the vast mechanical apparatus that is necessary to move oneself through the city, and that in other places would be a thing of wonder and amazement. One would say that it is a city made for searching out one's daily bread in bites, swallowing it in a hurry, and immediately jumping on the first victim to fall into our claws.

Thousands and thousands of human beings come to New York for a few months in search of a fistful of dollars before returning to the fresh air. They install themselves in the provisional fashion of a makeshift and cautious immigrant, ready to hoist sail at the least setback. And they are sitting there on the edge of their seat, as if they are in a hurry to leave, dry, pale, old, destroyed, . . . and poor, when death finally surprises them.

One day, in the afternoon twilight, I was looking at the big city from the Rockefeller Center. Everything hard about New York on the ground has a powerful delicacy from above. At the very moment of nightfall, the tall buildings seem constructed of a porous and fragile substance that could be crumbled in your fingers. As far as the eye can see, that steel and cement jungle offers its face, endlessly repeated. What gigantic harmony! Such feminine softness and peaceful calm enveloping like a veil so much bloody and armoured stone, pointing towards the clouds. Could it be some childish decoration that a slight breeze would disturb, moving the curtain where it's painted. Not at all. Turn your eyes towards the urban abyss and you'll see how the city heaves, how it ripples, how it turns over on itself and destroys millions of human beings who are fighting dramatically to impose themselves on the tumult. On that innocent afternoon, from the sour depths of its stomach comes a volcanic thunderclap, long and menacing:

> The day is ending, but New York knows it not.
> Just like Rome and Babylon.

PARIS

Paris? When you get to the airport, the procedure is perfectly simple:
'Have you anything to declare?', asks the customs-officer indifferently, expecting a negative.
'No I don't.'
A chalk-mark on the suitcase and on to the next passenger. Leaving is the same, except that they ask if we are carrying perfume. A simple 'no' – because we really aren't – and we're off on a free run to the plane.
The Paris of today doesn't seem, objectively speaking, very different from the Paris of ten years ago, on the eve of the war. German gunfire didn't actually do much damage there. All the buildings emerged unscathed from that nightmare, which so profoundly marked the face of other cities: Stalingrad, for example, in the Soviet Union, or Rouen, in France itself. Of course there is no lack of dramatic signs: the bronze was stolen by the Nazis from many of the statues to make ammunition, and on every corner the pedestrian comes across a bunch of flowers marking the spot where a hero of the Resistance was shot.
Until 1948 there had been rationing of some items, especially meat. You can now buy everything without restriction, though prices are high. What does the reader want to know? The boulevard Saint-Michel, the Place de la Concorde, the Pantheon, Nôtre Dame, the Sacré Coeur, the Seine itself, lapping the old walls of the city, as fine and subtle as if it were woven in the wind? Everything is there . . . Everything is still covered in that dark and noble patina that only time endows; everything enveloped in that mellow atmosphere, supremely poised, which makes Paris one of the most enchanting places in the world.
Nevertheless, penetrating a little more deeply into the Parisian spirit, you can sense that something has changed: the Frenchman living in Paris in, say, 1937 is not the same as the Frenchman there now, who went through the terrible experience of a second world war, and is deeply fearful of a third.
One day – some years ago now – I was with Alejo Carpentier in a little café near the Pont Neuf. I absentedmindedly started to whistle Riego's hymn – I'd just come back from republican Spain – when a woman's voice cut me short in a harsh tone.
'That music sounds bad under this roof', she said. 'Sing the Marseillaise, the hymn of the French people. My three sons died in the war singing it.'
Of course, I didn't want to respond. As a foreigner just arrived in the country, I wasn't going to complicate my life with a problem whose importance seemed

to me quite relative. Still, I didn't forget what had occurred, as always happens when circumstances not to our liking force us to keep our counsel.

Now, twelve years after that experience, I had another, quite different, but also of a populist nature. On the day of the inauguration of the Peace Congress, I took a taxi to go back to the afternoon session. I went up to a group of drivers who were chatting in a shelter and asked one of them to take me to the Salle Pleyel, in rue Saint-Honoré, where the assembly's deliberations were taking place.

'You're a delegate at the Congress?', the chap asked me, discerning with little difficulty my strong foreign accent and partisan's badge on my lapel.

'Yes, monsieur,' I answered.

'From what country?'

'From Cuba . . .'

The driver scratched his head, still holding his beret in his hand.

'Cuba? Oh, yes, Cuba! . . . That's in South America, isn't it?'

For the French in general, everything Spanish not actually in Spain itself belongs to South America. I explained to him, of course, that Cuba is in the Caribbean, and even spoke to him about José María Heredia, who wrote *Los trofeos*, but that didn't have any effect on him. So I abandoned any attempt at a more or less geographical explanation of our country, and started my own line of questioning. I spoke to him about the war.

'I was in the '14–'18 war and I know what it's like. I was in this one too. I lost my three sons in it.'

In the meantime we'd arrived at the Salle Pleyel, where a crowd of delegates from all over the world, many of them in their national costumes, were milling around the entrance to the huge building. I looked at the meter on the taxi. It showed 150 francs, about 45 cents. I held out a 300 franc note.

'Oh no, sir. You don't have to pay me,' he said, almost offended. 'You've come from far away to work for the same thing I'm working for, and my duty is to help you.'

You have to realize how much this means coming from a Frenchman!

On the following day, when the Congress was not sitting, a large group of delegates travelled into the regions on a sort of taking of the popular pulse. I ended up in Toulon – 100,000 inhabitants, central square right by the Mediterranean, French arsenal in wartime. In sum, a city with a long military history which stretches from the time of Henry IV to today, passing through Louis XIV and Napoleon.

The journey to Toulon from Paris is a long one by train, about the same as from Havana to Santiago de Cuba, since you get on the solid-looking *train bleu* in the Gare de Lyon at eight in the evening and don't arrive until nine the following morning.

The friends who drove me to the station had already warned me that I'd be making the journey in the company of a senator.

'He's also going to Toulon,' they told me, 'and he'll be speaking at the same meeting as you tomorrow . . .'

I resigned myself to this important prospect, though not with good grace, since senators tend to bore me rather. Meanwhile, time passed and the senator did not arrive. I was settled into my compartment, and the train was ready to leave, when my future companion suddenly appeared, as if out of thin air. He was a young black man, very short, who reminded me of our unfortunate painter, Peñita.[2]

He told me his name: Biakka Boda Victor, senator for the Ivory Coast. An African senator! Doesn't it sound like a fairy-tale, a very modern fairy-tale, with senators instead of princes and high-speed trains instead of slow and poetical carriages pulled by camels?

As the train drew out of Paris, Biakka Boda and I talked at length, as if we'd known each other all our lives. He is a doctor, born in Gagnoa in French West Africa. He went to primary school in the city of his birth and secondary school in Bigerville, at the Ecole Normale of La Gorée, on the island of that name. Finally, he took his diploma at the University of Dakar, in 1933.

'I love France very much,' Victor told me; 'and its culture is mine. But the French people in Africa are completely different from the French democrats you find in Paris. Our most serious problem is the one relating to the political rights of Africans. Until 1945 they were completely lacking and, of course, there was no legislation which could put them into place, even formally. The natives could be recruited like slaves for the French army or to work for public or private companies. The constitution of the Fourth Republic abolished the infamous Code Indigène and prohibited forced labour, which was just like slavery.'

But generally speaking, all this continues to be a dead letter, according to Boda Victor. On the Ivory Coast, just as in the other colonial territories, the suffrage is very limited. Women don't vote. Among the men, the only ones who have the right are ex-soldiers, planters (assimilated blacks), and local functionaries in public administration. Something similar happens in the administration of justice, with different tribunals for whites and blacks. Besides, terrible illnesses decimate the native population: smallpox, cerebral meningitis, sleeping sickness, yellow fever . . .

In spite of everything, Africa is awakening. The huge black man is slowly opening his eyes, stung by the light of our age, and is struggling to break the cords that bite into his flesh. Escaping the siege of colonial ignorance, some important figures emerge to become incorporated into the general picture of French culture. The poet, Fodeba Keita, the deputy Léopold Sédar Senghor, assistant professor of philosophy at the Sorbonne, and who represents his country, Senegal, at the Congress . . . Dudú Gueve and Dadié Bernard are excellent journalists, editors at Le Réveille in Dakar, and there are speakers and politicians of the calibre of Gabriel D'Arbussier, vice-president of the Congress. This black awakening is being channelled through an organization called the Democratic African Union, which includes many territorial extensions of a central body based in Dakar. The movement's leader is Félix Houphouet-Boigny.

'We ask,' Boda Victor told me that night, 'for something quite simple and perfectly just: that the natives be treated as equals with the French, not just in Paris, where it's always happened, but over there, in Africa . . .'

Unfortunately the Parisian sojourn couldn't be extended. There was hardly time for a quick visit to the three exhibitions which during this summer had captured

2. Alberto Peña, black Cuban painter from the 1930s, who died in poverty.

the attention of a public deprived of its holidays, which hadn't been able to escape the urban prison. One was of Picasso, who continues to be as 'picassian' and difficult as he was before he became a communist; another of Matisse, the grand old man, who is going on for eighty, but who draws as if he were twenty; and finally a very full one of Gauguin (to my mind the most important) on the occasion of his centenary. That exhibition made an enormous effort. It tried – with success – to bring together the whole, huge range of the great artist's work, dispersed not just over France, but over many other European and American countries. So they had brought pictures from England, Belgium, Switzerland, Czechoslovakia, Germany, Holland, Norway, and the United States.

The Gauguin exhibition also included wooden engravings, several ceramic pieces (among them a black Venus), and various manuscipts and documents. And finally, a beautiful and rare walking stick, decorated with Polynesian heads and the artist's initials engraved in red: P.G.O.

But time was flying, so I had to pack my bags and leave . . .

PRAGUE

The traveller visiting Czechoslovakia for the first time gets the impression of walking into a huge museum which had gathered its strength and animation under the influence of a subtle but obdurate will. For Americans (including those from the North), such a feeling is even keener because the life of our continent is like the cry of a new-born baby alongside the venerable stones on which the European spirit generally resides. Paris? Well . . . Paris is a multiple city, and being so, it receives into its bosom all kinds of different currents, which the *boulevard* or the Academy, the dancehall or the *atelier* channel into a universal stream. Ancient and modern – 'audacious, cosmopolitan' – it is still the centre of bourgeois culture, whose brilliant colours recall those of some organic matter in the process of decomposition.

But Prague, which is a very European city, is not Paris . . . which is very Parisian. In the oldest part of town, spread out along the Moldau, the centuries seem to sleep their durable history, a history of stone: that history which eventually becomes an examination platitude. The whole Czech country is suffused with the memory of Charles IV – 'the first European on the Bohemian throne' – whose dynamism as a builder broadened the vision of the local spirit which had persisted from the time when the city was little more than a fort surrounded by the shacks of Jewish fishermen.

Reminders of feudalism are everywhere; not of course in people's behaviour – and even less so now, but very much so in the historical documentation, in the severe and noble past, dominant in the atmosphere of that marvellous set of relics.

When we fly over Bohemia or over Slovakia, our eyes are caught not just by the constant repetition of the urban pattern – luminously white cottages with red roofs – but by solitary old castles, collapsing slowly with their steeples and battlements, mute witnesses to a past medieval splendour. Later, they figure in profuse number in the 'programme of visits', enough to become something of a fairly pleasant nightmare. Jorge Amado, the Brazilian novelist, rejected them outright. 'I prefer,' he said, 'to see life: I want to know what Czechoslovakia is like today . . .'

The country – 150 thousand square kilometres and 13 million inhabitants – is populated by two distinct groups, the Czechs and the Slovaks, whose political organization stems from the ninth century, under the Great Moravian Empire. The empire was finally destroyed by the invasion of the Magyars, who dominated Slovakia for a thousand years – until 1918 – while Bohemia developed under German influence.

Such a difference in origin is of course noticeable in the character of the two peoples. When I was in Bratislava, the Slovak capital bathed by the waters of the Danube, they said to me:

'Do you know how to tell a Czech from a Slovak?'

'No.'

'It's very simple. When a Czech gets drunk, he climbs on the table and goes to sleep; when a Slovak gets drunk he climbs on the table and dances . . .'

The Slovaks put it down to their Hungarian blood that they're happier and more lively than the Czechs – who pride themselves on being serious, hardworking and studious; the former are Catholics, the latter Protestants; the Czechs drink beer, the Slovaks wine . . .

As a result of the First World War, Czechoslovakia emerged in 1918 as an independent republic, free at last of its traditional bonds. Then came the Nazi occupation, which provoked a dramatic liberation movement. Since last year, through the revolutionary events of February, it has been transformed into a popular democracy. Today it is a huge socialist experiment, of which I certainly saw some signs during my stay in the country.

I remember, for example, that after dinner at the Hotel Paris in Prague, somebody mentioned the Workers' Diplomatic School . . .

'What's that?', I asked, somewhat surprised.

'Just what it sounds like. We are undertaking an interesting experiment: the creation of a diplomatic corps drawn from the working class. Would you like to visit these workers in their school and see for yourself the future diplomats?'

'You bet! Let's go straight away!'

We didn't go immediately, but two days later. One morning a young man and a very charming young woman came to pick me up at the hotel, and invited me to follow them. Before long the car we travelled in was going up the slope into Prague Castle, which overlooks the city. In an instant we were in front of an ancient building – an old feudal palace – on the top floor of which was what we were looking for, the *Delnicka Diplomáticka Skola*, that is to say, the Workers' Diplomatic School . . . A staircase, a small room, and then another, which was the office of the director, Yankú Vladimir, a young man with blue eyes, blond hair and an intelligent face.

'All this is brand new,' he warned me, through the interpreter, Miss Reinhaltová. 'The school was opened on the 13th of June this year, so it's not yet a month old . . .'

'Do you have many students?'

'Fifty-four.'

'Classes?'

'Every day. It's a boarding school. The students live here and come from different parts of the Republic. They've been selected from the workers who have given most proof of their love of the study of social problems. Each factory proposes a certain number of candidates, who are rigorously examined and selected . . .'

'How long does the course last?' I asked again.

'A year. When the academic studies finish, they go on to the Ministry of Foreign Affairs, where they make contact with what we might call the core of their career.'

'Apart from political and technical disciplines, what other subjects do they follow?'

'Czech literature, world literature; figurative arts, music, history, geography. Some aspects of general culture, which they'll extend later.'

'Do they study French?'

'No; English and Russian.'

After I'd filled several pages of my notebook, Yankú Vladimir gently interrupted me:

'My dear friend, time passes and something important is still missing. The students are waiting for you . . .'

'For me?'

'For you . . . They've been waiting for an hour and I fear they may be getting impatient. Besides, it seems as if they are going to give you a little something to do.'

We went out into a short corridor that led us to the classroom. We went in and the students, three girls among them, got noisily to their feet. The director then told me that the students wanted to ask me some questions about Cuba.

I willingly agreed, of course, surrendering myself to the voracity of those young people, in whose eyes our country perhaps appeared enveloped in a distant mist out of which poked the swaying and golden tips of the coconut palms.

But the questions were not of the touristic or picturesque variety. How did Cuba get its independence? Do the blacks and whites mix socially? Why hasn't Prío's government broken relations with Franco? Are the workers organized? A real regulation bombardment . . . I'd hardly replied to one question before another was posed. Many of them had their notebooks and took careful notes.

Finally they wanted me to recite them a poem.

'But you won't be able to understand it!' I replied.

They stuck to their guns. They wanted to 'hear Spanish verse'. I read them the poem, and then had to give them a summary, which Miss Reinhaltova translated for them.

Another day I visited Prague University, where I was taken by Jaroslav Kuchválek, who teaches Spanish language and literature in the Faculty of Philosophy. I went to his class and spoke to his students, young men and women. Among the latter were some singularly beautiful girls, who sang, to their own guitar accompaniment, songs in a very good Spanish, which didn't surprise me since Kuchválek, their teacher, speaks it perfectly, and even with a marked Madrid accent . . . What was amusing was that after my talk they made me sing myself, and in 'plainsong', that's to say with no accompaniment, since I've never played an instrument.

Until the Nazis arrived (killing off all cultural expression), university teaching in Czechoslovakia had a formalist character, theoretical and academic. When the country was liberated in 1945, the old establishment that the invaders had closed down was opened again. Except that a great wind of healthy suspicion was beating at its walls. Progressive student leaders, like Kazimour, first, and then Pelikan, played a role similar to that of Mella's at Havana University, although none of them met the tragic fate of the inspirational Cuban student.

It was also in that same Prague University that I witnessed one night an event in which I took a lively interest. In a huge room, one of the biggest there, a motley crowd squashed together: soldiers, students, teachers, workers, but also no lack of young middle-class people. And for what? A poetry reading. A competitive reading in which six or seven poets participated and where every poem and even every line was judged, and which was the occasion for a heated discussion.

The poets were on a kind of stage, presided over by the famous Vitězslav Nezval, author of the *Nocturnal Poems*, among which is the already classic one devoted to the North American inventor, Edison.

Naturally it was impossible for me to follow the lines of the debate in Czech, but a Spanish-speaking friend kept me in touch with the gist of the discussion. The heart, or nub, of that discussion was as follows: What new directions are currently opening up for national poets as a result of the revolutionary transformation taking place in Czechoslovakia? It was curious to observe the interest with which the audience, made up of such diverse parts, followed the intricacies of a discussion which had at its centre subtle literary speculations. The name of Nezval was often heard, and you could see him turning in his seat or protesting passionately in a language which, although it was unintelligible to me, was impressive in its fluency.

Through his lyrical leanings, Nezval belongs to the generation of Czech poets grouped together in the school known as Poetism, active since 1922. He was really its most important figure, as he would later be in Czech surrealism. Although he is a man committed to the political change that took place a year ago in his country, there is still in his writing many of the formalist elements characteristic of both schools. This year Nezval published a new book – *The Big Clock* – which in the judgement of his critics contains many poems written in a style that is 'taboo'. Poets of the new generation admired him, but don't imitate him. Young Czechs know his earlier poems by heart, but demand that he now sings of the new times with more conviction. The author of *Nocturnal Poems* doesn't refuse, but maintains that poetry conceived within socialist realism should not mean simple propaganda or sloganizing . . . as produced by the youngsters who criticize his. And Nezval draws support from the words of the Minister of Information himself, Kopecky, who, talking about them, wrote without any beating about the bush: 'They think that it's enough to scatter through the poem without rhyme or reason our most current expressions, such as "shock troops", "brigades", "political meetings", "national committees", "tractors", "combine harvesters", etc., for such abortions to be called poetry . . .'

MOSCOW

After two months in Czechoslovakia I went back to Paris. After a week in Paris I left for the Soviet Union in the company of Juan Marinello and his wife, Pepilla.

We flew in a French plane as far as Prague. Then on a Soviet one – bright yellow, with a hammer and sickle in red on a flag on the tail – we covered the last, and longest, stage.

In Prague a group of Czech athletes competing in Moscow got on our plane. In front of me sat the famous Emil Zatopek, world champion in the 10,000 metres, with his wife. Next to me, across the aisle, Miroslav Horcic, with whom I exchanged a few words in a French which was not exactly that of Voltaire . . . I note that the group all eat conscientiously: cheese, bread, chocolate, boiled eggs, ham, sausages, tomatoes . . . What do I know? The champion swallows everything that comes near him, without pause. In the middle of the flight the athletes organize a kind of training session, which consists of them throwing around from their respective seats a small red ball. It seems as if this exercise amuses them, because they're all very happy. At quarter to three in the afternoon (Eastern time), the plane lands in Lvov to make the only stop on the flight: half an hour. The athletes all get off with youthful rowdiness (especially the young women, who are very pretty), and start their ball-throwing exercise on the tarmac. It's drizzling and is cold, even though the 'summer' is well-advanced. The flight continues without the least mishap – travelling, it's true, always at very low altitude – and we reach Moscow at quarter past eight . . . in the evening, since during summer it doesn't get dark till near ten.

At the airport were Nicholas Gabinsky, literary critic; the permanent secretary to the Writers' Union Commission for Foreign Relations, Apletin; Pavlenko, a writer; and a woman, Ivanovna Zencova. We went by car from the airport to the Hotel Moscow, where we were staying. I ended up with a lavish apartment – room 647 – with two beds, bathroom, shower (which I hadn't seen since Havana and Prague: in Paris they are prohibitively expensive) and a large drawing room with its own writing desk. Almost as soon as we arrived, dinner was served: caviar, salmon, a very tasty soup called *salianca*, and fried meat. As well as ice cream, mineral water, wine, and vodka. Supper was very lively and finished late, at twelve, after which I went off to rest. First, however, I went out onto the balcony of the hotel to admire the towers of the Kremlin, whose impressive architecture is quite close by. At night they offer a marvellous spectacle, topped as they are by their own ruby-red stars, lit up from inside.

The following morning we set out to get to know the city. First the river Moscow, wide and majestic. Opposite, following its course, the walls of the Kremlin which, seen in the light of day, appears of an overwhelming size: it is not of course one 'fortress', but rather a group of them, making up a veritable city. Then, a few yards away, facing Red Square, the famous church of Saint Basil, with its onion-shaped, multi-coloured towers. The tallest, in the middle, has a golden cupola. Someone points out this detail.

'I'm not surprised,' I reply. 'In Havana the cupola of the National Capitol is also made of gold.'

Nobody believes it.

But I was less interested in the buildings than in the people, the movement of the city, the nature of the urban space. New York? Paris? Buenos Aires? No . . . Moscow is above all like Moscow. Although if some comparison had to be found, not for the whole, but for certain parts, I would say that it slightly resembled Mexico City.

The man in the street, the ordinary pedestrian, is also quite different from those in other cities. Men and women dress modestly: the former in shirt and trousers or, if need be, a suit – that is, jacket and trousers – without a tie on the sideways buttoned shirt, which they call *rubashka*. The women still wear short skirts, but the jacket is high-necked and fastened, giving them a serious appearance, quite surprising, not just for someone from the tropics, but for someone who has just left Paris.

You don't see, as you do everywhere in France, pairs of lovers connected by the lips, who seem to be sucking the life out of each other for interminable periods of time, to the indifference of the police.

'It's not our way,' they explain to me.

'O.K., but if somebody did it, what would happen?'

'Nothing; but everyone would rightly point out that there are more intimate places, designed for just that kind of thing.'

The taxis are characteristic. Grey in colour over more than half of their bodywork, they have on their upper part a strip like a draughtboard. They are large and clean, like those in New York. In Paris, as you know, they are dirty, tatty, noisy, but at the end of the day very charming. And on the subject of transport, one has to mention the city railway – the metro or subway – which is the biggest in the world. The stations are disconcertingly luxurious, and if not warned in advance, you'd think that they were palatial drawing rooms designed for great receptions. One of the loveliest and most spacious bears the name of the poet Mayakovsky.

The streets of Moscow are of course like those of anywhere else: some are wide, some are narrow, some in between . . . But my attention was attracted in particular by Gorki Street, where, indeed, Ilya Ehrenburg lives; Semenovskaia, with its houses surrounded by gardens; Ojotniriad, which runs along between tall buildings and tree-filled parks. On the shopping streets a great crowd of people, puffing and blowing, are constantly going in and out of the stores. What do they buy? Everything we buy over here: luxurious coats (some costing 14 or 15,000 roubles) or modestly priced dresses; gold jewellery and precious stones, of the kind displayed in the shop windows of Calle de San Rafael in Havana. Have the autumn dresses arrived, or is there a sale starting of men's stitched shirts, which would be hot for our tropical climate, but which are there seen as refreshingly cool; or, finally, can you buy yet the rubber-soled shoes which are indispensable for the rainy weather due any minute? The beehive of men and women means nothing at all, as long as the large hundred-rouble notes, with the picture of Lenin, pass from hand to hand . . . !

In the food shops there are also windows where they display not the merchandise itself but a reproduction in wood or plastic. There's no attempt to deceive the passer-by, because the reproductions are often very crude: they are always just a sign, an indication. Anywhere there's something that looks like a cheese, the real cheese will be inside . . .

On the evening of the very day I arrived, I went to the 3-D cinema about which so much has been heard. The film was screened in a small room near the hotel. As the reader knows, it's still all experimental, based on the work of a Soviet engineer, Ivanov. When the film is projected onto a special screen, made of perpendicular fibres, the figures acquire volume, that is to say, they don't appear 'flattened', as in the normal cinema. Sometimes, when it's a matter of bodies turning towards the audience, you have the unsettling impression that they're going to collide with you, that you could put your hands on them. This happens with a trampoline which some children jump on to in order to leap into the sea: we see them coming inwards and 'falling' a few feet from where we're sitting; we almost feel the water splashing us . . . The same thing happens with the branches of a tree, whose leaves flutter, moved by the wind, above our heads. But the experience still upsets one's vision and in the leaflets they hand out at the entrance you're advised to keep your body upright, which isn't always comfortable. Despite that, it's an unforgettable sight.

Lenin's tomb, does the reader ask? One day, the programme of visits offered two extraordinary prospects: that, precisely, was one of them; the other was the museum that carries the name of the founder of the Soviet state.

The Lenin Museum occupies a huge building constructed in red stone and is spread over three stories, which house the huge amount that has been collected of what belonged to the famous statesman. Portraits of his parents and of him at all different ages, a model of the house where he was born, his first school books, his student notes, personal letters (among them his correspondence with Gorky), first editions of his writings. An interesting document: Lenin's communiqué, when he was already in power, refusing an increase in his salary from 600 to 800 roubles. There are also many personal objects: his hunting gun, his overcoat, his shoes, his fountain pen, the kitchen utensils he used during his Siberian exile, his famous beret, a scythe for cutting grass, a pair of oars . . .

The mausoleum with Lenin's remains is to be found, as is well-known, on Red Square. Day by day, for twenty-five years, a vast human cordon has stretched along the walls of the Kremlin: they are visitors from all parts of the country and students from schools, institutes and universities who come to contemplate the famous remains. Out of special consideration we gain dispensation from such a long wait. Our guide, Gabinsky, approaches the official in charge of guarding the mausoleum, whispers some words in his ear, and a path opens for us: we go forward without more ado.

Lenin's tomb, built out of red and black granite, seemed to me – though I don't know for sure – about five or six metres high, its lines simple and severe. When you go in, you have to climb up and down various flights of steps before finally reaching a fairly large chamber where the corpse is laid. It is stretched out inside a glass casket which provides a vacuum. The body receives a cold, strange, extraterrestrial light, which illuminates it from head to toe and which forms an impressive contrast with the semi-darkness that dims the room. Lenin is dressed in black, his head uncovered and shaven, his face serene, but with a sad undertone, his arms stretched out alongside his body, his right hand half-closed, as it was in death. His overall appearance, with the short red beard and mongolian moustache, is markedly natural: you would say that he is asleep.

About the theatre? Well it was a pity. In the summer there is very little artistic activity in Moscow (the same is true all over Europe). It therefore turned out to be impossible to treat myself to the famous ballets, for which I'd been sharpening my teeth since before I'd arrived. Patience is called for, or a December visit, when it's fifty degrees below! In the circumstances I only managed to see a Spanish ballet, based on a certain episode during the Napoleonic invasion. It seemed to me brilliant and well-directed, but perhaps a little over-loaded with anecdotes.

What did impress me as extraordinary was the puppet show directed by Obrazov. The night I saw it they put on a tale from Gogol, *Christmas Eve*, adapted by Speransky as a three-act play. The music is by Rocknietov and the dances by Zamodur. The piece has moments of extraordinary poetry, such as the stealing of the moon by the devil and his cousins in order to darken the earth. The characterization – all with puppets, of course – is so perfectly sustained that you come to identify with them and even to follow their thoughts and intentions. Finally Obrazov presents a spectacle of his own, a variety show, with outstanding numbers. What a success this man would have if he brought his art to America, where we don't even suspect its existence!

Rather than a 'study' visit, the Soviet stay was an instructive stroll. Four weeks pass by in a flash in a country which has 200 million inhabitants and is made up of fifteen republics. Museums, workshops, factories, colleges, universities, theatres: everything passes by like a marvellous ribbon, from which emerges, paradoxically, the deepest emotions. Stalingrad, with its broken facade, lifting itself from the ashes; the warm Georgian countryside, populated by passionate women with black eyes and sun-burned skin, as if they had been born by the Caribbean Sea; the old city of Tiflis, with its Turkish quarter of twisting, badly paved streets; the visit to the Kremlin millionaire, who guards the useless riches of all the tsars; the Black Sea, so calm and so blue . . .

What were the Soviet people like? An ingenuous question! They differ among themselves in so many ways . . . They don't have – they can't have – a uniformity of character, of customs, not even of language, since each republic speaks its own, and has its share of national figures. It's not the same to be born in the north, next to the polar icecap, as to come into the world in the heat of the south, which produces dark, unpredictable, passionate beings.

Despite everything – and interestingly enough – the people are unified, even though the streets of Moscow are a picturesque showcase, a babel of the most varied types.

The impression I received on the very first day I arrived was that of finding myself in an extremely simple, sober, and cordial atmosphere. Deep down, there are many points of similarity with the North American people in their practical sense of life, in the absence of complication in everyday human contact and even in a certain childish joy characteristic of young nations.

For those of us who come from the capitalist world and are formed in it (despite our revolutionary convictions), socialist life is always offering experiences that are at heart amusing and which serve to remind us of 'our origin'. On the first day of my immersion in the Soviet ambit, while we were crossing the city, one of my companions pointed out to me a huge, new, white building.

'Whose house is that?' I asked, absent-mindedly.

'What do you mean, whose house?' he exclaimed, quite shocked. 'It's owned by the Soviet state. You'll see that it's many houses, not just one, built as accommodation for the workers.'

In fact Moscow is full of buildings of this kind. Their appearance from outside – small windows with lace curtains and a flowerpot – conveys an impression of definitive calm, just like the houses of the comfortable lower middle class.

On another occasion I committed a similar gaffe. I wanted to buy a woollen blanket, attracted by its lively colours and skilful weaving. I went with my guide into the shop where I'd seen it (underneath my hotel), but soon expressed my mischievous conviction that we would find the same piece at a 'reasonable' price somewhere 'less luxurious'. When all's said and done, this was a business situated inside a very important hotel, where things were bound to cost more.

'It would be useless,' replied my friend. 'The price is the same all over Moscow, because it's fixed by the state.'

When they gave me an envelope with two thousand roubles, in payment for my author's rights with respect to the translation of some poems from *El son entero*, my main concern was to guess how much it would be in dollars.

'And so this would work out at, we could say, out of curiosity . . . ?'

'Two thousand roubles.'

'Yes, I know . . . But two thousand roubles, how much would that be in . . . ?'

'You want to know in dollars?'

'Just so,' I sighed, in relief.

'Well it's two thousand roubles. Don't forget, comrade, that the rouble is our currency.'

It had finally sunk in. I said no more.

TÉTÉ-MICHEL KPOMASSIE

'A Spirit from the Mountains'

*The Togolese writer Tété-Michel Kpomassie was not the first Black visitor to
the Arctic. Perhaps his most illustrious predecessor, after Olaudah Equiano,
was the American, Matthew Henson, companion of Robert Peary on several
voyages of exploration over nearly twenty years, culminating in their successful
assault on the North Pole in 1909. Half a century later the teenage
Kpomassie was inspired by a book on Eskimos he found in an Evangelical
bookshop in Lomé. In his travelogue* An African in Greenland *(1981), he
explains how the semi-nomadic Hausa traders gave him the idea of slowly
working his way north via Accra, Abidjan and Dakar. Helped by an
accountant in Paris, who became a kind of 'father' to him, he continued his
journey, and eventually arrived in Copenhagen, six years after leaving home.*

My final preparations had been simple. A stroll around Nyhavn, a picturesque
district near the harbour, enabled me to pick up an old pair of American army
boots at a bargain price, an overcoat with a quilted lining, two woollen pullovers,
and two pairs of mittens. This was the extent of the equipment I assembled to
answer the call of the north. I suppose I was travelling light. My adoptive father
had presented me with an ancient folding camera that he had owned for a quarter
of a century. Finally, I bought some paper for a diary. All this was squashed into
a rucksack.

I had decided to travel by ship: it would be rash for someone like me suddenly
to come up against intense cold after only a few hours' flight, whereas a sea voyage
of several days would allow me to adapt gradually to the climate. Quite a sensible
idea, coming from one so often accused of lacking common sense.

The *Martin S*, a cargo and passenger boat, had been in port since May, loaded
and ready to make her first voyage of the year. She was bound for Julianehåb, one
of the first towns in southwest Greenland. I bought my ticket for that destination.

In fact, my plans were almost as ramshackle as my frail equipment, for though
I knew I wanted to live with the Eskimos, I still had only the vaguest idea as to
just where I should stay in that vast land. I decided that if I landed in the far south
I could then make my way northward up the west coast and so live in several
townships.

That Greenland is the biggest island in the world, with an area of 2,175,600 square kilometres, is merely abstract knowledge giving no idea of its real size. It takes a few comparisons to give a more solid impression. The distance from Cape Farewell, the southernmost point in Greenland, to Cape Morris Jessup in the north is the same as between London and the mid-Sahara. Its breadth is equal to the distance from Paris to Copenhagen. It is an immense desert with only thirty-five thousand inhabitants. Only the coast, consisting of rocks and high mountains indented with deep fjords, is habitable. The interior (five-sixths of the total area) is entirely covered by the *inlandsis*, or continental ice, which can be as much as 3,200 metres high and 3,500 metres deep. If it were all to melt the world's oceans would rise ten metres and drown whole coastal cities. Because of the huge mass of this glacial cap, we still don't know if Greenland is really an island, or an archipelago covered with eternal ice.

The ship left port on the afternoon of June 19 in foggy, dreary weather. At the dock ten people, all warmly clad, waved good-bye. Soon Copenhagen had disappeared and I began to feel closer to the Far North. But it was just the start of my adventure.

There were only nine passengers. An easy fellowship developed, and an excellent atmosphere prevailed on board right from the start of our journey. Among the eight other passengers were two Danish women (a mother and daughter, who were going to visit a relative), a Greenland woman and her child, and a pastor. There was also a young Dane called Chris, a skilled construction worker, who was taking his craft to the Eskimos 'to help them live better in more modern houses'. Adam, a Greenlander of thirty-two, had been working as a cook in Sweden and was going to spend his holidays in his native land after a twelve-year absence. His wife, a Swede, and his daughter of eight had stayed behind. But the passenger with the most surprising mission was a young Greenland woman called Tuperna, who had been taking a one-year course at an institute for beauticians in Denmark. Now she was returning to Narssaq, her native village, to open the first hairdressing salon!

It was not long before I had the first surprise of the trip. On our first day at sea, the ladies sunbathed until nine o'clock in the evening: on the second day, until ten o'clock; and on the third day, until eleven! After we had said good night on deck, I would go down to my cabin and read by the light of the sun. The brief, pale 'night' that followed (night only in name) would soon fade like mist. Towards three in the morning, it was daylight again; bright sunshine filled the cabin with its warm red rays. The short night grew shorter day by day as we neared Greenland. 'If it goes on like this,' I told myself, 'there'll soon be no night at all.' Every two days, when we got up, the ship's clocks were put back one hour in accordance with the changing time zones. I was astonished to find that it's only nine o'clock in the evening in Greenland when it's midnight in Paris and eleven o'clock in the evening in my native land. That set me thinking: with the total absence of night for six months in Greenland, how much sleep did the inhabitants get? For the time being, this question seemed insoluble. As for myself, I had already lost all track of time and never knew quite when to go to bed.

Right from the start, the fine weather promised a real pleasure cruise. Every morning a charming Danish hostess woke up the passengers for breakfast. Like guests in an hotel, we strolled along to the dining room, one by one. The white tablecloths, with their rows of napkins either knotted or folded like bishops' mitres, gave the room a festive air. After lunch, we would retire to the smoking room and then go to our cabins for a siesta. The whole interior of the cargo boat was attractive, and each of the cabins, matching the rest with their walls of varnished pine, had its own toilet and shower. In addition to the bunk, there was a divan, two armchairs, a low table anchored in the centre, and olive-green carpeting on the floor. The *Martin S* was new; this was only her second voyage.

On the fourth day, we were still able to lie out in the sun until eleven at night, but that pleasure disappeared on the following day. The sea turned rough for the first time, alternately worsening, then calming again. Finally a gale blew up and kept on blowing. The sea swelled, and the waves raged and thundered over the decks. Doors kept slamming shut. Everyone kept to his cabin. I rushed into mine to vomit, then lay down on the bunk. The other passengers were throwing up into the scuppers. I couldn't find a comfortable position on my bunk: its angle was determined by the ship, which kept pitching and tossing. That lasted all day. In the toilet next to my cabin, the water in the toilet bowl rose and fell with the rolling movement of the boat; suddenly dropping out of sight, it would shoot back without warning and spurt up to the ceiling. When you went to leave the toilet, the alarming angle of the floor prevented you from stepping forward; then the boat would slowly roll in a sickening lurch that hauled on the door and snatched the handle from your grasp. The door would swing wide open to let you through before shutting with an ear-splitting bang, and you would find yourself propelled towards your bunk, which broke your fall.

We were a handful of human beings far from land, imprisoned in a ship that plunged and reared and was dwarfed by mountainous waves. The thought of sinking nagged at us all, though no one mentioned it. None of my previous voyages had reduced me to such dark despair.

The 'night' of Wednesday, June 23, was extraordinary: a night of wild commotion. Objects kept tumbling over with tremendous crashes, and luggage ploughed from one end of the cabin to the other, while the whole vessel creaked and groaned. Next morning the sea suddenly became as smooth as a millpond. The air turned so cold that it started to cramp my breathing: we were approaching the barrier ice. Towards one o'clock in the afternoon, we spotted the first ice floes.

These were ice blocks of varying shapes and sizes, drifting here and there as the waves took them. The smallest looked like swimming swans, and some were like crouching camels rocking gently from side to side. Some were white, others green or blue. A brilliant sun, cold as steel, glittered on them and transformed the sea into a fairy-tale world: a vast ice-blue expanse strewn with great chunks of crystal. A dazzling glitter seethed and multiplied.

Half an hour later, these blocks were the size of anthills, and the much larger submerged parts formed enormous azure masses in the glaucous depths as they passed us. A little later on, they had reached the height of hills: these were the fabled icebergs, transported by the polar current that flows along the coast. Soon we could see hundreds of them, and their size never ceased to astonish me.

Meanwhile the smaller masses were becoming more and more densely packed. By evening, we could see only one vast sheet of ice spread all across the sea, with white mountains rising here and there. Creeping through this pack ice, the ship left a narrow channel in her wake that quickly filled again with slabs of ice. Her sides became colder and colder. Then came dense fog, and we stopped in the midst of the ice during the brief night, awaiting daybreak and better visibility.

Next morning, Saturday, June 26, the sun rose at two o'clock, shining so strongly that it dispersed the fog and we were able to move again. The ship resumed her slow progress, interrupted by bumps, stops, and starts. Your hands went numb as soon as you took them out of your pockets; a raw cold bit at your ears, your nose; your face felt frozen to the touch. My breathing became more and more laboured, and painful stabbing sensations in my nostrils made it agony to inhale deeply in that frosted atmosphere. I put on my thickest pullover, then my woollen mittens, and as the soles of my American army surplus boots weren't thick enough to keep out the icy chill of the decks, I wore two thick woollen socks on each foot.

That Saturday, after seven hours' endurance and hard navigation, we sighted land: Cape Farewell, the southern tip of Greenland! Mountains rose in the distance behind a slight mist, and the sight gave us all fresh hope.

But the captain, who usually wore a broad smile, radiating confidence, had a grim look and stuck to the bridge. This was because many vessels had been shipwrecked near Cape Farewell, after riding out storms: the icebergs still lay in wait. I still remember the party the captain organized on board on the evening of our arrival off Julianehåb, to celebrate the successful end of our journey. (The *Martin S* was shipwrecked the next year, while I was still in Greenland.)

We arrived on Sunday, June 27, towards noon. The sun seemed much warmer when the ship finally emerged from the immense sea of ice and sailed up the fjord to Julianehåb. In front of us, the bare, snow-capped peaks of tall grey mountains were silhouetted against blue sky. Some were haloed in mist. In the fjord, a few small icebergs were floating in the tranquil water.

Julianehåb is still called K'akortoq, 'The White One'. This Eskimo name, the image of the wilderness of white, was given it because the masses of ice and the icebergs that drift down both coasts pile up in this area. Embedded in an ice-pack a hundred kilometres wide and from three to ten metres thick, they prevent ships from reaching the east coast for months – sometimes for ten months at a time.

When we had sailed up the fjord, the first sign of K'akortoq was a collection of about thirty little houses made of wood and painted yellow, green, blue, or red. They were scattered at the foot of a huge mountain, in the midst of green lichens looking as soft as a lawn and sprinkled with yellow flowers. This tundra, the sole vegetation clinging to the rocky soil of that arctic land, casts an irresistible spell over the traveller who has just spent so many days at sea. The great mountain hid other houses which became visible after the ship had entered the harbour – a sort of wooden landing-stage with a warehouse of brick and stone. K'akortoq (from here on I shall call it by its Eskimo name) consists of about three hundred and fifty houses, all made of wood and horribly alike, perched on the flanks of huge rocks or scattered along the valleys. There are eighteen hundred inhabitants, making it after Godthåb, or Nûk, the capital, which itself has only five thousand inhabitants, one of the most populous 'towns' on the island.

We pulled alongside the landing-stage, and through the porthole of my cabin I could see the entire population gathered on the square beside the warehouse.

The men were of shortish build, though they were mainly half-castes, and clad in thick cloth trousers and pullovers or anoraks. The plump women wore European overcoats that came down to their ankles and headscarves and *kamiks*, or sealskin boots. They were holding an impressive number of chubby little children by the hand, their stout young bodies almost bursting out of their clothes. All stood silently watching the ship which, after an eight-day voyage – two of them spent battling against the barrier ice – was at last arriving in their village, bringing so many long-waited goods, especially – yes, especially – coffee, tobacco, and alcohol! But I mustn't get ahead of my story.

Never were inhabitants of a mountainous land more peaceful looking. They kept smiling, exchanged admiring comments on the *Umiassuâk*, the big ship, and laughed openly at the awkward walk of the passengers, who were staggering about the deck like convalescents.

I wondered what their first reaction would be on seeing me, a black man, leave the ship. They had never seen a man of my race, except perhaps in newspaper photographs. Like an actor carefully preparing for his first entrance, I took my time dressing in my cabin, putting on a thinner pullover under my overcoat. Unhurriedly I drew on my woolly mittens, pushed back the hood of my overcoat, and then, with my hands in my pockets, I made my entrance.

As soon as they saw me, all talking stopped. So intense was the silence, you could have heard a gnat in flight. Then they started to smile again, the women with slightly lowered eyes. When I was standing before them on the wharf, they all raised their heads to look me full in the face. Some children clung to their mothers' coats, and others began to scream with fright or to weep. Others spoke the names of *Toornaarsuk* and *Qvivittoq*, spirits who live in the mountains . . . That's what I was for those children, and not an Inuk like themselves. Like children the world over, they spontaneously spoke their minds about me. Unfortunately, I can't say the same for the adults. Proud and secretive, they masked their feelings behind an unchanging smile, mild but enigmatic. Not one of them corrected the children, yet the mothers' calm gave some of the children confidence, and, as they saw me approaching, they too tried to smile – a hesitant, not very reassuring smile.

The crowd opened to let me pass. It was then that I distinctly heard a woman speak the word *kussannâ*, a flattering term that I didn't understand at the time, but which means 'handsome'. Handsome in what sense? For the children I was a fearsome supernatural being who came to exterminate the village. Besides my being black, it must have been my height – five feet eleven (1.80 m) – that contributed to the fear I inspired in the children, whose parents were little more than five feet three (1.60 m). Perhaps too for that woman, a small woman living with small men, I was handsome precisely because of my height. So my height impressed them, but in different ways according to their age. It spread terror in the children, astonished the men, and was attractive to one woman who at that moment was probably summing up the opinion of all the other women. Two days later the radio station in Godthåb, the capital, announced the arrival of an African in the country in these terms: 'He is a very tall man with hair like black wool, eyes that are not slanting but arched, and shaded with curling eyelashes.'

The new employer of Chris, the young Danish builder, took us to his house for a beer. All the children left their parents' sides and followed us. More of them came out of every house; soon I had such a procession of them behind me that K'akortoq's scanty police force was obliged to follow us in a patrol car moving at walking pace to keep the children from trampling the 'foreigner' underfoot. The scene made me think of the Lilliputians surrounding Gulliver. I had started on a voyage of discovery, only to find that it was I who was being discovered.

Adam was welcomed by his parents.

'I'm going to find you somewhere to stay,' he said as he left us.

He came back to see me at the home of Chris's boss and announced that everybody wanted to put me up! But when his own sister, aged twenty-eight and married, heard that he was looking for lodgings for me, she absolutely insisted on having me stay in her house.

We walked past the little wooden church. Soon the house came into view. Like all the buildings there, it was isolated, standing about fifty metres apart from the other houses. Because of the uneven ground (formed of bare rocks worn down by glacial erosion) and a stream running nearby, the house stood on a solid foundation of brick and stone. Three wooden steps led up to the entrance.

We found ourselves in an unheated entrance hall about two metres long, with clothes hung up on nails. Black rubber boots were strewn across the floor, and I could see plastic buckets lined up along the wall, next to a barrel. Without knocking, Adam opened the second door, which gave access to the living room. A little woman, all smiles, came to welcome us.

'*Velkommen*,' she said in Danish.

'*Tak*' (thank you).

We settled down in comfortable armchairs.

'Cigarette?'

'No, thanks, I don't smoke.'

She lit one herself.

Green plants and pots of geraniums decorated the window ledges. On a low table was a combination radio and gramophone. A big sealskin was spread on the floor, the animal's claws gleaming between the legs of a sofa that filled a quarter of the room. The wooden walls were plastered with family photographs, pictures of Jesus, and large coloured portraits of each member of the Danish royal family.

My hostess dragged heavily on her cigarette.

'Does your friend drink coffee?' she asked Adam.

'*Ab*,' he replied.

The young woman at once brought in some cups and a coffee pot from the kitchen. I was expecting Nescafé, but this was real fresh-ground coffee. Its mellow and penetrating aroma took me by surprise.

'How could she have made coffee in less than a minute?' I asked Adam.

'In all the houses here, the coffee pot stands ready on the stove in case of visitors.'

Within a few minutes, we had each drunk five cups of coffee served with biscuits. After the third cup, she poured a few drops of *akvavit* into the coffee. The talk became lively, and Adam drew on all his Danish and English as interpreter.

'Mikili' (Michel), said my hostess, turning towards me, 'my name is Paulina. I've told Adam that you will stay here with me. Is that all right?'

'Fine.'

'You can bring your luggage this evening. Come and see.'

She took me upstairs to the second floor, where there were two rooms facing each other.

'You'll take that one,' she said, pointing to the room on the right.

It had a metal bed covered with white sheets, clean but not ironed, and an eiderdown. There was a chair beside the bed. That room was Paulina's and her husband's, but before our arrival in the house Paulina had moved out their belongings and put them in the children's room on the left, so as to give me the better of the two rooms.

'Hanssi and I will sleep in the children's room opposite,' she said.

'What about the children?'

'They'll sleep on the floor.'

I protested, especially since Hans, Paulina's husband, who was out at work in the naval dockyard, had not been consulted. But Paulina would hear no arguments.

'Anyhow,' she said, 'Hanssi is nearly always drunk, so he might as well sleep on the floor. Do you know what *imiak* is?' she asked eagerly when we were back in the living room.

'No.'

She disappeared into the kitchen, brought three glasses, and filled them with a yellowish liquid that she scooped in a bowl from the barrel I had seen in the entrance hall.

'This is *imiak* – Greenland beer.'

I took a little sip from the glass that she had filled to the brim. The drink had a sour taste that reminded me vaguely of dry cider.

'*Mamapôk*' (Is it good)? she asked rather anxiously.

'*Ab, mamapôk*,' I said.

We went on alternating cups of coffee and glasses of *imiak*.

'Adami,' Paulina said briskly, 'go get some food.'

Adam brought a dish full of big slices of some sort of meat from the kitchen and deposited it on the round table.

'This is *mattak*,' Paulina told me.

'*Mattak*?'

'Yes – raw whale skin.'

The slices of meat were as thick as papaya pulp or the flesh of a melon. We each took a slice and clamped it between our teeth; then, holding the other end in one hand, with a knife we cut off a bite, Eskimo fashion – that is, cutting upwards close to the lips, so that you run a great risk of slicing off your nose in the process.

Mattak consists of two adjoining layers; the outer part (the natural skin of that type of whale) is of a matte white, had the firmness of cartilage, and is rather tender, soft, even succulent, while the pinkish inner layer is on the contrary very hard to chew.

This new diet caused me considerable alarm. I wondered if I was to be fed on nothing but whale skin during my stay in Greenland. I could still change my mind if I wanted to. The ship, which was to call at two other ports before returning to Denmark, would be staying for several days at K'akortoq. It crossed my mind to go straight back to Europe, but I hesitated. Could I suddenly give up what had taken me so long to achieve, just because of a bit of raw whale skin?

So I ate my portion of whale skin, and my hospitable hostess asked me if I liked *mattak*. Fear of disappointing her made me reply, 'Oh, yes!' Whereupon she gave me, all to myself, a whole plateful of the stuff, to which she added an enormous quantity of yellowish, blood-tinged seal blubber. Very slowly and with great difficulty, but smiling appreciatively, I managed to finish the larger part of this food, which was not made palatable by any spices, not even salt. Inwardly fearing a frightful stomach ache, I berated myself for my excessive politeness, but without it I couldn't have won the precious friendship of my hostess so quickly.

Paulina went back into the kitchen, where she had so many surprises in store for me, and brought out some *ammassat*, little dried fish resembling skinny herrings. These salmonidae, sometimes known as caplins, are also eaten with seal blubber. I found them better without that delicacy, but Adam and his sister disagreed.

'Here,' they told me, 'you must eat plenty of fat – it helps keep out the cold.'

I left Paulina's house in the late afternoon, accompanied by a belching Adam.

'Bring your luggage this evening,' his sister told me again.

All in all, I was pleased with that first visit. The welcome couldn't have been warmer. I went back on board the ship duly escorted by children and police. All this time, in fact, the children had been thronging around the house.

The first thing I did was to go see the captain again and ask if I could continue to eat on board during the few days the *Martin S* would stay in port.

'At least once a day,' I pleaded. 'To vary my diet.'

He granted me this favour, and even added that I could use my cabin, too, for two or three days.

Like a swarm of bees around a hive, young girls wearing brightly coloured anoraks and tight-fitting jeans invaded the ship, going into the Danish seamen's cabins. I could hear one girl saying outside on deck: 'But where's the cabin of Mikilissuâk (Michel the Giant)?' Then one of them came in.

A few moments later she was fast asleep on my bunk. The door opened again a bit later, and a smiling little man with a rebellious lock of hair dangling over his forehead came into the cabin, accompanied by Adam. It was Hans, Paulina's husband.

'*Igloo-mût*' (Let's go home!) he said.

The girl woke up and protested:

'*Namik*! He's going to stay with me. Aren't you, Mikili? I live alone with my father.'

'But my wife has already made his bed!' Hans retorted furiously. 'Mikili, *igloo-mût*! My children will come and fetch your luggage.'

I tried to explain to the charming, disappointed girl that Hans's wife really had offered me hospitality already. I had accepted and I had to keep my word.

So I let myself be hauled off by Adam and his brother-in-law. They didn't take me home right away: we went for a while to chat in the 'café-bar'. There, young mothers were drinking beer, with blond children sitting beside them or on their knees – the consequences of too many visits to the boats . . .

I returned to the ship only to attend the captain's party. There I met some of the local Danes. Apart from girls, no Greenlanders were invited. The drink flowed like water. Chris spent the night in his cabin with a young native woman who was three months pregnant. As for me, I left the ship a little before the party ended. Hans was waiting for me, sitting on a stone near the warehouse, and guided me to his house.

Such was the welcome I received on the first day of my long stay on the western coast of Greenland.

John Wickham

1962

'Notes from New York'

John Wickham (b. 1923) was born and educated in Barbados. He has travelled widely in the Caribbean, Europe and North America, and worked for the World Meteorological Organization in Geneva for several years. He has enjoyed a long association with the Barbadian literary journal Bim *– where this and other short travel pieces were first published – and succeeded Frank Collymore as its editor in 1974. He is best known as a writer of short stories; his collections include* Casuarina Row *(1974),* The World Without End *(1982) and* Discoveries *(1993).*

Set down, not against one's will, especially not against one's will, in any place, one cannot hope to learn anything of the nature of the place or of the prevailing spirit of its people by asking direct questions. The chances are that many of the answers received will be false: false, not by intention, nor even by accident, but by the sheer inevitability of the alchemy that transmutes the simple posing of a question into the unconscious taking up of the embattled positions of moral, intellectual and cultural opposition. And the chances are immeasurably improved by the fact that America and thus the individual American now find themselves, for better or for worse, caught in the full glare of a world scrutiny in which no gesture goes unnoticed and no word unanalysed.

In such an atmosphere then as this present one the edginess, the self-excusing, the hasty effusiveness which immediately confront one come without surprise. Behind this big city sophistication, behind the comfortable living in this land of plenty, one suspects a raw edge, an uneasy self-consciousness. The picture is of a dashing fellow, faultlessly dressed in the best fabric, with a suppurating sore on his arm of which he alone is aware but which he cannot help feeling is visible through his camel hair coat.

The questions which one dares to ask then are those unarguably practical ones which admit of the least possible distortion: how high is the Empire State Building? Where is the terminus for the Greyhound express for the nation's capital? Which is the quickest way to the Bronx? What is the price of a haircut in Harlem?

'There's this tractors-for-prisoners deal,' said the cynical young man, his cynicism, I suspected, hiding a troubled awareness that New York, America, the whole world are not all they are whooped up to be. 'What do they expect to get out of that?' he asked. 'What they should do is to arrange a marriage between Marilyn

John Wickham, 'Notes from New York', *Bim*, 9 (34) (January–June 1962), pp. 135–40. Reprinted with the permission of the author.

Monroe and Fidel Castro: they've done this before, look at Grace Kelly and Rainier and who got anything out of that?' I could not resist saying that that would be merely exchanging one Monroe Doctrine for another.

'Have you read Sartre's book on Cuba?'

'No, should I?'

'Yes, by all means, it's in paperback. What have you seen in New York?'

'Nothing but the airport when I arrived last night.'

'And what did you think of that?'

It was too big to see and all I could remember was a wooden-faced, heavily made up young woman in a uniform saying through her nose, 'Welcome to the United States!' and a customs officer who was wearing a hearing aid.

'Whatever you do, you must visit the Metropolitan Museum and don't fail to see *Raisin in The Sun* and there's a dance recital tomorrow by the School of Performing Arts and soon there will be this Shakespeare Festival in Central Park and you mustn't miss *Camelot* and *The Blacks* and they're showing *Black Orpheus* at a place on Broadway and off Broadway at The Circle In The Square someone is doing *Under Milk Wood*.'

In Central Park one afternoon, hoping to escape the humidity, which, to believe the radio and television announcements, lay at the root of all discomfort, and armed against boredom with James Baldwin's *Nobody Knows My Name*, I was approached by a little coffee-coloured girl of hardly more than seven. Her face was incredibly dirty with all the sticky marks of cheap candy, her hair was untidy and she herself was the picture of neglect. How, she wanted me to tell her, could she get to the playground with the big swings? Since I had, not a moment before, noticed them on my way it was easy to show her the footpath on the other side of the cinder track along which the status-seeking New Yorkers, astride their rented-by-the-hour mounts, strive to acquire the look of having been born in a saddle at places in the country. It is a harmless, pretty and, for the saddle-horse stables smelling of hay and horse sweat on Eighty-ninth Street, profitable affectation.

As the little girl's dirty grey corduroy dress disappeared among the trees I wondered suddenly whether her mother knew where she was and whether she was allowed to brave the hustling traffic of Central Park West alone. So I clapped my hands and called her back. She came running and skipping to me.

'Does your mother know where you are?' I asked her. She nodded silently.

'Are you sure?' I insisted.

'It's all right, mister, she sent me!'

And so, when I came to think of it, she would have done. All along the streets between Amsterdam Avenue and Central Park the Puerto Rican mothers, grandmothers, aunts, sisters, babies and big loutish brothers sit the summer out on their filthy pavements among the rubbish of discarded beer cans, empty cigarette packages, baby carriages, bicycles and baseball bats. The rubbish, the toys, the pavements, the front steps, everything is soaked by the jet of water from an open fire hydrant, at which a swarm of mischievous small children are soaking themselves and every passer-by to beat the summer's heat. The cars parked along the street are dirty wrecks, none of them, but for one fin-tailed freak, this year's model. From the doorways a volley of staccato Spanish is hurled out into the street from the mouths of the dolled-up babes (Brigitte Bardot, the Sex Kitten, is the current image) and the toothless, suckling, draggletailed crones. They can't, one is almost certain, possibly understand one another and small wonder that in the public schools the Puerto Rican youth is made to take Spanish for its foreign language.

From any house in any of these streets where the city authorities have been forced by a violent Saturday night riot to concentrate the attention of their welfare department, from a house, say, next door to the stable stench, it is not hard to imagine the shrill female Spanish equivalent of 'Get the hell outa here and go to the goddam park, will yuh!' And a little dirty faced child, crying tears that stain her face and leave her eyes bright but bewildered, issues forth to chance her little life against the traffic for a go on the big swings. Against the green grass and under the trees where the squirrels leap from branch to branch, in full view of the bare shouldered girls stretched as motionless as fallen Venuses in the sun, the little grey figure searching for Swingland is pathetic and incongruous. For such incongruities neither the effusions of Hollywood nor the brought-back-home tales of the American Wonderland had proved an adequate preparation.

Nor had anything of Richard Wright or Langston Hughes or Countee Cullen or James Baldwin quite proved an adequate preparation for Harlem on a Sunday afternoon: the multitude of churches, each distinguished from the adjoining tenement by the obscenity of its coloured glass windows; the slick chicks walking out with their slick-haired, tinted haired, boy friends; and along the pavements the snowball carts, the black pudding vendors, the drunken fat women, the glassy-eyed drug addicts, all in their Sunday summer stupor. Beneath all this surface smoulders a massive antagonism hardly concealed by the hymn-singing contralto coming from a first floor window. Everything, from the remarkable singleness of expression on the faces (a mixture of fright and petulance) to the scribblings on the advertisement posters, contributes to the impression of latent antagonism. Across the huge poster advising the acquisition of the art of Judo for self defence a Harlem wit had savagely and bitterly scrawled: 'Judo ain't shit, better get a razor!' Across the aisle of the Harlem-bound bus a dusky southern voice drawled, 'Ah done tole her ah jest don' eat, ah jest don' eat . . . she can keep her lil' ole steak . . . ah want to get me a pair of them cheap summer shoes, y'know them pretty ones, yellow or blue or pink and maybe a pocket book to match and two or three of them light summer blouses and ah've *got* to take something for the folks and ah've got to pay the rent so's ah'll have some place when I git back. He *said* he would take care o' that but you cain't ever be sure. Ah'd rather pay it myself before ah leave.'

And through the ghetto jungle of tension, modulated by the blaring juke-boxes and heightened by the signplates of the spiritual advisers and fortune-telling mesdames and by the almost endless parade of the exhibitionist homosexuals, through all this the New York City Police patrol in pairs, guns at their sides, twirling their truncheons, watching the parade.

Of such overheard scraps of conversation, such scribblings and such chance encounters in parks are impressions formed. True, it takes more than these, much more than these, to achieve any sort of functional relationship with any place, but even in one's home town no real relationship is possible without the absorption of such random and haphazard snippets as these and unless their place in the fabric is acknowledged, understood and resolved. The snarling, swarthy motorist, leaning out of his car to curse the violator of the red traffic light ('When you see the red light, you stop, you stoopid fat bastard!') joins hands somehow with the elegant woman on the bus, sullen, offensive, ('Lady, will you *please* let me pass?') the driver intoning all the while, 'Move to the back of the bus! Move to the back of the bus!' Even the pleasant faced trainman on the Long Island train into New York, exasperated beyond his patience by the woman passenger who kept asking whether he was sure that the train was going to stop at Bridgehampton, even he couldn't keep the snarl out of his voice. 'Lady,' he said, 'will you give me the money and let me get on with my work: it's just seventy-four cents, that's all, seventy-four cents, we'll get you there. Anyone would think you're going to Chicago or some place!' And so one comes to recognise the snarl, masked sometimes by the merest veneer of politeness but often blatant on street corner or in supermarket, strident and aggressive on the television commercials, as part of the vernacular.

On the pavement outside Macy's at the rush hour a man stops suddenly, an unlighted cigarette in his mouth. He feels anxiously in all his pockets without success. I offer him a match and the pink face quivers in nervous embarrassment as he lights the cigarette. Then he smiles and goes on his way.

A little old woman, Jewish in every feature of her tired and wrinkled face, walks along the road around the baseball field in Central Park where, it seems, all the Puerto Rican youth of the city is engaged in baseball battles (though, from the noise you would think it is more than baseball they are playing). As she walks along, oblivious of the noise and the youth and the bright summer, she mutters to herself, 'Fife dollars, fife dollars!' in such toneless exclamation that no one hearing her can tell whether she is on the giving or the receiving end of the five dollars, whether she is regretting an unwarranted extravagance or complaining against the inadequacy of five dollars as compensation for whatever services it is she has given.

Two elderly women walk along Columbus Avenue. They walk fast and all that can be heard is the end (or is it the beginning?) of a sentence: 'He had sausage and eggs and a cup of coffee.'

On Forty-ninth Street near Broadway an actor paces to and fro along the pavement. His eyes are glued to the script he has before him as he learns his lines and gestures with his hands.

One can't help thinking that all these disjointed scraps and scenes, these snatches of sentences, caught, as it were, in mid-air outside their frames of reference, are all part of a phenomenon that is substantially more than the arithmetical sum of its parts, all part of the idiom of this city.

According to my friend, the cynical young man, New York is not a city, it is only an arrangement of contiguous villages. But whatever it is, one is constantly being reminded that it is not the United States. What then is?

The Greyhound bus left New York for Washington from Fiftieth Street. Along the Jersey turnpike at sixty miles an hour and soon we were passing wide fields in which the corn was bustin' out all over. The broken down shacks in some of the fields brought the South to mind. Past the motels the bus sped, never once stopping, past Joe's Motel, Motel Carlton, Aberdeen Motel, Sun Valley Motel, a hundred of them, each with its billboard of advertisement (TV, Steak Dinners,

Sea Food, Open-air Grill) and swimming pool of blue water around which spread acres of glistening sun-tanned flesh. The swift succession of these new inns of America nudged the mind inevitably to that fabulous two-year odyssey of Humbert Humbert and his Dolores Haze. And, as if this hint were not enough, on the adjacent seat across the aisle a thirteen-year-old nymphet inexpertly smoked cigarette after cigarette (did she have to empty the package before she got home to her Mom and Dad in Washington?) and screamed to her less adventurous and protesting partner of the same age and sex, 'I tell you I don't care what they do, I don't care!' And no one in the bus seemed to care either nor even seemed to notice how like art life can be when it makes up its mind.

A sandwich house in Washington proclaimed all sorts of sandwiches – steakwich, fishwich ('Wichcraft,' whispered the ever present Nabokov); in a new film a millionaire built a 'boatel', a 'beauteria' in Brooklyn (by this token, would the roti stands in Port of Spain become roterias?) flaunted its advertisement. Are these the authentic America of today? There is no way of knowing for sure. Or is it the New Yorker magazine, now without Thurber and Ross but still (despite such recent deviations as Nadine Gordimer's 'The African Magician' and A. J. Liebling's piece on Archie Moore, the Seasoned Artist) retaining the well known tone of cynical sophistication? The thought occurs that this tone is only a polished and more grammatical dialect of the vernacular snarl. Or does America, the authentic America, somehow reside in a sort of new-frontier curiosity? The curiosity that leads the intelligent woman at the party, having heard that Barbadians have a distinctive accent, to ask sweetly, 'Will you talk some Bajan for us?' ('Not,' I replied, gripping my gin and ginger firmly, 'not in this cold blood!'). The radio announced the other day that there were seventeen million cases of mental illness in America: is this part of the Authentic America? Or is America, by chance, most accurately described as my nine-year-old daughter described Coney Island on a sweltering July day – 'Just like Carnival with all the bands mixed up!'?

And yet one has a nagging suspicion that, for all its diversity, for all the immensity of its distances, there is one America. The tenor of much of James Baldwin's 'Nobody Knows My Name' supports this suspicion, the satirical near-to-the-bone patter of the new comedians like Mort Sahl and Danny Thomas, the popular anxiety over Berlin, the national response to Jackie Kennedy, all these plus the terrible unifying force of television on such events as the excursions into space and the US–Soviet sports meeting in Moscow, all these seem to be indications that there is, after all a single America. The trouble comes in finding it.

Sometimes in one's eavesdropping search for the elusive paradigm of this country, one stumbles against a solid chunk of reactive material which betrays the presence of valuable ore in unsuspected places. This summer, at the annual Shakespeare Festival in Central Park, they did *Much Ado About Nothing*. As with most of the plays and spectacles on show, no one could fault the production on the score of technical excellence, the pure mechanics of the thing. Yet, notwithstanding the smoothness and efficiency of the presentation, it was not always obvious that this was Shakespeare. Where, one was tempted to ask, had the poetry got to? However, on the evening that we saw it in the ice rink in the Park, with the General Motors neon sign high over our shoulders announcing not only the year's cars but also, periodically, the moment's time and temperature, there was one scene of high drama. In the denouement when Claudio, the lover, in atonement for having besmirched the fair name of his betrothed, is made to promise marriage to her hitherto non-existent cousin, Leonato asks him:

Are you yet determined
Today to marry with my brother's daughter?

Claudio gives a ringing answer:

I'll hold my mind were she an Ethiope.

At which it seemed as if a great hush descended upon the audience. Did one read too much in what might merely be a missing of the words or was there quietly at work a troubled tribal conscience whispering of integration and freedom riders and peace corps?

JOHN LA ROSE

'A West Indian in Wales'

The Trinidadian John La Rose (b. 1927) worked as a schoolteacher and then with an insurance company, but his radical political activities led to his dismissal, and he was banned from other West Indian islands by the British authorities. He contested a seat in the General Election of 1956 as candidate of the West Indian Independence Party, of which he was General Secretary. Forced into exile after its defeat, he went first to Venezuela in 1958 and then to Britain in 1961.

In London he founded the influential bookshop and publishing house New Beacon Books. His own publications include several volumes of poetry – Foundations *(1966) and* Islets of Truth Within Me *(1971). He was also one of the founders of the Caribbean Artists Movement. This piece appeared in the last issue of its journal,* Savacou, *which has been described as the first anthology of Black British writing.*

Names like Williams, Griffiths, Jones, I had always known. They were for me English names, or at least, names in English. If your name was de la Rosa or Maingot, the linguistic filiation was equally precise: Spain or France. The shape of the words and their sounds had sown their special location on the map. As an islander, conscious of myself and my spot of earth (small islanders always are), there is some deep curious need to discover the earth and a special place upon it.

I do not know when I realised that Williams went with Wales, but it must have been about the same time that I began to learn that Cuffy was Kofi; that all white people were not the same and that some white people hated others even on our own island, and even in my own school.

He taught me Greek and did me the honour of giving me an exalted mark in the 90s out of a 100 in an exam. Knowing by then the difficulty of accents and my ignorance, I knew I had not deserved the mark. He obviously did not think I had yet come to that stage of awareness. His English, however, was peculiar to his place, like ours. He even said mon-arch instead of mon-ark on one occasion, and I faulted him mentally without overtly disclosing the detection. Then one day, like the child of Yeats he was, he burst into a violent condemnation of the English for their oppression and bloodletting in Ireland. His tongue rolled over that word with filial affection. Then I knew, and things had changed utterly.

John La Rose, 'A West Indian in Wales', *Savacou*, 9/10 (1974), pp. 109–11. Copyright © John La Rose 1970. Reprinted with the permission of the author.

No Welshman ever bore down upon me with the same fury. And though there were many in the country, none had shattered the mould of my early opinions in that way.

My first sortie into Wales was on a strangely useless mission. Bertrand Russell was to have presided at a press conference in London. I was asked to go up and meet him and bring him down as the organisers in London were afraid that his transport might break down en route. As it turned out our presence was superfluous and his original transport flew like a racing pigeon leaving us to saunter quietly through the insular beauty of the Welsh country. So much of the volcanic land reminded me of the Caribbean islands. On that first visit, we noticed the last pub where I, like other travellers, was warned to stock up before crossing the border. Yet the moment of crossing was difficult to remember; there were no frontier guards, no papers to present, no men with arms at the ready. It was like going from Devon to Dorset.

Our first journey was at night, with car lights which did not work very well, as we then thought. We crept in the dark past Bala having headed carefully from Shrewsbury to Llangollen. When we got to Ffestiniog late that night, I knew that this would be as far as we could ever conquer Wales. Whatever I had known of Welsh nomenclature before, the evidence in the place names I glimpsed as we sped past convinced me that this was a language the English could not easily dominate. The land, the nobles, the castles, yes; but not the language where people enclose their most intimate being. It was within these confines that the Welsh could most easily preserve themselves from outside predators and discover the other world for their dreams.

We were determined this second time to hug our undigested memories tightly within our skin and relive those moments we had retained. The time of year differed by about four weeks. Previous to this it had been late autumn with the bronzed brilliance of leaves in the trees, but now it was late summer and cold days. The land around Llangollen still held its undisturbed brooding calm and beauty. The river flowed close to the road singing lullabies over stones; rushing and restraining itself when out of breath; refreshing the land with crystal water.

Bala and the lake were still there, looking fragile, yet tough in their expanse and power. The land hilly and stony and sheepladen. Somewhere in my religious training I had learned, 'Feed my lamb, feed my sheep.' The old Welsh shepherd I saw was doing just that. The first shepherd I knew had been called Jesus and in his photograph, he stood with a long crooked stick the full length of his body. This old Welshman drove a car and blew a whistle to control his many stonewalled sheep pens. As he stood on the wall, I wondered how many hands had calloused, how many back-muscles had bruised, how many spirits had been broken to build those low flung pyramids. The lake washed the feet of this ancient land, rugged and manicured, steeped in the sound of footfalls, struggling through the march of memory. 'O long is the march of men and long is the life and wide is the span.'[1]

This time our journey took us beyond Penrhyndeudraeth, past the expansive sandflats of Portmadoc and the artificial curiosity of Portmeirion into the snug village of Aberdaron in the Lleyn promontory. Around Criccieth, a castle embattled

1. From Martin Carter, 'University of Hunger.'

in *son et lumière* surprised us perched against the sky. Its builders had probably expected invaders from the sea.

Aberdaron was our base and we explored the land and sea around like burrowing moles seeking to unearth the tragedies of time and circumstance.

This was land without people. We who were there in late summer were intruders (so a Church of Wales minister told us), wanted for our economic substance and nothing else. You could not tell this from the pleasant reception we were given. It must have been a profounder malaise than passing eyes, even peering eyes, could discover. Roaming Columbuses, we appropriated the substance of the place with our eyes. It was a place covered with slate.

> *All headstones are black slate*
> *Griffith Jones 1948–1965*
> *Hugh Jones 1945–1966*
> *The sea drove its heavy tongue into the land.*[2]

Roads crisscrossed the land everywhere, as in Barbados. Narrow well-kept roads brought on to the headlands and the long sandy inlets and bays like Nefyn and the whistling sands at Porth Oer and Abersoch. This was a Costa Brava, a coast, beautiful, rugged, wild like Trinidad's North East coast. Memory crossed the seas and returned.

Everywhere men worshipped God in their chapels and tabernacles, guarding their evangelical individuality against intruders. Snowdonia lay somewhere in the background and it surprised me that Mount El Tucuche in Trinidad was as high, though less well known.

We sat on the cliff opposite Bardsey Island and reminisced. The pilgrims had tramped this way in prayer, risking the crossing over the narrow fickle sound to the sanctuary all men long for. A Second World War gun emplacement now guarded their memory. The pilgrims' faith lay buried in the ground. Only a lonely farm and fancy bore witness to that time. But the time itself in its context of continuum, of the long march of man, of the long life of man with its persistent strength of longing and dreaming, was with us newborn and fresh as the grass beneath us.

Few crops grew to feed the few that remained. Halfway to Pwllheli from Aberdaron the road turned sharply into tangled tropical forest. But the shoppers in Pwllheli buying cards and tourist bric-a-brac saved a careful eye for Welsh tweeds and bedspreads.

We had spread our mudded carwheels over the land and had seen as far as our spirits dared to press. What would remain of us and our visit would be even more insubstantial than the broken staffs of faithful pilgrims buried somewhere in the ground. Insubstantial and substantial as the paradox of life itself.

2. From John La Rose, 'Intruder.'

'In the Falling Snow'

Caryl Phillips (b. 1958) was born in St Kitts, but came to England at an early age, was educated in Leeds and Birmingham, and read English at Oxford. He has written for film, television and the theatre, but is best-known for his award-winning novels which range widely across the centuries and continents of Black history: The Final Passage *(1984),* A State of Independence *(1986),* Higher Ground *(1989),* Cambridge *(1991) and* Crossing the River *(1993). He is currently Henry Luce Professor of Migration and Social Control at Barnard College, New York.*

The European Tribe *(1987) is an account of a year's travel in Europe, a 'notebook in which I have jotted various thoughts about a Europe I feel both of and not of'. The narrative begins in Casablanca and ends in Moscow, while the intervening chapters find him in Spain, France, Italy, Ireland, Germany, Poland and – as here – Norway.*

> *In the falling snow*
> *A laughing boy holds out his palms*
> *Until they are white.*

RICHARD WRIGHT

By the time I reached Oslo's Fornebu airport I was tiring badly. I had spent the greater part of a year travelling, but I consoled myself with the thought that at least I would not have to endure the drudgery of a long queue at passport control. I had treated myself to Club class, and assumed therefore that I would disembark before most passengers. Ahead of me were two young American businessmen. They were swiftly processed with a smile. I stepped forward and presented myself. With one hand resting on my unopened passport, the customs officer fired a barrage of questions at me. How much money did I have? Where was I going to stay? Did I have a return ticket? Had I been to Norway before? Was I here on business? I threw down my return ticket and stared at her, my body barely able to contain my rage. 'Stand to one side,' she said. I stood to one side and watched as she dealt with each passenger in turn. There were no questions asked of them.

When everyone had gone through, she picked up my passport and ticket, and then left her counter. Five minutes later she reappeared in the company of a male officer. 'How much money do you have?' he asked. I don't know. 'How much

Caryl Phillips, *The European Tribe* (London: Faber and Faber, 1987), pp. 100–5. Copyright © Caryl Phillips 1987. Reprinted with the permission of Aitken and Stone Ltd.

money is in your bank account?' Which bank account? I asked. 'Do you have any credit cards?' Yes. He nodded as though disappointed. 'Please wait here.' They both disappeared. On their return they found me looking down at the space between my feet, afraid of what I might say if I caught their eyes. 'You can proceed now.' I did not move. 'Go on, you can proceed through customs control.' I looked up and took both my passport and my ticket from the man. The sentence began from the soles of my feet and travelled right up through my body. 'You pair of fucking ignorant bastards.' 'Come with me, sir.' I was instructed to reclaim my luggage, which were the only two pieces left on the revolving belt. In gaoler-like silence, they frogmarched me into the customs hall where I was searched. A middle-aged English woman who had witnessed the episode turned upon my escorts. 'You should be ashamed,' she said. At least it was clear to somebody else what was happening. The scene could not be dismissed as paranoia, or as a result of my having a 'chip on my shoulder'.

They ushered me into the chief's office. I stood and listened as the pair of them explained, in Norwegian, to the chief the reason for my presence. As they spoke all three of them kept glancing in my direction. Eventually, the case for the prosecution came to an end. The chief put down a sheaf of papers and came over to face me. 'You must behave like a gentleman,' he told me. 'This', I assured him, 'is how gentlemen behave when they meet arseholes.' He asked me if I found it culturally difficult to deal with a woman customs officer. I burst out laughing. He suggested that I 'leave now'. Leave for where? 'Oslo, or wherever you will be staying.' I picked up my luggage, but had one final question for him. I asked if his staff would be treating Desmond Tutu, who was due to collect his Nobel Peace Prize in a week's time, in the same manner. 'You may leave now.'

Any ideas I had of a free and easy Scandinavia had already been destroyed. Like her neighbours Denmark and Sweden, Norway is now having to come to terms with people of different cultural backgrounds, and inevitably this is producing an unpleasant backlash. Out of a population of 4 million, Norway has 80,000 immigrants, 63,000 of whom are from Europe or the United States. This leaves 16,000 non-whites, mainly originating from Pakistan and the Middle East. The non-whites constitute only 0.35 per cent of the population, yet a recent poll in the daily newspaper *Aftenposten* showed that 87 per cent of Norwegians did not want any more immigrant workers to enter the country; 33 per cent preferred not to see immigrant workers in the street; 52 per cent wanted them to abandon their cultural traditions and adjust to Norwegian life; and 94 per cent of them said they would not welcome an immigrant into their homes.

Norwegian resentment revolves around the usual fears of immigrant hygiene, unemployment, sexual fears, and displeasure at having to finance the social welfare support system that maintains some immigrants but far more Norwegians. Unfortunately, a similar bitterness exists in both Sweden and Denmark, where acts of racist violence are becoming more commonplace. Norwegian magazines, like *Innvandrer Informasjon*, which seek to promote racial harmony by featuring articles illustrated with pictures of Africans in Scandinavian clogs, are no substitute for political will. It would appear that Ibsen's century-old observation (in *Ghosts*, 1881) of his fellow countrymen still holds true: 'It isn't just what we have inherited from our father and mother that walks in us. It is all kinds of old and obsolete beliefs. They are not alive in us; but they remain in us none the less, and we can never rid ourselves of them.'

In a way, I came to Norway to test my own sense of negritude. To see how many of 'their' ideas about me, if any, I subconsciously believed. Under a volley of stares it is only natural to want eventually to recoil and retreat. In a masochistic fashion, I was testing their hostility. True, it is possible to feel this anywhere, but in Paris or New York, in London or Geneva, there is always likely to be another black person around the corner or across the road. Strength through unity in numbers is an essential factor in maintaining a sense of sanity as a black person in Europe. But, I asked myself, what happens 300 miles inside the Arctic Circle in mid-December, with nothing but reindeer and Lapps for many miles in any direction? I knew they would stare, for it is unlikely that many of them would have ever seen a black person before. Only then would I find out how much power, if any, was stored away in the historical battery that feeds my own sense of identity.

From the beginning my 'experiment' went crucially wrong. I flew to Tromsö, a town about 200 miles inside the Arctic Circle where I hired a car. It began to snow quite heavily so I checked into a hotel, then decided to find a nightclub. The first person I met in the club was a Trinidadian woman. I had foolishly underestimated the extent of the Caribbean diaspora. She was as shocked as I was, and anxious to strike up a conversation. I soon discovered that she was thirty-one, had three boys aged nine, eleven and fourteen, whose father was a Norwegian from whom she was now separated. She had met him in San Fernando, Trinidad when he was sailing through the Caribbean. Her move to Norway had caused a permanent breach with her parents and her life here with him had recently fallen apart. She was drunk, and oblivious to the leering contempt with which other men in the club watched her. Then she remembered her children. They did not like her to go out at nights, so she urged me to speak to them on the telephone. My voice would prove that she had met a West Indian and justify her neglect.

Her phone call was brief, and she returned to confess that she was anxious to leave her children and have some fun on her own. When the eldest boy reached sixteen she would be free. 'I'm still good-looking, aren't I?' she asked. 'I still can have a life of my own, but you know, I love Tromsö more than anywhere. I hate Trinidad.' She paused. 'But I have my own life now.' I asked her what she liked about Tromsö. 'The nature,' was her reply. I began to feel for the three boys waiting at home. Like a potter's wheel that has suddenly been jammed to a halt, West Indians have been flung out into history and tried to make good wherever they have landed. She was the saddest case I had come across. Defying every thing that I know about the caring attitude of Caribbean women to motherhood, she was lost and ailing. As I made ready to leave the club she took my arm. Did I want to meet her children? They might be asleep if we stayed and had another drink or two, and that way I would be able to meet them in the morning. I suggested that she ask somebody else and left.

The next day I drove for hours. The snow lay thick, the landscape a chilled whitewashed canvas with no human beings, just a metal forest of rickety trees, and an odd mirror-glass lake breaking the monotony. Fifty miles north-east of Tromsö I stopped for petrol in a small town. It was mid-afternoon and pitch black. The ninety minutes of winter daylight had long since passed. Turning to face me, the woman attendant dropped the petrol pump in shock. Did she imagine that I was going to molest her? I picked up the pump and gave it back to her. She made some gesture to indicate that her hands were greasy. I smiled. From the car cassette player I heard Bob Marley singing 'Redemption Song': 'Emancipate yourself from mental slavery' did not refer to black people.

I arrived back in Oslo the day Bishop Desmond Tutu received his Nobel Peace Prize. On the television he talked about the need for moral action by the West with regard to South Africa, stating that a concerted and unified economic and political embargo was essential. He made the demand in the knowledge that the vested economic interests of the West would make such action unlikely. Norway trades openly and extensively with South Africa. Their lack of moral fortitude, and that of the rest of Western Europe, will inevitably help contribute to a bloody and protracted finale to this current chapter of South African history. Norway's presentation of a Peace Prize to Bishop Tutu seemed curious. Pontius Pilate washing his hands?

The following day I attended a 'Desmond Tutu Celebration' in Oslo's 'People's Hall'. Organized by the Norwegian Trade Union movement, the festivities were attended by representatives from the church and state, the laureate and his family. Again he spoke passionately on the need for 'economic pressure' and, naturally enough, he received a standing ovation. There then followed a series of performances that included a Norwegian 'punk' band, a black American singer who delivered a barely recognizable version of Stevie Wonder's 'I Just Called To Say I Love You', and a Scandinavian poet. Just when the evening seemed lost, seven blonde-haired Swedish schoolchildren strode on to the stage and proceeded to clap hands and, without accompaniment, sing a medley of African folk songs. Bishop Tutu and his family rushed to join them on stage. The spontaneity and vigour of their performance warmed an otherwise frosty evening. In this unexpected scene, there was, at last, hope.

After the celebration, I found myself sharing a table in an Oslo late bar with a drunk Norwegian. He complained to me that his fiancée had recently 'run off' to do Third World aid work in Kenya, and was now refusing to come back. In a lilting and desperate voice, he asked me how black and white can grow to understand each other. I could only tell him the truth; in many ways, we already did but that a touch of mutual respect always helped. We shook hands on it. My ten minutes of solitary peace were soon disturbed by a drunk Eritrean 'brother', who informed me that I must not stay in Europe too long as I would just get old and be pointed out as 'an old nigger'. He suggested that I go back to where I came from. He was 'studying' in Norway. I asked him how long he had been here. 'Fourteen years,' but he was quick to explain that he had only stayed for so long because he knew how to deal with the white man. An hour later I watched as they carried him out. He was unconscious before his drunken body reached Norway's sub-zero streets.

4

Tours of Duty

W. E. B. Du Bois

'The Fields of Battles'

In December 1918 W. E. B. Du Bois was sent to France by the National Association for the Advancement of Colored People to investigate claims of discrimination against black troops and to defend African interests at the forthcoming peace conference. His part in the first Pan-African Congress in February 1919, which attracted 57 delegates from fifteen countries, is well known. But at the same time he also published a number of articles on 'The Black Man in the Great War', in the NAACP's journal, The Crisis. *This appeared in April 1919.*

I have seen the wounds of France – the entrails of Rheims and the guts of Verdun, with their bare bones thrown naked to the insulting skies; villages in dust and ashes – villages that lay so low that they left no mark beneath the snow-swept landscape; walls that stood in wrecked and awful silence; rivers flowed and skies gleamed, but the trees, the land, the people were scarred and broken. Ditches darted hither and thither and wire twisted, barbed and poled, cloistered in curious, illogical places. Graves there were – everywhere and a certain breathless horror, broken by plodding soldiers and fugitive peasants.

We were at Chateau-Thierry in a room where the shrapnel had broken across the dining-table and torn a mirror and wrecked a wall; then we hastened to Rheims, that riven city where scarce a house escaped its scar and the House of Houses stood, with its laced stone and empty, piteous beauty, high and broad, about the scattered death. Then on we flew past silence and silent, broken walls to the black ridge that writhes northward like a vast grave. Its trees, like its dead, are young – broken and bent with fiery surprise – here the earth is ploughed angrily, there rise huts and blankets of wattles to hide the ways, and yonder in a hollow the Germans had built for years – concrete bungalows with electric lights, a bathroom for a Prince, and trenches and tunnels. Wide ways with German names ran in straight avenues through the trees and everywhere giant engines of death had sown the earth and cut the trees with iron. Down again we went by riven villages to the hungry towns behind the lines and up again to Verdun – the ancient fortress, with its ancient hills, where fort on fort had thundered four dream-dead years and on the plains between villages had sunk into the silent earth. The walls and moat hung gravely black and still, the city rose in clustered, drunken ruin here and in

W. E. B. Du Bois, 'The Fields of Battles', *The Crisis*, 17 (6) (April 1919), pp. 268–9. Cassell wishes to thank The Crisis Publishing Co., publishers of *The Crisis*, the magazine of the National Association for the Advancement of Colored People, for authorizing the use of this work.

yellow ashes there, and in the narrow streets I saw my colored boys working for France.

On, on out of the destruction and the tears, down by bewildered Commercy and old Toul, where a great truck hurrying food to the starving nearly put our auto in a ditch, and up to Pont-à-Mousson where Joan of Arc on her great hill overlooks the hills of mighty Metz; then to Nancy and by the dark and winding Moselle to the snow-covered Vosges. In yonder forest day on day the Negro troops were held in leash. Then slowly they advanced, swinging a vast circle – down a valley and up again, with the singing of shells. I stood by their trenches, wattled and boarded, and saw where they rushed 'over the top' to the crest, and looked on the field before Metz. Innocent it looked, but the barbed wire, thick and tough, belted it like heavy bushes and huddled in hollows lay the machine-guns, nested in concrete walls, three feet thick, squatting low on the underbrush and scattering sputtering death up that silent hillside. Such wire! Such walls! How long the great, cradling sweep of land down the valley and over the German trenches to the village beyond, beside the silent, dark Moselle!

On by the river we went to the snow-covered Vosges, where beneath the shoulder of a mountain the Ninety-second Division held a sector, with quiet death running down at intervals. The trenches circled the hills, and dug-outs nestled beneath by the battered villages.

We flew back by the hungry zone in the back-wash of war – by Epinal and Domrémy – Bourbonne-les-bains and Chaumont and so – home to Paris.

'Stray Days'

Virginia-born teacher and administrator Addie Hunton (1866–1943) was sent by the YMCA to undertake educational and welfare work among Black American servicemen in France. Arriving in the summer of 1918, she stayed on after the Armistice to participate in the Pan-African Congress in Paris in February the following year. Two Colored Women with the American Expeditionary Forces *(1920) was written with her colleague Kathryn Johnson (dividing the chapters between them). It records the daily lives of combatant and non-combatant troops (including the 813th Pioneer Infantry Regiment), on duty and on leave, their relationships with both the US military establishment and French civilians. In this, the penultimate chapter, the book provides a rare glimpse of the authors' own experiences.*

There were days of travel from one post of duty to another, and days of recreation that took us away from the camp for a little but seldom away from the soldiers themselves. Army restrictions were as numerous and as intricate as the barbed wire entanglement of the front. But in spite of limitations, and in some instances because of them, we had many novel and interesting experiences in what we called Stray Days.

Waiting, as simple as it seems, could sometimes be one of the most trying ordeals of a soldier's life. This was true of those who reached France in the heat of the conflict to become in some small way a part of it. Arriving in Paris and finding it sorely pressed by the foe, one immediately became a part of the anxious throng within its gates, with scant desire for sight-seeing or visits to places of interest during those tense days. This was especially true if one had known that city when it was all life and light, before the pall of suffering and dread had fallen over it.

Now one preferred to sit in the Garden of the Tuilleries, if the bomb and shell of the enemy permitted it. Looking out upon the huge dark form of the Louvre or letting the eye wander past the remains of the palace to the Place de la Concorde, it would be most natural that the thoughts or conversation would turn to the long struggle of France for the attainment of an ideal democracy. Usually the conversation would be with a wounded soldier or sad old civilian of the French who would add much to our knowledge of his people and their history. Or, in

Addie W. Hunton and Kathryn M. Johnson, *Two Colored Women with the American Expeditionary Forces* (Brooklyn: Brooklyn Eagle Press, 1920), pp. 241–52.

those same oppressive days, we would ride past the palatial residences with their fast-closed windows, on the Champs Elysées, out to the Bois de Bologne. Sitting there with face toward Napoleon's Arc de Triomphe, one would come to understand that kingdoms and principalities, builded by selfishness and tyranny, survive but a day. Through the gruesome crucible of the Bastille and guillotine, France had won the democracy that she was now battling to preserve. The grim insistence of this determination could be seen in the wounded men that were ever near us.

But when the French had finally won, life and light once again filled Paris, and with it the urge and joy of long days of sight-seeing for the Americans. Soldiers 'on three days' leave' wanted to see luxurious Versailles whatever else was omitted. Others preferred Fontainebleau with its stately palace, or St. Denis with its hundreds of royal tombs. All wanted to go to the tombs of Lafayette and Napoleon. One would find the Chapel of the Invalides crowded with soldiers looking down upon the great sarcophagus of the Emperor, while a Y man related the history. Now and then as we listened, we felt that the shade of the great warrior might be protesting all unseen against some of these original interpretations of his life.

Aside from the best-known places of interest, one liked to go out to Père la Chaise with a group of men and show them its wonderful beauty, even though a cemetery – show them the graves of great scholars and artists of France, even those of its great lovers like Héloise and Abelard. Often the day would be closed with a restful ride on the Seine, where, somehow, one came into more intimate touch with historical Paris and a keener understanding of it than from any other point. The long dark form of the Louvre, the beautiful Notre Dame with the nearby Hotel de Ville, and the gold-domed Hotel des Invalides are among the dominating views of the famous little Seine, and in them is summed up much of the death and resurrection of a nation. But outside of Paris the footsteps of the world seemed to turn toward Rheims. Rheims with its far-famed cathedral, all war-despoiled, became a place of pilgrimage not only for the devoted French, but for the thousands of foreigners on their soil. Towering above the ruined city, the cathedral, so rich in artistic value and historical associations, stands all shattered and torn. Thirty years to restore, they told us there! Somehow as we looked upon it, standing proudly erect in spite of its ghastly wounds and piles of wreckage heaped high about, it seemed strongly emblematic of its wonderful people, who even then had begun the herculean task of restoring their villages and towns. Aside from walking through the ruins to reach the cathedral and our ride to the fort and battlefield with its never-ending trenches, we have two distinct memories of our visit to Rheims. First, it was a wonderful way to celebrate the birthday of one of us; and second, a secret service man, posing as a Frenchman, completely won our confidence. Once before in Paris when one of our number had a dinner in honor of the Liberian delegates to the Peace Conference, we found close at our side an American in faultless evening dress. He quite amused us by the way he pretended to be engrossed in his dinner and book, while he really gave himself to listening. A little diplomacy, and his calling was discovered. But at Rheims it was all different. Sprawled on a bench in real French attire with wine bottle in hand, this man spoke perfect French. It was the hottest day we had ever experienced in France, so he opened the conversation with questions about the weather in different sections of the United States, thus locating us. Then came other questions about colored people, their relations and feelings to their country. After a while our little party went to purchase postcards, and when we returned our erstwhile Frenchman had become an unmistakable American. He laughingly revealed his identity. Now, perhaps it was the environment, but, at any rate, we had all stood the test that day of being rather good Americans; even the 'buck' private who accompanied us seemed to have forgotten the many grievances of his kind and spoke with a kind of glow upon his face of his home in Baltimore. Our secret service man was well pleased with our Americanism, but we felt rather chagrined that we had missed so splendid an opportunity to share with him certain truths about colored folk at home that he probably had not learned.

Seeing Rheims, one also wished to see the city so close by and so closely linked to it for all the war. But we had seen Chateau Thierry first. One Saturday afternoon the two writers were started from Verdun with 'movement orders' for Paris. But the spirit of adventure was very strong in them. They were in a region that within a year had changed the map of the world and added miraculous pages to history. They were in a sector where their own men, side by side with the French, had fought bravely to victory, so that to see it only from the fast moving train was hardly possible. At Chalons they descended, and so full of their adventure were they that the difficulty of securing suitable lodgings in that city, overcrowded with American officers and soldiers, did not disturb them. Two Frenchmen carrying their baggage, contentedly jogged along with them, now and then offering a suggestion. The old cathedral, one of the finest in France, and the old buildings of the city were well worth the time spent in hunting a place to sleep. Next morning they hurried over to the ruined city of Chateau Thierry with its little Marne that had twice held the world in breathless anxiety. How glad they were to join there two other Y women and a Y man who were also out for a day of recreation! Already they had found the headquarters' company of the '813th,' and the colonel of that regiment granted the use of two camions or wagonettes in which they all raced to Belleau Woods. There Messrs. Kindal and Parks, with Miss Thomas and Mrs. Williamson were faithfully serving those companies of the '813th' that were building the cemetery there and of whom we have spoken. There, too, we found Dr. Wilberforce Williams helping the regular staff. Never was a dinner served in the properly appointed way eaten more joyously than the one to which those ten secretaries sat down that Sunday in Belleau Woods. It had been gathered from devious sources by the soldiers of the regiment and brought to the Y hut, so that the courses would not have pleased an epicurean taste. However, there were few fragments left from that meal.

We have told about the soldiers at Chateau Thierry and Fere-en-Tardenois, but we have not told about our race from one place to the other, about thirty miles, with stops here and there to find our way, pick up hats and caps blown away, and to repair the camions.

That night we slept at Epernay and that is still another story. There, too, we found the city crowded by Americans. We thought we would sit in the depot all night, but the sleeping crowd and steamy atmosphere drove us forth into the clean night air. We were just endeavoring to drive a bargain with the owner of a *voiture* for its use as a sleeping carriage, when a tiny French lady in voluminous black bombazine swept us away to her small apartment with its big feather bed. The next day, having satisfied for the time our desire for sightseeing, we most demurely handed in 'movement orders' at the Paris office.

During the war Epernay, like Bar-le-Duc and Chalons, was always just on the rim of that gulf of fire and smoke that swept Eastern France. For the most part these cities escaped with only an ugly scar here and there. Verdun saved them, for could the Crown Prince but have realized his dream, they, too, would have been as Soissons, Rheims and Chateau Thierry, mere heaps of ruins.

There were other trips over battlefields and through their tunnels that most of those who went to France had the privilege of making. But it was away from the beaten paths of travelers, and especially along the west coast of France, that these Stray Days afforded us the greatest pleasure. At St. Nazaire there were days when we would leave the noise of the camp and wander down long shady roads, by high stone walls that hid from view beautiful cottages and gardens, down steep inclines to the sea, stepping from boulder to boulder till we would be far out. Then we would rest with the breeze full of the salt of the sea blowing about us. Sometimes we would talk of home and loved ones over there in the west, sometimes of our work, but oftener we would be silent. Looking up we might see a khaki-clad form high above that would come down to us at a frightfully rapid pace. There were lovely moonlight nights when we would stand by the sea-wall on the ocean boulevard and watch the transports that so often filled the harbor, resting on the glistening waves. But there were other nights when, clad in storm raiment, we enjoyed equally as well seeing the great waves dash over the wall and across the boulevard in turbulent anger.

Now and then there would be a whole day in which we could leave the camp entirely. Then we could go to one of the many little seaside resorts about us – Pornichet, for instance, with its great stretch of white beach, quaint and quiet inns and tempting sea food. There one would go to sleep with the roar of the waves in the ears and the salt of the sea filling the atmosphere.

Now and then there would be need of supplies for our hut that the local *magasins* or shops could not supply, and it would afford a chance for a shopping expedition to the quaint and historical old city of Nantes. Once there we would spend most of the day in the crowded but wonderfully attractive shops. Then we would seek for a *voiture* with a versatile and talkative owner who would show us the points of interest in the old town that had known so much of persecution and despotism. The river Loire, now filled with supplies for the army, was once filled with barges in which hundreds of human souls were drowned. Nantes was one of the important war bases, and was always crowded by Americans.

Another outing took us to Vannes on the Brittany coast, one of the oldest towns of France. In Celtic times it was the capital of Venetis and it takes the honor of giving Venice its name as well as colonizing the Adriatic. Because its inhabitants resisted Caesar with so much vigor he said of them 'they have bodies of iron and hearts of steel.' Looking at the every-day life of those inhabitants of the Brittany coast, one feels that time has brought few changes in conditions and customs. The men driving their cows and sheep on market day, the women and children riding in the carts or walking about the towns, all in the native costume of their class, close the door on the present and, for a time, make one a part of the past. Its old stone gateways and courts, its old squares and old passages and more than all else, its old men and women with their clattering wooden shoes, reveal how little the outer world has penetrated to that ancient spot.

A half day only left for Vannes, and Carnac with its Druid Stones almost thirty kilometres away! How was it to be done? We could not miss seeing such a wonder. There was but one way, and well for us that we did not know then all the army regulations or we would have missed this place now engraven in our memory. But we did not know, so we did the one thing possible, hired an automobile with chauffeur – both French – and sped to Carnac. It is neither beautiful nor ugly, but it is wonderful to see hundreds of gray stones rising skyward out of the heather-covered fields. So regular the rows, so silent the surroundings that one can almost believe the legend that makes them an army turned to stone. There is much of tradition and history in all of this part of Brittany.

Finnistere offered many advantages for outings with the great military port of Brest as the starting point. To be in Brest in winter was to feel the gloom and penetrating chill of England with the addition during the war period of mud everywhere – earth ground into sinking mire such as only vast and constant movements of men and machinery could produce. It was the greatest port of the war, and men were always there by the thousands. We climbed high above the city one winter evening to visit the men at Camp Lincoln. As we spoke to them that night we saw their faces out of the shadows made by the flickering candles. Months later we spoke again, but in a well-lighted auditorium that had been built for the men as the result of the persistent and successful efforts of Secretary Cansler and his associates. Brest itself is full of historic interest, beginning with the sombre Chateau and its dungeons. But all around it are picturesque spots that lure one away from the town in summer days. One Saturday four Y women and twelve soldiers went by automobile north from Brest about twelve miles and reached the remote village of St Mathieu. They were then at the most westerly point on the Continent, named by the natives '*Loc Mazi pen ar Bed*,' or the cell of St. Mathieu at the end of the earth. But the most important thing there is the ruins of a great monastery constructed in the sixth century. It was bombarded first by the English and again during the French Revolution. On all the Continent we had seen nothing more picturesque than that great roofless monastery with its cloisters and pretty Gothic windows. Covered with moss and ivy, it stood a monument to the monastic order of its day. Nearby was a lighthouse and all about us were mines, for the village held a strategic position at the entrance to the English Channel. Beneath the sea-wall was a submarine passage that had had its uses in other wars as well as in the last one. From there we rode on to Conquet, a typical little fishing village of the north coast. We ate dinner in a big old room jutting far out on the sea, where the mist fell about like rain.

How in the memory of thousands of doughboys and welfare workers lingers the picture of Lyons! With its lovely bridges, parks and boulevards, with its great Cathedrale de Fourvière perched high above it, more than any other place it was the 'City Beautiful' for the men who rested there en-route to southern France. It was with Dijon, beautiful beyond compare, after the barren of camp life.

There were days in Southern France where, in addition to the interesting outings that were ever a part of the regular program, we made other journeys. Some of our number traveled to Grenoble and to beautiful Nice on the

Mediterranean, others went over those picturesque parts that border Spain and some stood by Lake Geneva and spent a night at lovely Chamonix under the shadow of Mont Blanc, marveling at its stupendous beauty. There were vales and grottoes, lakes and mountains to which we went, but there was always the soldier and one used these Stray Days largely to gather new strength, new vigor for the important task back in the Y hut. One might go many miles away from camp life, but the vision of those thousands of virile lads with soul and body steeled for the hour could not be lost and always sent one back to them with an eager longing to serve better than before.

SIDNEY BECHET

'First Sight of Europe'

Sidney Bechet (1897–1959) was born in New Orleans. A talented child, he was already an accomplished clarinettist when he arrived in Chicago in 1917. His first trip to Europe, with the Southern Syncopated Orchestra, as recorded in his posthumously published autobiography, Treat It Gentle *(1960), is described below. He subsequently returned to Europe for extended periods – performing in France, Germany and Russia – and settled permanently in Paris in 1951. One of the first great celebrated jazz soloists, he was a pioneer of the soprano saxophone, and left a large body of recorded work.*

I was playing in the Deluxe at Chicago after I left playing with Joe Oliver about 1918, and Will Marion Cook came there one night. He sat around and listened to the music and after we had finished playing he asked me, did I want to go to New York to play with him.

He was a fine man and a good musicianer, Will Marion Cook. When he was young he played violin and he used to give concerts, classical music. And when he was around sixteen, I think it was he told me, some teacher came up to him and said it was a pity that he hadn't learned the violin proper, because if he had he would have been a wonderful violinist. So from then on he thought he would come to Europe to take lessons, and he went to Dvořák. And Dvořák listened to him play and then said, 'Listen, I'm awfully sorry. I like you very much, but I have boys here in my class eleven and twelve years old. And if you wanted to take lessons from me you would have to start way back with the twelve-year-olds.' So Will accepted that and came back to America. When he got home he went in for a contest, for a scholarship, playing violin. And when it was over one of the judges said to him that if he hadn't been coloured he would have won the scholarship for sure. Well, that burned him up, and he broke his violin and never played no more. He just composed and conducted. He wrote some very good numbers – *The Rain Song*, *My Lady's Lips*, *Mammie of Mine* and things like that. He wrote an awful lot of numbers, and he never wrote a bad one. I wonder why they are hardly played now.

When I got to New York I showed up to play, and Will knew I couldn't read notes. I could look at the page and tell where the music was going, but I never had learned things note by note – I couldn't play it that way, The music, it's almost like it don't want any parts: it wants to be all of itself. Leastways, you gotta *feel* it like it was all at once.

Sidney Bechet, *Treat It Gentle* (London: Cassell, 1960), pp. 125–33.

Will knew about this, so he got me aside and told me: 'Son, I want you to listen to the band a couple of times and I'll let you know when to rehearse.' I told him I didn't need a rehearsal and he looked at me and said, 'If you got the nerve, go ahead.' That was all he said, and that's all there was to it. All the band needed was to go over a few of my pieces to learn my solo parts. That was mostly for numbers like blues. The *Characteristic Blues*, that was one I played. That's how it was put together and we went on at the Metropolitan.

But Will had some kind of trouble over contracts and things, and we all broke up for a while till he could get it all straightened out. So to fill in time I went and played with Tim Bryen on Coney Island. We all wore very fancy uniforms and the pay was good. Tim had a regular clarinet player, named Kincaid; and this Kincaid, he had a curved soprano saxophone. I liked the tone of this saxophone very much, so full and rich. I'd tried one in Chicago when I was playing at the Pekin but I hadn't liked it, and I think there must have been something wrong with it. Well, I liked this one Kincaid had, and from that time I got more and more interested in the soprano saxophone.

After a while Will got round all the trouble, and he decided to take this band, the Southern Syncopated Orchestra, to London. He asked me if I wanted to go along and I told him yes. But while I was getting packed up someone told me there was a terrible soap shortage in Europe, and particularly in England, on account of the war. So the next time I saw Will I said I'd still come along, but I must have $500.00 advance. He was a bit surprised, but he gave me the money, and when we sailed most of my baggage was made up of four vast crates of soap.

We sailed in a cattle boat; the trip took fifteen days and we were all as sick as dogs. We got there in June of 1919 and we played at the Royal Philharmonic Hall. That's where I met that Swiss conductor, Ernest Ansermet. He used to come every performance. He'd sit there in his box and after it was over he used to go on backstage and talk to Will. Many a time he'd come over to where I was and he'd ask me all about how I was playing, what it was I was doing, was I singing into my instrument to make it sound that way? We talked a whole lot about the music. This man, he was trained for classical, but he had a real interest in our music. There was just no end to the questions he could think to ask about it. I don't think he missed a performance all the time he was there. And then he wrote a piece about us and he said – I've still got it by me now – he said, 'The first thing that strikes one about the Southern Syncopated Orchestra is the astonishing perfection, the superb taste, and the fervour of its playing.' And then he went on, 'There is in the Southern Syncopated Orchestra an extraordinary clarinet virtuoso who is, so it seems, the first of his race to have composed perfectly formed blues on the clarinet ... I wish to set down the name of this artist of genius, as for myself, I shall never forget it – it is Sidney Bechet.' Well, I don't know about this genius business; like I said, I've always played the music I know the way I feel it, and I was mighty glad at the way Ernest Ansermet understood right off what we were doing.

And another thing I did when I got to London was to buy a *straight* soprano saxophone. I was walking around with Arthur Briggs when I saw one in the window of an instrument maker. We went in, and I ran through *Whispering* on it: this was the first number I played on it. I liked this saxophone as soon as that London instrument maker gave it to me, and Will Marion Cook, he liked it too.

So he had some special arrangements made so I could play this; *Song of Songs* one of them was called. This was a piece of good luck for me because it wasn't long after this before people started saying they didn't want clarinets in their bands no more. And there was I all set with my saxophone.

We played there at this Philharmonic Hall about a month. This orchestra, you know, it was big: there was thirty-six pieces all together. It had twenty singers, it had violins – the whole thing. And we had a business manager, George Lattimore. It was really a show. Then one day Will came up to me – that was in August of 1919 – and very quiet-like told me there was to be a special performance at Buckingham Palace, a Command Performance, that's what you call it. And I had to perform, he told me. He was going to take a quarter of the band and feature a quartet around me. Well, I didn't know what to say to a thing like that, walking right into a King's palace. I didn't know what to expect, but the way it turned out, it was just bigger than another place; it was like Grand Central Station with a lot of carpets and things on the walls. Only it had more doors. By the time we got to play I was thinking I'd gone through enough doors to do me for a month. There was this butler all dressed up and he led us through all these doors and finally he showed us out into the garden where we was to play, and after that it was like any other. Once we got started we had the whole royal family tapping their feet. There was over a thousand people there. And Will told me later that he'd asked them what it was they'd enjoyed most, and the King said it was that blues, the *Characteristic Blues*.

But there was a funny thing I was thinking there between numbers when I was looking at the King. It was the first time I ever got to recognize somebody from having seen his picture on my money. After that, every time I bought me a gin I'd look at the money. He wasn't on all of it. There'd been these other kings, and there'd been this King's grandmother, and they'd left some money with *their* pictures. But this King, it was George V, he had his picture on a lot of this money, and when I bought something I'd take a look at it. It was a funny thing looking at your money and seeing somebody you'd know.

Well, after that we had an engagement for three or four months at the Philharmonic Hall in London and then for a week at the Coliseum. We should have gone over to Paris then, but things didn't work out and the orchestra sort of broke up and all changed around. There was a lot of legal trouble, too, and it wasn't good. Benny Peyton, the drummer, he formed a little band from some of the men in Will's orchestra; the Jazz Kings, he called it. There was Benny, Henry Sapiro on banjo, George Smith violin, Pierre de Cayo piano, Fred Coxito on alto saxophone, and me. We played at the Embassy Club, a smart place where we had to wear white tie and tails. And it was then, too, that I first took part in a recording. We recorded for the Columbia Company; but they made a mess of it and overcut the waxes so the records were never issued. Then the big orchestra got reorganized; Will Marion Cook had left by then, during all these disagreements; Lattimore was running it, and the conductor was a man called E. E. Thompson, who used to play trumpet a bit too. Then we did go over to Paris. That was my first time in Paris. We played for a couple of months at the Apollo Theatre in Montmartre in 1920. It was only just in 1950 that I played there again. It was a funny thing coming back to that same place after all that thirty years.

A thing like that – you come in the same door and you're in the same place and nothing seems to be changed. It could be that other time thirty years ago all over again. You could try to forget and then you could pretend it was the same time. But all the time you know how much has changed. You're not trying to kid yourself. You don't believe you can go back. What you're doing when you pretend, that's a way of feeling how much change there's been. It's a way of realizing, like. But that's getting ahead. That's another time. When we got through there we went back to London, and we played through the summer at the Kingsway Hall, and again at the Philharmonic. That's where I had me a lot of trouble. The way it ended, I was deported from England. That was a hell of a thing.

There was this fellow I knew, his name was Clapham. He was a classic piano player. One night when I got through playing I walked out and I ran into him, and we got to talking. 'Sidney,' he told me, 'where are you going? You're not going to turn in yet. Let's go out someplace and have some fun.'

Well, we walked along a ways thinking to stop off somewheres for a gin maybe and on the way we met two girls. Two tarts they were; 'tarts', that's what they call them in England. These were two we knew from having been around there. One of them I'd been with before a time or two.

We all got to talking and after a while we went up to this Clapham's apartment and we got to fooling around. Clapham, he played the piano and we all of us had a few drinks playing around at this and that, just the way it is when you're having this kind of a party. After a while Clapham stopped playing the piano and he wanted his girl to go with him into the next room, but she wouldn't go, she just didn't want to. Well, I was with my girl and we'd been talking and kissing some, just fooling around, and I'm wanting to make things more serious, but she didn't want to. Well, the way it goes sometimes, one thing leads to another and all at once she bit my hand and I slapped her. I didn't slap her hard. We were just messing around together and all at once I felt this bite and I just made a natural move like, what you call a reflex. It wasn't anything big: after all, we'd been with one another before. The only thing about it was there'd been this little argument.

But she was a little drunk and she got excited and started to holler. The way people are, when you're liquored up like that, even if it's not really drunk; it seems like things just get to happening their own way. There's nobody doing any thinking. My girl, she started out to holler and her girl friend jumped up and began to scream, and the landlady ran out and called the police. And the first thing you knew there were people all over the place. It seemed like no matter where you looked there were fifteen people coming at you from that direction.

So the next thing, we were in jail and I was just sitting there picking my teeth and waiting. I didn't think I needed a lawyer . . . I hadn't no intention of raping her. What did I have to do that for? I hadn't done nothing at all. We'd just had a silly man–woman kind of dispute. My hand, it was bit first.

The police, though, got to this girl. They got to her, threatened her, made her say there was this rape business. They told her they'd pick her up and bring her in any time they saw her. Well, she didn't want any of this business. As soon as she'd slept off what liquor she'd had she didn't want anything to do with it. But there wasn't much she could do. They knew she was a whore. She just didn't have any way to protect herself. But that's something I've learned: it can be a bobby or it can be a policeman or it can be a gendarme, but I don't care what language it is – a cop is nothing but a cop, and he's bound to do things his way. Whatever it is he gets in his head, that's the way he'll have it be.

I didn't know about all this till after the next morning. That's when this case came up, and I was hauled into court; I kept trying to explain but all I could hear was rape, rape, rape. It seemed like there was no court at all for listening to what I had got to tell.

The members of the band had come around and they wanted to go bail for me, but it seemed the court wouldn't let me have bail. They got all kinds of charges and reasons and words why they wouldn't do it, but after a whole lot of talk they finally let me out. Oh, they had all kinds of reasons. They said I was going to be in on a deportation charge; and assault and battery they had that too. The judge said there was no point in letting me out as they'd have the case cleared in a couple of weeks and then I'd be up for deportation. Finally, though, it was fixed up for an appeal and I was finally clear to go until that came up.

When the appeal came up, I had a fine lawyer and I won the case in no time at all. They couldn't even say this was the first time I'd been with the girl. So there was no charges against me, but the judge who was doing the case, he wouldn't clear the deportation charge. That judge, he was one of those men – I've seen plenty like him – he could know exactly how a thing was, he could know altogether different in a way, objective-like, but when it came down to him and his court, all he could see was that police authority that practically makes it like it's *his* authority. And, you know, there's a pride a man's got for a thing like that. It takes him.

And there was another thing happened too. While I was there in that court, the judge was asking me all kinds of questions and I was trying to answer, but I didn't understand all it was they'd made it up to look like. What do I know about all these legal ways? Then at one point the judge, he told me, 'Why don't you explain yourself?' and I said, 'Your Honour, I'm all balled up.' That's what I said. All balled up. But my God, you should have seen the judge. Later, it was explained to me: in England, *all balled up*, that's a bad expression, it's a hell of a thing to say, you just don't use it. Well, my lawyer he got to the judge and explained to him how in America, all balled up is just something confused, it's being like a ball of twine that's wound up around itself. He told him it was an expression anybody could use in America. But the judge, he'd heard it his own way, and he was remembering it his way.

And at that time too, back there in the early 'twenties, England was having all this trouble with foreigners and agitators and one thing and another; they were doing all they could to get foreigners out of the country. And that's how it was. I was told I was being deported, and I was handed over to this uniform and to that uniform, and after I've been kept around a while, there's some more uniforms and then I'm taken to the train and I'm put on a boat, and that's how I got back to New York.

But there was one thing. One of those things you just don't forget. When we got off the train there was some delay and I was walked around a bit by this officer-like that's delivering me over and we pass a pub and I invite him in for a drink. He says he don't mind, so we go inside, and I order up a couple of gins and when they're brought to us I put this coin on the table, this half-crown and there's this king's picture on it lying there on the table, like I could look at a snapshot and say, 'Why, I know this feller.' In a memory way, I could still see him sitting there tapping his feet while we was playing. But I'm feeling now that it's nothing I care for. Just leaving that half-crown, it's too much of a tip for two gins, but I don't want it. I just leave it there on the table. And when I'm on the boat I look through my pockets for all the English money I've got, all the coins, and I just chuck them overboard.

Maybe that's some kind of foolishness. But after I'd done it, somehow I was happier in myself. A coin, that's something with two sides, and I'd seen both of them. You put a lion in back of a king, that's a big thing, but you look behind the lion, *if* you could look behind the lion, there's nothing to see but cops, and I'd seen all the cops and judges I'd been wanting to see. So there I was on a boat going back to America. And in spite of all the trouble I'd had, I was lucky in one way. For not long after that, in October 1921, the band was all going over to play in Ireland when the ship they were travelling in got hit and sunk. And eight of the band got drowned, and they lost all their instruments. It was a terrible thing. If I hadn't been back in America, God knows, I might have gone on too with those poor boys who were drowned.

'First Days in the USA'

An African Savage's Own Story, *first published in* Scribner's Magazine *in New York in 1929 and a year later as a book, purports to be the autobiography of a 'black Jew' from West Africa, who ran away from home and stowed away on a ship bound for Glasgow in 1896. Adopted by a well-to-do family, the 'poor wee naked black creature' was introduced to 'civilization'. Although he returned to his homeland twice over the next few years, taking several wives (including Gooma, mentioned briefly in the text below), he felt somewhat out of place. It was as a theatrical 'African chief' – at the Lady Godiva pageant in Coventry in the English Midlands – that he seemed to find his calling. In 1909, left £1000 in his former master's will, he embarked on the next phase of his life as an entertainer-cum-lecturer, which took him to the United States.*

Contemporary reviews were somewhat sceptical of the book's claims, and recent research by David Killingray and Willie Henderson has shown that its author was in fact a Joseph Howard Lee (1887–1947), born in Baltimore. There is little evidence that Lee ever visited Africa, but there are good reasons for believing that he lived and worked for a time in Great Britain as an 'African' entertainer under various names. Some of the incidents described in the book certainly took place, and a local newspaper reported the appearance of one 'Amgoza' as a live anthropological exhibit in the University of Pennsylvania Museum. His subsequent account of his service in the British Army in Palestine and Egypt between 1918 and 1920 appears to have some basis in fact. On the other hand, his frequent arrests and imprisonment for sexual offences are only obliquely referred to in his book. He died in Attica Prison, New York.

I went from Glasgow to London. While living in London, I made the acquaintance of a man by the name of Austin, who liked me very much and taught me many things, among which was the foundation of astrology, which he knew to perfection.

I did not realize the value of money, and so, instead of putting my thousand pounds in the banks, I carried the cash in my pockets. How the white people stole from me! They short-changed me, and they overcharged me! I know now what they did, but I did not know then.

I went from London to Liverpool. While in the latter city, I frequently crossed the ferry to New Brighton. In New Brighton I met a woman, a Mrs. Collins, who

Bata Kindai Amgoza Ibn LoBagola, *LoBagola: An African Savage's Own Story* (New York: Alfred A. Knopf, 1930), pp. 320–33.

travelled in a show. She owned a travelling cinematograph show and induced me to go with her to attract people to see her show. I did not see why I should not do as she asked, and, in fact, I thought it would be fine sport; so I went along. Her people taught me how to dance, and then they dressed me up in a white suit and made me dance on a platform outside the show. By travelling with the show I saw many towns in England.

I soon got tired of that kind of life, perhaps because I did not earn anything. I do not recall ever having received any money for my work. I did get my 'eats,' and I slept in a wagon, much as gypsies do. The lady bought me a new suit of clothes, but when she learned that I was going to leave, she took the suit away from me. I abandoned the show in a small town called Bewdley, in Worcestershire.

The folk in Bewdley liked me very much and were kind to me. It was in this town that I first learned to ride a bicycle. It happened one day that a man by the name of Mr. Jenks, a barber by trade, who, as a sideline, rented bicycles, lent me a bicycle, and I went a riding. I did not know how to ride, but I was eager to learn. So I went to the top of a steep hill, got on the bicycle, and started to go down. When I reached the bottom of the hill, the bicycle was around my neck, and I had many cuts and bruises. I have been able to ride a wheel ever since.

I visited a small town near there, a place called Kidderminster. This town was then a carpet-weaving place.

One Sunday afternoon, while standing on the platform at the railway station, I saw a train crowded with cheering men and women, who were waving good-bye to their friends, who stood weeping on the platform. The boy I was with told me that the people on the train were all off for America. I think he said that they were going to 'one of our colonies.' The tale the boy told me about the place was exciting. That was the first time that I had heard there was a great, new land where men and women went to establish new homes. I wondered why my young master had not taken me to it, since he had taken me to almost every other place worth while.

The boy went on to tell me that in this new country most of the people were outlaws. He said that everyone walked around with guns and with revolvers on their hips. Perhaps he believed these things himself; certainly he told me as if he believed them. The picture that he drew of the new land was far different from anything I had seen in England, or anywhere else. According to him, America was a wild country. I asked him why all those people should go there if it were such a wild land. He replied: 'To civilize the people there.' That thrilled me, and I was eager at once to go and see that land and help civilize the people. I did not tell the boy my intentions.

I had no benefactor to dictate my going and coming, and I did have some money left; so within a week I secured my passage to that 'outlaw country' America.

During the whole time that I had lived in Scotland and in England, I had never seen another black man. I remembered seeing blacks from Dahomey on exhibition in the Dahomey village in Paris, when my young master had run away with me; but before then, and since then up to the time that I am speaking of, no one had ever mentioned to me that there were black people living in the world outside my own land, Africa.

I embarked on the steamship *Haverford*, at Liverpool, in 1909, bound for Philadelphia, in savage America. I landed in Philadelphia in the spring of that year.

Now I was confronted for the first time in my life with the problem of colour. Up to that time no one had ever mentioned my blackness to me; it had not been thought of, so far as I knew, except as a curiosity. The thing that puzzled me now was that I was not spoken of in this new country as a black man; I was called a 'coloured' man.

I wandered about, after having been released by the dock authorities, and at last came into a district called Kensington. I immediately thought of Kensington in London. But what a difference! I then heard, for the first time since I had been out of Africa, that familiar word 'nigger.' I went to about forty houses, as well as to public hotels, but everywhere the people turned me away. Some said: 'We do not take niggers here'; others were not quite so harsh. At that time, however, the words did not seem harsh to me, for had I not seen 'niggers' before, out on the Gulf of Guinea?

I happened to meet a kind woman who was very patient, and explained to me everything as far as she could make me understand her. It happened that she was a woman from Kidderminster, where I had conceived the inspiration to come to the outlaw country. When I told her that I had recently been in Kidderminster, she wept and said that it was her birthplace, and that she longed to return on a visit. According to her, the district of Kensington was not the place in which I should look for apartments or lodgings. She said that the people there would not let a 'coloured' man, meaning 'black man,' live there, and that I should expect to live in a black man's house. She added knowingly: 'This is not the old country.'

She started me off. I left the street car (meaning 'tramway') at Fairmount Avenue and Thirteenth Street. I walked into a cigar-store (meaning 'shop'), which was actually owned by a 'coloured man.' He was kind to me and called in another 'coloured man,' who, incidentally, was not black, but white. How could they call *him* coloured? What a mix-up!

This white 'coloured man' took me to his house in P___ Street. The place looked more like a lane than a street. It did not take me long to find out that his house was a gambling-house. At that time I did not realize that such a house was out of place. It affected me as almost everything else did that I came across that was new.

The white-coloured man became my landlord and my keeper. He lived there in the company of a girl. I thought she was white, like him, but I did not know what to call her in this land of confusion. The little house was nearly always filled with other coloured men and women of all shades; they did a great deal of drinking and playing some card-game for money.

It was there that I got my first impression of America. I was surprised that everything was so different from what the little boy had told me at the station, back in Kidderminster. Needless to say, my money soon went in that house in P___ Street. When I wanted to buy anything, my landlord did the buying for me, in order to 'protect' me 'from getting robbed,' as he put it.

He was an excellent dresser, and his idea was for me to look spick and span also. I frequently received lectures from him as to how I must appear in America. Whenever I bought a suit of clothing, through him, he bought one also, from my money, which he held 'for safe keeping.' My money soon went and I had no means of getting more. My landlord tried to induce me to write to Scotland for funds. That I could not do. He became angry because I had no money to pay him for my lodging. I did not know how to work, and I had no talent; at least, so I thought.

One day I was out walking with my landlord, and we both stopped to look at a signboard. It was in front of a dime museum. The thought occurred to him that I might get a job there. I remembered how I had delighted crowds in front of the travelling show of Mrs. Collins; so when he asked me if I could do something funny, I said yes, because the idea pleased me.

Now, in my home in Africa we have a medicine made from the sap of the papaw-tree; its name in my vernacular is *throy-on*. It is chiefly used for healing open wounds and cuts. It acts like a 'New Skin' solution. I have often used it, and I had used it especially on the occasion of my ordeal, when I was tested by fire in regard to my flower, Gooma. At that time I managed, through the help of one of my father's women, to smear my whole body with this stuff before the ordeal. The medicine has a milky appearance. Now, I am not certain whether it was the action of this medicine upon my skin that did it or not, but I know that when an oily torch was lighted and applied to my fingers, arms, and legs, the fire did not hurt me. That was about the strongest proof that I was telling the truth, according to our way of thinking. I remembered that I could burn my fingers with a lighted match without feeling any effect. I told the white-coloured man that I could do this. He was delighted; he took me inside and showed me to the head man. Of course the head man wanted to see me touch fire and not get burned, so I did it in front of him. He was also delighted. My keeper explained to him that I had come out of the bush of Africa.

They planned to dress me up in skins and feathers, much the same as Mr. Sumner had done in Coventry when I had ridden in the Lady Godiva procession. I was supposed to dance a native dance, but that is very difficult to do without the accompaniment of a tomtom. I was also supposed to talk a little about my native land. Now, I knew nothing specific about my own home; that is, I did not know its latitude, longitude, or altitude; I had had no real instruction about my own land. I could not talk concisely about any particular thing. I made up a nice little talk, however, with the assistance of the head man of the museum, about missionaries in my country, although there are none there. I was supposed to tell the people to keep their money at home and not to send it to Africa for the missionaries. I was advised to say that I came from Dahomey, a land which everyone had heard about, and not to talk about any other part of Africa, because people would not believe me if they did not know where the place was. I got thorough instructions.

My audience was always sympathetic, especially amongst Jews, agnostics, and working-men. Though I did not realize it then, my talk was of a highly controversial nature, and not at all a talk about the customs of my people.

One day a theatrical agent saw me at the dime museum. He thought that I would make a good feature for a theatre. He took me away from the museum and put me in a first-class motion-picture theatre. Needless to say, my native dancing was quite a novelty, but it was my talk about the missionaries and the money that made me notable at that time. To tell the truth, I had no idea what I was saying and what its importance was, for up to that time I had never seen a missionary. I did not know what a missionary did. So I followed instructions and simply played to the gallery. I played in that theatre two weeks, the first being the regular engagement, and the second by the request of the public. My salary was thirty-five dollars a week at the theatre. It had been twenty-five dollars at the dime museum.

From that time on I was called upon by many managers to play at their theatres, and I was quite a success as a vaudevillist. All the money that I earned I had to give to my keeper, who was supposed to put it away for me. He surely did put it away. He allowed me to keep three dollars a week, so you can see how he was prospering, and all from my labour.

I was contented, nevertheless, until the coloured man began taking me, every Saturday night, inside a pool-room and cigar-store combined. In that place I always met a crowd of men gambling. I had never known what gambling was before then, but the men soon initiated me into all the games. I remember the names of the games that I was taught to play: four-card monte, open poker, and dice, called 'craps.' The dice game attracted me very much, but I never won, especially then. Even now, when I stoop low enough to indulge in that national pastime 'coloured golf,' I never win, because I really do not know how to play it, or how to bet. I have won once or twice, but usually a little later I lose my money anyway, so it is a case of 'Heads I win, tails you lose.'

On the ship that brought me to America, I happened to meet a Mr. K___. He became interested in me when he heard me sing the Scotch song 'Stop yer ticklin', Jock' for a benefit on shipboard. He gave me his card and told me that if ever I should come to his home town, which was Pittsburgh, Pennsylvania, I must call to see him. I had forgotten the man until one day I was engaged to perform at a very exclusive club, the Mercantile Club, on Broad Street, Philadelphia. I made such a hit there that some of the members invited me to come down from the stage and sit with them at the table and eat. It was at this table that I saw that same Mr. K___, a Pennsylvania Senator. He was telling everybody that he had met me on the ship coming from Europe. That put my stock up a hundred per cent.

One of the members became interested in me and asked if he could do anything for me. Now was my time to complain about my keeper and to let them know that I was dissatisfied. I told them all about what went on in the little house in P___ Street, and how I had to give all my money to the coloured man. The gentleman was sorry for me. He asked if I wished to go back to my own country, and I said yes. Why, I do not know. What should I do back in my own home? Whom had I to see there? I simply said yes for the sake of answering. Really, I was getting on all right in America, only my circumstances upset me – making such a lot of money and then not being able to keep what I made. That was the only trouble.

The gentleman said: 'All right! I shall see that you get home.' That made me happy.

After making other appearances in public I was called to the office of that gentleman, and he informed me that my passage was being arranged, and that I should sail for Dahomey, via London. I could hardly contain myself, but why I really do not know.

During my stay in Philadelphia I had the honour of meeting several learned gentlemen, among them Professor J___, of the University of Pennsylvania, and Dr. G___, of the University of Pennsylvania Museum. These men asked me to give information about the social organization of the people of Dahomey, where I was supposed to come from. Well, I supplied them with what I knew of that country, but I was not certain whether what I said was accurate or not, because there is as much difference between a Dahomeyan and one of my people as there is between a flea and an elephant. At that time I was not asked questions about my own people. I took it for granted that I was to talk about what the questioners wanted to know about. They did not know how to question me. Therefore I talked to them just as I had talked to the audiences that I had been appearing before. When they asked me questions about the Dahomey language, I told them what I knew, and added anything I could think of. I did not imagine that the men wished anything but entertainment. I had no idea that I was supposed to be any more accurate in imparting information to the men who were assigned to question me at the University of Pennsylvania than I had been when talking to a common crowd at a theatre.

Some questioners were very kind to me. One was Dr. S___ and another was Mr. W___. Neither of these men asked me anything except concerning the place they understood that I hailed from. Not a word was said about my own antecedents; they asked about the Yoruba language, of which my knowledge was very limited. When I found that I could not answer about matters in Dahomey, I simply said anything that came to me, but never once did it dawn upon me to talk of my own people and their customs. Not long after that time, I was invited to speak in the Department of Anthropology, at Exeter College, Oxford. My subject was to be fetishism. Now, I have specific information about that subject, and, needless to say, I made a hit. The professor who had invited me to speak was delighted, and so was everyone else. I had been asked to talk about something that I knew about. I suppose the good gentlemen of the University of Pennsylvania discussed me, and I am sure that it must have dawned upon them that they were in error in the way they sought information. They took it for granted that I knew the things that they questioned me about.

When I left them, that good man Mr. W___ gave me an excellent letter of introduction to Professor M___ of Oxford University.

HUGH MULZAC

from *A Star to Steer By*

Hugh Mulzac grew up in the Windward Islands in the West Indies and set his sights on a life at sea from an early age. His travels as a young merchant seaman took him as far afield as Australia, the Black Sea, Chile and Baltimore, where he met his first wife. His wartime service was rewarded with American citizenship in 1918 but – apart from a brief interlude as chief officer of the Yarmouth *(aka the* Frederick Douglass*) on Marcus Garvey's Black Star Line – he found racial discrimination meant his master's licence was worth little. His fortunes improved with the United States' entry into World War II, during which he became well known as the captain of the* Booker T. Washington, *an important symbol of inter-racial harmony which supplied Allied forces in Europe and North Africa. In this extract from his autobiography, he tells of his experiences aboard the* Polk, *sailing round the world in the late 1930s as the international situation rapidly worsened.*

It will seem strange to many that it was not until the late '30's, at the age of 52, that I began to develop a political philosophy. There are many reasons for this. There was my natural conservative 'British' background, with all its emphasis upon 'learning', manners and a deeply inbred loyalty to the crown. This was more intuitive than conscious. In actual fact, one could not be a seaman in the early years of this century without learning to despise British imperialism and its handiwork throughout the world. I saw the terrible effects of exploitation in most of the countries of the world, but did not understand economic and political relationships.

Another reason for my political naivete was that throughout these years I had but one goal: to sail as master of an ocean-going ship. It did not take me long to understand that the principal difficulty was my color, but it took *decades* to learn that I could not wage this battle *individually*. For too long I regarded my goal as a personal crusade, not realizing that my fight was the fight not only of all the *colored* races, but of poor working people, black or white, and that it could be advanced only by the advance of all. For too long I fought my lonely battle for recognition with one arm tied behind my back.

This is not to say I never worked with others. I joined everything there was – the NAACP, social action groups in neighborhood churches, civic reform associations, fraternal organizations, and every trade union for which I was eligible from 1907

*Hugh Mulzac, *A Star to Steer By* (New York: International Publishers, 1963), pp. 120–7. Reprinted with the permission of the publishers.

on. There was hardly an evening ashore when I did not go out for a committee meeting of one kind or another. But I was, throughout those years, driven by personal ambition and never understood my struggle in its wider *social* context.

The formation of the NMU changed all this. For the first time I realized how it felt to be free to speak my piece at a union meeting without consciousness of color; free to compete for a job by throwing in my registration card against a white seaman; free to run for union office, if I chose. And most of all to walk aboard a ship with my shoulders thrown back in the clear, deep knowledge that no company official could reject me because I was not white.

This whole crystallization began to take place immediately prior to and during my service on the *Polk*, which accelerated these discoveries. Despite the fact that the President Lines had signed contracts with three different unions covering the deck, engine, and steward's departments there was a healthy union attitude aboard ship. We didn't walk around with chips on our shoulders and challenge the officers to knock 'em off, but neither did we quietly accept the abuses that had prevailed before the strike. 'Beefs' were settled with department heads or held in abeyance until the union patrolman could come aboard in a United States port. Union meetings were held frequently and attendance was compulsory, so that we worked as an organized body. The experience of working with a group of vigilant union men, determined to fight for their rights – and further, winning frequent victories – sparked my political development.

Work on the *Polk* was extremely hard. Even under the new contract, members of the steward's department could be worked nine hours in a spread of 15; that is, any nine hours between 6 A.M., for example, and 9 P.M., with six hours off in between. We carried 280 passengers and a crew of 95 – 375 people to be fed three times a day! Nor were the galleys the modern, gleaming salons of today; they were small, crowded and hot, devoid of contemporary work-savers such as electric potato peelers, mixers, and ovens.

There were no days off. If you took a day off you were logged four for one. One trip in Havana only two of my 18 galley helpers showed up for the evening meal and three of us had to prepare dinner for the passengers. There was only one problem we didn't have – insufficient stores. Five large freezers were jammed to the bursting point with fresh meats and vegetables, and the steward, fully aware that the crew would steal whatever was not delivered to the table, allowed us to feed well. But nine hours a day in a crowded, steaming galley, seven days a week, month in, month out, is work indeed. I never fried an egg or flipped a pancake without wondering 'What in hell am *I* doing *here*?' One can't work this way in a militant atmosphere without wondering about the meaning of work, exploitation, and the future – especially when one is 52!

There were two other conditions on the *Polk* that aroused my political and social consciousness – the route we traveled and the character of the passengers. The *Polk* was on a round-the-world schedule, putting into 20 or more ports in more than a dozen countries, territories, and possessions. Usually the tourists, ashore only for the day, headed for the fanciest hotel or shopping district. At our first stop, Havana, they set a course straight for the *Nacional* or Sloppy Joe's, and spent most of the day in an air-conditioned bar, with, maybe, a daring sortie or two to buy a piece of lace, straw hat, or a bauble. The following day at sea they could be heard 'analyzing' the problems of Cuba – the workers were lazy and filthy, the weather was too hot, prices too high, and Cuba was lucky America had taken such an interest in it – otherwise it would be even worse off! They learned *nothing* of. this island's dictatorship which had been completely taken over by American sugar interests; its once rich, multi-crop land converted into a one-crop estate which could employ the workers only a few months of the year. An Englishman could have formed equally valid views of America from a day in the Waldorf-Astoria bar!

From Cuba we headed for Panama, or more accurately the Canal Zone; except for another reckless excursion to Cristobal or Panama City it was as close to Panama as any of the passengers ever got. Here again, they knew nothing of Panama when they arrived and learned nothing while they were there. Of the whole domination by the United States from the time Teddy Roosevelt had organized the revolution to chip away this piece of Colombia, through the 'gold and silver' discrimination against native workers, to the iniquitous terms of our treaty with Panama, they were entirely innocent – and disinterested.

Then we steamed up the coast to San Francisco, across to the Hawaiian Islands, and on to Yokohama.

In 1938 when I visited Japan for the first time on the *Polk*, some 90-odd million Japanese were living on five islands whose total land area was less than that of the state of California – and only 12 percent of it arable. Japanese military and business circles were already well embarked on the program of expansion which was to erupt in the attacks on Pearl Harbor and the Philippine Islands just three years later.

Few of the *Polk* passengers gave any thought to the problems of war or peace. That Korea had been enslaved by the Japanese since 1905, that Japanese armies had already occupied large parts of China, that its military machine had moved into the islands of the South Pacific, almost none knew or cared – they were interested only in the 'quaint charm' of Japan, a rickshaw tour of the parks and gardens, a visit to the Ginza for bargains, and finally, for no trip would have been complete without it, a visit to Tokyo's *Yoshiwara* or Yokohama's *Homoku* sections, where numbered 15-year-old prostitutes were exhibited in store windows and could be 'ordered' by number for four yen the whole night! This was 'doing' Japan.

By contrast it is well to point out that by 1939 the seamen and West Coast longshoremen had already declared their own strict embargo against the shipment of scrap iron and oil to Japan, while the rest of the world was blithely trading with the aggressor. The bombs that rained over Pearl Harbor on December 7, 1941, were, in a very real way, our own steel chickens coming home to roost.

Steaming on, we reached Shanghai, the world's prime cesspool of imperialistic greed and international throat-cutting and intrigue. When Mao Tse-tung's armies liberated all of China in 1948–49 few seamen were as surprised as the diplomats. There was no country with such extremes of rich and poor. While wealthy *compradores* dallied with their mistresses in the elegant salons on Nanking Road the bodies of starved citizens were collected daily by the 'street cleaning' trucks throughout the occupied section. Extraterritoriality prevailed – legal French, English, and American islands in the vast Chinese sea. Human beings were thick as lice and as easily deprived of life. I have seen taxis, rented on a monthly basis by a few United States Marines, go careening up Nanking Road, knock over a rickshaw, and not even stop to determine whether anyone was hurt. No matter what the crime, Americans were tried in American courts and freed by American judges, for what was the life of a Chinese?

Coming up the Hwang Pu, deck crews often broke out in the bitter song, to the tune of 'Let Me Call You Sweetheart':

> Meet me at the slop chute, on the old Whangpoo,
> Bring along your dipnet, there's enough for two,
> There'll be mashed potatoes and a good beef stew . . .
> Meet me at the slop chute on the old Whangpoo.

The slop chute, of course, is the garbage scupper from the galley which empties into the sea. When we arrived in Shanghai I saw what happens to the sampan owners who gathered at the ship's side to catch the discharged garbage with their dip nets. Captain Hawkins, a master in the usual tradition of contempt for the poor, ordered the bos'un to turn the fire hoses on any of the frail little craft that approached the 20,000-ton *Polk*, and to sink them if necessary. One sampan containing a pretty Chinese girl and a man who we later learned was her husband nevertheless managed to cling to a dangling line. A Japanese patrol boat pulled up and a sentry killed the man with a single shot. Then the patrol boat overhauled the sampan and the sentry beat the girl into insensibility with his rifle butt. This sort of thing happened daily on the Shanghai waterfront. Vendors on Nanking Road sold pictures of Chinese revolutionaries caught by Chiang's troops before the Japanese invasions, their severed heads lying in the street where they were caught alongside their still kneeling bodies!

The tourists talked about these things of course – and in the next breath were chortling about the 14-course dinner they had at the Palace Hotel, complete with champagne, for only eight *mex* – about 40 cents in 'gold,' with the yuan fluctuating from 17 to 22 per dollar. Or the men, out of hearing of their wives, boasted about the beautiful White Russian girls they had met at the Casanova club, whose favors they had enjoyed for a quarter! No one missed the seventh floor of the Sincere Company, a large local department store where Chinese girls, parading with their *amahs*, could be bought by the day, week, or month for a few dollars – or sold into perpetual prostitution for so magnificent a sum as $100.

And so it went around the world – in Hong Kong, Singapore, Calcutta, and Bombay; Port Said, Naples, Algiers, Gibraltar, and home. Ancient Rome could not have produced a more decadent, arrogant, and stupid class of patricians than those whom the *Polk* carried, trip after trip. They were absolutely impervious to the degradation and human misery around them. I once overheard a traveler in Madras exclaim, as she stepped over the bodies of suffering and dying Indians, 'My! It's all so *colorful!*' It was as if India were a vast movie set and the Indians were dying to entertain her! The bored business men regarded the world as a vast plantation for the extraction of profits, while their wives supposed it was an elaborate bazaar held to tantalize them with bargains!

Wherever the *Polk* went conditions were much the same. The chronic starvation was greater or less; one or another type of epidemic periodically chopped down the poor. The oppressors were Americans, Englishmen, Germans, Belgians, French, or Dutch, but they were inevitably oppressors, and they were inevitably white. In every port the *Polk*'s passengers blithely headed for the Cathay, Raffles, or Shepherds for political orientation over cocktails; searched relentlessly for souvenirs to dazzle the folks back home and complained about the 'white man's burden.'

I remained aboard the *Polk* for seven trips as chief cook while the world steadily disintegrated. Hitler's invasion of Austria, the Munich Pact and 'peace in our time,' the dismemberment of Czechoslovakia, and Franco's triumph in Spain, the beginning of the Japanese–Soviet War in Manchuria, and the invasion of Poland came as a horrible counterpoint to our endless entering and leaving of ports, union meetings protesting this or that, and the idiocies of the passengers. But even the tourists became a little grimmer as we left Port Said in the spring of 1940 bound for Italy. Suddenly 'the hand that held the dagger plunged it into his neighbor's back' . . . Mussolini declared war on France and we entered a Naples at war. Troop trains and fighting ships put in and out of the harbor daily. Throughout the city there were large posters of Hitler and Mussolini and at night bands of Italian workers crept along the dark streets splashing the poster with mud and gouging out the eyes of the painted heads of Hitler and Mussolini – a symbol of the fate that would befall both before the war was over. Jaunty fascist soldiers paraded through the streets. Years later, though I couldn't then have guessed under what circumstances, I was to have a renewed acquaintance with these soldiers when they were in a different mood.

1938, 1939, and 1940 were thus the crucial years in which, for me, the myriad forces of history began to stand out, starkly and definably. Seven trips around the world on the *Polk*, slaving in a steaming galley with the tinkle of passengers' laughter filtering through the galley doors, my master's ticket still unused in my pocket, confronted in port after port with the misery and degradation of the world's poor, the fatuities of the rich, and the banal sophistries of capitalist diplomats for which the workers would sooner or later have to pay with their lives, crystallized suddenly in acute truths, sharp as a bayonet. I began to realize in a humble and powerful way that my allegiance did not lie with states, kings, or national boundaries *but with people!*

How stupid it was, I realized, even to owe one's loyalty to *one* people, a *particular* people, even Afro-Americans! Was not our fight for a decent life for ourselves inseparable from the struggle of Indonesians against the Dutch? The Congolese against the Belgians? The Algerians against the French? The Kenyans against the British? Or the Cubans against Batista and his American cohorts? Or the Haitians and Dominicans against their respective dictators? The essential thing to grasp seemed to me then, and seems to me still, that we are *one people* in *one world, and that our battles are inseparable.* The murder of Emmett Till injured a Kenyan, made *his* fight for freedom harder, as the jailing of Jomo Kenyatta was an insult to us all.

And now, in 1940, dictators fresh from triumphs in Spain and China were loosed upon the world again – and I was frying eggs for cafe society rich on a pleasure boat!

As these ideas took shape I resolved to quit the *Polk* and fight once more to sail in my rating. When we returned to the United States in August the country's mobilization was well under way. Orders were flowing into the shipyards for new destroyers and dry cargo vessels, and again there were newspaper reports that licensed seamen would soon be needed. I couldn't help smiling at the irony of my position – like millions of others, the only time my country could really use me was when it was at war! In the years from 1918 to 1941 I could, for all anyone cared, go hang. But now I began to suspect that another opportunity to sail on deck was in the making and I resolved to be ready when the call came.

Nicolás Guillén

'A Baseball Player, Machine-Gun Captain'

One of many leading Black intellectuals to rally to the cause of Republican Spain during the Civil War, Guillén reported on the conflict for the Cuban newspaper, Mediodía. *Among his companions was the American poet Langston Hughes, who also wrote of their meeting with this baseball star turned machine-gun captain, in* I Wonder as I Wander *(1953).*

•

Do you remember Basilio Cueria, that huge mulatto who played catcher for Marianao? He's swapped the diamond for the trench. He's no longer looking for the ephemeral glories of baseball championships; now he's living through the highest glory possible – fighting fascism in Spain alongside the men who are suffering all over again in the cause of liberty. He's now machine-gun captain in the First Combat Brigade of the 46th Division of the Popular Army.

Cueria's father was from Asturias. His mother was black. From both sides, then, he inherits his rebelliousness against the invaders of a working people. From Asturias the impetuous ferocity, the durable resolve, the unbreakable will. From Africa the pain of a flesh oppressed for centuries, the stormy spirit, quashed by slavery but finally breaking through in search of a revolutionary outlet. Oppressed white skin and oppressed black skin join in Cueria as mixed blood, like a unifying symbol in the face of an enemy which is common to workers of all races. What difference is there between a miner who defends his piece of land in the north of Spain with obstinate fingernails, and the black persecuted in the Caribbean or Brazil or his own burning continent by the greed of the *civilized* powers? None at all. Both have the same fate. The same martyrdom awaits them both. The same economic anguish. The same desperate need, in the end, to fight to defend themselves.

We have to etch a simple truth in the spirit of our people: beyond the colours red, yellow, black, and white, there is terrible material inequality, monstrous misdistribution of the wealth of the world; and we must struggle to make that distribution more equal, more fair. Where should this happen? Everywhere. In China, against Japan and against the Chinese who turn their backs on their own people; in Venezuela, against the governments who allow the English and Germans to greedily suck up all the oil; in the Caribbean, against the greed for cane, sugar,

Translation of 'Un pelotero, capitán de ametralladoras', from Nicolás Guillén, *Prosa de Prisa* (Havana: Editorial Arte y Literatura, 1975), vol. I, pp. 107–10. English translation copyright © 1998 Peter Hulme.

bananas, mines, demonstrated by the USA; in Spain, against Italy and Germany, who dream of taking control by fire and sword of a land that should only belong to those who work and defend it.

Cueria is a representative of this conflict. Fortunately, the world is full of people like him, who have quickly overcome a negative, selfish, and short-sighted position and have reached a level on which they can understand their tragedy, and from which it's been possible for them to comprehend the broad horizon of the struggle in which humanity is today engaged. The number of these men gets ever larger, growing irresistibly. One day they will cover the earth and will finally become masters of their own lives.

Basilio Cueria was born very near Havana, in Marianao, son of the parents already mentioned, just over forty years ago. From very young, he showed a greater aptitude for baseball than for anything else, and in this sport he came to be a star of major dimensions. In a certain way, you could say that baseball has been the most influential activity in his life, shifting it into very different spheres, and even projecting it towards a total re-creation in a field of major human responsibility. Baseball led him to the army between 1917 and 1920, as the leading figure in the line-up of a military team; the same sport led him to seek permission to leave Cuba to form part of Molina's famous Cuban Stars, with whom he toured the south of the States: Savannah, Jacksonville, Atlanta; and then because of our 'small world championship' he would always come home to reinforce his club, Marianao, when it played Havana and Almendares, the classic matches against what the fans regarded as their eternal rivals.

'Afterwards', says Cueria, ' when I left the team in Cuba, I went to live in the United States. I spent three years in Jacksonville, and in 1926 I went up to New York and began to work in Long Island in a factory that made heaters. But I soon went back to baseball, to play with the Havana Red Sox, with Ramirito Ramirez. Then with another club I toured Canada, playing in Saint John, Quebec, Montreal, Toronto . . .'

1928 went by. Cueria tells me that he decided then to leave the sport. Instead of coming back to Cuba, he stayed in New York alongside the revolutionaries plotting against Machado. He knew Leonardo Fernández Sánchez, joining enthusiastically in all the political work of the Cubans there, in which he proved very useful.

'Did you go back to Cuba after the overthrow of Machado?'

'No. I stayed in New York. I was there till Wednesday, 20th January, at twelve o'clock at night, when I left on the "Berengaria" for France in order to help the people of Spain.'

'Who persuaded you to give this help? Were you getting bored in New York? Did you fancy an adventure?'

'None of those things you suggest. If you want to know, it was simply my position as man of the people. I know that those Spaniards, by whose side I could die when I least expect to, are men of the people just like me. Don't you think so? That's why I came. And it's here that I've spent the greatest moments of my life. You can be as sure of that, as that I'm talking to you now . . .'

'And what have you done? Who have you fought with?'

'I came into Spain with the International Brigades, in the Lincoln Batallion, where I spent five months. But I always really wanted to get to where I am now, the First Combat Brigade, which for me represents the real shock troops of the Spanish revolution. One day, finally, this proved possible. Comrade Candón visited the Jarama front, where we all were. He saw me, and when he recognized me (because we'd known each other in New York) and found out that I had knowledge of machine-guns, he invited me to go with him. I agreed at once. My transfer was arranged. A few days later, we were under fire. They made me lieutenant and now, with the capture of Quijorna, they've promoted me to captain. It was general Miaja himself who promoted me. "Where are you from," he asked me. "From Cuba, sir," I answered. And then he said to me, "Good, very good; I'm very pleased that comrades from a country like Cuba should volunteer to come to Spain to fight for liberty." That was an emotional moment for me . . .'

'Finally, Cueria, what are your plans for the future? Will you go back to Cuba, or are you thinking of staying in Spain?'

'Look, when it comes to the future nobody can be sure, unless you're a fortune-teller. But my intention at the moment is to go back to Cuba when all this is over, once we've won, which we will for sure. And nothing would make me happier than seeing my loved ones again – I haven't seen them for so long. My family, and my friends in the team, like Oms, Fabré, José M. Fernández . . .'

Cueria was silent for a moment and then, as if he were talking to himself, he said in conclusion:

'If they don't kill me, I'll go back.'

from *Mississippi to Madrid*

James Yates grew up in Mississippi, but ran away from home aged 16, jumping freight trains to Chicago. As a dining-car waiter, he was active as a union organizer, and, moving to New York, became involved in fund-raising on behalf of Ethiopia after the Italian invasion. Following the example of two friends, he volunteered for Spain, and though delayed by difficulties in obtaining a passport (because Mississippi did not keep records of the births of Black children, he had to obtain an affidavit to testify as to his place and date of birth), he travelled to Europe in February 1937. He worked as a truck driver, mainly for the anti-fascist German brigade, the Thaelmann. Wounded, he returned to the United States before the end of the war. In this extract from his autobiography, Mississippi to Madrid, *Yates describes his return to Spain over thirty years later.*

Ever since returning from Spain my passport was withheld from me by the US government. Finally, as a result of the decision in the Paul Robeson case, I was able in 1971 to again obtain a passport and to travel outside of the US. I decided to make a trip to Europe on a Yugoslav freighter. It would be a good way to start writing. The journey from New York to Riejecka, Yugoslavia, lasted twenty-six days, during which time we sailed in the Mediterranean Sea off the coast of Spain. I wondered how I could come to Europe and not visit Spain, the place where for the first time in my life I experienced what it was to be a free man. Whether or not to return to Spain was not an easy decision to make. After all, it was still a fascist country ruled by Franco. I decided, nevertheless, to go to Spain for a two week visit.

I took a midnight train out of Paris. About daybreak the train arrived in Marseilles. When I looked at the small map of France which I carried with me, it appeared that it would not be long before I would once again be in Spain. A hot and cold feeling overcame me when I considered what might happen to an enemy of Franco. By the time the train reached Perpignan, a small city located about thirty miles from the Spanish border, I had decided to get off in order to give myself time to reconsider. I took a room in a small hotel and slept for a few hours. Later, in a small cafe where I went to have dinner, I was surprised to hear the people all around me speaking Spanish. Listening to them talk I realized that I could understand much of what was being said. I beckoned to a man at the next table,

*James Yates, *Mississippi to Madrid* (Seattle: Open Hand, 1989), pp. 165–72. Reprinted by permission of Open Hand Publishing Inc. Copyright © 1989 by Open Hand Publishing Inc.

then greeted him in Spanish. I asked, 'Are you from Spain?' to which he answered, '*Si, Si.*'

'How long have you lived in France?' When he answered, 'Ever since the end of the Spanish Civil War,' I knew he was just the person I had been looking for. I began by telling him that I was one of the Americans who had fought in Spain with the Abraham Lincoln Brigade. His eyes bulged and he began to beckon to others to come over. Everyone in the cafe was standing around my table and to my surprise they began to ask me about people. 'Do you know Steve Nelson?' 'Where is Wolff?' 'What has happened to Salaria Kee, the Black nurse?' They talked about the aid sent by the Lincolns, after they returned to the US, to the thousands of Spaniards who crossed the border to escape Franco. I asked for their advice, 'Is it all right to visit Spain?' They assured me there would be no problem.

The next day I continued on my journey. Our first stop was the border town of Port Bou, where all train passengers were required to go through customs. Everywhere I looked there were police in their green uniforms and black three-cornered hats. No doubt there were just as many plain-clothes police too. After clearing customs we boarded another train which moved slowly over the same tracks that I rode over when I left Spain forty years earlier. There were differences. This time the train windows were intact and no Italian gunboats waited in the Mediterranean to shell the train.

As we approached the outskirts of Barcelona, I began to see the horrors the war had wrought. Miles of empty buildings stood as though they were official monuments to the war. The train rolled into the same station that had suffered a heavy bombing the night I left for home.

I took my heavy suitcase from the rack and carried it as I made my way down the long walk to the large iron gate leading to the waiting room. As I approaching the gate one of many tall men who were standing around lunged at my bag. I was shocked, but then suddenly realized he was saying, 'Taxi, taxi.'

'*Si, si hombre.*' He led me to the taxi stand. I climbed into a taxi and told the driver, 'hotel,' and made him understand it must not be an expensive one. To my surprise the man who led me to the taxi climbed in beside me. Having a private porter accompany me to an inexpensive hotel was a new experience for me. Seeing thousands of poor people walking the streets, it all became clear to me. There were no jobs and this was a way to make a few pesos.

The taxi deposited me at a hotel just off Las Ramblas. It cost only a dollar and a half a day. There I was given a clean room. Looking out the window at the hundreds of people strolling up and down Las Ramblas I realized that none of them were standing in groups and talking as they used to do before Franco.

Late that afternoon, just before sunset, I took a stroll and then sat on a bench overlooking the Plaza Catalonia. Standing all around the plaza were the officers in green with their machine guns. As I walked to my hotel along the back streets I saw armored trucks waiting as though ready for action.

At three o'clock in the morning on my third night in Spain I was awakened by screams from a man who I could only presume was being tortured just a few rooms away from mine. There was no way I could sleep the rest of that night. I was experiencing just a little of what life under the fascist regime was like. I wanted to leave the hotel, but doubted if it would be any different in another one.

I decided to leave Barcelona, but had to wait for the arrival of an important letter which I was expecting from Paris. I had been checking for mail each morning at the American Express and was relieved when I found that my letter had at last arrived. Then my worst dream came true. The German woman who was in charge of the mail said, 'Wait, I have something else for you.' I heard something falling and ringing like marbles hitting the floor. It turned out to be buttons that said 'Free Angela Davis.'

Before coming on this trip I had been working for the release of Angela Davis from prison. So, I decided when making my plans for the trip that it would be a good idea to bring along a suitcase of Angela Davis buttons to distribute in Europe. Having run out of the buttons I ordered more and requested that they be sent to me at the American Express in Paris. I left word there that only letters should be forwarded to me in Spain – no packages. Now here were the buttons. They had been forwarded to me here by mistake. My first thought was, 'Oh Lord, what is this? Here I am in fascist Spain with Angela Davis buttons. What if this gets reported to the authorities?' All the while walking back to the hotel I wondered what to do with the buttons. Then I pulled myself together. I had faced Franco before in the Civil War forty years ago. I spent the rest of the day sitting on many benches and somehow leaving a button behind at each one. By sundown all of the buttons were gone.

The scenery on the bus trip from Barcelona to Valencia was very beautiful, just as it had been in 1937. The orange groves still stretched down to the sea on one side of the road and up to the mountains on the other side. However, there were differences. Then, at every stop a crowd would gather to greet us and give us gifts of oranges – the only thing they had to give. Now there were many roadblocks. Visitors were treated respectfully, but the natives were detained and given a good going-over. All papers had to be in order.

Once in Valencia, I found a hotel where I rested for a few hours before going for dinner. In the hotel bar I met some soccer (called 'football' in Spain) players. Franco gave one thing to the people of Spain: support for sports. The main sport in Spain is 'football'. It is also the main topic of conversation. This is a clever trick to keep the people from thinking about the government. The 'football' players I met that evening were from Orihuela. When they asked where I was from I told them, and said I had been in Orihuela before, but was pleased they did not ask me when that had been. As much as I wanted to, there was no way I could have told them that it was during the Spanish Civil War.

After speaking in Spanish with the 'football' players, I was surprised to hear English being spoken. I turned around and saw four Black women seated at a table. They were pleased to have me join them, and I ordered a round of drinks. When the women told me they were from Ohio, I said, 'I have a friend in New York who is from the Midwest, but I don't know where.'

'Walter Garland.'

One of the women, whose name was Sarah, spoke up and said, 'I know his wife. She and I belong to the same club.' Oh, what a glowing feeling overcame me when I knew I was about to learn the whereabouts of my friend Walter. It was like a knife had entered my heart when she said, 'Walter died two years ago.' I could not hold back my tears. We all mourned together.

The next morning, while walking in the park, I saw an old man with a walking stick sitting on a bench. I thought to myself that perhaps it would be possible to talk with him. All of the Spanish people I had attempted to talk with were polite but uncommunicative. As I sat down next to him on the bench, I said, '*Buenas dias.*' Then I was silent for a while before I asked, 'Are you from Valencia?'

'No. I am from Bilbao, in the north of Spain.' He went on to tell me that he was a retired railroad worker and had moved south for the warmer climate.

'How are things here in Spain?' I enquired. To which he replied, 'Bad, bad,' and within the next few moments he got up and walked away. I couldn't blame the people for not talking with anyone they did not know well. Franco had the prisons filled. People with no criminal record received sentences of forty years. Their crime was that they had fought in the Republican army.

Shortly after the old man left I resumed my walk and searched for some of the places I had known in the city forty years earlier. For a while I was completely lost. Then I came across a familiar well where people were still coming to fill their buckets and jugs, just as their forbears had done for centuries. From there I was able to find my way to the old railroad station, which had remained the same as I remembered it. Just behind it was the bullfight stadium, which also had not changed. From there I walked to the main part of town where I rested in one of the outdoor cafes.

The next morning I headed by train to Madrid. As the train wound its way slowly around the steep mountain curves, I saw two church steeples and a few chimneys still standing amidst the pine trees, reminders of the villages that had been destroyed by Hitler's bombers.

After four hours of traveling slowly through the hills and past steep gorges, the train picked up a bit of speed as we traveled across flat farmland. A roadway ran parallel to the train tracks just as it had during the war when we conveyed food to the millions of people in Madrid while the city was under siege. The deep trenches that had been dug then to give us some protection were now almost all covered with trees. Looking now beyond the trenches, I watched the peasants as they harvested wheat. Forty years ago they had toiled in those same fields in full view of the low-flying enemy planes.

I had planned to stay in Madrid for a few days, but a few hours was enough for me. German influence on the Spanish culture seemed to have destroyed it. Most of the people I saw were elderly Germans. In the dining room of the hotel where I stayed overnight, even Spanish food had been removed from the menu. I longed for some *garbanzos* and for *arroz con pollo.*

Leaving Madrid I caught a glimpse of the cemetery where many of the Internationals were buried. I sadly recalled bringing the body of one of the Germans from the Thaelmann Brigade here. He had been killed in the battle of Brunete.

The first stop the train was to make was at El Escorial, which had been the headquarters for my battalion. Through the train window I could see off to the right a monument which had been built by Franco in honor of the fascists who died in the Civil War. To the left was a road sign pointing to Brunete. Oh, what a feeling came over me knowing that just nearby were lying for all time the bones of the Americans and other Internationals who had died in the struggle for freedom in Spain.

As the train pulled out of El Escorial, I saw once more the ancient burial place of Spanish kings and nobility. It had not been bombed, although the towns and villages surrounding it were completely destroyed. I had never before experienced such silence on a train. I read a newspaper and glanced up occasionally at a man who stood at the door of our compartment that held six people. I could sense the fear of the Spanish people around me, for whom this train journey could be their last opportunity to escape Spain's fascist government.

When we arrived at the border town of San Sebastian, everyone had to show their travel documents. There was no way of knowing who would be detained. As the train started up again and moved into France, a storm of loud cheers broke out. Passengers got out the guitars and castanets that they had tucked away, and there was music and gaiety all the way to Paris.

Albert Luthuli

'Two Journeys Abroad'

Albert Luthuli (1898–1967) grew up in Groutville, Natal. He studied at Adam's College, and continued on as a teacher there for fifteen years. He returned home to successfully stand for election as Chief of Umvoti Mission Reserve in 1935. Politicized by his work as administrator and magistrate, he organized local sugar producers and joined the African National Congress in 1945. In this extract from his autobiography, Let My People Go (1962) – written with the assistance of Charles and Sheila Hooper – he tells of two trips abroad: to India in 1938 and the USA ten years later.

In 1952 he gave up his state-paid position as Chief to become the president of the ANC. Arrested many times in the following years, he was confined to Groutville for five years in 1959, being allowed out of the country only briefly to fly to Oslo to receive the Nobel Peace Prize – the first African to do so – in 1961.

Before the Dutch Reformed Churches departed for the wilderness, my membership in the Christian Council bestowed on me my first journey beyond the Union's borders. In 1938 I was one of several delegates (four of us Africans) to the International Missionary Conference in Madras, the main purpose of which was to discuss the place of the indigenous church in missionary endeavour.

The leader of our delegation was a Dutch Reformed Minister. Even when South Africa had been left lying far behind in the wake of our ship, white South African attitudes clung to him. We, for some reason, were travelling second class, while the Europeans travelled first. On the first Sunday out the delegation leader sought us out to say, 'Well, gentlemen, the white passengers might object if you were to come to the first class to worship there. Would you make your own arrangements here?'

We accepted this. It was nothing new. It scarcely aroused comment until other white delegates came to inquire about our absence. We told them the reason and they were taken aback. On the following Sunday we were invited across to the first-class lounge for multi-racial worship. The boat did not sink.

I remember this same man saying to us during the voyage, 'Personally I have no colour-bar. I'm quite ready to associate freely with Christians of different race. But in South Africa, having regard to the situation there, I would not invite any of you to my house if the neighbours objected.'

---

*Albert Luthuli, *Let My People Go: An Autobiography* (London: Collins, 1962), pp. 78–85. Reprinted with the permission of HarperCollins Publishers Ltd.

A sad comment, I thought, on the battle between Christian principle and what the neighbours think. But there has been a sequel, one which raises my spirits and which is, perhaps, peculiarly Christian. After years of silence (following the Dutch Reformed breakaway) this minister and his wife have sought us out and kept regularly in touch with us by visits and correspondence. I still hope to return his visits if a time comes when I am free to move about again. In his case, the neighbours have not won.

The Conference itself was a great privilege, bringing as it did contact with Christian leaders from all over the world, some of them giants. I think that what made the deepest impression on me was not the high level of debate (it was high), but the thrill of seeing world-wide Christianity in miniature. For the first time I *saw* the result of the command: 'Go ye into all the world and preach the Gospel.' What had hitherto been vague became precise. Added to this was my delight in a sense of the vigour of Christianity. It was alive and active, grappling with its problems and facing its challenges. We do not see much of that in South Africa.

I was sad about South Africa. When I learned (for the first time) that there are African Anglican Bishops in West Africa, I thought it an adverse comment on South Africa, where so far there are none after this long time. Why? Has the Church been unable to train Africans, or has it tried only half-heartedly? Or has the rigour of the West African climate made Europeans feel more temporary there, readier to hand over and go?

In India we found evidences all round us of aggressive Christianity. There were schools and colleges everywhere, and the Church had found it possible to produce mature indigenous Christian leadership. Perhaps the challenge of highly developed Eastern religion spurred Christians on to great efforts. In South Africa the Church has tended to accommodate itself to the general secular pattern of the country, it has been content to supply a modicum of elementary education, and generally it has waited for its African converts to push it from behind, to alarm it into belated action.

The spectacle in India of the Church seriously tackling poverty (how desperate a poverty!), the Church undertaking agricultural projects, the Church organising home industries and social services, all this made me aware of our sluggish pace in South Africa. I came home an incisive critic of South African Christianity. I still am one. It does not diminish my loyalty.

The hospitality of India and Ceylon and the munificence of the Christian community, were overwhelming. In Ceylon I was for ten days the guest of a devout Anglican widow, the owner of an extensive estate and a large mansion. To her great regret her only son was a Communist. I remember how she said to me, 'Chief, I have gone beyond grief now about my son. He's a good boy. He could have misused our wealth, but he works, he cares for the servants in ways which put me to shame as a Christian. I had hoped he would be an Anglican priest. But he's a good son.'

The poverty of India appalled me. It was so much worse than what I know in South Africa. Beggars followed us for miles, people slept huddled in the streets, the country dwellings were often crude huts. But if I felt helpless in the face of such destitution, Indians were trying to combat it. In one suburb of lovely houses we learned that the teachers there had formed a building society and provided housing. The Society of the Servants of India was busy, too, using voluntary self-taxation to relieve the poor. The imagination and spirit in these efforts impressed us deeply.

One cloud hung over the Conference – the cloud of war. Tension was evident in a reserve between Chinese and Japanese delegations. Even so, the very fact that they were able to meet as brothers in such a situation bore vivid testimony to the potency of Christianity.

I came back from India with wider sympathies and wider horizons.

Ten years later I enjoyed a second reprieve from the tense complexity of my homeland. As on the occasion of my first visit beyond the confines of South Africa, the invitation arose out of my church activities. This time, however, in 1948, I was invited to go to the United States to undertake a lecture tour about Christian missions, under the joint aegis of the American Board and of the North American Missionary Conference.

The opportunity delighted me. With it came my first experience of air travel. My wife accompanied me to Johannesburg where I was to board the plane which left at midnight. I remember my departure vividly. Because it was dark I could not even catch a last glimpse of her. As the plane took off I felt an acute pang of loneliness and isolation, a voyager going into the void.

My arrival at New York made it speedily evident that my knowledge of geography had deserted me while I packed. I packed in winter. I arrived in blazing, humid summer – equipped to meet it with a winter wardrobe!

I was soon immersed in the first part of my programme, which took me to a number of summer camps, mainly for young people. I was most impressed by the way in which the churches in the States were meeting the challenge of young people, not only by providing for their needs, but by deploying them wisely in the active work of the church. This accent on youth was new to me, and it seemed both worth-while and successful. For a couple of months I was fully occupied in visiting these camps and talking to young people. As a member of the staff of each camp I found myself counselling groups of young white boys – another new experience. At one camp my group (boys and girls this time) stole the show on Talent Night. We put the emphasis on Africa and ended by singing *Nkosi Sikelel'i-Afrika*.

Everywhere I went the interest shown in Africa was immense. I was able, I think, to satisfy curiosity about South Africa, but the questions which were asked about the rest of the continent made me much aware of my ignorance in those days about Africa as a whole, and of the extent to which white South Africa sealed us all off from the rest of Africa.

After this I became for a while the property of the North American Missionary Conference. According to its itinerary, groups of speakers toured numbers of large American cities and I found myself called on to address huge gatherings in such places as Boston, Chicago, Minneapolis, and Washington, D.C. I was taxed more than the other members of my group, but when sheer fatigue drove me to the point of rebellion, I was told, 'Blame that on the people's eagerness to learn about Africa.'

It may be that the presidential election going on at the time stimulated American interest in Africa. One of its themes was the development of under-developed countries. I hoped then, as I do now, that the U.S.A. was concerned with the uplift of people and not with the dragooning of Africans into the Western camp for reasons of international politics; nor solely with the exploitation of material resources. I said this repeatedly to Americans with whom I discussed the matter.

I think it is still pertinent. We are subjected to intensive wooing by both East and West. But what we want now is to be ourselves, to retain our personality, and to let our soul, long buffeted by the old scramble for Africa, grow free. African leaders must be wary of the material enticement of her people. We do not live by bread alone, however alluring the sight of bread may be to the hungry.

While we were in Washington the Australian Embassy held a reception for us, and there I met the Secretary of the South African Legation. It was strange to be accosted in Zulu so far from home, and perhaps stranger to be treated as I would not be at home – certainly not nowadays – by a Government official. At his invitation I visited the South African Legation twice, where I was quite normally treated. I remember this conversation:

'How are you getting on in the U.S.A., Chief?'

'Well,' I replied, 'that's not for me to say. It's really for the people I've spoken to to judge. I find it hard to divorce church affairs from politics. The Americans ask questions, you know, and I reply honestly to the best of my knowledge. I cannot answer as though the church lived in a political void.'

'On the whole, Chief,' was the reply, 'you're doing very well.'

I wondered how they knew.

Although it was not a part of my programme, I asked to visit the south, where I was entertained at three colleges. I had little opportunity to meet ordinary country people, but during visits to country areas I was able to form some idea of the conditions under which American negroes live. I was interested to notice that in certain places farmers were not only taught how to farm but were given state financial aid, regardless of their colour – and that in the Deep South. I was interested, too, to encounter the sort of institution which would have been dear to the heart of Dr. Loram. The emphasis was all on the manual crafts. I have no scorn of these, but they do not seem to me to justify university degrees.

I think, however, that I spent more time in answering questions than in having my own curiosity satisfied. My negro friends were very eager to hear about South Africa, and their readiness to help resolved itself many times into the question, 'Can we come over there to assist you?'

'It would be heartening if you could,' I used to reply, 'but for one thing the South African Government wouldn't let you – certainly not with that motive. For another, you'd find yourselves foreigners in the continent of your origin. But we're glad of your interest in any case, and to the extent that you fight segregation here, you help indirectly. The more democratic America becomes, the better for those whom she influences. We need the interest of your churchmen too. There's a tendency for your white missionaries among us to drift away – they sometimes get identified with the whites.'

I did not meet the issue of colour at all in the north. Naturally, I lived for the most part in the homes of Christian people where one would not expect to meet it. But even in hotels and shops, people were people. In a mild way I was conscious of a colour-bar in the south.

In Atlanta I asked if, by way of relaxation, I might go with my hostess to a cinema.

'Chief Luthuli,' she said, 'you've asked a difficult thing of me. You see, our cinemas are segregated and the shows are poor in negro cinemas. But the main thing is this: I have vowed never to spend a cent of my money on upholding segregation. I will not buy segregation. I'd love to take you. I hope you understand why I can't.'

'Lady,' I replied, 'I understand you only too well.'

In one institution an exaggerated sense of race – or rather, of nationality – displayed itself rather oddly. Here I preached a sermon one Sunday morning and on the following day made a tour of the classrooms. As I came to the end of my tour, the teacher who was with me said hesitantly, 'One student here has refused to attend your lecture to this class; I'm reluctant to tell you why.'

I pressed her for the reason, and she replied, 'Yesterday in your sermon you said, "I'm glad to be amongst my people." This child has taken exception to that. She says *she*'s not of Africa.'

'It's good that she feels she belongs here,' I said, 'but I blame you for not teaching her all the facts about herself.'

It was in Washington itself that the full and utter absurdity of the colour-bar really manifested itself. Train travel to the south (and back) was segregated. This meant that negro Americans were separated from white Americans by curtains. They travelled in the same compartment, but curtains hung between them. Then in Washington the curtains were removed. The same passengers journeyed onwards in the same compartments, still breathing the same air, but now they could see as well as hear each other.

During my stay I was able to address a number of groups of Americans not connected with the churches; and then, reluctantly, I had to take my leave – reluctantly because of the many friends I had made, and because it was refreshing to enjoy normal relations with white people, and to notice that no heavens fell. I had already extended my time in the States by three months. Even so, I still had to refuse invitations to speak as far afield as Canada and the Pacific Coast.

I came back via Lisbon. Both ways, to my great regret, I failed to set foot on English soil, but on my return I did spend a day in Lisbon. 'A lovely, lovely city,' I said to myself, ' – and no wonder. Its loveliness is partly fashioned out of the toil of Africa. Africans who do not know much loveliness have helped to make it look like this.'

This was my last visit to the outside world, at least for the time being. I returned in the year when the Nationalist Government of Dr. Malan came to power. Formerly whites had discouraged travel abroad by Africans. Now it is made excessively difficult, with only rare exceptions. The argument is, of course, that 'natives who travel get spoilt.' We are said to become misfits. Contact with whites in America or Europe is supposed to go to our heads.

My journeys to India and America did not, as such things are believed to do, fill me with a new discontent, or any half-desire to escape. I was asked often enough whether I would not like to stay in the U.S.A. I had only one reply: 'No. The very challenge makes me say I have work to do at home. I like to travel. But South Africa is my home, and I hanker after nobody else's.'

It may be that travelling has made me see South African issues more sharply, and in a different and larger perspective. Even so, I have not been seized by the urge to shake my people's oppressors and bang their heads until they recognise that people are people. I would like the recognition to come to them naturally and peacefully.

But perhaps the desire in any African for normal human relations – not group relations – is itself proof that he is 'spoilt.' If that is so, I can only reply that I was not spoilt abroad. I was spoilt by being made in the image of God.

PHILIPPA DUKE SCHUYLER

1960

from *Adventures in Black and White*

Philippa Duke Schuyler (1931–1967) was the daughter of the Black journalist George S. Schuyler and the wealthy white Texan Josephine Cogdell. She revealed her talents as a pianist and composer from a very early age, but as an adult found that it was only by touring abroad that she could win the recognition she deserved. She travelled extensively, not only as a concert performer but also as a journalist, reporting on world events from the countries she visited.

In the early 1960s, her long-standing ambition to become a 'mainstream' success in the United States led her to change her name and acquire a Portuguese passport – allowing her to 'pass' as white, escape the association with a controversial father, and lose the 'child prodigy' tag. In 1966 she was invited to play for US troops in Vietnam, and alongside her concert appearances reported on the war for the right-wing Manchester Union Leader. She was killed in a helicopter crash over Da Nang.

Her books draw on her travelling experiences and include Who Killed the Congo? *(1962) and* Jungle Saints *(1963) on Africa, and* Good Men Die *(1969) set in Vietnam.* Adventures in Black and White *(1960) covers her international performing career in the 1950s, but is organized geographically rather than chronologically. 'Tours are not straight lines, but mazes,' she writes in the Introduction. 'This book is a series of snapshots of adventure, of exotic people, ideas, and scenes caught swiftly in passing.' And she explains the title as follows: 'This is how I have lived for over a decade, in sixty countries, in black and white moods, among black and white people, and with my only permanent companion, a black and white keyboard.'*

Santiago, truly lovely, has more and more striking modern buildings going up each day. The transparent jade waters of the lucid Mapocho river are overlooked by the aloof rocky slopes of Cerro San Cristobal.

Never have I seen so many crippled, blind, legless and armless people in the streets of a major city, though, as in Santiago.

Once, when I got lost returning to my hotel from the Teatro Municipal, I found myself in a strange alley among decrepit buildings.

The alley, dirt-encrusted and malodorous, was heaped with garbage, old rags, smashed barrels, broken glass, and ordure piled in the gutters.

---

*Philippa Duke Schuyler, Adventures in Black and White (New York: Robert Speller and Sons, 1960), pp. 66–8. Reprinted with the permission of the publishers.

The crumbling, stained houses leaned over unsteadily, their shadows spreading like wolves' teeth.

Soon I emerged into an irregular courtyard that centered around a cracked stone fountain at which lounged seven men.

One had a black beard, two were Indians, one a legless cripple, one had a face covered with eruptions, one had a gross belly like a swollen wine-skin.

They moved into action on my appearance, and soon relieved me of my scarf, gloves and brief-case.

Some announcements of my last concert at the Teatro Municipal were stuck between the pages of the music. Apparently the Indian could not read. Running one finger through his long straight black hair, he turned it in every direction. Then he looked at the music from every possible angle. The other Indian lighted a kerosene lamp, and the two of them stared at the music, with puzzled intensity, as though it were some kind of map. 'Qué es esto?' the Araucanian muttered.

'It's the music I use –' I explained that I was a pianist, stammering as I searched for the right words. My tongue twisted on the Spanish phrases. When they finally understood, despite my Castilian accent, that I was a musician, the fifth man, whose face was covered with crusted red sores, laughed raucously, and the Araucanian said, in a malicious voice, that I had better play something then. He pointed to a wooden case that stood on the mendicant's cart. He lifted it down to the ground. It was a small white four octave hand organ, with two pedals.

He pushed an empty wine-case toward it, for me to sit on. I pushed the pedals, and touched a key. It sounded with a flute-like tone. They all gathered around me, passing a winebottle among themselves. I began the Triana by Albeniz. It went beyond the extent of the organ's keyboard. I began a Bach Fugue. It sounded beautiful on the organ, disciplined, sad, meditative. I grew lost in its thematic architecture, and the tones soared forth. I thought of Wordsworth's lines:

> Action is transitory, – a step, a blow,
> The motion of a muscle, this way or that –
> 'Tis done, and in the after-vacancy
> We wonder at ourselves like men betrayed:
> Suffering is permanent, obscure and dark,
> And shares the nature of infinity.

Then I played a passionate Triste from La Pampa in Argentina, and a haunting, romantic song from Patagonia. They were very pleased by this. They smiled, with some appearance of humanity, and said: 'Más! Toca más! Que ella toque bien!' I played more Chilean pieces, while they winked, clapped their hands, and stamped their feet.

The Indians, as they drank from several wine bottles, grew less grim and almost friendly. I continued playing, by the flickering light the kerosene lamp shed on the yellow keys, as they sang the melodies in loud voices, evidently enjoying themselves. More Indians emerged from the shadows and began to dance.

This might have lasted forever, had not some sudden screams, followed by what seemed like bullet-shots, caused my audience to disperse in all directions.

They disappeared into the shadows so fast one might have thought they had never been there.

One of the Indians gave me back my scarf, gloves, and briefcase, and pushed me toward the edge of the court where there was a stone archway I had not seen before, in which was set a small oak door, studded with nails. He hit a bronze knocker that was on it. The door opened. He led me in, and it closed behind us. A woman with a candle in her hand was standing there. He spoke to her, in a torrent of words, and then the two led me down a long hall till we reached another door. He opened it. It let out onto a fairly busy street. He put his hand outside, pointed to the right, I went outside, and he shut the door behind me.

I walked a little way, and found a taxi which took me to my hotel.

5

Africa

'Arrival at Lagos'

Emigrationism – which sought to assist fugitive slaves and other free Blacks to settle in neighbouring countries (in the Caribbean, Central America and Canada) – was a significant current in the US anti-slavery movement. Proposals in the late 1850s to extend its scope to include Africa, however, attracted strong criticism, not least because they seemed close to the policies of the American Colonization Society, whose abolitionist credentials were suspect, to say the least. Advocates of the new schemes, such as Martin R. Delany and Henry Highland Garnet, did not propose mass emigration, but hoped to establish small settlements of carefully chosen Black Americans who would bring Christianity and technical expertise to the 'motherland' and organize the cultivation of 'free cotton' in competition with the exports of the slave South.

Robert Campbell (1829–1884) was born in Jamaica, and taught at the Institute for Colored Youth in Philadelphia. In 1859, he and Delany went to investigate the possibilities of establishing a settlement in what is now western Nigeria. His account of the trip, A Pilgrimage to My Motherland, *from which this extract is taken, is more conventionally descriptive than Delany's propagandizing* Official Report of the Niger Valley Exploring Party, *but it was Campbell and not his colleague who returned to Lagos two years later and remained there until his death, using his skills as a printer to publish a journal,* The Anglo-African. *As his Preface promised: 'After what is written in the context, if I am still asked what I think of Africa for a coloured man to live and do well in, I simply answer, that with as good prospects in America as coloured men generally, I have determined, with my wife and children, to go to Africa to live, leaving the inquirer to interpret the reply for himself.'*

On the 21st July, early in the afternoon, our ship anchored off Lagos.

Our arrival was at the most unpropitious season of the year, the bar being then worse than at any other time. We found it impossible to effect any communication except by signals. The next day some natives were persuaded to come off from the beach, the bar being still bad; they carried off the mails secured in a cask, and I, leaving my packages in charge of a man who accompanied me from Manchester,

Robert Campbell, *A Pilgrimage to My Motherland; or, Reminiscences of a Sojourn Among the Egbas and Yorubas of Central Africa, in 1859–60* (London: William John Johnson, 1861), pp. 17–23.

ventured to go on shore in their boat, which, however, I would not have done had I been aware of the great risk I incurred.

Could one but have divested himself of the sense of danger, the scene was magnificent – the huge 'swells' chasing each other, and our little barque now riding victoriously on the crest of one, then engulphed in a deep chasm between two others, rising high on both sides. It is perhaps impossible for men to evince more dexterity than these natives in the control of their canoes, especially on approaching the beach. There were twelve men paddling with two others, one steering and the other in the prow, watching the approaching surges, and directing accordingly. When near the beach the last, with much ceremony, pours a few drops of rum on the water, and a great deal more down his throat, after which he very vehemently harangues, first, I suppose the demon of the water, to which the rum was offered, and then his crew, cheering them for their work. There was another native on the beach, who gave directions of some sort to the steersman, by strange gesticulations. His appearance, as he stood above a group of companions, himself mounted on an inverted surf-boat, with his loose garments waving in the air, presented a subject which would have delighted an artist, and was indeed wildly picturesque. It is necessary to watch carefully the regular successive rise and fall of the waves, in order to prevent them breaking over the boat. Within a few yards of the beach they stop, 'backing water,' and watching intently their leader; then at a signal from him, they dash forward vigorously on the top of a wave. As soon as the canoe touches, simultaneously they are in the water, and seizing their frail craft, in an instant bear her high and dry on the beach.

The bar of Lagos is dangerous, chiefly on account of the large number of sharks which are always ready to make a repast on the bodies of the unfortunate occupants of any boat capsizing there.

The difficulties of the bar are not, however, insuperable; small vessels can always easily sail over it into the fine bay within, where they can load or unload with little trouble and without risk. But it is not so easy to go out again, as then it would be necessary to 'beat' against the wind; but a small steamboat could at once take them out in tow with perfect safety. I was informed that slavers used always to enter the bay; they could, of course, afford to wait for a favourable wind with which to get out. On landing I was kindly received by a Mr. Turner, a recaptured slave, educated at Sierra Leone by the British, and now a respectable merchant at Lagos.

After partaking of some refreshments, provided by my hospitable friend, I was conducted to the house of Lieut. Lodder, R.N., the acting Consul, to whom I brought a letter from Lord Malmesbury, Minster for Foreign Affairs in the late Administration. My reception was cordial, and I was afforded convenient accommodation at the consulate all the time I continued at Lagos.

A disgusting spectacle presented itself at the entrance of the river: on the right margin stood two bodies, transfixed by poles passing through their mouths. They were nearly dry, and strange to say, were not disturbed by buzzards, although a great number of these birds – fortunately very abundant in Africa – were flying about them. They were two of five men who were executed for robbery. One of them was the son of a chief, and his connexion with the party gave rise to a great 'palaver,' his friends contending that in consequence of his birth, he should not suffer a malefactor's death; while others contended that his crime had degraded him to the position of other men, like whom, he should answer for his offenses.

Lagos is a small island about six miles in circumference, located on the West Coast of Africa, in the Bight of Benin, Gulf of Guinea, lat. 6 deg. 26 min. N., long. 3 deg. 26 min. E. Like Bathurst, on the Gambia, it is very low, and formed by an accumulation of sand, in some places lower than the surface of the river; it is very swampy, from the infiltration of water. Like many localities on the coast of tropical countries, it is unhealthy. The prevailing disease is fever, with chills; with common prudence, however, there is nothing to fear in this disease; but if the person suffering from it will blindly persist in the use of alcoholic stimulants, the consequence might be serious. I am sorry to say that Europeans and others generally indulge far too freely in these beverages. In too many instances, I believe, the climate is blamed for the evils thus created. After passing through what is called the acclimating process – which lasts during twelve or fifteen months – one is seldom troubled again with fever.

The population of Lagos is estimated at about thirty thousand; there are about fifteen hundred emigrants from Sierra Leone, the Brazils, and Cuba; all these are themselves native Africans, brought from the interior and sold on different parts of the coast. Those from Sierra Leone are recaptured, and the others redeemed slaves. Few are more than half civilised. The white inhabitants – including English, Germans, French, Italians and Portuguese – are about twenty-five. A few very fine houses have been erected near the water-side, and others were being built at the time of our departure. They use, as money, small shells (*Cypria Moneta*), called cowries by the English, *owu* by the natives, this being also the general term for money. The value of the dollar and its fractions, as well as English currency, is well understood and appreciated; it is fast getting to be the same at Abbeokuta.

The present King of Lagos is called Docemo. He was placed in the position by the late Consul Campbell, after his brother Kosoko was deposed for warring against the English, and for his participation in the slave-trade. Kosoko has still a few adherents, particularly among the European inhabitants favourable to the slave-trade; only the guns of H.M. gun-boat 'Brune,' lying always in the river, preserves the present King his position. Kosoko lives not far from Lagos; he is said to be cruel and tyrannical, and still claims to be the legitimate king of the place.

On the morning of the 1st of August I made a visit to his Majesty King Docemo. Lieut. Lodder, R.N., the acting Consul, sent a messenger to his Majesty, informing him of the intended visit, and asking his permission, which being obtained, a party – consisting of the Commander of the 'Brune,' the Paymaster of H.M. steamship 'Medusa,' the acting Consul and myself – proceeded. We were received in the reception-room, and some chairs, intended solely for such occasions (for neither the King nor the members of his household sit on chairs), were offered us. After waiting a few minutes his Majesty, tastefully arrayed in a cloth of plaid velvet, and gold embroidered slippers, presented himself, and was introduced to his visitors respectively. The interview lasted about an hour. I told him briefly, through the interpreter, our object in visiting Africa, which seemed to give him much pleasure; so far as his dominions extended, he said, immigrants might select land suitable to their purpose, and he would gladly give it. I thanked him for his offer, and then spoke for a few moments of the great results which must flow from the development of a country like his, so blessed with resources. In reference to an American who came with me from Manchester, he inquired whether he understood using oxen for agricultural purposes; when answered in the affirmative, he seemed rather incredulous. The other gentlemen had also business to transact with the King, which rendered our conversation rather brief.

When I had been a few days at Lagos, Mr. Williams, a somewhat intelligent native – interpreter to the Consul – invited me to see his farm on the mainland, a few miles across the river. Accompanied by two other persons, we left early in the morning, before breakfast, expecting to return in two hours at most. Reaching the land, it was still necessary to journey a few miles to the farm. Though yet early, it was warm, and the walk tiresome, so that I was obliged to rest myself on a stump, while my companions proceeded to a little distance to plant some seeds. Seeing a bird which I wanted to preserve alight a few yards off, I tried to come within shot of it; before able to do so, it pursued its flight. I followed and eventually shot it; but in attempting to return, I unfortunately took a direction leading away from my first position. I wandered about for more than an hour, shouting all the time at the top of my voice to attract attention; for my ammunition being in the possession of my companions, I could not fire my gun for that purpose. I soon found myself in an almost impenetrable jungle, the shrubbery and vine so thickly interlacing, that it was with the greatest difficulty I could break through; the ground, too, was swampy, and I sometimes sunk nearly to my knees. By this time my friends were as busy seeking me. I never felt more joyful than when I heard their voice in response to my own. From hunger, fatigue, heat of the sun, and excitement, I returned home, about 2 P.M., with severe headache and fever. The next day I was worse, and continued ill for several days. The reader has here my first initiation into the African fever, and I might add that not a few may trace their first attack to similar imprudence.

In such a climate a stranger should never leave his home before breakfast, nor undertake very vigorous exercise before he has passed the ordeal of acclimature.

1887

A Month in Egypt

After returning from Britain to the United States in 1847, Frederick Douglass settled in Rochester, New York, and consolidated his position as one of the leading anti-slavery campaigners, founding his own newspaper, The North Star *(later renamed* Frederick Douglass' Paper*). During the Civil War, he recruited young men for the Union Army, and in later years held a number of government posts, including that of Minister to Haiti (1889–91).*

In 1884 he married his second wife, Helen Pitts, and in September 1886 they travelled to Europe. Their tour took in England, France and Italy, where they decided to extend their itinerary to include Egypt and Greece. During their trip, they each kept journals, which remain unpublished. This extract from Douglass's diary covers the Egyptian leg of their journey.

[Text in square brackets has been added to aid comprehension; punctuation has been silently edited to the same end; but no attempt has been made to correct or standardize Douglass's spelling, which is inconsistent.]

Febry 13. On board the steam ship *Ornioz* bound for Egypt. This morning at eight o'clock Helen called me to the Bullseye to catch my first view of Stromboli, a volcanic mountain, conical shaped, [rising] abruptly from the sea. There were white clouds about its base, but the morning light rested upon its summit – and made it beautiful. Soon after this there loomed in the distance the mountainous shores of Sicily and those of Southern Italy. Messina on the one hand and Corigio on the other and the Straits between them in front of us. It was a deeply interesting spectacle and the morning was well fitted to heighten the effect. I could but congratulate myself that born as I was a slave marked for a life under the lash in the cornfield that [I] was abroad and free and privileged to see these distant lands so full of historical interest and which those of the most highly favored by fortune are permitted to visit. I find myself much at ease on this steamer. I am known to passengers and officers and all alike seem to wish to make my voyage pleasant to me. It is now blowing pretty hard and our good ship is tumbling about on the sea in a manner which makes it hard to write. We did not get a glimpse as we hoped in passing Sicily, of far famed Etna. We were told that it was hidden by the clouds. We hope for better luck on our return.

Monday 14 Febry. If right in my estimate of the length of time I have been in the world, I am now 70 years old. Aside from a cold and a little hint of sea sickness,

---

*Frederick Douglass, Diary, 1886–7, Frederick Douglass Collection, Library of Congress.

I am quite well strong and cheerful. This is a trying day for Helen and many other ladies on board. The wind is strong and the waves very high. Few seem ready for dinner. My colic is better than most for I am able to go at the sound of the Bell. I am a little surprised at the wild behavior of the Mediterranean. I expected better things of her. To night I saw the light on the Island of Crete. I suppose there was no light there when Paul sailed along its coast. It is strange that starting life where I did and old as I am that I shd be plowing this Classic Sea and on my way to the land of Moses and the Pharoahs – where Joseph and his brothers went for corn and Jos. was treacherously sold by his brothers into slavery.

Tuesday 15 Febry. The wind has fallen and the sea has gone down. Helen is well on her feet again. We hope to be in Port Said tomorrow morning. Our morning which began bright is now over cast with heavy clouds and the Barometer is going down. Many are writing home this morning to be mailed I suppose at Port Said – as most of our passengers are bound to Australia. Notwithstanding English reserve, I am not at a loss for all the company I want. I answer reserve with reserve and approaches with approach. My friends are one of the ship owners Mr Anderson and Mr J. C. and Mrs Murry – real hearty and sensible people. Miss Borden from Fall river is on board and is going up the Nile. She is a great traveller and is very agreeable. Five months ago this morning on the deck of the *City of Rome* Helen and I bid fare well to the Shores of America, not with expectation of finding our way to Egypt and I dare not now say how much farther South and East we shall go before we turn our faces homeward – such is life!

Wednesday Febry 16 1887. Arrived at Port Said: the queerest of queer places. The entrance to the Suez Canal. All nations are here represented – a place to study Ethnology. Our ship is just now coming to the wharf. Forty or fifty service boats have already surrounded the ship and their inmates are clamouring like wild fowl of every possible note to the passengers to buy their oranges, lemons, figs and other fruit. Soon several dhows loaded with coal to the waters edge to coal our ship for her further voyage. They are soon boarded by a perfect swarm of Arab laborers, frocked, hooded, or fezed, barefooted and barelegged to the knees, to bring, in baskets on their heads, the coal on ship board. Heavens! what a wild clamour – what a confusion of tongues, all going at once and each endeavouring to drown the voice of the other, but the work goes bravely on, and one is astonished at the strength, cheerfulness and endurance of these sable children of the desert. I saw among them several genuine Negroes and they seemed not a whit behind their fellow workmen either in noise or physical ability. When our coal was in, we moved on silently down the canal towards Ismalia. But through what a barren and desolate land do we thread our way? Not a blade of grass, not a tree, not a single dwelling. No sign of human or animal life, except a distant row of Pelicans looking on the plain like a line of foam on the Shore of a sea. On, on we go slowly and noiselessly, on a narrow stream of pure blue water, cut through the wide waste of sand whose limits lie far beyond the range of vision. Night comes and we anchor till morning since we are not permitted for reasons of safety to proceed in darkness. The stillness of the day is continued in the night and much more impressive by the darkness that has fallen upon the desert. Morning came warm and bright and we proceeded on our way. Our steamer is followed for miles by a little boy screaming for *Bachiude*. No sign is given as to where he came from or where he will go. He looks as if he had risen out of the Sand. The passengers through him bread and oranges. He pockets them in his scanty clothing and runs on as if nothing had been given him. The amazing thing was that he never was satisfied with his gains nor tired of his running.

Thursday Febry 17. Ismalia. We reached this place about 12 miday. Too late for the train to Cairo – and must remain here till tomorrow. We were taken ashore from the *Ornioz* by a small steamer and have taken lodging for the night at the Hotel Des Basins de Mer, a small bed but good food at three dollars per day. I hardly think we can see in any part of Egypt any thing more Egyptian in the manners, customs and appearance of the people than we see here. We saw to day a caravan of camels bearing their burden over the sand. It vindicated the truth of many pictures of this side of Eastern life. We saw several veiled women bearing jars of water on their heads just as women probably did in the days of Abraham. The market house here is quite worth seeing, even though we shall see larger ones of the same kind when we shall reach Cairo. Ismalia is a new town sprung up on the prospect open[ed] by the Suez Canal. The conditions for growth is not favorable. I saw a Greek patriarch walking [in] a flowing robe here to day wearing a peculiar cap. I find it hard to look with patience upon people who thus parade their religion in their clothes and who evidently wish to exact homage on account of such pretentions.

Friday 18 Febry. We quitted Ismalia to day at 12 o'clk for Cairo and a six hour ride brought [us] to our destination. This ride will not soon be forgotten. It was through the Bible famous land of Goshen. For the most part a land of unequalled fertility of outspread fields of green vegetation and of flourishing and picturesque palms. Here we saw the same kind of plow used two thousand years ago, for the people here, like the laws of the Medes and Persians, change not. Everything we see reminds [us] of the days of Moses. I do not know what color and features the ancient Egyptians were but the great mass of the people I have yet seen would in America be classed with mulattos and Negroes. This would not be a scientific description but an American description. I can easily see why the Mahometan religion commends itself to these people for it does not make color the criterion of fellowship as some of our so called Christian nations do. All colors are welcomed to the faith of the Prophet. I am stopping at the New Hotel, so called. Pretentious on the outside, expensive, but not well kept. I got my first glimpse of a pyramid to day as we approached Cairo by the train. It was a little disappointing, but I will wait for a nearer view. On our arrival in Cairo we were met in the street by a grand Holiday procession – Friday is the Mahometan Sunday – which block[ed] the street so completely that we were unable to go on for nearly the half of one hour. Our patience however was rewarded by seeing the Khedive – and having from him a gracious bow – and what is better to see the struggling, jostling, noisy and eager mass of his turbaned subjects pushing there way between carts, carriages, donkeys and carriages at risk of life and limb. We could not have a better chance of seeing an Egyptian crowd. Though noisy and without form, utter chaotic, it was good natured – each one took the push of his neighbor without offense. The officer that endeavored to clear the way for the Khedive used a whip instead of sword or Bayonet. The sound of the whip upon some of the long skirts was sharp and loud, but no body was hurt.

Saturday Febry 19. Called upon Mr Cardwell the American Consul General. Was very courteously received by him. Visited two Mosques. We were not allowed to enter without putting [on] sandals so that infidel shoes shd not touch their sacred courts. We saw several washing their feet and afterward kneeling and kissing or touching the floor with their forehead. In one respect these Mosques are to be commended. They have no images or pictures of Saints or God, make no effort to personify Deity.

Visited the tombs of the Mamelukes and on our way saw various forms of squalor, disease and deformity – all manner of importunate beggary. It was truly pitiful to see a people thus grovelling in filth and utter wretchedness. We also visited the Bazars, where all manner of fabrics are manufactured and sold. Here men were smoking their long pipes drawing the smoke through water and selling or rather offering their wares for sale. The most painful feature met with in the streets are the hooded and veiled women. It is sad to think of that one half of the human family should be thus cramped, kept in ignorance and degraded, having no existence except that of minister[ing] to the pride and lusts of the men who *own* them as slaves are owned, and worst is they seem to like to have it so.

Sunday Febry 20. Attended and spoke a few words to the Sunday school of the U. P. Church mission. It was good to see in Egypt about two hundred of these people assembled to receive instruction from Mr and Mrs Harvey, both Americans. Egypt, that gave knowledge to western Europe two thousand years ago was now sitting at the feet of the West and receiving instruction from a part of the Western world then unknown! From the heights of her citadel we see the Libyan hills and the Cheop[s] Pyramids. The view is very inspiring.

Monday Febry 21. Went to the house of Dr Graich. Saw his museum of Egyptian curiosities. Called on the daughters of Arch Bishop Whately who have been here twenty five years teaching school. Excellent women doing excellent work.

Tuesday 22d. In company with Mr and Mrs Shankland went to the Gizeh and climbed to the top of *Cheops*, the highest Pyramid in the Valley of the Nile. Its height is four hundred and seventy feet. The ascent is both difficult and dangerous and I would not undertake it again for any consideration.

Wednesday Febry 23. Called with Miss Cousier on several Egyptian families in the morning and in the afternoon went to Heliopolis and saw the famous Ostrich Farm and the beautiful obilisque of red granite, the only visible remains of the once great city of *On*.

Thursday 24. Went the Museum in Cairo. The largest and best assemblage of Egyptian antiquities now extant. The Room of the Mummies is startling when we think we are looking at people who lived and moved in this Valley, three thousand years ago. In the evening we took supper with Mr and Mrs Harvey, missionaries, afterward prayer meeeting.

Friday 25 Febry. Wrote during the forenoon. Sent one letter to Mrs Crofts and one to Rosetta. In the afternoon went to see the Howling Dervishers at worship, the Coptic Church and the Jewish synagogue – and then took a ride on the Shubra Road. There was much to remind [me] in the worship of the Howling Dervishers of the colored Methodist camp meetings in the South. There were many spectators present and the worshippers got a good bit of money by their queer performance, which by the [bye] did not seem insincere. They evidently thought their worship was pleasing to their God. One man spun around like a top forty or fifty times without stopping. I thought he would certainly fall to the floor but he did not, but, after resting a few minutes proceeded with his whirling till the close of the meeting. Another man worked himself up to a perfect frenzy, jumping up and down and at last fell to the floor rigid as one dead. During all the worship their beating on large tambourines, blowing on a reed instrument, a kind of chant and momentary interjections of recitations from the Koran. The whole performance was sad to behold. Sad to think that rational being[s] could be made to believe that such physical contortions could be pleasing to God or secure his favour. Yet how much better is the form of worship adopted by many other denominations. And is it not strange that man should imagine to secure Divine favor by telling God how good & great he is – and how much they love and adore him. God is glorified not by such worship but by a spirit of obedience to the laws of our being as established by the Almighty and written in the very constitution of things. Burnt offerings, incantations and muscular action silence [illegible word] and degrade manhood.

Saturday Febry 26. Went this morning to Mohameden College where twelve thousand pupils studying the Coran and preparing to teach its doctrines to the benighted sons of men. I saw about two thousand of them in the court and college building reading their morning lesson. They wore the peculiar dress and turban of the Mahomedan and presented a striking spectacle. If sincerity is any proof of the truth of their creed they certainly give that proof – but alas! sincerity is no proof. The most revolting imposture has been defended by equal earnestness and sincerity. The followers of the Prophet can pray as loudly and preach to as many miracles as the Christian can – they even exceed the Christian in religious attention to ceremony. We also went to see the Mohammedan *Bible* house, where you may see the Coran in all languages. It is a great sight. Two hundred millions of people are said to receive this Sacred Book, the Coran.

Sunday Febry 27. Attended a Presbyterian service conducted in Arabic in the morning. Did some promenading in the afternoon. Wrote to Charley and went to see a great tree called the Banian Tree. The peculiarity of this tree is that its branches extend to the ground, take root and spread indefinitely.

Monday 28 Febry. We rode away over a delightful road on donkeys [to] the Ghezireh Palace and Gardens and Grotto. It well repaid the trouble, though for my part the ride on Donkeys among multitudes of people in Oriental costume and crowds of Camels and Donkeys making a striking [tableau] of Egyptian life was more interesting than Palace, Garden or Grotto.

Tuesday March 1st 1887. This has been one of the most interesting days we have spent in Egypt. This morning we set out at half past seven on a journey of sixteen miles. Three to the Railway Station for Bedrashen and thence six miles on the backs of Donkeys to the site of ancient Memphis and the Necropolis of Sakkara. The Donkey ride was a hard one but the results were very satisfactory. We first came to the site of Memphis and there we saw a piece of sculpture which [I] suppose has no equal in the world: a statue of Rameses forty two feet in height and here [and] there fragments of broken architecture and sculpture. But the chief place of interest was several miles away. It was the Necropolis of Sakkara with its pyramids and tombs. The tombs are truly architectural wonders.

Wednesday 2d March. Went to witness parade & sham battle by British troops stationed in Cairo. The people of Cairo were not attracted to see the fine show. They are evidently not over pleased with the presence and power of British soldiers, though in truth, they are probably much better off with them than they would be without them.

Thursday 3d March. Went to look at [a] Dahabiyeh in company with Miss Agg. and Miss Richardson. We are to go with them in it on an eight days trip up the Nile. In the afternoon walked with Helen through Bazar.

March 11th. Have just returned from a five days trip up the Nile as far as Beni Hassan. While there were few points of special interest reached during the trip, the excursion upon the whole owing to the general character and history of the country, the peculiar character of the people met with along the shores of the great river, the strange appearance of the towns, the varied scenes presented by the barren and desolate land, mountains assuming all sorts of shapes sometimes resembling vast fortifications and at others reminding us of enormous animals, was one of the [most] interesting and delightful made during my tour abroad. It is not strange that people of Egypt almost deify the Nile – without it there country would become a barren waste. The Nile feeds, clothes and shelters them, from it they get water to drink, water to bath, to wash their cloths, from it they get their fish, the mud to build their houses & the fertilizer to repair the waste of the soil in production. It is to them the source of life and whatever of health and prosperity for which its people have to be thankful. It is [a] great highway over which their products find their way to market – and its bosom night and day is covered with curiously rigged vessels with wing-shaped sails going to and from Cairo. Our trip was made upon a Dahhabeyez, christened by Miss Richardson and Miss Agg. as the *Meni*.

14th March Monday. Arrived at Alexandria. Hotel Bonnard. Tuesday 15th March. Called upon Mr Ewing, missionary; also upon Judge J. B. [illegible word] took a pleasant ride with him in company with Judge Brinkhouse. Afternoon lunched with [illegible word], saw Pompey's Pillar and the site of the Alexandrian Library.

Wednesday March 16. Took passage on board the Egyptian steamer, *Sarchie* for Athens. The weather beautiful, the passengers pleasant and we hope for a prosperous voyage. The thought of soon treading the classic shores of Greece is very exhilarating.

W. E. B. Du Bois

1924

'Africa'

Liberia in West Africa has loomed large in the history of the United States since the American Colonization Society began assisting freed slaves to resettle there in the 1820s. The various settlements combined to form an independent Republic in 1847 which was home to several leading Pan-Africanist intellectuals of the nineteenth century, including Alexander Crummell and Edmund Wilmot Blyden. In the 1920s Marcus Garvey's 'back to Africa' schemes fell foul of the Liberian Government, but his arch-rival, W. E. B. Du Bois, received a warm welcome as special envoy of US President Coolidge in 1923 as this account of his visit, first published in The Crisis, *shows.*

The account subsequently appeared in The Dusk of Dawn (1940), *where, following an examination of his family history, Du Bois admits that 'with Africa I had only one direct cultural connection and that was the African melody which my great-grandmother Violet used to sing'. He is thus led to ask the question posed by the poet Countee Cullen, 'What is Africa to me?'*

I have just come back from a journey in the world of nearly five months. I have travelled 15,000 miles. I set foot on three continents. I have visited five countries, four African islands and five African colonies. I have sailed under five flags. I have seen a black president inaugurated. I have walked in the African big bush and heard the night cry of leopards. I have traded in African markets, talked with African chiefs and been the guest of white governors. I have seen the Alhambra and the great mosque at Cordova and lunched with H. G. Wells; and I am full, very full with things that must be said.

December 16, 1923
Today I sailed from Tenerife for Africa. The night was done in broad black masses across the blue and the sun burned a great livid coal in the sky. Above rose the Peak of Tenerife, round like a woman's breast, pale with snow patches, immovable, grand.

On the boat – the *Henner* from Bremen – I am in Germany and opposite is a young man who fought four and a half years in the German army on all fronts – bitter, bitter. War is not done yet, he says. He's going to Angola.

W. E. B. Du Bois, 'Africa', *The Crisis*, 17 (6) (April 1924), pp. 247–51. Cassell wishes to thank The Crisis Publishing Co., publishers of *The Crisis*, the magazine of the National Association for the Advancement of Colored People, for authorizing the use of this work.

We are six Germans in this little floating Germany: a captain, fifty or fifty-five, world roamer – San Francisco, Klondike, all Africa, gemütlich, jovial; a bull-headed, red necked first officer, stupid, good, funny; a doctor, well bred, kindly; a soldier and business man, bitter, keen, hopeful; others dumber and more uncertain. We drink Bremer beer, smoke, tell tales and the cabin rings.

December 17
On the sea – slipping lazily south, in cloud and sun and languorous air. The food is good and German. The beer is such as I have not tasted for a quarter century – golden as wine, light with almost no feel of alcohol. And I sense rather than hear a broken, beaten, but unconquered land, a spirit bruised, burned, but immortal. There is defense eager, but not apology; there is always the pointing out of the sin of all Europe.

My cabin is a dream. It is white and clean, with windows – not portholes – and pretty curtains at berth, door and window; electric light.

December 19
The languorous days are creeping lazily away. We have passed Cape Bojador of historic memory; we have passed the Tropic of Cancer, we are in the Tropics! There is a moon and by day an almost cloudless sky. I rise at eight and breakfast at eight thirty. Then I write and read until lunch at 12:30. About 1:30 I take a nap and coffee at four. Then read until 6:30 and supper. We linger at the table until nearly 9. Then reading, walking and bed by 10.

December 20
It is Thursday. Day after tomorrow I shall put my feet on the soil of Africa. As yet I have seen no land, but last night I wired to Monrovia by way of Dakar – 'President King – Monrovia – Arrive Saturday, *Henner* – Du Bois.' I wonder what it all will be like? Meantime it's getting hot – *hot*, and I've put on all the summer things I've got.

December 20
Tonight the sun, a dull gold ball, strange shaped and rayless sank before a purple sky into a bright green and sinking turned the sky to violet blue and grey and the sea turned dark. But the sun itself blushed from gold to shadowed burning crimson, then to red. The sky above, blue-green; the waters blackened and then the sun did not set – it died and was not. And behind gleamed the pale silver of the moon across the pink effulgence of the clouds.

December 21
Tomorrow – Africa! Inconceivable! As yet no sight of land, but it was warm and we rigged deck chairs and lay at ease. I have been reading that old novel of mine – it has points. Twice we've wired Liberia. I'm all impatience.

December 22

Waiting for the first gleam of Africa. This morning I photographed the officers and wrote an article on Germany. Then I packed my trunk and big bag. The step for descending to the boat had been made ready. Now I read and write and the little boat runs sedately on.

3:22 p. m. – I see Africa – Cape Mount in two low, pale semi-circles, so pale it looks a cloud. So my great great grandfather saw it two centuries ago. Clearer and clearer it rises and now land in a long low line runs to the right and melts dimly into the mist and sea and Cape Mount begins Liberia – what a citadel for the capital of Negrodom!

When shall I forget the night I first set foot on African soil – I, the sixth generation in descent from my stolen forefathers. The moon was at the full and the waters of the Atlantic lay like a lake. All the long slow afternoon as the sun robed itself in its western scarlet with veils of misty cloud, I had seen Africa afar. Cape Mount – that mighty headland with its twin curves, northern sentinel of the vast realm of Liberia gathered itself out of the cloud at half past three and then darkened and grew clear. On beyond flowed the dark low undulating land quaint with palm and breaking sea. The world darkened. Africa faded away, the stars stood forth curiously twisted – Orion in the zenith – the Little Bear asleep and the Southern Cross rising behind the horizon. Then afar, ahead, a lone light, straight at the ship's fore. Twinkling lights appeared below, around and rising shadows. 'Monrovia' said the Captain. Suddenly we swerved to our left. The long arms of the bay enveloped us and then to the right rose the twinkling hill of Monrovia, with its crowning star. Lights flashed on the shore – here, there. Then we sensed a darker shadow in the shadows; it lay very still. 'It's a boat,' one said. 'It's two boats.' Then the shadow drifted in pieces and as the anchor roared into the deep five boats outlined themselves on the waters – great ten-oared barges black with men swung into line and glided toward us. I watched them fascinated.

Nine at Night

It was nine at night – above, the shadows, there the town, here the sweeping boats. One forged ahead with the stripes and lone star flaming behind, the ensign of the customs floating wide and bending to the long oars, the white caps of ten black sailors. Up the stairway clambered a soldier in khaki, aide-de-camp of the President of the Republic, a custom house official, the clerk of the American legation – and after them sixty-five lithe, lean black stevedores with whom the steamer would work down to Portuguese Angola and back. A few moments of formalities, greetings and goodbyes and I was in the great long boat with the President's Aide – a brown major in brown khaki. On the other side the young clerk and at the back the black, bare-legged pilot. Before us on the high thwarts were the rowers: men, boys, black, thin, trained in muscle and sinew, little larger than the oars in thickness, they bent their strength to them and swung upon them.

One in the centre gave curious little cackling cries to keep the rhythm, and for the spurts, the stroke, a bit thicker and sturdier gave a low guttural command now and then and the boat, alive, quivering, danced beneath the moon, swept a great curve to the bar to breast its narrow teeth of 't'chick-a-tickity, t'chik-a-tickity' sang the boys and we glided and raced, now between boats, now near the landing – now oars aloft at the dock. And lo! I was in Africa!

December 25
Christmas eve and Africa is singing in Monrovia. They are Krus and Fanti – men, women and children and all the night they march and sing. The music was once the music of revival hymns. But it is that music now transformed and the silly words hidden in an unknown tongue – liquid and sonorous. It is tricked and expounded with cadence and turn. And this is that same trick I heard first in Tennessee 38 years ago: The air is raised and carried by men's strong voices, while floating above in obligato, come the high mellow voices of women – it is the ancient African art of part singing so curiously and insistently different.

And so they come, gay apparelled, lit by a transparency. They enter the gate and flow over the high steps and sing and sing and sing. They saunter round the house, pick flowers, drink water and sing and sing and sing. The warm dark heat of the night steams up to meet the moon. And the night is song.

Christmas day, 1923. We walk down to the narrow, crooked wharves of Monrovia, by houses old and grey and steps like streets of stone. Before is the wide St. Paul river, double mouthed, and beyond, the sea, white, curling on the sand. Before is the isle – the tiny isle, hut-covered and guarded by a cotton tree, where the pioneers lived in 1821. We circle round – then up the river.

Great bowing trees, festoons of flowers, golden blossoms, star-faced palms and thatched huts; tall spreading trees lifting themselves like vast umbrellas, low shrubbery with grey and laced and knotted roots – the broad, black, murmuring river. Here a tree holds wide fingers out and stretches them over the water in vast incantation; bananas throw their wide green fingers to the sun. Iron villages, scarred clearings with grey, sheet-iron homes staring grim and bare at the ancient tropical flood of green.

The river sweeps wide and the shrubs bow low. Behind, Monrovia rises in clear, calm beauty. Gone are the wharves, the low and clustered houses of the port, the tight-throated business village, and up sweep the villas and the low wall, brown and cream and white, with great mango and cotton tree, with light house and spire, with porch and pillar and the green and color of shrubbery and blossom.

We climbed the upright shore to a senator's home and received his wide and kindly hospitality – curious blend of feudal lord and modern farmer – sandwiches, cake and champagne.

Again we glided up the drowsy river – five, ten, twenty miles and came to our hostess. A mansion of five generations with a compound of endless native servants and cows under the palm thatches. The daughters of the family wore, on the beautiful black skin of their necks, the exquisite pale gold chains of the Liberian artisan and the slim, black little granddaughter of the house had a wide pink ribbon on the thick curls of her dark hair, that lay like sudden sunlight on the shadows. Double porches one above the other, welcomed us to ease. A native man, gay with Christmas and a dash of gin, danced and sang and danced in the road. Children ran and played in the blazing sun. We sat at a long broad table and ate duck, chicken, beef, rice, plantain and collards, cake, tea, water and Madeira wine. Then we went and looked at the heavens, the up-twisted sky – Orion and Cassiopeia at zenith; the Little Bear beneath the horizon, new unfamiliar sights in the Milky Way – all awry, a-living – sun for snow at Christmas, and happiness and cheer.

January 1, 1924

As I look back and recall the days, which I have called great – the occasions in which I have taken part and which have had for me and others the widest significance, I can remember none like the first day of January, 1924. Once I took my bachelor's degree before a governor, a distinguished college president and others. But that was rather personal in its memory than in any way epochal. Once before the assembled races of the world I was called to speak in place of the suddenly sick Sir Harry Johnston. It was a great hour. But it was not greater than the day when I was presented to the President of the Negro Republic of Liberia.

Liberia had been resting under the shock of war. She had asked and been promised a large loan by the United States. She had conformed to every preliminary requirement and waited when waiting was almost fatal. It was not simply money, it was world prestige and high protection at a time when the little republic was sorely beset by creditors and greedy imperial powers. At the last moment, an insurgent Senate preemptorily and finally refused the request and strong recommendation of the President and his advisors and the loan was refused. The Department of State made no statement to the world and Liberia stood naked, not only well-nigh bankrupt but peculiarly defenseless amid scowling and unbelieving Powers.

It was then that the United States made a gesture of courtesy; a little thing, merely a gesture, but one so fine and so unusual that it was epochal. It sent an American Negro to Liberia. It designated him Envoy Extraordinary and Minister Plenipotentiary – the highest rank ever given by any country to a diplomatic agent in black Africa. And it named this Envoy the special representative of the President of the United States to the President of Liberia on the occasion of his inauguration, charging the envoy with a personal word of encouragement and moral support.

It was a great and significant action. It had in it nothing personal. Another appointee would have been equally significant. Liberia recognized the meaning. She showered upon the Envoy every mark of appreciation and thanks. The Commander of the Liberian Frontier Force was made his special Aide and a sergeant, his orderly. At 10 A.M. New Years morning a company of the Frontier Force, in red fez and khaki presented arms before the American Legation and escorted Solomon Porter Hood, the American Minister Resident, and myself as Envoy Extraordinary and my Aide to the Presidential Mansion – a beautiful white verandahed house waving with palms and fronting a grassy street.

Ceremonials are old and to some antiquated and yet this was done with such simplicity, grace and seriousness that none could escape its spell. The Secretary of State met us at the door, as the band played the wonderful Liberian National hymn and the soldiers saluted. He took us up a broad stairway and into a great room that stretched across the house. Here in semi-circle were ranged the foreign consuls and the cabinet – the former in white and gilt with orders and swords; the latter in solemn black. Here were England, France, Germany, Spain, Belgium, Holland and Panama to be presented to me in order of seniority by the small brown Secretary of State with his perfect poise and ease.

The President entered – frock-coated with the star of a European order on his breast. The American Minister introduced the Envoy and the Envoy said:

YOUR EXCELLENCY:

The President of the United States has done me the great honor of designating me as his personal representative on the occasion of your inauguration. In so doing, he has had, I am sure, two things in mind. First, he wished publicly and unmistakably to express before the world the interest and solicitude which the hundred million inhabitants of the United States of America have for Liberia. Liberia is a child of the United States, and a sister Republic. Its progress and success is the progress and success of democracy everywhere and for all men; and the United States would view with sorrow and alarm any misfortune that might happen to this Republic and any obstacle that was placed in her path.

But special and peculiar bonds draw these two lands together. In America live eleven million persons of African descent, they are citizens, legally invested with every right that inheres in American citizenship. And I am sure that in this special mark of the President's favor, he has had in mind the wishes and hopes of Negro Americans. He knows how proud they are of the hundred years of independence which you have maintained by force of arms and by brawn and brain upon the edge of this mighty continent; he knows that in the great battle against color caste in America, the ability of Negroes to rule in Africa has been and ever will be a great and encouraging reinforcement. He knows that the unswerving loyalty of Negro Americans to their country is fitly accompanied by a pride in their race and lineage, a belief in the potency and promise of Negro blood which makes them eager listeners to every whisper of success from Liberia and eager helpers in every movement for your aid and comfort. The uplift and redemption of all Africa is in a special sense, the moral burden of Liberia and the advancement and integrity of Liberia is the sincere prayer of America.

May I, finally in thus expressing to your Excellency the good wishes of my country and its President, be permitted to add my own personal sense of the distinction put upon me in making me the humble bearer of these messages. I have now the honor, Sir, to transmit to you the personal word of Calvin Coolidge, President of the United States of America by the hand of Charles E. Hughes, Secretary of State.

GEORGE S. SCHUYLER

'Monrovia Mooches On'

*George S. Schuyler (1895–1977) grew up in Syracuse, New York, and after
leaving school spent six years in the army, most of it in Honolulu. In the early
1920s, following a series of manual jobs, he began writing for the radical
magazine* The Messenger *and the* Pittsburgh Courier, *for which he was a
columnist and leader-writer for many years. Although best-known today for
his novel,* Black No More *(1931) – which satirized the leading figures of the
Harlem Renaissance – he also earned some notoriety as a journalist, his
increasingly anti-communist stance embarrassing even the newspaper which
employed him.*

*He travelled widely as a reporter within the United States and overseas,
and his assignments included a 600-mile trek through Liberia which he made
in 1931 to gather evidence of the state-sponsored conscription of young men to
work on the plantations of the island of Fernando Po in the Gulf of Guinea.
His second book,* Slaves Today *(1932), was based on his experiences there, as
was this 'lively and disrespectful description of Liberia's rag-tag capital' (as he
describes it in his autobiography). It appeared in 1937 in the short-lived
monthly magazine* The Globe. *Offering 'Intimate Journal-Travel-Romance-
Adventure-World Interest: Original Features from all over the world', its
contributors included Ezra Pound, William Saroyan, Paul Morand, Langston
Hughes, H. E. Bates and William Carlos Williams.*

Monrovia, Liberia, enjoys the dubious distinction of being the world's only capital
founded and maintained for a century on charity and loans. First the American
Colonization Society, then the United States government, then two loans from
London, a third from an international consortium, and the most recent from
Firestone, with a half million dollars annually from missionaries, have enabled
an oligarchy of a dozen families, their retainers and henchmen, to exist without
physical toil in an atmosphere of shabby gentility. This income is augmented by
primitive agriculture and increasingly frequent forays into the hinterland to
squeeze food, fines, and taxes from the two million aborigines. This mendicant
tradition has so taken hold that it is a virtue to borrow but a vice to repay. After
all, why should the citizens repay loans when the government has never done so?

After nine days of gossip at sea you await with great curiosity your first glimpse
of Africa's last free black city. You belly to the port rail, eagerly sniff the land odor

---

George S. Schuyler, 'Monrovia Mooches On', *The Globe* (July 1937), pp. 10–16.

from the distant expanse of green jungle, and watch occasional columns of smoke curling lazily into the blue. Forgotten are drab Liverpool, that turbulent crossing of the Bay of Biscay, and the school of leaping porpoise to starboard.

You are prepared to discount some of the tall tales you have heard when from the distant haze green-clad Cape Mesurado rises dramatically out of the surrounding bush, the snowy surf pounding the sandbars at its feet. For Monrovia surprises you with its rather pretty display of pretentious white buildings with bright red roofs peeping out from groves of giant mango and cotton trees. This seems a charming, idyllic climax to a dull voyage.

Then, misgivings! The engines stop two miles from the shore. The white steamer drifts like a swan on the pond-like sea, and the anchor roars into the deep. Through your binoculars you see a long, rakish Kru boat put off from shore and detour two miles inside the sandbar until the dozen half-naked oarsmen shoot it through a natural breach into the open sea. An American-born citizen, you hear, once offered to pay for cutting a channel directly opposite the town, but the administration spurned him. He belonged to the Opposition Party which could not be permitted to get credit for any move so unprecedently progressive.

With Liberia's lone star flag fluttering fore and aft, the revenue cutter approaches. The glistening backs of the chanting oarsmen move rhythmically as they pull close. A barefooted helmsman, with cap visor over one ear and ragged breeches flapping in the breeze, shouts commands while three uniformed and solemn Negroes sit imperturbably in the rear seat. The ladder is lowered. The officials climb aboard. Baggage is lowered amid much shouting and commotion. You make the tricky descent into the open boat, and the five-mile journey to the shore begins.

Monrovia's charm recedes the closer one approaches. Soon the enchantment lent by distance has vanished. Enroute you pass the smallpox isolation pen, a single large hut surrounded by a high wire fence. Here the afflicted are callously left to shift for themselves without adequate food or medical attention. A disturbing introduction, this, to a republic whose proud motto is 'The Love of Liberty Brought Us Here.' To which some wag has added, 'And the Lack of Money Keeps Us Here.'

Part of the shore is lined with the tumbledown shacks of Kru town, Monrovia's slum, where resides much of the 10,000 population. The city proper sprawls over the Cape with little semblance of order. It is a rash of mean dwellings and more pretentious concrete-block architectural horrors, many of them out of plumb. What you thought were red tile roofs are really rusty tin. There is almost no evidence of the great natural wealth the country is reported to possess. Monrovia is definitely down at the heels.

Against a background of ugly weather-beaten warehouses, a motley crowd gathers at the landing place. Uniformed officials, bespectacled and briefless attorneys, barefoot soldiers sporting red fezzes and wrap leggins, with rifles of 1900 vintage, ragged aborigines with scabby skins, visiting chiefs from the hinterland and swathed in striped robes and accompanied by umbrella carriers and interpreters, copper-colored girls in exotic prints revealing much of their charm, naked children playing amid ubiquitous trash, a half dozen helmeted traders and maybe two or three consular officials. The stifling atmosphere is filled with the jabber of two dozen languages and dialects.

Embellishing this picturesque scene are the half-sunken hull of a small battered steam yacht, formerly used as a revenue cutter, and a fringe of dugout canoes, and rotting scurf strewn along the beach. Clouds of red dust almost obscure the rambling capital above. Strange smells from garbage, dung, discarded cans, and rotting fish affront the nostrils. Over all a relentless midday sun presides.

Customs officials go through your baggage with the typical inquisitiveness of their kind, but you are more fortunate than many previous visitors. An explorer from the American Museum of Natural History sought vainly for a year to get his rifle out of customs. An American Negro bishop tried for three days without avail to get his baggage released but never found the 'right' official in. Finally, he slipped one of the officials a ten shilling note with a suggestive wink. When he got back to his residence, his unopened luggage was piled neatly in his room.

To officials whose salaries are often six months in arrears, the spectacle of American Negro immigrants 'returning' to the African Fatherland well provided with cash is a welcome one. One customs inspector used commonly to approach the captains of incoming American ships with the query: 'Well, how many you got this time?' When told, he would exclaim with satisfaction, 'Well, send them ashore, we'll pluck 'em!'

No idle boast was this. One immigrant who arrived with $800 and hurried to give up his American citizenship was back at the U.S. Legation three weeks later cursing the chiseling Liberians and begging aid to get back to America. A Negro physician from New York arrived with ample funds and an urge to protect the natives' health. Boldly he gave up his citizenship. Six months later Monrovian sharpers had cleaned him out. Desperate, he stole his American passport from the Liberian State Department archives and stowed away to the States. An American colored woman arrived with high hopes, a young son, and $500. A week later she was found poisoned to death, her son deathly ill from the same cause, and her money gone.

The Liberians have learned the fine art of poisoning from the versatile aborigines. For general safety it has became an unwritten law that the galls of all captured crocodiles must be buried in the presence of local authorities. But that is only one of the numerous poisons in general use. An American Chargé d'Affaires, who helped expose the slave traffic from which all the politicians profited, narrowly escaped poisoning on the eve of his departure in 1931.

One impoverished customs official once stormed aboard a ship threatening to impose a heavy fine for some alleged violation of the law. The captain countered by mentioning the presence of some very fine Yorkshire hams in the cold room. Just then a superior official clambered aboard and eyed his subordinate suspiciously. Alarmed, the fellow turned savagely on the captain, yelling aloud, 'Are you trying to bribe me? I'll put you in jail!' The captain flushed and sputtered with rage. When the superior officer was out of earshot, the subordinate cast aside his belligerence and whispered. 'All right, Captain. I'll take those hams now.'

Immigration officials are equally pleased when Kru seamen or contract laborers from Fernando Po plantations return home with the remnants of their wages. These lads must pay an entrance tax, a head tax, a church tax (even though a pagan), and any other taxes the nimble-witted officials can think up. Sometimes black seamen of British or French citizenship are held in Monrovia's awful jail and fined. Then there is hell to pay as well as an indemnity for the 'mistake.'

If by accident a returned worker still has money, the barefoot gendarmes prepare to fleece him. One familiar charge is disturbing the peace. This includes any 'offense' from whistling in the dark to singing under the influence of palm wine. At the ramshackle police court the thoughtful judge usually fines the culprit the exact amount taken from him by the turnkey. Foreigners are frequently soaked for the most fantastic charges. One white motorist was fined several shillings apiece for the puppies a bitch dog he killed *might* have delivered had she lived.

There is a law against touching a person in an altercation. Once when the wife of a Firestone official upbraided some children for throwing stones on her verandah, one of the urchins challenged: 'Hit me! Go on and hit me! I wish you would hit me. I'd like to get some of Firestone's money, too!' The exceedingly litigious Monrovians are always on the alert for such opportunities. In a country where discharge from a job is legally construed as defamation of character, it can be understood why many firms fight shy of Liberian employees. A grand effort was made by a cabal of briefless lawyers to chisel $25,000 out of the Firestone company on this very ground. Everything was all set and the jury foreman was getting ready to announce the verdict when the judge got word from the Executive Mansion to lay off for fear of American intervention. He grabbed his hat, and yelling 'Case Dismissed!' ran out the door.

Leaving the customs house you come out on Water Street, the one and only commercial artery. It is paved only with boulders, dust, and rubbish, while down one side is an open drainage ditch where flies and mosquitoes load up with germs before pouncing on Monrovia's 10,000 inhabitants. Stores and warehouses line both sides of the street but they are run by French, Germans, Dutch, Hindus, Japanese, Syrians, English and Portuguese, in fact by everybody except Liberians, who rarely even work in them, being considered incompetent and thievish. 'Educated' Liberians rule but almost never work. None of the better class would think of carrying even a small package across the street, while such activities as cutting grass and weeds or painting one's house simply isn't in the book.

The other half dozen streets are paved exactly like Water Street, except that these less travelled thoroughfares have more weeds. Rocks and holes make walking or riding an adventure, especially at night. The strain upon the few dozen automobiles may be imagined. When something breaks it is a real catastrophe for there is no public auto repair shop. Firestone once obligingly opened one in Monrovia, but characteristically no one dreamed of paying for services, so the shop was closed.

Street cleaning and garbage collection are left chiefly to goats. These scavengers are everywhere and even scamper gayly over the President's verandah. Drinking water comes from wells often in proximity to outdoor privies. Some of the well-to-do have cisterns, and water is always filtered or boiled. Of course, there are no sewers. The League of Nations sent a health officer from the Gold Coast in 1931 to clean up the town. He scraped together 800 truckloads of trash, but having no trucks to remove it, he stuck little red flags in the piles. Three years later the piles were still there and may still remain. Prior to his coming, Monrovians absolutely refused to obey the regulations published by an American health officer sent out in accordance with the Firestone loan agreement. When the Secretary of War was asked why Monrovians did not clean up the city, he replied sagely, 'If we clean it up the white folks will take it away from us!'

Moving up the hill to Ashum and Carew Streets, one sees that Monrovia consists of a score of substantial government buildings, missions, legations, consulates, and residences, of the ruling oligarchy sandwiched between a conglomeration of half-finished, screenless, unpainted shacks with rusty tin roofs and windows frequently without panes. The servants customarily live in hovels underneath their masters' houses which are built high off on the ground. Many families have several child 'pawns' who serve them and their children and are often beaten unmercifully.

Some of the Monrovians have plantations a few miles out, but the wealthiest are naturally government officials. They sometimes send their children abroad to school. They are courteous and soft-spoken, and one is loath to believe the harrowing tales of terrorism visited upon the hapless natives in the bush. From the President down most of them have concubines. To provide for such numerous families, taxes in kind from the hinterland (rice, palm oil, cassava, chicken, cattle) are customarily divided between high officials. Those who get jobs as district commissioners at $800 a year always return wealthy from a session of fining the natives.

The only chance the lower orders have to steal is during the rainy season when the deafening noise of steady rainfall on tin roofs makes burglary a cinch for barefoot thugs. During the remainder of the year they mooch off their masters.

The churches are well attended, the average Monrovian being devout. Even the 367 soldiers whose chief duties are raiding native villages are compelled when in barracks to attend services each Sunday. Most of the officials are noted preachers. One of them, a Postmaster General, was an alumnus of Sing Sing. Another, while Vice President, had the account book of a creditor stolen and heaved into the sea. Next day he informed the fellow: 'If you can show me where I owe you $800, I'll be glad to pay it.'

There is no motion picture, but dances are held once a week in a barnlike structure for the better class; and down in Kru town over in Vai Town the natives dance every moonlight night. It is uncommon for the scream of pipes, the wild chants, and the rhythmic drumming to cease before dawn. Although tennis is popular, the lackadaisical Liberians have never assembled sufficient cash and energy to build a tennis court but cheerfully use that maintained by the European club. Sunday band concerts are held in the public park.

Monrovia is most gay at election time, on inauguration day, and when the bicameral legislature assembles. Bunting, boozing, and tropic bundling are then the order of the day. There is much excitement as silk-hatted, frock-coated legislators and officials promenade the dusty streets. Levees are held at the Executive Mansion where immaculately dressed whites and blacks assemble at opposite ends of the verandah and gossip about each other. At such time the 4-room Elizabeth Hotel thrives . . .

Otherwise Monrovians pursue the even tenor of their way: waiting for the weekly ship bearing fresh meat and canned goods, fighting off malaria and yellow fever, charting the currents of petty gossip that swirl and eddy through the crooked streets and lanes, borrowing money off unwitting strangers, and dreaming of another huge foreign loan on which to default.

In no direction have the Monrovian politicians revealed their cleverness more completely than in floating foreign loans. Against these they readily pledge their microscopic internal revenue and customs receipts, only a fraction of which reaches the loan officials. Mahogany, ebony, teak, ivory, rubber, gold, palm oil and diamonds have been an irresistible bait to the surprisingly naive international bankers. The ruling clique knew that with America's traditional friendship as white stepmother, their territory was safe from the rapacious French and British. So they never worried themselves about paying more than the interest on borrowed money, and sometimes not even that. The $500,000 loan of 1872 and the $500,000 loan of 1906 were repaid with the $1,700,000 international loan of 1912, which in turn was wiped out by the $2,500,000 Firestone loan of 1926. The squeezing of the American tycoons by the Anglo-Dutch rubber monopoly made the securing of a United States-controlled source of supply imperative. Firestone got his million acres and the Monrovian politicians made whoopee with what was left after the 1912 loan was paid. All the money is gone now but the governing clique chuckles over its shrewdness. For while this important American economic interest keeps colony-hungry Europeans aloof, the increasingly influential Negro vote in this country halts any move to make Liberia a Puerto Rico or Hawaii.

For all their tatterdemalion existence, these Monrovians are a proud, haughty, and hospitable lot, surprisingly like the Southern aristocrats who once owned them. They are jealous of their independence and determined to maintain it. They are extremely clever diplomats, as they must have been to retain their sovereignty against heavy odds. Each year as more of them travel abroad and their children return from American colleges, the Monrovians look more to progress and improvement.

Pretty soon the seemingly incurable yen to mooch and chisel will be curbed and an incredibly unique place will become just another capital.

RICHARD WRIGHT

from *Black Power*

Dedicated 'to the unknown African', Black Power (1954) is an account
of Wright's visit to the Gold Coast (now Ghana) as the British colony prepared
for independence. He describes meetings with members of the Convention
People's Party (closing with an open letter to its leader, Kwame Nkrumah),
opposition spokesmen, tribal chiefs, local businessmen, union officials. The
text – featuring epigraphs from a range of figures from Trinidadian historian
and politician Eric Williams to German philosopher Edmund Husserl – is
prefaced by a note in which he writes: 'I felt it was time for someone to subject
a slice of African life to close scrutiny in terms of concepts that one would use
in observing life anywhere. Thus, some conclusions arrived at in these pages
might well startle or dismay those who like to dote on 'primitive' people . . .
Africa challenges the West in a way that the West has not been challenged
before. The West can meanly lose Africa, or the West can nobly save Africa;
but whatever happens, make no mistake: THE WEST IS BEING JUDGED BY
THE EVENTS THAT TRANSPIRE IN AFRICA!'

One afternoon, after lunch, I walked down to the seashore where the stevedores were unloading freighters. I had to identify myself and get a pass before being allowed into the area where swarms of half-naked men were carting huge loads upon their heads. The nearer I got to the men, the more amazed I became. I paused, gazing.

Coming toward me was an army of men, naked save for ragged strips of cloth about their hips, dripping wet, their black skins glistening in the pitiless sun, their heads holding pieces of freight – parts of machines, wooden crates, sacks of cement – some of which were so heavy that as many as four men had to put their heads under them to carry them forward. Beyond these rushing and panting men, far out on the open sea, were scores of canoes, each holding twelve men who paddled like furies against the turbulent surf. Save for the wild beat of the sun upon the sand of the beach, a strange silence reigned over everything. I had the impression that the tense effort of physical exertion would not permit a man to spare enough breath to utter a word . . .

The wet and glistening black robots would beach their canoes filled with merchandise and, without pausing, heave out the freight and hoist it upon their heads; then, at breakneck speed, rush out of the sea, stamping through soft, wet sand, and run; finally, they would disappear over a dune of sand toward a warehouse. They ran in single file, one behind the other, barely glancing at me as they pushed forward, their naked feet leaving prints in the soft sand which the next sea wave would wash away . . . On the horizon of the sea, about two miles away, were anchored the European freighters and between the shore and those ships were scores of black dots – canoes filled with rowing men – bobbing and dancing on the heaving water.

Another canoe came toward the beach; the men leaped out, grabbed its sides to steady it until it touched the sand; again I saw that wild and desperate scrambling for the merchandise; again they lifted the boxes or crates or sacks or machine parts to their heads and came rushing toward me, their lips hanging open from sheer physical strain. My reactions were so baffled that I couldn't tell what I felt. What I saw was so useless, so futile, so inhuman that I didn't believe it; it didn't seem real. I felt no protest; I was simply stunned, feeling that someone had snatched back a curtain and I was contemplating half-human men as they had labored in the hot sun two thousand years ago with the threat of death or physical torture hanging over them. But I saw no whips or guns; a weird peace gripped the scene . . .

The harbor here, I was told, was much too shallow to allow ships to dock; they could dock, of course, at Takoradi, 170 miles away, but that would mean that the various shipping companies would have to send their freight by rail to Accra. That was why this beastly work had to take place; it allowed a higher profit to be made on the merchandise.

Each of the twelve men in each canoe held a short, splayed oar with three prongs; each man had to dip and pull this oar through the water sixty times a minute if the canoe was to keep afloat and move through the raging current, and each stroke of each man had to plunge into the water at the same time. There were some children working too, but not in the canoes; they waited at the water's edge and helped their fathers or friends or brothers to lift the heavy loads to their heads.

Nearby was a young black clerk dressed in Western clothes; he held a sheet of paper in his hands, and, as each canoe came in, he checked it off. I went up to him.

'Do they make much money working like that?'

'Each boat earns twelve shillings a trip; that's a shilling for each man, sar.'

'How many shillings can a man make a day?'

'If he works hard, sar, he can make seven.'

'But why do they rush so?'

'It costs a ship a lot of money to stay out there, sar.'

'When do they start work?'

'At daybreak. Not much sun then, sar.'

'Do you have trouble finding workers?'

The young man looked at me and laughed. Then he turned and pointed to a far crowd of half-nude men huddled before a wooden stairway leading up to an office.

'Do you lose many men in the sea?'

'Oh, no, sar! Those men are like fishes, sar. But we do lose merchandise – the company and the ships can stand it, sar. They're insured. Oh, sar, if you saw the beautiful automobiles that go down in that sea –'

A man passed with a sack of something lumpy upon his head, running . . .

'That looks like a sack of potatoes,' I said.

'It is, sar.'

'Why aren't they grown here?'

'I don't know, sar.'

'Is seven shillings a day considered good pay?'

'Well, sar, for what they buy with it, it's not bad.'

He wandered off, jotting down figures on his sheet of paper. I'd seen men tending machines in frantic haste, but I'd never seen men working like machines. . . . I'd seen River Rouge and it was nothing compared to this hot, wild, and hellish labor. It was not only against exploitation that I was reacting so violently; it frightened me because the men did not seem human, because they had voluntarily demeaned themselves to be spokes in a wheel.

I walked toward the exit, then paused and stared again at the fantastic scene, seeing it but not believing it. I felt no hate for the shipowners who had contrived that this should be; there was something here amiss deeper than cheating or profit . . . My reactions were elementary; the ships could have remained at anchor until they rotted, I wouldn't have cared. There are circumstances in which human life is no longer human life, and I'd seen one of them. And for this particular barbarity I had no answer, no scheme; I would not have gone on strike if I had worked there; I simply would not have worked there in the first place, no matter what . . .

I returned to my hotel and lounged in my room. Water seemed to stand in the air. I got up and went into the bathroom and picked up my nail file. Good God . . . It had turned red. I looked farther. All the metal in my toilet kit was a deep, dark red. I rubbed my fingers across the metal and a soft mound of wet rust rolled up. What a climate . . . What could last here? Suppose the Gold Coast was cut off from the Western world, for, say, ten years? Would not the material level of existence be reduced to that which existed before the coming of the white man? Practically nothing, under British colonial policy, was manufactured in the Gold Coast. Indeed, the only ostensible difference between the environmental conditions of the bourgeois blacks and the tribal blacks consisted in the possession by the upper-class blacks of a mass of imported British products in their homes. The British argument until now has been that the climate ruled out industrial production, but I was convinced that this was a British 'rationalization' to keep down potential industrial competition. I was sure that if the British *had* to industrialize the Gold Coast, they would have found a way of doing it . . . Until some effort was made to preserve metal against corrosion, this place was under a sentence of death. And I realized that whatever history was buried in this hot and wet earth must have long since decayed, melted back into the red and ravenous clay. No wonder that archeologists, no matter how long and earnestly they dig, could find little or nothing here. Throw the whole of Detroit into this inferno of heat and wetness, and precious little of it would be left in a hundred years.

Restless, I wander again into the streets and am struck by the incredible number of mere tots engaged in buying and selling. I've begun to feel that, as a whole, there is no period of 'youth' here in Africa. Here, at one moment, one is a child; then, almost overnight, at the age of eight or ten, one assumes the status of an adult. Children toil at minding smaller children, cooking, carrying water on their heads, trading in the market place, assuming responsibilities long before the children of the West. Perhaps 'youth' is a period of luxury which middle-class Westerners alone could give their children?

Maybe that was why one so seldom encountered what might be called 'idealism' in Africa? Perhaps there was no time for dreaming – and how could one get the notion that the world could be different if one did not dream? Though the African's whole life was a kind of religious dream, the African scorned the word 'dream.' Maybe the plant of African personality was pruned too quickly, was forced to bear fruit before it had a chance to grow to its full height? What would happen to a romantic rebel in an African tribe? The African takes his religion, which is really a waking *dream*, for reality, and all other dreams are barred, are taboo.

In the late afternoon a rainstorm broke over the city; it had been threatening for some hours and when it did come, it came down with a violence that made you feel that some malevolent being was bent upon harm. Nature here acts with such directness, suddenness, that the mind, in spite of itself, projects out upon natural events animistic motives. After the first cloudburst the rain settled down to a long, steady downpour. The air was still; I could almost feel the moisture enter my lungs as I breathed. It was not until after ten o'clock that the sky cleared and the stars could be seen, distant, mingled with clouds.

Again I poked about the alleyways of James Town. Now that the rain had stopped, the gregarious natives were returning to the streets. At corners women were lighting candles and huddling themselves beside their piles of staples. Plantains were being dropped into cauldrons of boiling fat. Finding myself out of cigarettes, I paused in front of a woman.

'A can of cigarettes,' I said, pointing.

She stared, then opened a can and took out one cigarette.

'No; I want to buy a can,' I said.

She turned and called, summoning help. Cigarettes were sold in round tin cans of fifty each and they were vacuum-packed against the moisture. A young girl came; she and the woman chatted.

'No; she sell you *one*.' The girl was emphatic.

'Why won't she sell me a can?'

'She can't.' Again she talked to the woman in tribal language, then she turned to me once more. 'She sell can for one pound.'

A tin can of cigarettes cost but seven shillings. Was she trying to cheat?

'That's too much,' I protested.

'You can buy *three*; that's all,' the girl said.

I finally understood the crisis that I'd brought into the woman's life. In this poverty-stricken area rarely did a native buy more than one cigarette at a time, and I had confronted her with a demand for fifty, which was wholesale business!

I pushed forward in the dark, down lanes of women sitting besides their boxes, their faces lit by flickering candles. As I strayed on I heard the sound of drums.

Yes; I'd find them . . . Guided by the throbbing vibrations, I went forward until I came to a vast concrete enclosure. The drums were beating behind that high wall . . . Could I get in? I went around the wall until I came to a narrow opening. Discreetly, I peered through and saw, far back in the compound, a group of people dancing to drums; kerosene lanterns lit up the tableau. Ought I go in? They were black and so was I. But my clothes were different from theirs; they would know me for a stranger.

A young man came toward me; he was about to enter the compound. He paused and asked:

'What do you want?'

'Nothing,' I said, smiling at him. 'What's going on in there?'

'You're a stranger, aren't you?'

'Yes; I'm an American.'

'Come on in,' he said.

I followed him in, noticing as I passed a row of dim-lit rooms that in some rooms only men were seated and in others only women . . . We came to a swirling knot of men and women; they were dancing in a wide circle, barefooted, shuffling to the demoniacal beat of the drums which were being pounded by a group of men near the wall. The ground was wet from the recent rain and their bare feet slapped and caressed the earth.

'Why are they dancing?' I asked the young man.

'A girl has just died,' he told me.

There was no sadness or joy on their faces; they struck me as being people who had to go through with something and they were doing their job. Indeed, most of the faces seemed kind of absentminded. Now and then some man or woman would leave the ring and dance alone in the center. They danced not with their legs or arms, but with their entire bodies, moving slowly, undulating their abdomens, their eyes holding a faraway look.

'Why are they dancing?' I asked again, recalling that I'd asked the same question before, but feeling that I hadn't had an answer.

'A young girl has just died, you see,' he said.

I still didn't know why they were dancing and I wanted to ask him a third time. An old man came to me and shook my hand, then offered me a chair. I sat and stared. The lanterns cast black shadows on the wet ground as the men and women moved slowly to the beat of the drums, their hands outstretched, their fingers trembling. *Why are they dancing* . . . ? It was like watching something transpire in a dream. Still another young man came and joined the two who now flanked my chair. They mumbled something together and then the young man who had brought me in stooped and whispered:

'You'd better go now, sar.'

I rose and shook hands with them, then walked slowly over the wet earth, avoiding the rain puddles. *Why are they dancing* . . . ? And their dancing was almost identical with the movements of the High Life dancing that I'd seen in the outdoor dance hall . . . At the entrance I paused and looked back; I was surprised to see that the young man had discreetly followed me.

'You say that a young girl has died?'

'Yes, sar.'

'And that's why they are dancing?'

'Yes, sar.'

I shook his hand and walked into the damp streets, my eyes aware of the flickering candles that stretched to both sides of me. Jesus Christ, I mumbled. I turned and retraced my steps and stood again in the entrance to the compound and saw that the men and women were now holding hands as they circled round and round. The young man stood watching me . . .

'Good night!' I called to him.

'Good night, sar!' he answered.

I walked briskly and determinedly off, looking over my shoulder and keeping in the line of my vision that dance; I stared at the circling men and women until I could see them no more. The women had been holding their hands joined together above the heads of the men, and the men, as though they had been playing London Bridge Is Falling Down, were filing with slow dignity through the hand-made arches. The feet of the dancers had barely lifted from the ground as they shuffled; their bodies had made sharp angles as they moved and I had been surprised to see that they were moving much quicker than I had thought; they had given me the impression of moving slowly, lazily, but, at that distance, there was a kind of concentrated tension in their gyrations, yet they were utterly relaxed. I had been looking backward as I walked and then the young man pulled the wooden gate shut and it was gone forever . . . I had understood nothing. I was black and they were black, but my blackness did not help me.

GWENDOLYN BROOKS

from 'African Fragment'

Gwendolyn Brooks (b. 1917) was born in Kansas and has spent much of her life in Chicago. Since her first volume of poetry, A Street in Bronzeville (1945), she has published extensively – poetry, fiction and autobiography. This extract is taken from the first volume of her autobiography, Report from Part One (1972). It describes her visit to East Africa in the summer of 1971.

Nairobi, Kenya.

Many many whites, sun-browned, wealthy, flying to the land of the black man.

When the whites on the plane speak of Africa they speak with an affected heartiness, with a glass possessiveness, with nervous bluster.

The first blacks I see in Africa enter the white man's big bird, quickly bob and dip about, cleaning out the trash.

Nairobi. I gulp down the Nairobi midnight air. I stride erectly from the plane to the airport. I tell myself, 'I don't care what anybody says; this is BLACKland – and I am *black*.'

In my room, a wastebasket covered with 'leopard' cloth. A 'Renoir' on a wall. (White women. Pensive white women, plumply sitting.) There is a fat elephant on my key.

Saturday night – the boom-booming of the 'Kenya Resident Band,' playing nothing in particular, but that very loudly. Loud, red, precipitate music. Howls, off somewhere, loud laughs . . .

On Sunday morning people, little troops of them, are out. I see them from my window. There is a bunch-dress woman, baby on back, walking beside her husband – who holds a two-inch daughterlet by the tiny hand. I leave the Panafric Hotel, strike out into the sunshine. It is cool enough to wear a jacket. I have put on my blue jacket, tying the belt behind me. Once off the pavement decline of the hotel, I begin to scream inside myself. I notify myself 'The earth of *Africa* is under my feet!' Above me, white clouds! Blue, blue sky!

A little boy behind his father on a bicycle at first smiles in response to my own hot just-out-of-the-U.S. smile, then changes his mind and sticks a white tongue out at me, clutching his father all the while.

*Gwendolyn Brooks, Report from Part One (Detroit: Broadside Press, 1972), pp. 87–122. Reprinted with the permission of the publishers.

Black people are everywhere, in bright-colored robes, long gowns tied at the waist, kerchiefs, western trousers and shirts and jackets, western short skirts and separates. I look about at my brothers and sisters, and I am aware of both a warm joy and an inexpressible, irrepressible sadness. For these people, who resemble my 'relatives' on Chicago's Forty Seventh and King Drive, or on Thirty Sixth and Calumet, or in the depths of the West Side, are neatly separate from me. In the New Land, my languages were taken away, the accents and nuances of my languages were taken away. I know nothing of Swahili nor of any other African language. Therefore, the chattering blacks around me might just as well be twittering birds. I say 'Good morning!' 'Hello!' 'Hi!' (For as yet I do not even know their 'Jambo!') Sometimes they smile, nod and mutter something, sometimes they look blankly at me and say nothing. Sometimes they carefully look away from me.

I think to myself 'How long it has taken me to secure for myself the accents, nuances, subtleties of the *English* language!' 'I do not have,' I say to myself, 'another fifty-four years to learn the languages that are rightfully mine!'

The men keep their hair short. (I see an exact copy of balladeer Terry Callier.) Many of the 'better off' black men wear black suits. The black cloth looks dull – almost rusty. It is to be observed that the people, in general, admire what is European. But the women's hair and headdress try to rebel – try *not* to 'abandon the hut.' I see the naturals – naturally – but no 'big' naturals. I see tall twists of colored cloth on the lifted heads of the women.

Sgt. Ellis Avenue . . . I see sudden bright recognitions, long warm steady handshakes. I walk and walk and walk. I take pictures with my daughter's little camera. This arouses, variously, curiosity, anger, suspicion, superior impatience. I can tell that some of the people are wondering why I am taking *their* pictures: after all, *I* am the oddity.

Bravely, I enter a downtown grocery store. I do not know enough about the money; I dread embarrassment. I buy cans of orange juice, and wafers and sardines. I buy '*Puf*!' And I manage very well. I offer the Indian saleswoman a large note, and she gives me change, without ever discovering how little I know about 'her' money.

Africa. A writer is tempted not to worry about 'writing it up'; is tempted just to 'let' it beautifully be!

'Mother Africa.'

The people here carry on their lives with – it seems – scarcely a thought of their stolen brothers and sisters over the way there, *far* over the way. They have their home problems. I think if all of us up and packed and CAME, some very careful explaining would have to be done. Some mighty sure lessons would have to come through. Otherwise their widening eyes and ears might EXPLODE.

Many Africans, stopping everything at midday, lie down in the nearest grassy place. Oblivious to opinion; faces down or faces up. In bright or dusty clothes.

The cars are after you. They rape as they wish, they rip around corners, aiming their passion here and there. They eye, and *aim*.

There is quietness around me. The voices may rise in rich laughter, but they are chiefly subdued. The young women's voices are appealingly soft, often lightly musical.

I do not see the 'pimp' walk affected by many young black men 'back home.' Here, the walk of a young man is usually full of fresh air and gentle bounce! Or it may be a sort of loose lope.

Gatheru: ' . . . Africans – after all, it IS *their* country . . .' When you really *feel* that, Africans of the straight blood, when all the millions of you really feel that, along with the knowing your woes will be done.

A little collection of fast walkers turns down a road. I turn, too. I follow them. They enter a comely church, All Saints Cathedral. I think, 'How happy my mother would be to know that, on my first Sunday in Africa, I am going to church.' In the church, the congregation is black, but there is mixed black and white sitting on the platform, and the somber choir is mixed black and white. For the somber black-robed black at the podium there is one fervent minute of emotional release: 'As Tubman said,' *he* says with rising stridency, 'oh mastuh – don't send yo' *son!* – come yo' SE'F!'

A small man at a newspaper 'stand' a few steps away from the church points to a pile of newspapers and asks *at* me '*New York Times?*' It is, I feel, an insult! What, in Africa, on my first day in Africa, do I want with the *New York Times?*

In an Indian bookshop. 'You look like a Tourist,' says the Indian bookshopkeeper to an Indian shopper in dark glasses and a tall wide floppy black hat. 'Oooh *oooh*,' she squeals. 'I certainly don't feel like one!'

Aren't they both tourists? Yes, they are tourists in this land that belongs to *blacks.*

The Third World concept seems to me, at this time, too large for blacks to tackle. There is now-*urgent* business. I want blacks – *right now* – to forge a black synthesis, a black union: so tight that each black may be relied on to protect, enjoy, listen to, and warmly curry his fellows. That, at this time, is business enough.

Back at the hotel. It is an expensive hotel, a 'tourist' hotel, and the life in it is certainly not representative of African life in Africa. My friend Era Bell Thompson, international editor of *Ebony Magazine,* has given me the telephone number of Margaret Kenyatta, mayor of Nairobi and daughter of Jomo Kenyatta, and it is my intention to ask her about families, African families ('may I stay with one of them?') and about students, African students ('may one of them show me every aspect of Nairobi, pleasant and unpleasant?'). It is her home number that I have and she is quickly reached. She is surprised to hear from me. (A letter of introduction that Era Bell has sent her is not to reach her until I am back in Chicago.) But she replies to my questions with an invitation to visit her at the City Council next morning . . .

I wash, change, and descend to the dining room. I am served a good meal by non-committal waiters. *Hurry hurry hurry*. Yield us your plate, so we can be rid of your presence, and can give 'your' place at table to another. The handsome dining room is crowded. I ask a waiter about the availability of coffee ice cream. He looks frightened, and begins a six-minute conference with another waiter, who immediately looks almost as harried . . .

'SONNY!' imperiously calls the 'superior white' man to the black man. SONNY! Come. Do my bidding, *slave* . . .

Upstairs. My room is on the fourth floor. Out comes my fat elephant key. I enter cautiously, looking up, down, and all around. Ravenous, zig-zagging insects, huge and strange, are what I am looking for, what I fear, anticipate. And in *spite* of the fact that I've lined all the window louvre openings with tissue, there is a disturbance in the globe! But I'm weapon-ready at least. I seize my 'Puf!', handy right there at the door. Armed with this canned courage, I stand upon a teetery chair, leer, and – *Puf! – Puf! – Puf!*

I have slain my first, and only, African beast.

It is dark here at fifteen minutes after seven. Most of my week here is going to be cloudy, and it will rain on two of my days.

When I go to bed – looking for flying spiders, jumping roaches and sprinting mosquitoes in every direction (in 'all' of Africa, I never saw these!) – I am cold. Cold in Africa! In my ignorance of my mother-home, this seems odd.

Only on this second night of my Nairobi visit do insistent pictures of my 'old' life nudge me. I am surprised by sharply illustrated memories of dandelions in my parents' Champlain Avenue back yard, so cherished in my childhood; sandpails; graduations; Chicago bus-boardings; Papa, who wanted no soup on the last day of his life, no fruit juice, but 'a lamb chop:' (we wouldn't give it to him – how cruel, thoughtless, or unimaginative); playmates loved and hated; Reverend Lightfoot at my wedding. But quickly these pictures pack themselves away. And again it is *Africa* that is real.

The City Council Building is a large and wide white beauty.

I have been brought to it from the Panafric Hotel by a handsome chauffeur in a handsome and long black limousine. On my arrival two stalwarts, one on each side, have escorted me up the fine wide stairs and up, up into Miss Kenyatta's outer office, where a pretty and efficient young woman with pleasant unsmiling-ness has coffee brought in to me, coffee with cream and brown sugar, by a young man in tan jacket who *does* smile.

When Miss Kenyatta comes in from who knows what great duty, she takes me into her private office. She has more coffee brought in to me. Anxiously she watches me as I drink it. 'Is that all right?' During our exchange she says this again and again. The translation is: I hope this which I am doing pleases and aids you.

She is strong. Her beautiful face and the attractive ampleness of her figure say Strength, Security, Means-To-Effect,-Begin,-And-Bring-To-An-End.

I look around me. A heater, named 'Valor'; red with still flame. On the wall to my left, a picture of Miss K., in her ceremonial robes of royal red and black. On the wall across from her picture is a large likeness of her father, the just Jomo, whose strength seems powerfully to start into the room, perhaps to say 'Now, *look*, Daughter;' or, perhaps, 'COUNTRYMEN!' I see open boxes of shining insignia – medals, decorations, possibly. These sit, quietly proud, under *her* picture.

What do we talk of? Of Era Bell Thompson, of her concern for Era Bell's weariness. ('She works too hard.') Of Era Bell's various writings. Of the possibility that I might want more coffee. Of the University of Nairobi, which I want to see and to which she telephones. Fredrick Waweru will talk to me at half past two, and, if possible, secure for me a young man or woman who will introduce me to Nairobi family life. We talk of poetry. Yes, she likes some poetry. She likes p'Bitek. 'Do you mean the man who wrote "The Song of Lawino?" Okot p'Bitek?' 'Yes.' I tell her of my excited admiration of this poet. She smiles, controlled empathy in her smile.

She takes me through a door in her office to a long room filled with gaily-covered couches and chairs (I remember green patterns, and white), where she has me sign her guest book. Then I am returned to the outer office, where she and her secretary speak to each other chiefly of the inadequacy of the telephones that morning – using the softly, affectionately confiding voices that I find so many Africans reserve for friendly conversation among themselves.

Margaret Kenyatta's chauffeur is instructed to take me to the University of Nairobi. Mr. Waweru, I am to find, is the assistant registrar. I tour the beautiful university . . . sit for a while in a large empty room in the Education Building – 'Ed. 120' – which is furnished with many chairs cushioned in deep-bright blue. I go out, stride across the grounds, smiling here and there. It seems that *all* of the girls have soft feminine voices! I leave the school grounds and very carefully cross a car-crazy street. I find a nice little shop, and go in to buy gifts for friends. I had been told by Nora, who had attended the university for six weeks the summer before, to trade with care and wit; so whenever the nice young man quotes a price, I look surprised, skeptical, delicately alarmed. He understands the game, of course, and plays with a quiet geniality. He lowers all prices, but not greatly.

Loaded with loot, I return to the university, and find Mr. Waweru.

To my requests to meet families, to be introduced to families, to be taken into homes, Miss Kenyatta's last word had been that 'these things' must be arranged – I should have written long ago, and 'something' might have been arranged, I am told by Fredrick Waweru: 'Your time is so short, and you gave no advance notice; the best time for these social meetings is on the weekend. Take my wife and me, for example. We would have been pleased . . . But my wife works as a nurse, and I'm busy here all week . . . My mother and father live far away . . . When are you leaving?'

'Saturday.'

'The weekend!' he exclaims in relief. 'You see?'

I see.

So. Miss K. knows no student to recommend to my company, and Mr. W., *if he hears of one*, will let me know.

'We don't want you disappearing,' says Fredrick Waweru. 'You don't want just anyone for a guide, because we wouldn't want you to just sort of disappear.'

'Good gosh, no!' and I shudder, remembering that I have just read in a newspaper there of the disappearance of two white Americans. When I exclaim and shudder, Mr. W. really opens up, and laughs with warm friendship before the image of it all: me disappearing, you see – utterly, utterly disappearing, with no trace ever and whatsoever . . .

He is generous. He informs me of the curriculum, of the different schools in the combine and of their offerings. He says that at the next graduation there will be at least ten doctors coming from their school of medicine. 'The next year this will be doubled; and soon . . .' He talks of the school of journalism. He says, too, in answer to my eager question, that poet p'Bitek is still a member of the university staff, but is, at the time, some thirty miles away. He makes a telephone call. The conversation, with whomever, is carried on in quick, cheery 'African' – Swahili? Yoruba? I certainly and sorrowfully do not know.

'Are you coming back to Nairobi from Dar es Salaam?' No; from Dar es Salaam I shall go to Cairo, and from Cairo to London, and from London to Chicago. 'P'Bitek will definitely be here at the university on the twenty-eighth and twenty-ninth, so, if you can rearrange your travel plans, he could see you here.'

In any event, I leave copies of Broadside Press books and Third World Press books for Okot p'Bitek and for Mr. Waweru himself, autographing those that are my own. (I had left copies of my books with Miss Kenyatta, who looked pleased to have them.)

I request a cab. Mr. Waweru summons a servitor, who on arrival is told to take me downstairs, and to get a cab for me. I shake hands with Mr. W., and look into his eyes for the last time. It has been interesting, observing those eyes; one is impressed by the level silence of the eyes. You *have* to think of the eyes of lions, looking with calm neither warm nor cool at the intruder, who may or may not be welcome. During our time together – about forty minutes – his messages have been well lined up, and he has spoken at a steady rate, fluent, but *not* super-fast as he tells me he fears.

Downstairs the cab is a long time coming. I stand in one of the arched doorways, watching the people. A small spinning girl, about four, with almost no hair, is engaged and petted by many passers-through. She throws back her head at each notice, and gazes coquettishly at her admirer. She gives words to each. African words. 'She, too, speaks an African language,' I muse despondently. 'I, at *fifty-four*, do not.'

I see worried-looking white professors, with lines across perspiring brows. I see big-naturaled, Edwardian-jacketed, tight-trousered, 'pimp' walking American 'dudes.' Here again are the strong but modest young African girls who, when they speak at all, speak with that shy musical softness I am beginning to revere. And I am fascinated by the African male students, short, tall, graceful or agreeably wobbly, who when they recognize each other greet each other with a warm affection so beautiful I wish urgently that I might be a part of it.

Profound handshakes, handshakes of earnest fellowship delightfully spice this campus.

'It's coming,' says a young man, leaning out of the wee office which holds telephones, a table, and two attendants. So I thank him, and go out to the road to find 'it.'

I do not want to see Miss Kenyatta again, distinctive though she is. I do not, on this little trip, want a thoroughly official flavoring of my impressions. I want my impressions to be spontaneous. At another time I could enjoy, if allowed, a richer acquaintance with this firm mayor of Nairobi – would enjoy talking honestly and piercingly (if that is possible: perhaps it is not) of matters that really scrape up out of the heart, rather than of coffee, poet preferences and mutual acquaintance.

Coffee *does* seem, however, a serious matter here! For a cloud had come over the face of Miss Kenyatta's cautiously friendly secretary when I first declined coffee *or* tea, so I quickly changed my mind and accepted the steaming coffee served with a pitcher of cream, a bowl of brown sugar crystals. Served in a green and white cup, on a green and white chipped saucer. And as for poesy – well, when I told Miss Kenyatta that I keep buying copies of *The Song of Lawino* to give away, she looked at me, for the first time, as though I *might* be a decent and interesting human being, instead of just another nosy, needling 'nited States-er, cluttering up her country and her time. 'Call me tomorrow,' she had said warmly when we parted, 'and let me know how you make out at the University of Nairobi. I am not a scholar, and I do not know much about these matters. But call me. Is that all right?'

I call the next afternoon. A man answers. He knows no English, and will not bring any one else to the telephone. But I want only to assure her that I have 'made out' just fine, just fine. And I do not call again.

In all the places I visit, in all the Nairobi streets I roam, I encounter only one dashiki-wearer. A man of about thirty, hymn-singing in the All Saints Cathedral. The Postoffice. A big, bleak-neat, busy place. To the cocky little plump-faced man-with-chin-hairs at the stamp window I say 'May I have fifty stamps for mail going outside the country?' He is in a mood to play, albeit coolly. He would look down on this 'Afro-American' if it were possible. But it is not possible. 'What country?' he scissors, tearing off the stamps. 'The United States.' 'Ho.' 'How much?' He looks at me with African, narrowed, coolly playful eyes. 'Not *too* much. *Not* too much. You can afford it.' 'Oh, yeah?' 'Yeah!' he replies, smiling at last, with warm wideness.

I love the game park.

The graceful animals do not watch us and they watch us.

I experience Part One and Part Two. Part One: the animals are behind fencing; lions, the chimpanzee, monkeys, the baboon, deer; the wart hog – who looks at me so appealingly, with such tender, communicating eyes, and whose feelings must be hurt when a Britishwoman pushes her baby past him *fast*, rushing the buggy as if in terror, and screaming 'OH! So UGLY! What an UGLY face. LOOK at that UGLY *face*!' Part Two. No bars. No fencing. Animals living freely, 'in their natural habitat.' Lions, leopards, deer, graceful and majestic, walk in front of the Land Rover, taking their time, glancing at us or not, as they choose – but at no time afraid of us. We see a lion completing a bloody meal, then turning on his side, to begin a nap. It is quiet. So quiet. I am sharing this game park tour with a British couple (no one else has signed up for this day), and for a few moments we all stop talking. How blessedly, incredibly *still* . . . Then lions, then deer, then *all* the animals, Sky, and hushing grass are harmony.

On July Twenty-fourth Simon Njenga drives me to the Nairobi Airport. He is friendly. 'I am Kikuyu.' It is an announcement.

'Did you *stay* at Panafric Hotel?' Awed puzzlement. 'Yes.' Pause. I look at him significantly: the look says 'You and I understand about being poor.' But I add to the look: 'It is very high there. The Panafric is a very expensive hotel.' He agrees, fervently. 'There are other hotels. Good hotels, not so expensive. The Brunas Hotel, and the Grosvenor Hotel. They are very good hotels, much cheaper than Panafric.' I thank him, making a note of the names. 'Did you pay – all from yourself? – all your own?' '*Yes.*' 'And in Dar es Sa*laam* – you will also stay at hotel?' 'No; I'll stay with friends. They will introduce me to people. I want to meet many people.' 'Yes. Yes! That will be much better for you.'

He tells me of 'Nairobi things' I've missed. 'I could have shown you many places, many things. Next time' – he gives me his card – 'use my card; call me.'

Thadious M. Davis

'Double Take at Relais de l'Espadon'

Thadious M. Davis (b. 1944) is a poet, editor and critic, author of a major study, Nella Larsen: Novelist of the Harlem Renaissance *(1994). This poem first appeared in an anthology of African-American women poets, accompanied by the following note: 'Relais de l'Espadon is a tourist hotel on Gorée, an island three miles off the coast of Senegal. Gorée is known as "the island of the slave trade".'*

On the Ile de Gorée, M. Diop elegant
in steel-gray cardigan
bowed his greeting, waved me be seated
inside a shaded courtyard opening to the sea
With quiet ceremony he offered me tea
Senegalese style   hot and sweet
served neat like shots of whiskey
His fine manner and regal bearing
subdued the space around us

In a generous flourish of slender sepia hands
he adopted me, one of the lost tribe
Graced with relief from a tourist's day
I dreamed of a long time coming
then blossomed reclaimed
A Wolof daughter admiring his formal ease
that bore no trace of my many fathers
shuffling through Louisiana mud
my fathers bent by labor, bowed in servility

After lunch, we sat thigh-to-thigh
riding the ferry to Dakar
Ignoring moisture and heat, we struggled to speak
His flawless French   but no English
drew hesitant response

From *Black Sister: Poetry by Black American Women, 1746–1980*, edited by Erlene Stetson (Bloomington: Indiana University Press, 1981), pp. 277–8. Reprinted with the permission of the author.

Our language: gestures
flowing reserves of sudden caring
I followed his eyes scanning the wake
Gorée, golden globe of afternoon, flickered into view
And I began the long journey backward
Relais de l'Espadon   slaver's mansion
stood restored, a sunlit pastel
yellow walls and rose shutters
jailing stone patios swept by sea air
Salt water welled within old wounds
preserved memories   my father's house of many rooms
Blood and bone stiffened before we sighted port
I surrounded myself with a prison of kin
My human fortress still fighting sea and separation

M. Diop disappeared into the city
His straight proud back, graceful and controlled,
left me wondering
    Is he the father I might have had
    Is he the son who shackled my father and me

6

Home

MARY SEACOLE

from *Wonderful Adventures of Mrs. Seacole in Many Lands*

*Daughter of a Scottish army officer based in Jamaica, Mary Seacole
(1805–1881) learnt folk medicine from her mother, who ran a boarding-house
in Kingston. Well travelled, she found her medical and surgical skills were
much in demand during the cholera and yellow-fever epidemics in the
Caribbean in the early 1850s. She was in England when the Crimean War
(1854–56) broke out and she hoped to serve as a nurse with the armed forces.
When official permission was refused, she made her own way to the battle
zone with a distant relative, Thomas Day, setting up the 'British Hotel' and
providing food, drink and medical supplies to the Allied troops during their
one-year siege of the Russian port of Sebastopol. She was as well-known in her
day as Florence Nightingale, and her autobiography was an instant success.
The final chapter reprinted here finds her pondering the future that awaits her
following the armistice.*

Before the New Year was far advanced we all began to think of going home, making
sure that peace would soon be concluded. And never did more welcome message
come anywhere than that which brought us intelligence of the armistice, and the
firing, which had grown more and more slack lately, ceased altogether. Of course
the army did not desire peace because they had any distaste for fighting; so far
from it, I believe the only more welcome intelligence would have been news of a
campaign in the field, but they were most heartily weary of sieges, and the prospect
of another year before the gloomy north of Sebastopol damped the ardour of the
most sanguine. Before the armistice was signed, the Russians and their old foes
made advances of friendship, and the banks of the Tchernaya used to be thronged
with strangers, and many strange acquaintances were thus began. I was one of
the first to ride down to the Tchernaya, and very much delighted seemed the
Russians to see an English woman. I wonder if they thought they all had my
complexion. I soon entered heartily into the then current amusement – that of
exchanging coin, etc., with the Russians. I stole a march upon my companions
by making the sign of the cross upon my bosom, upon which a Russian threw
me, in exchange for some pence, a little metal figure of some ugly saint. Then we
wrapped up halfpence in clay, and received coins of less value in exchange. Seeing
a soldier eating some white bread, I made signs of wanting some, and threw over

Mary Seacole, *Wonderful Adventures of Mrs. Seacole in Many Lands* (London: James Blackwood,
1857), pp. 188–97.

a piece of money. I had great difficulty in making the man understand me, but after considerable pantomime, with surprise in his round bullet eyes, he wrapped up his bread in some paper, then coated it with clay and sent it over to me. I thought it would look well beside my brown bread taken from the strange oven in the terrible Redan, and that the two would typify war and peace. There was a great traffic going on in such things, and a wag of an officer, who could talk Russian imperfectly, set himself to work to persuade an innocent Russian that I was his wife, and having succeeded in doing so promptly offered to dispose of me for the medal hanging at his breast.

The last firing of any consequence was the salutes with which the good tidings of peace were received by army and navy. After this soon began the home-going with happy faces and light hearts, and some kind thoughts and warm tears for the comrades left behind.

I was very glad to hear of peace, also, although it must have been apparent to every one that it would cause our ruin. We had lately made extensive additions to our store and out-houses – our shelves were filled with articles laid in at a great cost, and which were now unsaleable, and which it would be equally impossible to carry home. Everything, from our stud of horses and mules down to our latest consignments from home, must be sold for any price; and, as it happened, for many things, worth a year ago their weight in gold, no purchaser could now be found. However, more of this hereafter.

Before leaving the Crimea, I made various excursions into the interior, visiting Simpheropol and Baktchiserai. I travelled to Simpheropol with a pretty large party, and had a very amusing journey. My companions were young and full of fun, and tried hard to persuade the Russians that I was Queen Victoria, by paying me the most absurd reverence. When this failed they fell back a little, and declared that I was the Queen's first cousin. Anyhow, they attracted crowds about me, and I became quite a lioness in the streets of Simpheropol, until the arrival of some Highlanders in their uniform cut me out.

My excursion to Baktchiserai was still more amusing and pleasant. I found it necessary to go to beat up a Russian merchant, who, after the declaration of peace, had purchased stores of us, and some young officers made up a party for the purpose. We hired an araba, filled it with straw, and some boxes to sit upon, and set out very early, with two old umbrellas to shield us from the midday sun and the night dews. We had with us a hamper carefully packed, before parting, with a cold duck, some cold meat, a tart, etc. The Tartar's two horses were soon knocked up, and the fellow obtained a third at a little village, and so we rolled on until mid-day, when, thoroughly exhausted, we left our clumsy vehicle and carried our hamper beneath the shade of a beautiful cherry-tree, and determined to lunch. Upon opening it the first thing that met our eyes was a fine rat, who made a speedy escape. Somewhat gravely, we proceeded to unpack its contents, without caring to express our fears to one another, and quite soon enough we found them realized. How or where the rat had gained access to our hamper it was impossible to say, but he had made no bad use of his time, and both wings of the cold duck had flown, while the tart was considerably mangled. Sad discovery this for people who, although hungry, were still squeamish. We made out as well as we could with the cold beef, and gave the rest to our Tartar driver, who had apparently no disinclination to eating after the rat, and would very likely have despised us heartily for such weakness. After dinner we went on more briskly, and succeeded in reaching Baktchiserai. My journey was perfectly unavailing. I could not find my debtor at home, and if I had I was told it would take three weeks before the Russian law would assist me to recover my claim. Determined, however, to have some compensation, I carried off a raven, who had been croaking angrily at my intrusion. Before we had been long on our homeward journey, however, Lieut. C___ sat upon it, of course accidentally, and we threw it to its relatives – the crows.

As the spring advanced, the troops began to move away at a brisk pace. As they passed the Iron House upon the Col – old for the Crimea, where so much of life's action had been compressed into so short a space of time – they would stop and give us a parting cheer, while very often the band struck up some familiar tune of that home they were so gladly seeking. And very often the kind-hearted officers would find time to run into the British Hotel to bid us good-bye, and give us a farewell shake of the hand; for you see war, like death, is a great leveller, and mutual suffering and endurance had made us all friends. 'My dear Mrs. Seacole, and my dear Mr. Day,' wrote one on a scrap of paper left on the counter, 'I have called here four times this day, to wish you good-bye. I am so sorry I was not fortunate enough to see you. I shall still hope to see you to-morrow morning. We march at seven a.m.'

And yet all this going home seemed strange and somewhat sad, and sometimes I felt that I could not sympathise with the glad faces and happy hearts of those who were looking forward to the delights of home, and the joy of seeing once more the old familiar faces remembered so fondly in the fearful trenches and the hard-fought battlefields. Now and then we would see a lounger with a blank face, taking no interest in the bustle of departure, and with him I acknowledged to have more fellow-feeling than with the others, for he, as well as I, clearly had no home to go to. He was a soldier by choice and necessity, as well as by profession. He had no home, no loved friends; the peace would bring no particular pleasure to him, whereas war and action were necessary to his existence, gave him excitement, occupation, the chance of promotion. Now and then, but seldom, however, you came across such a disappointed one. Was it not so with me? Had I not been happy through the months of toil and danger, never knowing what fear or depression was, finding every moment of the day mortgaged hours in advance, and earning sound sleep and contentment by sheer hard work? What better or happier lot could possibly befall me? And, alas! how likely was it that my present occupation gone, I might long in vain for another so stirring and so useful. Besides which, it was pretty sure that I should go to England poorer than I left it, and although I was not ashamed of poverty, beginning life again in the autumn – I mean late in the summer of life – is hard up-hill work.

Peace concluded, the little jealousies which may have sprung up between the French and their allies seemed forgotten, and every one was anxious, ere the parting came, to make the most of the time yet left in improving old friendships and founding new. Among others, the 47th, encamped near the Woronzoff Road, gave a grand parting entertainment to a large company of their French neighbours, at which many officers of high rank were present. I was applied to by the committee of management to superintend the affair, and, for the last time in the Crimea, the health of Madame Seacole was proposed and duly honoured. I had grown so accustomed to the honour that I had no difficulty in returning thanks in a speech which Colonel B___ interpreted amid roars of laughter to the French guests.

As the various regiments moved off, I received many acknowledgments from those who thought they owed me gratitude. Little presents, warm farewell words, kind letters full of grateful acknowledgments for services so small that I had forgotten them long, long ago – how easy it is to reach warm hearts! – little thoughtful acts of kindness, even from the humblest. And these touched me the most. I value the letters received from the working men far more than the testimonials of their officers. I had nothing to gain from the former, and can point to their testimony fearlessly. I am strongly tempted to insert some of these acknowledgments, but I will confine myself to one:–

Camp, near Karani, June 16, 1856.

My dear Mrs Seacole, – As you are about to leave the Crimea, I avail myself of the only opportunity which may occur for some time, to acknowledge my gratitude to you, and to thank you for the kindness which I, in common with many others, received at your hands, when attacked with cholera in the spring of 1855. But I have no language to do it suitably.

I am truly sensible that your kindness far exceeded my claims upon your sympathy. It is said by some of your friends, I hope truly, that you are going to England. There can be none from the Crimea more welcome there, for your kindness in the sick-tent, and your heroism in the battle-field, have endeared you to the whole army.

I am sure when her most gracious Majesty the Queen shall have become acquainted with the service you have gratuitously rendered to so many of her brave soldiers, her generous heart will thank you. For you have been an instrument in the hands of the Almighty to preserve many a gallant heart to the empire, to fight and win her battles, if ever again war may become a necessity. Please to accept this from your most grateful humble servant,

W. J. Tynan.

But I had other friends in the Crimea – friends who could never thank me. Some of them lay in their last sleep, beneath indistinguishable mounds of earth; some in the half-filled trenches, a few beneath the blue waters of the Euxine. I might in vain attempt to gather the wild flowers which sprung up above many of their graves, but I knew where some lay, and could visit their last homes on earth. And to all the cemeteries where friends rested so calmly, sleeping well after a life's work nobly done, I went many times, lingering long over many a mound that bore the names of those whom I had been familiar with in life, thinking of what they had been, and what I had known of them. Over some I planted shrubs and flowers, little lilac trees, obtained with no small trouble, and flowering evergreens, which looked quite gay and pretty ere I left, and may in time become great trees, and witness strange scenes, or be cut down as fuel for another besieging army – who can tell? And from many graves I picked up pebbles, and plucked simple wild-flowers, or tufts of grass, as memorials for relatives at home. How pretty the cemeteries used to look beneath the blue peaceful sky; neatly enclosed with stone walls, and full of the grave-stones reared by friends over friends. I met many here, thoughtfully taking their last look of the resting-places of those they knew and loved. I saw many a proud head bowed down above them. I knew that many a proud heart laid aside its pride here, and stood in the presence of death, humble and childlike. And by the clasped hand and moistened eye, I knew that from many a heart sped upward a grateful prayer to the Providence which had thought fit in his judgment to take some, and in his mercy to spare the rest.

Some three weeks before the Crimea was finally evacuated, we moved from our old quarters to Balaclava, where we had obtained permission to fit up a store for the short time which would elapse before the last red coat left Russian soil. The poor old British Hotel! We could do nothing with it. The iron house was pulled down, and packed up for conveyance home, but the Russians got all of the out-houses and sheds which was not used as fuel. All the kitchen fittings and stoves, that had cost us so much, fell also into their hands. I only wish some cook worthy to possess them has them now. We could sell nothing. Our horses were almost given away, our large stores of provisions, etc., were at any one's service. It makes my heart sick to talk of the really alarming sacrifices we made. The Russians crowded down ostensibly to purchase, in reality to plunder. Prime cheeses, which had cost us tenpence a pound, were sold to them for less than a penny a pound; for wine, for which we had paid forty-eight shillings a dozen, they bid four shillings. I could not stand this, and in a fit of desperation, I snatched up a hammer and broke up case after case, while the bystanders held out their hands and caught the ruby stream. It may have been wrong, but I was too excited to think. There was no more of my own people to give it to, and I would rather not present it to our old foes.

We were among the last to leave the Crimea. Before going I borrowed a horse, easy enough now, and rode up the old well-known road – how unfamiliar in its loneliness and quiet – to Cathcart's Hill. I wished once more to impress the scene upon my mind. It was a beautifully clear evening, and we could see miles away across the darkening sea. I spent some time there with my companions, pointing out to each other the sites of scenes we all remembered so well. There were the trenches, already becoming indistinguishable, out of which, on the 8th of September, we had seen the storming parties tumble in confused and scattered bodies, before they ran up the broken height of the Redan. There the Malakhoff, into which we had also seen the luckier French pour in one unbroken stream; below lay the crumbling city and the quiet harbour, with scarce a ripple on its surface, while around stretched away the deserted huts for miles. It was with something like regret that we said to one another that the play was fairly over, that peace had rung the curtain down, and that we, humble actors in some of its most stirring scenes, must seek engagements elsewhere.

I lingered behind, and stooping down, once more gathered little tufts of grass, and some simple blossoms from above the graves of some who in life had been very kind to me, and I left behind, in exchange, a few tears which were sincere.

A few days latter, and I stood on board a crowded steamer, taking my last look of the shores of the Crimea.

LANGSTON HUGHES

'Happy New Year'

The prodigious output of Langston Hughes (1902–1967) includes poetry, novels, short stories, plays, journalism, translations and anthologies. He is one of the most widely travelled of all the writers represented in this volume. His autobiographies, The Big Sea *(1940) and* I Wonder as I Wander *(1956), are effectively travel narratives, taking in the author's experiences in Mexico, Cuba, Haiti, France, Italy, Spain, West Africa, Japan and the Soviet Union. Here is the final chapter of the later volume, which finds its author in Paris at the end of 1937 on his way back from the Spanish Civil War, where he was correspondent for the* Baltimore Afro-American *newspaper.*

I arrived in Paris just in time for Christmas. The holidays were pleasant. Some Negro friends invited me to Christmas dinner – a wonderful home-cooked dinner it was, too. During the holiday week I saw the Cartier-Bressons, Nancy Cunard, Bricktop and the Roumains. Louis Aragon introduced me to George Adam, who had begun to translate my short stories into French, and I met Pierre Seghers, my publisher. For almost five years now I had earned a living from writing, so my dream was beginning to come true – to be a professional writer – and it had been my good fortune so far not to have to write anything I did not really want to write. Meanwhile, my interests had broadened from Harlem and the American Negro to include an interest in all the colored peoples of the world – in fact, in all the people of the world, as I related to them and they to me.

I liked being a writer, traveling, meeting people, and looking at main events – like the depression in America, the transition from serfdom to manhood in Soviet Asia, and the Civil War in Spain – in it all, but at the same time apart from things, too. In the Soviet Union I was a visitor. In the midst of a dreary moral-breaking depression in America, I lived in a bright garden cottage at Carmel with a thoroughbred dog and a servant. In the Civil War in Spain I am a writer, not a fighter. But that is what I want to be, a writer, recording what I see, commenting upon it, and distilling from my own emotions a personal interpretation.

Unconsciously, in doing this I found that music helped me, and everywhere I looked for it, and listened. All over Paris that winter there was Negro music –

Langston Hughes, *I Wander as I Wonder: An Autobiographical Journey* (New York: Hill and Wang, 1993), pp. 400–5. Copyright © 1956 Langston Hughes. Copyright renewed © 1984 by George Houston Bass. Copyright introduction © by Arnold Rampersad. Reprinted by permission of Hill and Wang, a division of Farrar, Straus & Giroux, Inc. and by permission of Harold Ober Associates, Inc.

Comptom Glover at Harry's New York Bar, Maceo Jefferson at the Big Apple, Georgie Johnson at the Boeuf sur le Toit, and anybody and everybody dropping by to play piano or blow a horn at Frisco's place – the popular coal-black Negro with the lighthouse smile. Una Mae Carlisle, Rollin Smith and Valaida Snow were singing at Montmartre clubs, and French jazz bands all over town were trying their best to beat it out like the Negroes. Meanwhile, I went to see Mauriac's *Asmodée* at the Comédie Française, and to hear the ancient Yvette Guilbert and Damia at the music halls, and Maurice Rostand reciting his poems, and to the Boule Blanche on the Left Bank to watch the Africans dancing.

But Paris did not seem as happy that winter as it had been in the summer. There was much talk of war in the air – not just war in Spain. The Parisian intellectuals declared Spain was only a training ground for Hitler and Mussolini, a place to try out Nazi bombing planes and educate Fascist pilots. The coming war, they predicted, would be everywhere. The charming but sad Jacques Roumain said, 'I expect the world will end.'

'I doubt it,' I answered, 'and if it does, I intend to live to see what happens.'

He smiled, 'You Americans!' he said.

But many Americans felt then as apprehensive as did the Europeans. A number of long-time residents of Paris were considering packing up to come home. I myself had wanted to spend the winter in France, but I'd had to send most of my money to Cleveland. Letters from my mother said that she was no better and that since my brother was back in college at Wilberforce, she hated to live alone, so she wrote that she had given up the house to move with some cousins. A great woman for linking her fate with cousins, my mother! But her illness worried me, so I thought I'd better go straight home and see about her. There wasn't much choice, anyhow, as I had just about enough money left to pay my passage. But this was not the first time I'd found myself in Paris practically penniless. I'd been so during my first weeks in the city long ago when I jumped ship and came there in 1924 looking for work. And since then I had been broke or almost broke in so many other cities around the world – and still had fun – that my personal predicament didn't worry me much. Sitting one night in the Bar Boudon on rue Douai, where the Negro musicians gathered, I remembered once during my childhood in Kansas my grandmother had given me an apple that had been bruised and so had a brown spot on it. I didn't want to eat the apple.

My grandmother said, 'What's the matter with you, boy? You can't expect every apple to be a perfect apple. Just because it's got a speck on it, you want to throw it away. Bite that speck out and eat that apple, son. It's still a good apple.'

That's the way the world is, I thought, if you bite the specks out, it's still a good apple.

In Paris, I stayed at an Ethiopian hotel – the only 'colored' hotel in town – which amazed the Negro newspaperman, John Davis, when he stopped in Montmartre on his way to interview the Emperor Haille Selassie in exile near London.

'In Paris,' he said, 'of all places to stay in a colored hotel! Why?'

'For fun,' I said. The hotel was amusing, with bushy-haired Ethiopians, Sudanese, Algerians and other non-Parisian characters coming in and out, and a panorama of Montmartre from its windows.

John Davis said he had to interview Haile Selassie the next morning at nine at His Highness's country place in England, so he took a night plane for London. But I learned from Davis later in New York that, when he arose very early the next day in London to drive out to see the Emperor, and got there promptly at nine, he was told that the appointment was for nine o'clock *Ethiopian time* – which meant four that afternoon. 'Damn it all,' said Davis, 'I could have had an extra night in Paris!'

Before his departure from Paris we had gone night-clubbing along rue Pigalle and had met a charming girl who said she was from Java, part Dutch and part Javanese, but who spoke hesitant English and broken French with a Georgia drawl. John Davis whispered to me over the champagne he had bought that he was sure she was colored, from somewhere in Dixie, passing for Javanese in Paris, which amused him greatly. The girl was so exotic-looking that I doubted she was American, and disputed his insistence on it. I was wrong. Later I ran into the girl in New York talking perfectly good Harlemese, and not passing for anything on Lenox Avenue where she was quite at home.

On New Year's Eve I went to the Paris Opera alone. Why I chose to hear *Samson and Delilah* that particular night, I don't remember now. Perhaps it was the only evening that I could get a ticket at the Opera before sailing for America. I didn't enjoy the performance much. My seat in the gallery was very high, far away from the stage and behind a pillar. The music rose beautifully to my location, but the singers and the ballet seemed miles off. The sets were ponderous and old-fashioned. When Samson pushed the temple down, each piece seemed to take a full minute to descend separately on quite visible wires into a heap of obviously artificial scenery. Visually the *Folies Bergères* did a thousand times better on sets. The Opera Comique was better, too, to observe from the gallery. I wondered why I had not gone there instead of to the Grand Opera.

After the Opera, I had intended locating a party that some Martinique friends of the French Guiana poet, Leon Damas, a protégé of Gide's, were giving in the Latin Quarter. But when I started down into the Metro, I found that I had left the address of the party at my hotel. Rather than go back to the hotel and get it, since it was nearly midnight, I decided not to go to the party. Instead, I walked down the almost deserted Boulevards toward the Madeleine, thinking there might perhaps be a midnight mass there with organ music in honor of the New Year. Midway between the Opera and the Madeleine, I noticed a slightly limping figure approaching me, head down in his overcoat collar for it was cold. I remembered that limp from Moscow. It was Seki Sano, the Japanese theater director I had met at a Meyerhold rehearsal. We were surprised to see each other. To exchange news, we went into the glass enclosure of a sidewalk café and ordered drinks. All but one of the tables on the glass-encircled winter terrace were empty. At that table a rather pretty woman sat alone. Through the glass outside we could see the lights of the lonely boulevard, for very few people were passing in the chilly darkness. Quite unlike New York on New Year's Eve, downtown Paris as midnight approached was very quiet. The French remain home on holidays.

Seki Sano said, 'I read a year or two ago in the Moscow papers about your being expelled from Japan. I'm sorry that happened to you in my country. But I am expelled, too. I cannot go back.'

'I'm sure someday you can go back,' I said, 'and I, too, if I want to go.'

But Seki Sano was not so optimistic. 'There are too many people wandering around the world now who can't go home,' he said. 'Lots of them are in Moscow. More are in Paris – people from the Hitler countries, from the South American dictatorships, from China, from my own Japan. No exiles from America – though I wouldn't be surprised if the day didn't come.'

'That's one nice thing about America,' I said, 'I can always go home – even when I don't want to.'

'*Bonne année!*' said the waiter bringing our drinks. 'It's the New Year!'

Sure enough, faintly, somewhere out in the Paris night, we could hear bells tolling the entrance of 1938, so we lifted our glasses. But the woman at the nearby table suddenly began to cry.

Seki Sano said, 'Pardon, madam, but won't you join us?'

The woman sobbed thank you in an accent that was not French. Russian, maybe? Or German? We did not know. An exile, too, like Seki Sano? We did not ask her. She had been drinking coffee. The waiter brought her cup to our table as she rose.

The woman finally managed a smile. She sat with us quietly until the bells stopped ringing, then thanked us again and said good night. She disappeared alone down the boulevard toward the Madeleine. Seki Sano and I shook hands and parted at the corner across from the Café de la Paix. He was going to the Left Bank and I to Montmartre.

Slowly I walked through the lightly falling snow that had begun to sift down over the Paris rooftops in scattered indecisive flakes. The streets were very lonely as I passed the Galleries Lafayette and the Gare Saint Lazare and turned up the slight incline leading to Montmartre. Even the little clubs and bars along the way were quiet.

Where could everybody be, I wondered. How still it was in this old, old city of Paris in the first hour of the New Year.

The year before, I had been in Cleveland. The year before that in San Francisco. The year before that in Mexico City. The one before that at Carmel. And the year before Carmel in Tashkent. Where would I be when the next New Year came, I wondered? By then, would there be war – a major war? Would Mussolini and Hitler have finished their practice in Ethiopia and Spain to turn their planes on the rest of us? Would civilization be destroyed? Would the world really end?

'Not my world,' I said to myself. 'My world will not end.'

But worlds – entire nations and civilizations – do end. In the snowy night in the shadows of the old houses of Montmartre, I repeated to myself, 'My world won't end.'

But how could I be so sure? I don't know.

For a moment I wondered.

Andrew Salkey

from *Georgetown Journal*

*Among his many varied writings, Salkey wrote two fascinating travel books.
They are finely detailed, almost hour-by-hour, accounts of two separate visits
to the Caribbean from London, incorporating transcripts of interviews and
conversations, summaries of speeches, and extracts from local newspapers.
Voyages 'home' in a sense, though they take him not to Jamaica where he
grew up, but to two countries he had never been to before.*

*Havana Journal (1971) records a month spent in Cuba as delegate to an
international gathering of writers, scientists and technologists in January 1968.
Georgetown Journal (1972) covers a two-week visit to Guyana in February 1970
as invited guest of the new Republic to attend a Caribbean Artists and Writers
Conference. His travelling companions included John La Rose and Sam Selvon.
The theme of 'homecoming' is a recurrent one: in this short extract he meets
two artists who have returned from London and New York to the Caribbean,
trying to disprove the received wisdom that it is not possible to do this
successfully.*

Tuesday 17th. February, 1970: I went to bed, some time after two o'clock, Tuesday morning, carelessly flopped across a bare divan, and fully dressed. I awoke at about six-thirty to the noises of rain dousing my head and pillow, a rolled bath-towel; dogs barking from the direction of the backyard of Peter D'Aguiar, the former leader of the United Force and former Deputy Prime Minister of the Coalition Government; roosters crowing their authoritarian rule all round the Kitty High School, at the top of which our flat was situated; and with a choir of bird-song, the kiskadee prominent among the singers, overlaying the morning babel.

I smiled at Parboo, with whom I was sharing a vast verandah-style bedroom, and who, thinking I was asleep, had thoughtfully got out of bed to close the window above my divan.

'You' home, now, ol' man,' he said. 'You see how rain wettin' you, an' you hear all them dawg an' cock crowin'? Englan' don' sound so, at all!'

We talked. John had been anxiously trying to contact me, for quite a while after the party. He wanted me to join him at Mrs. Alves in Station Street. Sam, too, had been trying to locate me.

---

*Andrew Salkey, *Georgetown Journal* (London: New Beacon Books, 1972), pp. 106–8. Reprinted with the permission of the publishers.

Parboo gave me a set of four large plasticrome transparency prints of the work of four Jamaican painters: a scene of washerwomen at a stream by Barrington Watson; a harbour view by Albert Huie; a mythological pastoral vista by Carl Abrahams; and a beachscape of three fishermen hanging their seine for drying by Parboo himself. While reading the biographical details, at the bottom of each print, I discovered the added fact, in Parboo's entry, that he had also studied with George Grosz, Fernand Léger and Yaseo Kuniyoshi, and that he was one of the founders of the Contemporary Jamaican Artists' Association, a vigorous group of painters and sculptors whose radical move, away from the traditional art patronage of the Island, has struck a decisive blow against the stranglehold of the narrow exhibition-bureaucracy in Kingston.

Parboo pushed his head through his window, and shouted to the Guyanese painter and Art teacher, Donald Locke, whose flat we could see across the way from Bill's front door. When Donald came over, he teased me about London as only a former fellow exile is able to do, making use of the intimate details of place, class and racist stories, folded into the bitter-sweet of the experiences recalled.

Because he and Parboo had turned their backs on the doubtful pleasures of being abroad, and had returned home, I wanted to hear about Donald's re-entry into Georgetown.

'How's it been?' I asked.

'Bai, they say you can't ever return to you' yard, nuh,' he said. 'Those who go and stay away for a long time can't really make the crossing home, even though they actually do. Well I'm trying to prove that cute little aphorism untrue, and it's giving me a bitch of a hard time. Parboo knows what I mean.'

'How you mean, papa?' Parboo said. 'I could write a whole *rass* library full o' wha' it mean', yes, an' every blessed book would tell a separate story o' shit an' bad luck.'

'But, you're both at home, in spite of everything?' I said.

'That's true,' Donald said. 'And as far as I'm concerned, I intend to stay right here and do my thing, at Queen's, where I teach, and in my own work, outside the College, whatever the pundits say, whatever pressures develop, whatever happens. And things' not easy, now, either, any way you look at them.'

'Easier than back in JA,' Parboo said. 'The ol' titty touris' trade can subvert you if you don't watch you'self, an' I musn't run it down too heavy, 'cause if we didn't have it to call on, all a man like me would be dead from starvation, a'ready.'

'Would it be very different had you stayed in London, Donald, or you, Parboo, in New York?'

'Man, I only need New York for regular trips, and *bam*, I cut back home, where all the shit is,' Parboo said. 'You believe it but I'm a home boy, now, you know, for good, with all the salt you' got to suck through wooden spoon. All the same though, the place want' a bomb put up it' batty hole an' blow the shit out to sea!'

Donald said, 'Bai, it don't need no guru to tell you that the days when all we boys used to go 'way an' stay *done*! That's behind us. What's in front of us is home an' the Caribbean, an' makin' the place mean something. Hear me? We' got more than enough lying down outside, right here.'

'You see all that Interior you' got?' Parboo said. 'Man, i's that we need up by my two-by-four place. We need something to cancel out all them still-life shit an' all them pretty-pretty *rass* that the Art School offerin' the young people. An' we want an enlighten' attitude to Art an' artist right through the society.'

Donald said, 'It's up to us, Parboo. We'll make it. We've got to.'

I had no doubt that Donald was right. I understood Parboo's dejection. His own situation was oppressed by a philistinism of an inordinate kind and power.

BERYL GILROY

1989

from *Boy-Sandwich*

*Beryl Gilroy (b. 1924) emigrated to Britain from Guyana in the early 1950s.
Her experiences as the head of a London school are recorded in her* Black
Teacher *(1976). Following postgraduate studies she worked as a child
psychotherapist. She has published children's fiction, a volume of poetry, and
several novels including* Frangipani House *(1986) and* Stedman and Joanna
(1991).

Most of Boy-Sandwich *(1989) is set in London, and revolves around the
relationship between the narrator, Tyrone, a British-born Black teenager, and
his grandparents, who languish in an old people's home. Finding a valuable
painting among their stored belongings, he is able to finance their return to
the Caribbean, along with his parents, and, on a year out between school and
university, Tyrone himself and his girlfriend Adijah – recently seriously injured
in a racist arson attack. Both his parents and grandparents find a new lease
of life, as does Adijah; and his mother is flattered by the attentions of 'Cookie'
Tollgate, the local solicitor. But for Tyrone, the 'Island' does not feel like
'home'.*

I continue along the road which is like most people – asleep. Cats and dogs that
have been hunting and carousing through the night are slowly going home. An
old woman, clucking like a tired-out mother hen, feeds her chicks handfuls of
corn. Another supervises a few browsing lambs.

Widow's-Dip is a pretty place – a little cove nibbled in the side of the Island by
the sea and then surrounded by mounds of tufty sand-grass and beds of tiny yellow
flowers, slightly larger than buttercups. I sit in the shade watching nature. Time
passes. The day grows older.

I notice Stephy in the distance out of the corner of my eye. She is a cousin twice
removed. Cousins once removed are called 'brothers and sisters' in the islands.
Everybody seems to know and rely on Stephy, and of all the young girls I have met
she is one of the few that does not have a child clinging to her. Always neat and
tidy, every strand of hair in place, she is very correct in her behaviour. It is as if,
like a good strategist, every move is planned. But sometimes she seems a quietly
sleeping volcano biding her time. And then there are those days I think of as her
market days. As she watches, as she participates in the village happenings, those
oval-shaped and clear brown eyes are buyer's eyes, closely examining what is on

*Beryl Gilroy, *Boy-Sandwich* (Oxford: Heinemann, 1989), pp. 113–18. Reprinted with the
permission of the publishers.

offer at the stalls of life. Only her fingertips touch the things she likes until she is ready to snatch. Even if she has no money for her purchases, she will always find a way to get the pick of the bunch.

The heat of the sun is still mild enough to be enervating and, aware of Stephy's presence, I let my mind revisit London, while I wait for her to make her move. On the sand opposite the crabs sidle away as small chicken-hawks hover close.

'Hello, Tyrone. What you doing here? It's just past day-dawn.'

'And you, Stephy. I can ask the same.'

'I see you pass my door. I follow you. I make it nearly eight.'

'Nice, clean morning. Come sit down.' She sits down.

'How do you find living here? Don't you want more than this?' I quiz.

'I trying to go to America. I have a brother there but the sponsoring take a long time. I have to wait and see.'

'Are you in the Party?'

'Yes, you have to. But you know what that mean? First they own you and then they really own you. I keep away.'

'What do you do for sport? For pleasure?'

'We play rounders and go once a month to disco in the town. There is a US base near here. Sometimes I go to their dance. You know how to dance soca? Picktown soca?'

'I like Picktown. It's a quiet place, soca or no soca.'

The lie nearly singes my tongue.

'Every man to his own. I born here, I want to go from here. Home is for when you young and when you old. In between you go and grow somewhere else. Where's Adijah? You not often alone.'

'She don't like it too hot. She was in a fire.'

'Yes, we see it on TV. Twelve people – young people – burn!'

'She was playing music there. She jumped. It was touch and go for her.'

She feels sorry. I can see. She nestles beside me. She is feeling flames – mine and hers.

'You like hot sun? It soon get hot,' she says dreamily.

We lie there, two curious young people sharing a need, the need for home, facing the need to escape from home. I kiss her tentatively. She does not kiss me back. She just accepts it. There is no dissent. No discord. She accepts me totally. There are no words, just harmony and then ecstasy. She is delightfully receptive to me. I lie there enjoying the after-glow – riding high but suddenly she springs up, dusts herself and disappears as she had come. A crack of twigs. A whiff of the scent Adijah has given her. I can see that she feels conquered – yet again.

I hear the hidden despair in her receding footsteps and then there is silence. Momentarily my sense of maleness ebbs and flows in all its power and then I too feel stigmatised and guilty. In reality I should be experiencing a powerful feeling of conquest. Stephy is special and she has not repulsed me. I am Tyrone Grainger, another Island rake in the making. Suddenly the whole enterprise of coming home turns into a farce. The Island seems a confused mess. The longer I stay the more frequent such acts of betrayal would become and more and more young women seeking a way out of the press of their circumstances would yield to my demands.

'Cookie' flashes like neon lights before me. I am becoming a bit like him. The way I look at the young girls I pass, my fantasies out of control!

I feel a sharp change culminating in a hatred for the Island. Grandpa's, Grandma's, my parents'. Their Island. I hate the way it shuts me in, and the sloth-like passage of time that lulls me into a false sense of ease and insensibility. I hate the betrayal of young people and the very many illiteracies about black Londoners like me. Most of all I hate my misunderstanding of the idea of home. I don't belong here. And this morning, with the murmuring waters and racing clouds in the distance, I know it. I am British and believe it. I too scramble up to a new realisation. I dust myself and walk resolutely home. I want to call myself British for the first time in my life.

Adijah sits eating her breakfast in the garden, and fussing about the flies and other tiny creatures that see fit to offend her. Flecks of sunshine break through the leaves and pattern her hair while butterflies settle on the nearby hibiscus flowers. She has become an Island girl, at ease amongst the sunshine, the pineapples, the melons, the insects and the flowers. Sensing something, her eyes question me. I smile and say flatly, 'I am going home.'

'Home,' she sneers as she bites into a crescent of watermelon, gulping down both flesh and juice while ejecting the beetle-black seeds on to the ground. 'What kind of insult is that? Your home is here – isn't it?'

'I am going home,' I say again. Only in a flatter tone and with more resolution. 'I am going back to England.'

She ignores me. It is as if her ears are just decorations on her head. I repeat myself. Still she ignores me. I can see that her lips are set, and her eyes as hard and as stubborn as her mood. I go upstairs to think. The money has been amicably sorted out and there is no anger or discontent between my family and myself. Everyone has been agreeable to the three-way split.

Outside, the breakfast game of dominoes is in full swing, with Big Mal in his element and chortling at the possibility of a win over my grandparents. In the distance on the wide brown-burnt grass, Stephy plays with her dog. I go back to Adijah, angry that she is winding me up by ignoring me.

'This is no joke, Adijah,' I say quietly. 'I am going. Don't play games. This is a serious time for us. You had better stop and listen.'

'What did you say?' she asks, mixing menace with spite in her voice. I repeat myself.

'Take me seriously, I'm going back . . .'

Before I can finish she screams, 'Shut bloody up!' as if she has been attacked by a swarm of those little wasps which nest in the shrubs growing by the roadside. Marabuntas, the Island people call them. There are torrents of tears, sobs and more scatological language that would make the devil blush if such a thing were at all possible.

My father rushes out to us. 'No need for such language, Adijah, in my home. Who is going where?' She points to me. Since her accident she has become 'hair trigger' and waspish but my parents always ignore her outbursts.

She sobs, 'He is not touring as we planned. He's going back, to the racism, the dole and the National Front – the dirt and the despair. Remember the eviction?'

'And the unemployment, the grime, the history and your university – King's College,' I say. 'Some go back now, some later.'

She then remembers that she is expected to return as well and a bewildered look overruns her face.

'I am going back to what I understand and can deal with.' I speak more softly after my point has been made.

There is now a tight knot of family surrounding me. They are strangling me with the closeness of their presence. My grandmother, the tears shining like daubed glycerine on her face, feels let down. Like my grandfather she sees me as a fixture, a part of their conscious mental life; but I have failed my father yet again. This time I am going away. 'Away' means distance although he has 'gone away' himself in more ways than one.

'Stop talking foolish,' he says, a milky note in his voice. 'Why're you going back to England? It's a third world country. A bit more up-class than this but still third world. And one is as good as another. Besides, it's always warm here. And is always cool-time. No bustling. No fussing. Everything's cool.' He sniggers like a teenager. It doesn't suit him one little bit. His age is showing.

My mother goes on about never knowing where I would jump next. She recounts all my stupidities from the time I was born. I suck my teeth sneakily to show my anger at the attack upon my whole mode of being in this world. But Adijah hears me. 'Don't suck you teeth at your mother!' she yells. 'You pompous twit. No respect for parents! No nothing! You're not too big for a cuff from your mother. Round your thick ears!'

'Look,' I say, throwing up my hands. 'There's nothing here for me to think about or feel other than helpless about. There's only boredom, stagnation and deviousness here, and you're becoming a cantankerous old bully.'

'Who stop you from thinking?' my mother yells. 'People with brains think anywhere – everywhere – all the time! They don't get bored. They don't stagnate.'

'Since he sold that picture he fancies himself as a financier. He's nothing but a huckster.'

Adijah seems suddenly overcome by her own behaviour and by her own loss of control.

'This is home, Tyrone!' Grandma coaxes in an effort to console and reconcile.

'It is our home,' Grandpa says. 'But it is not Tyrone home. London is what he know. He must not sleep wid our eyes.'

Grandpa is the only one trying hard not to emasculate me. I remember him quietly telling me how gangs of racists used to surround the house in which he lived, effectively stopping his mates from going to work and the night-shift workers from going indoors to sleep. He alone knows what I feel with loving anti-racists around me like garish wrapping paper.

'How can he go back? Yes, how can he go back? He is not used to suffering on his own.'

Their voices rise and fall in unison, in counterpoint.

I listen wearily. They must leave me to decide and act on my own, for myself. I must shape my life without interference. I must grow and achieve for myself alone. Not by being pushed from behind by four pairs of pernicketty, meddlesome hands. I have done as I said. I have chosen to look out for my grandparents and that has been accomplished without regret.

'Everybody is getting out of England and you are rushing in where angels fear.' Adijah uses her voice like a jagged knife when it suits her.

'People are risking their lives to get there,' I reply calmly. 'Think before you talk, Adijah. Besides, your family is doing rather nicely, moonlighting on the dole!'

'Leave my family out. My father is retired. My brother pays his taxes.'

'I'm sure he does,' I reply pointedly. 'Now and then.'

Zenga Longmore

from 'Carnival Cavalcades: Dominica'

In Tap-Taps to Trinidad, British actor and singer Zenga Longmore describes two journeys to the Caribbean from her home in Brixton, South London. On the first, she and her sister and her husband stay with his brother in Jamaica. This, her second trip – accompanied part of the way by her brother Abbas Jusef – finds her island-hopping west to east from the Dominican Republic to Trinidad, where she is a guest of an aunt she has not met since childhood.

Identifiably Black, she is widely assumed to be returning 'home', although she is in fact not of Caribbean descent. Towards the end of the book, an Englishman on the flight home asks if she had travelled to 'find' herself. She replies: 'Find myself! I got totally lost. In every island I was a different person. "High" in Jamaica, "Mestizo" in the Dominican Republic, "Mulatto" in Haiti, "Black" in Dominica and St Lucia, "Mulâtre" in Martinique and Guadeloupe, and in Trinidad I was none other than a "red skin nigger". Such is life, and such is the unhealthy obsession with race, a colonial legacy that brutalises the Caribbean from top to toe.'

I was very much looking forward to staying in Dominica because I knew that the carnival would be in full swing by the time we arrived. It was all too exciting to be true. I hoped it would be a soothing carnival, quelling the nerves and resting the eye.

The journey over the windy Caribbean sea, however, made me forget about the carnival, and indeed about anything at all apart from staying alive.

We were in a four-seater plane, and it seemed as if a Force Eight gale was raging without. The plane swooped up and down with big dipper ferocity, throwing the passengers back and forth in their seats. Everyone laughed at my screaming at first, then they became bored and irritated, turning in their seats to give me dirty looks.

'How come they're not frightened?' I kept having to ask myself, before closing my eyes and yelling out to whom I hoped was a benevolent God.

Abbas sat complacently by the window cheerfully telling me to look out and admire the view. The view was a dot in the distance. As we approached, it turned into a mountainous island, green with lush vegetation.

Our little plane dived downward into the tiny airport, and we had arrived. I wobbled out on shaky legs and breathed in long and deep. The air was so much clearer and fresher than it had been in the Dominican Republic, with cool breezes.

---

*Zenga Longmore, *Tap-Taps to Trinidad: A Caribbean Journey* (London: Hodder and Stoughton, 1989), pp. 129–42. Reprinted with the permission of the Maggie Noach Literary Agency.

The little calypso band of men dressed up in colourful costumes to welcome the tourists from the plane were wasted on me. Pretty young women danced and handed out carnival leaflets, but I was too much in a state of nerves to be able to appreciate the sweet gesture, so I stomped grumpily past them, hardly giving the musicians a second glance.

The first thought that struck me on stepping from the airport was, 'England'.

Cars drove on the proper side of the road, and the phone boxes were red with royal motifs. The accent of the cab driver was standard English but with a delightful lilt.

Rastafarians strolled around in the gloaming, eating fried chicken and dumplings. I saw more Rastas that one night in Roseau, than I had done in all my weeks in Jamaica. The idea of finding a Rasta in Haiti or Santo Domingo was totally unimaginable.

Our hotel, a Victorian timber building, was right in the centre of town. 'Welcome back to Dominica! I'm *so* glad you've chosen to stay in our hotel. You come back home for carnival?'

'We have come for the carnival, but Dominica is not our original home.'

The hotel staff looked a little puzzled. If we were not from Dominica, what were we doing here? Only tourists came for a holiday, apart from visitors who were of Dominican extraction; and tourists were white.

All the hotel staff were friendly in the extreme, and I felt safe in the glow of their motherly care. I was home.

Proper food was being sold in the dining-room, good old-fashioned curried goat and rice, with 'ital', or natural, juices. How good it was to hear English being spoken once again; to be able to listen in on other people's conversations and understand every word. Yes, I decided I liked Dominica, I liked it very much.

That night, Abbas lay abed phoning his girlfriends in London, and I set out alone to savour the fruits of the carnival.

Roseau struck me as being a very fine town, with wooden houses in the Creole style, and narrow streets ablaze with flowers and charm. Already a carnival mood invaded the air. Revellers dressed in all manner of costumes patched together wandered around, and the tiny bars poured loud soca music into the warm night air. Couples clicked fingers and twitched hips to the rhythms, all making their way to the Carnival King competition, to be held in a vast stadium.

As I came into the enormous stadium, it seemed to me that the whole of Roseau's 20,000 strong population had gathered there to elect the reigning monarch of calypso. I sat on the dry grass, wedged between two drunken old men.

Now Dominica has a very high class of drunken old men. Search the Caribbean from top to bottom, and their eloquence remains unequalled. Even after the show had started they refused to stop talking. Not that I minded.

All the songs the calypsonians belted out were richer in political content than they were in rhythmical swing.

For nearly five hours, I was preached to by very pretentious sounding calypsonians about the economic factors of the banana produce, taxes, investments, and Margaret Thatcher's involvement in the economic stranglehold that Britain has imposed upon Dominica. At first I tried to understand what was going on, but with swift alacrity I gave up the struggle, and settled down to chatting with the old men, eating spiced fish and drinking cold beer.

'So I spec' you be staying for the jumping tomorrow, little brown miss.'

'Jumping?'

'Ehgn! See how she ignorant about her own isle. When floats come 'long down the roads, everybody follows them and jumps in the streets. Lord Jesus! Jus' because you live in England for a while, doesn't mean to say that you shouldn't – hic – learn 'bout the country that you are or-ig-in-ally from.'

'But I am not or-ig-in-ally from Dominica.'

'Oh, darlin'. Don't be so 'shame of your roots. Hear me now. You know what carnival is and why?'

'Yes.'

'Tell me then.'

'Something to do with Shrove Tuesday and Lent.'

'Stupid. Stupid. Stupid this girl is. You think we should carry on talking to such a stupid person?'

His friend looked me up and down then shook his head, but the old man went on regardless.

'After Lent when all the fasting was going on, there was a big celebration and a masquerade, and all this partying was called carnival.'

'That's what I just said!'

'Liar you liar! You said Christmas!'

A Rasta was singing a song addressed to Miss Charles, the Prime Minister, running down everything she'd ever done, but the chorus went, 'We love you, we adore you.'

'So how you like our music?'

'Too political by three quarters.'

'You don't like politics?'

Before I had time to answer, the old man launched into a heavily involved speech about the pitiful state of Dominica's falling economy, blaming it all on Margaret Thatcher, but he loved, he said, the Queen.

'The Queen, hoh yeah! The Queen is good. I like the Queen plenty plenty, but old Thatcher, she hate black people like we, and she is doing her best to ruin the country. We sell all our bananas to England. All our cocoa crop goes to England too, but when the cocoa comes back to us as Milo, we pay something like ten times more than what we sold it for – heh, Danny –'

'Yes man.'

'Ten times more isn't it?'

'Yes man.'

'See. You come from a rich land of sookooyas, y'know, vampires, and I come from a poor land of honest people who can't make decent livings because of the greed of a far-off nation. What do you make of that? Come round to my house tonight, meet my wife, and I'll educate you good and proper. You strike me as being a little bit simple.'

'Thanks awfully for the offer, but I have a sick brother waiting at the hotel who needs me.'

'Well, meet me another time, and we can talk.'

I thanked him and made to leave. I had imagined there would be dancing at the concert, but found instead a bored audience, who very often did not applaud when the songs had reached an end. I was more than a bit miffed at being called simple, and needed to pore over an improving book to restore my faith in my little grey cells. Besides, I was powerfully tired, and more than a little tipsy.

On the way home I stopped for a long time to gaze in wonder at the pretty little river that ran through the town. Not a soul passed me without greeting me in some way. I suddenly felt so happy I thought I was going to explode, but at the same time I also felt the burden of guilt that happiness always seems to bestow. 'What have I done to deserve this?' I kept thinking. Maybe it was the contrast to Haiti and the Dominican Republic that shocked me into an unnatural state of giddy pleasure. My faith in the Caribbean was restored.

The next day I saw a startling sight. Policemen were ambling about the streets *without* carrying guns! I had forgotten that that breed of police existed, and it was gratifying to remember that they did.

The Islamic world has a belief that nothing should be perfect. An intricately woven carpet that has taken years to complete will be purposefully flawed by the weaver, because it is thought that a manmade object that is ideal in every way is an offence to Allah, who alone should be the creator of the perfect. Mankind the world over seems wilfully to mar the good and the beautiful, whether man- or God-made, and the Dominicans are no exception. It did not take me long to discover Dominica's one flaw – tourists.

The tourist industry is the blight of any country. Apart from the ugly hotels and the ruined landscapes that inevitably accompany the tourist trade, there is also the problem that everyone in the country who has any truck with tourists tends to become phoney, because people always imagine that tourists cannot appreciate the genuine attributes of their country. The English become laughably cockney or Bertie Woosterish when American tourists are anywhere around, thinking that that is what the Americans like, and the sad fact is that it actually *is* what they like. In Zimbabwe, the false 'African Villages' that are built for the tourists are chock-a-block with clucking Europeans and clicking cameras, whereas the *real* African villages are totally ignored as if they didn't exist. This practice of the locals establishing the sham to please the tourists is upheld all over the globe.

Although I tried to steer clear of the tourist areas, to do so in Dominica was a near impossibility.

Sitting in one of the smart hotels by the beach, Abbas and I were quite shocked by the arrogant way in which the tourists treated the local people, and I am sorry to say the worst culprits were the English. Waitresses, almost reduced to tears, were mercilessly shouted at by harsh-voiced men and women complaining about such piffling details as a pin-size stain on the table cloth. This disagreeable state of affairs was worsened by the grovelling attitude that the Dominicans adopted towards their European customers.

None of the tourists liked me at all. First they would ask me what part of Dominica I was from, and when it transpired that I was a tourist just as they were, I would be looked upon with mistrustful eyes. Black people were here to provide a dash of local colour, and serve them rum punches, not sit among them as equals. It was all wrong.

Unfortunately, because there were no cars to hire owing to the number of carnival tourists, Abbas and I were forced to take excursion tours around the island.

Dominica is the hilliest island in the Caribbean, with 365 rivers, one for each day of the year, and there is nowhere in the world that can match its loveliness. It is impossible not to fall under the spell of this beautiful island.

Trafalgar Falls, with its two large waterfalls, was a splendid sight. Tiny little boys 'guided' us in a very intelligent fashion, naming all the plants that abounded around the falls, occasionally pressing their fingers into various shrubs to demonstrate how the leaves folded up.

'That is the woman falls, and that is the man,' said an eager little boy.

'Why is one the woman, and one the man?'

The child blushed prettily: 'Because the woman is fatter.' He was right. One stream of water gushing downwards was short and fat, and the other was long and skinny, but both were staggering in their beauty.

Another beauty spot Abbas and I visited was the Emerald Pool. Set in the splendour of a primeval forest, a strange eerie mood is created around the turquoise pool. Tarzan-like creepers wend and twine around the ancient rocks, and one is aware of the wood spirits who lurk in the steamy air. Sadly, however, once we reached the Emerald Pool itself, the water was so full of French tourists washing their hair in the waterfall, that the sight was completely ruined.

The beaches were aswarm with locals and tourists alike, swimming in the clear sea. Many tiny fishing boats bobbed up and down alongside the opulent yachts in which the tourists had sailed into the harbour. 'Professional Rastas' (as Little Mannie had called them) were helping the tourists anchor the boats; many of them were being treated to a rum punch in return for their favours.

One of the Rastas, a tall skinny fellow with very dark skin and gingery hair, hung around Abbas and me telling us to pay his friend to take us around the island.

'Let my friend take you around, man, c'mon, don' be shy.'

'No,' I joked, 'we just want to sit in the hotel for three weeks, we don't want to see the island.'

'Oh c'mon, man, you can't jus' sit in the hotel! That does be boring, get around, man, an' see all the sights. You been anywhere yet?'

'No.'

'You naw been to Trafalgar Falls or Emerald Pool or anywhere else?'

'No, and we don't want to go either. It's much better just to stay in the hotel, and not go out at all.'

The young man shook his head in disgust. Abbas sat drinking coconut water feeling very embarrassed, wondering how I could allow myself to appear such a dim-witted tourist.

'You naw even want to go and see the Indian Reserve?'

'Nope.'

'Where you from, England?'

'Yep.'

The Rasta shot me a meaningful look, as though to say, 'typical!'

He then dived into the water and swam over to one of the yachts, and next thing I knew he was leaning over the railings of the vessel with a rum punch in one hand, and a sausage on a stick in the other.

After our drink we walked to the local school to get a good nose around.

Blaring from the school hall was loud soca music, and faint shadowy figures were visible from behind the thick curtains.

'It is the boys having their own little carnival in there. When carnival comes around, all the boys dress up as girls, and we all have plenty fun,' said a young child.

The child then said it would be all right for us to have a look around the classrooms.

Written on the blackboard in the first class we entered was, 'It's party time, it's boogie time!'

Ah, that was more like it, I thought, remembering with a shudder the ominous maths in the Haitian school. The Dominican teachers obviously had a more advanced idea of what school was all about.

'Morning, boys!' I intoned austerely at a group of boys kicking a ball about in the playground.

'Morning, ma'am,' they chorused, stopping their game to salute me.

Just as I became rather frightened by a group of young boys who didn't jeer behind my back, a series of muffled sneers could be heard as I turned through the gate.

'Serves you right for thinking you're Joyce Grenfell,' laughed Abbas. Abbas was going to the carnival that night with a shy young girl called Rita. Tonight was his last in the West Indies, and he was determined to finish his trip by stepping high, wide and plentiful.

After a sumptuous meal at a posh hotel where Jean Rhys once lived, Abbas and I went our separate ways.

The little streets were hung with bunting and flowers, and floats of all kinds paraded up and down, each one vibrating with addictive harmonies. Carnival Queens, dressed in brilliant flouncy costumes, simpered coyly beneath the shadow of extravagant flowery hats. An impressive Gulliver's Travels float edged its way slowly through the heaving crowds, displaying a gigantic Gulliver model strapped to the bottom of the lorry, with gaudily dressed Lilliputians jigging around him. More and more floats squeezed through the revellers, each one more fanciful than the next.

Everyone danced with furious abandon, some waving their arms in the air in ecstasy. 'What have they got to be so joyous about?' I kept asking myself. Then, all of a sudden, I was infected with the spirit of joy that had possessed the rest of the throng. The crowds were so thick, that once caught among them, it was impossible to leave without a struggle, but, instead of the atmosphere becoming claustrophobic, it became headily exciting, and one felt drunk with pleasure at being a part of this whirlpool of revelry.

Some of the people dressed as gladiators, some as Harlequins, but the popular pet was the devil. In ancient folklore, music and dancing were thought to be Satan's work, so no Carnival can be complete without the Prince of Darkness keeping an eye on things. Red tights and horns were the order of the night, and many a handsome devil could be caught bumping and grinding till dawn.

Grannies, old men, and children alike, all partook of the celebrations, and the way some of the old folk danced with one another, made you wonder whether life did not begin at seventy.

'Hey, let me dance with you.'

A squat, red-eyed young man grabbed me round the waist, and danced in the Dominican style, where the man stands behind the woman holding on for dear life, and they both shimmy with a frantic whirling of hips.

'You know why I like you? It is your complexion. I only like black people, and I only like people of your colour. You naw know how I wish I was your complexion.'

'Hey, what have you been smoking?'

'Only tobacco. It's true! Do you think I like being so dark? No, no, no. I want to have your gold colour.'

'Well, isn't that strange. I would love to be darker, so it only goes to show we're never satisfied with what we're born with.'

A thin mist of rain, that falls constantly in forested Dominica, was descending gently, so I used that as an excuse to leave the dissatisfied man and have a drink at a local bar.

A young woman asked me for my hat and sun-glasses, and gave me two cans of beer in exchange. She spoke in a sing-song voice of her hatred of English politics, and her love of Dominica.

'I been to London once, it crowded, ugly and smelly. All the people are rude, and nobody helps anyone else. A woman could be lying naked in the streets, and the people will just walk past her pretending they haven't seen. Everything is money, money, money. Beauty and kindness they have all forgotten. I blame the government. Bad, isn't it, ehng?'

'None too hot,' I replied.

Her friend introduced himself as Colbert, and insisted I dance with him.

'Why do you waste your time gossiping with women at a carnival where the people are supposed to jump?'

We danced behind the floats for hours on end. Every now and again, he would pull me aside, saying, 'Let's get away. There's white people here, and I don't like to be around them.'

The white people looked very self-conscious, but glowed with pride as if they were thinking, 'How exciting to be among all these blacks. Wait till I tell the folks back home!'

Maybe I misjudged them, but I can't say I was over-enamoured by any of the tourists I met.

'Do you like white people?' asked Colbert, eyeing me gravely.

'Some of them are all right. My mother's really nice.'

'Your mother's w – oh, sorry, sorry, sorry. I – I – I – didn –'

'That's all right, just so long as it never happens again.'

Although Colbert bowed his head and swore he would rather cut out his tongue than offend me, he continued his habit of dragging me away from the white people. I myself had the sneaking suspicion, that if I lived in Dominica, and the self-satisfied tourists were the only whites I encountered, I too would have developed an aversion for white people, and I can guarantee that most *white people* travelling the West Indies would feel the same.

Colbert was very drunk. At midnight he proposed to me, and because I had also had one over the eight, I accepted him.

'I just want to spend the rest of my life with you. Can we marry?'

'Oh, all right then, if I mushed.'

'I have to go see my friend now. Meet me at the Beehive Club at one in the morning, then we can talk about the de-*tails* of the wedding.'

'Will do.'

I lurched back to the hotel in a shameful state of debauchery. A muscular Rasta waved an enormous python at my face when I reached the steps of the hotel. Women screamed in panic, but I wearily brushed both man and snake aside. Colbert would have to find another fiancée that night. I was going *straight* to bed.

'It's *you*!' said a startled voice behind me. 'I thought you said you weren't going out of your hotel, not even to the carnival.'

I turned, and through bleary eyes made out the form of the Rasta at the beach.

'I changed my mind.'

'Well, you can't go to your bed now. Come back and join the carnival.'

'Sorry, I'm going to die in a minute.'

'You'll only die if you sleep. If you dance you'll live.'

'Will I?'

'Eh hehng.'

We threw ourselves back into the crowds, and 'jumped' for a long time. The Rasta, whose name was Halbert, was right: I lived.

Many of the dancers had crippling deformities. Some of their legs were so bandy as to resemble sideways Vs. Whether they suffered from rickets or not, they joined in the fun, and sang along to the records.

The atmosphere, by now, had become extraordinarily sexual. Couples 'wined' so intimately they seemed only a step away from making love. (The rub-a-dub-dub of London blues parties had nothing on the winings and grindings of the Dominica carnival.) Hips were thrust against one another in the most suggestive manner, and a teenage girl was doing something rather shocking to the wheels of a lorry. She turned to shout at Halbert telling him he was too rough for me. Halbert laughed loudly, and gabbled a stream of patois to her.

Dominican patois is a form of broken French with a few English and African words thrown in. The population, as in Jamaica, is bilingual.

A hand gripped my arm, and I wheeled round to see the gripper, and encountered a pair of tortured eyes. The eyes belonged to my 'fiancé', Colbert.

For a moment we stood hypnotised, then Colbert stared unbelievingly at Halbert.

I couldn't explain Halbert away as my brother, and I certainly could not explain why I was in the streets, and not at the Beehive, so I did the next best thing.

With a cheery wave to Col and Halbert, I sprang over a muddy wall, and ran pell-mell back to the hotel, as fast as my weakened legs could carry me.

I burst into the hotel, crashing into the receptionist who held me by the shoulders in a motherly embrace, and asked, 'Who you running from?'

'I've er – seen a snake.'

'A snake?'

I peered out of the hotel into the crowds to see if there was any sign of the seething Colbert.

Halbert was lurking by the steps of the front porch, looking at me sadly, with large, luminous eyes.

'Why you run so?'

'Sorry about that, I suddenly remembered I'd left something on the stove.'

'I know why you ran so. You met that guy and you remembered you s'posed to meet him tonight. But I know the guy, he's from country, he won't hurt you. Let's go to the Beehive.'

'I can't!'

'Listen, man, if he's there, jus' say, 'cool out, man'.'

'Sorry, no can do.'

'Well, come to another club with me.'

'Where?'

'Not too far, we'll get a lift or a bus.'

I agreed.

Roseau is like a village, with everyone knowing everyone else, so it was easy for Halbert and me to sponge a lift off the first passer-by who was lucky enough to own a car.

'Firs' we go to my house, where you can chill out, irie?'

Halbert lived about a mile away from the town centre, and in the moonless night, it was impossible to see more than an inch ahead. The night seemed dramatically still and quiet, save for the tropical insect noises, and the faint swish of an unseen sea.

Halbert held my hand, leading me downwards into his village. I could make out rocks and sand with my feet, and every so often would step on a goat, or a bad-tempered sleeping dog. Gingerly I picked my way downwards. How Halbert knew his way in the blackness was impossible to fathom.

A dull thud resounded, and I realised that a door had been pushed open.

'Ben' your head low now, because the ceiling it plenty, plenty low.'

I bent almost double, and remained rooted to the spot until Halbert lit a kerosene lamp, and instantly we were swathed in a warm, amber light.

I looked around to find myself in a shanty shack, with a hard mud floor, wooden walls, corrugated iron roof, and a plenty, plenty low ceiling.

There was no furniture except a bed made from foam rubber scraps, with just an old army coat for covering. In the corner was a besom made from a bundle of sticks, and a plastic carrier bag lying in the middle of the room contained Halbert's clothes and other worldly possessions. I was quite amazed. Halbert cut so fine a figure, it was hard to believe he was so poor. His clothes were trendy in the Rasta style, khaki shorts, a neatly pressed Hawaiian shirt, and a red, green and gold band tying back his pale locks.

Halbert smiled a twinkly grin at me, and at that moment, two things occurred to me. One was how unbearably handsome he was, and the other was maybe I shouldn't have agreed so glibly to come to his house in the middle of the night.

I cleared my throat.

'Lovely pictures you have on the wall . . .'

The walls were entirely covered with large prints of Haile Selassie and the Lion of Judah, with snippets of the Rasta doctrine all in curly writing.

'So you really are a true Rasta, those are not just designer locks.'

'I and I a true Rasta. I worship Haile Selassie. I have no dealings at all with Babylon or artificial ways of life. Everyting in me life is 'ital', an' me don' never touch meat. I and I a peaceful man, descended from the Israelites, like all me black brethren, an' me tribe is the tribe of Levi. Jah Ras Tafari, King of Kings.'

I didn't think it fitting that I should ask him why his accent had become Jamaican all of a sudden, so I merely nodded and tried to look sage.

'Do you smoke ganja?'

'I smoke the weed of wisdom, yes.'

'Ah.'

'Come over to my mother's house, first, and we can watch a bit of TV, then we can go over to the club.'

Back up the inky steps we trod, until we found ourselves on the street. Halbert began to sing an improvised rapping song about the carnival, and we both snapped our fingers in time to the rhythm.

His mother's house was a squalid block of flats a half-an-hour's walk away.

The interior, though, was neat and cosy. As so often happens, the dwellers had defied the evil schemes of the architect, and had actually succeeded in making the hideous design of the building look reasonably decent, inside at least.

The floors were covered in sparkling white lino, and on one of the formica divans lay a long, sleeping body of a man.

'My brother, that. My mother, sister and her two kids are sleeping in the next room. Don't scream when you see any more cockroaches, 'cause you'll wake them all up. No matter if you wake my brother up.'

The brother grunted in his sleep.

'You wanna cuppa tea?'

'Yes, please.'

I switched on the TV and stared at an American cop series in a sort of coma.

Halbert came back into the room with a mug of steaming brew. I took a sip, and spluttered into the cup. Not that I meant to be rude, but my taste-buds were deeply offended. When you're expecting an honest to goodness cuppa tea, and you receive a watery mixture tasting of chocolate and chemical, good manners go the way of all flesh.

'What's the matter, ehng? You don't like tea?'

'I love it, but this . . .'

And then, of course, I remembered in a flash. In the West Indies all hot drinks are called tea, and worse still, they are plied with as much sugar as a cup can hold. This particular tea was chocolate Nesquick tea, made with tepid water.

Halbert and I sat chatting about his lazy brother. We were both sure his brother was really awake, despite the loud snores, so our snide comments about him became more and more outrageous in their character. It ended up with Halbert criticising the top of the hapless man's head, at which point the brother awoke, eyes ablaze. Halbert and I darted from the room, and ran into the hot night.

'My brother wants me to cut off my locks, he don't like my religion, but I would sooner dead than lose my faith in Selassie I. Once I eat meat, I'm as good as done.'

After a fairly long walk we reached the club, or should I say we reached a tiny room with no lights or customers. I'm not sure if it had staff, I can't remember. However, there was very loud music playing from an amplifier on the bar: old-fashioned Jamaican reggae.

Halbert and I sat in the corner sipping beer from dented cans.

The door suddenly burst open, and a glassy-eyed man threw himself into the room, and shook Halbert by the arms.

'Captain Hook a coming!'

Halbert dived behind the bar, and Mr Glassy-eyes flattened himself against the wall.

A car screeched past the club, and the sound of its engine was soon fading into the distance.

Two white eyes peeped over the top of the bar swivelling right and left. The newcomer cautiously vacated his wall, and both men drifted back to my table.

We sat for a short while without speaking.

'So – er – what was all that about?'

'What about?' came the reply, fifteen minutes later.

'That 'Captain Hook' business.'

'Captain Hook don't like we, and if he see us here he may try to kill we.'

'But who's Captain Hook?'

'A detective. He don't like Rastaman. If he caught us here drinking in an illegal club like this, he would beat we like he did last time. The man is wicked. He is evil. Do you know what him do to my friend here? He took a long stick and he jab him in the neck with it. Still he has the scars. George, George, man, show her the scar.'

George swept back his locks, unbuttoned his shirt front and pointed to his neck. I peered in the darkness, but could only vaguely make out the gleam of his gold chain.

'See the marks? That's the type of man we're dealing with.'

George took a deep swig of my beer, and said, 'And if he see that we sit here with a tourist he'll get all the more vex. He love tourist girls, and it'll make him mad to see we chatting to one. That's why I come to warn Halbert.'

Halbert clasped George's hand in gratitude.

Maybe I had been mistaken about Dominica's benevolent police force.

Halbert and I took a mini-bus back to my hotel and arranged to meet the next day, early in the morning.

The carnival was still raging away, but although the street was throbbing with 'jumpers' I only had eyes for Halbert, as his skinny figure swung away through the dancers.

SEKAI NZENZA-SHAND

'Following the Tracks Back'

Sekai Nzenza-Shand was born in Zimbabwe. She trained as a nurse in England before moving to Australia in 1985, where she studied politics at the University of Melbourne. Her publications include a novel, Zimbabwean Woman: My Own Story *(1988) and a number of short stories. In* Songs to an African Sunset *(1997) she writes: 'Although I had gone home on holiday at least every two years, I was beginning to see myself as an outsider – someone who did not belong there any more. Yet I did not feel I belonged in multicultural Australia either.' Longing to be 'anonymous', she decided to return to Zimbabwe with her Australian husband, Adam, and settle there for good. The book tells of her experiences working for an aid organization in Harare and her visits to her native village, where she hoped to 'reclaim something of myself that I had lost during years of living in the West'.*

The road home was as difficult as I remembered it, a rough three-hour drive over the corrugations, not helped by the fact that we were travelling in one of Charles's huge old BMWs which could not have been less well adapted to this journey.

Adam was used to driving on rough roads back home in Australia, but I could tell from his expression that he had never seen anything like this before. The road was really only intended for the village buses that plied this route twice a day. It began as a neat, two-lane strip of tar, but that was short-lived; a single-lane tarred stretch continued uncertainly for a while, until abruptly the dusty road took over. You could always tell when you had left the commercial farms owned by the whites because the tarred road and electricity poles would end. After that, you were in the Tribal Trust Lands, now known by the more politically correct title of Communal Lands. The change of name had meant little to the people: it had really just been a case of changing masters.

The BMW did not like the dirt road and nor did my husband. He did not see the magnificent blue of the Wedza mountains, the picture-postcard villages, and the little children running out to greet the car. He only saw the potholes, the jagged rocks and the deep culverts where the rains had turned road into river bed. This was not the honeymoon drive he had in mind. Travelling at thirty kilometres an hour produced vibrations that drowned out the stereo and when, after half an hour, the dashboard fell away in our laps, we had to forget about music altogether.

We stopped frequently to clear away rocks or to survey the road ahead, which at every turn potentially concealed axle-snapping obstacles.

Still, we were getting closer to home all the time. Soon we were in sight of the mountain, Dengedza, that overlooked my village; familiar faces appeared on the roadside. The road had become smooth and my husband was clearly enjoying himself now – he was even smiling and commenting on the scenery. I didn't have the heart to tell him about our driveway.

On reflection, it was less a driveway than the result of a rockslide. Not that we stopped to reflect too much when the rock struck the bottom of the car: a big rock all right, but hardly big enough to stand out against the hundreds of others that were scattered across the final 200-metre stretch to the homestead.

Our homecoming was rapturous. I hadn't been back for a while, and my mother ran out from the kitchen to greet us, ululating and dancing, raising dust as she came. My brother Sydney, his wife, Mai Shuvai, and their children heard the commotion and came running up from their huts to see what it was all about. Bathed in the purple light of late afternoon, it was a perfect scene and I felt a peace and happiness that only being home can bring.

Then somebody saw the oil pouring into the red dust underneath our car.

'Maiweeeeee!' (My mother!) screeched Mai Shuvai irrelevantly as she tried to stem the flow of hot oil from the sump with cotton wool. The cotton wool was replaced by a tin mug, which quickly overflowed and was replaced with a pot, and then a still bigger one. Soon just about every kitchen utensil was filled with the steaming oil.

To me, this scene had a familiarity about it that if anything made me feel more at home. Life in the village was an ongoing cycle of crisis and resolution. Nothing, except sickness and death, could disturb the overall pattern. As time was rarely an issue, wasting it meant virtually nothing at all; therefore, there was no urgency to find a solution to our problem. This was the art of life in the village.

But for my husband, being 150 kilometres from civilisation with a broken car, no tools and no hope of a passing BMW mechanic was nothing short of a major crisis, an absolute show-stopper. After he finished yelling and kicking the dust, he just sat down and stared into the distance, trying to resign himself to the prospect of an indefinite stay in the village. Here was a person who had never experienced the feeling of being abandoned by twentieth-century technology.

The people in the village did not understand what all the fuss was about. Tomorrow at four in the morning, the bus back to Harare would come by the village, waking everybody with its three-note horn blaring out 'Strangers in the Night.' If the car could not be fixed, the white man could simply get on the bus for the six-hour journey back to town.

Uncle Chakwanda, who had arrived from the main village, appointed himself mechanic to our stricken automobile. He had never fixed anything more complex than a windlass or a paraffin lamp but he led Adam away in search of 'parts' to fix the oil sump. Adam followed him, his shoulders drooping, all his power as a civilised westerner visibly ebbing away. An hour later the two of them returned with a half-tube of two-part epoxy cement, with which Uncle Chakwanda intended to restore the damage to the pride of German engineering the following morning.

'It will never work. This old man must be bloody crazy,' said Adam, laughing without an ounce of mirth. 'Has anybody else got a car around here? Maybe there's a farmhouse somewhere that has a phone.'

Everybody laughed at the sight of the white man covered in oil and dust, looking wildly around for some sign of hope – an electric light in the distance, an aeroplane flying overhead, some ingenious technology to help him out of his predicament.

Two or three beers and a bath in the warm water from the borehole lifted Adam's spirits enormously. He and I sat with our backs against the whitewashed wall of my mother's house, watching a huge white moon rise behind the hill, casting long, flat shadows on our little homestead.

Years before, we young girls longed for these full moon nights, when we would meet in the forest, down in the valley far from the kitchen fires, to dance and talk of romance and the future. There were leopards in the forest back then, hidden amongst huge dark trees which stretched out to the horizon. It was wartime and sometimes we would hear the guerillas passing quietly in the scrub, heading into the village to get food, supplies and perhaps the warmth of the older women. We would hold our breath until they passed and then our songs and laughter would slowly start up again, lilting through the trees back to the huts. In that half-light, the faces of my friends had been innocent of the hardships that were to come: teenage motherhood, the decades of drought, long years of war and a revolution which meant very little to rural people.

It would seem that I was among the last children to share the secrets of the forest, the last generation to hope for better things. The forest was virtually gone now. Even the big trees that did remain seemed somehow smaller, twisted and gnarled, their limbs distorted by the yearly harvest of firewood. Where there was once forest there was now just naked earth, cut with erosion gullies which increased with each rainy season. The songs of the village girls had been replaced by the mournful chanting of the white-clad followers of the Apostolic Faith. Times were hard and many people were seeking consolation in this Old Testament-based religion. Perhaps they were looking for the spirits that had disappeared with the forest.

That night, we were to attend an all-night ceremony honouring the spirit of a long-dead ancestor. The *bira* was to be held in the main village, a line of huts towards the river. Walking there with Adam and Sydney, I noticed that the drought winds had seared the chalky soil and that there were no crops in the fields, as there should have been at this time.

As we drew near we could hear the sound of drums and voices coming from the kitchen hut, naturally amplified by the mud bricks and thatch. Groups of men sat outside by fires, drinking *doro*, village beer, a sweet and heady seven-day brew. The drinking of beer has always been a part of Shona life, creating a fellowship between people that cannot be erased by the hardships of life in the village.

People were coming in from all parts for the ceremony, as *biras* were the central social activity in the village – apart from funerals, which seemed to dominate the calendar these days.

Faces of half-forgotten relatives, classmates, neighbours, domestic workers, teachers came out of the darkness to meet me. Greeting upon greeting was exchanged for more than ten minutes as we moved towards the kitchen hut, where a ragged choir of over thirty married women were singing up a storm by candlelight, in celebration of the ancestor's *mudzimu* or spirit. Three male drummers were pounding out solemn rhythms which from time to time would spontaneously spill into an upbeat tune led by one of the stronger singers.

The air in the small hut was heavy and sensuous – a pervasive smell of body odour and wood smoke enveloped me. Herd boys and schoolgirls drifted past the open door, sneaking looks at the singers. Every so often noted village dancers, both male and female, would bound into the centre of the hut to perform; the rest of us watched them laughing and singing. Two short planks were passed from hand to hand as clap sticks, to fill out the band.

The villagers were slowly getting used to the fact that Adam was not in fact an albino, as an elderly man had speculated upon our arrival, but my husband from Australia, the one whom my brother Sydney had been bragging about at previous beer sessions. I could imagine Sydney, the village geography teacher with his dirty suit and tie askew, regaling his fellow drinkers with stories about the time he went to Australia to attend our wedding. 'We had prawns for supper and ice-cold Australian beer all night. And I danced with white ladies in a very civilised atmosphere!'

Even before his brief Australian trip, Sydney's book-learnt knowledge of the world was unrivalled in the area. Now with his tales of visits to race meetings and red-light sex shops where white women paraded topless in front of him, he was an absolute legend. And besides all that, Sydney had seen the sea, something that virtually none of these men would ever do.

From the darkness came a new group of visitors, walking purposefully towards the kitchen. The fire-sitters filed in behind these newcomers and I noticed that there was one person at the centre of this procession whom everybody was looking at. The figure was obviously a man but he was dressed in an ill-fitting woman's white gown, like the church ladies used to wear in a bygone era, and his head was covered by a bonnet tied down tight at the sides. He clutched a hatchet which he was waving vigorously, gesturing to his relatives to prepare the way for his return to the family. The appearance of the 'ancestor' on the dance floor visibly affected many of those present, even though the spectre was probably their cousin or uncle. Adam was astonished by the dressed-up man and keen to return to safety, away from the hatchet being waved around.

In Shona culture, someone will dress in the style of a dead person and imitate the mannerisms of this ancestor while dancing, in a ritual that is calculated to awaken the spirit of the dead person in his fellow celebrants. The ceremonies usually last all through the night and are a key element in maintaining village harmony, good seasons and fertility.

The belief in ancestral spirits is woven into village law. Families can demand compensation for wrongs committed long ago to an ancestor by another family; the descendants of people who failed to stop someone being killed in their village are considered guilty of a crime against the ancestors; and a man who insults his mother will face continual bad luck, even after her death, until he puts things right. You ignore the ancestral spirits here at your peril, whatever the white missionary might tell you on Sundays about worshipping idols. People who observe the customs find that the ancestors look after them, as many freedom fighters reported during the war for independence.

The *bira* continues the long dialogue with the ancestors which stretches up to the Great Spirit. The Great Spirit is Mwari, the supreme deity in traditional Shona belief. It is not possible to talk directly to him; people have to ask the ancestors to mediate on their behalf. If Mwari is unhappy about someone's conduct, they ask his forgiveness by paying libations to the ancestral spirits. It is for this reason that Christian missionaries had so much success in Zimbabwe: their sales pitch included unmediated dialogue with God – no more middlemen to go through. Many people found this direct dialling highly appealing.

The beer was still flowing when we began our walk back to the homestead. Sydney was reluctant to leave while the pot was being passed around, but he came with us all the same. As we crossed the fields, he recited a list of developments at his school that Adam and I were to organise by the time of our next visit.

The sky was full of stars, more than my husband had ever seen in the city. 'There's a satellite,' he said, with great satisfaction.

My family's village is not really deserving of the name. It is made up of my mother's homestead and my brother Sydney's house, which is down the hill. Sydney stayed in the village so he could teach at the local school, where his wife also teaches. They have six children, three girls at boarding school and three boys still in primary school.

The homestead buildings consist of my mother's grass-thatched hut, and a six-room, corrugated-iron-roofed house; I remember assisting in moulding bricks for this house when I was ten. Then there is the granary and a shelter for our borehole.

Traditionally, our house should have been one of a long line of grass-thatched huts facing a line of sleeping houses. But after my father returned to his village from his teacher training, he and my mother regarded themselves as more civilised than everyone in the main village near the river. So in 1965 they moved up the hill to build a modern house, away from my grandfather and his many wives. For years, this house was the model home in the area, remarked upon for miles because we slept on beds and used pit latrines, which were unknown in most villages at the time.

As children we were required to grow at least one tree each. We grew mangoes, oranges, guavas and lemons. When the trees were in season, Amai had to bury some of the fruit because it all ripened at the same time and could not be preserved.

It was a pleasant, happy home. We mixed with the local kids only at primary school, or when we were herding cattle in the valley or swimming in the river; basically, we kept to ourselves a lot. Our library, housed in my parent's bedroom, was made up of books given to my father by the missionaries. We grew up on authors like Rider Haggard, Enid Blyton, Daniel Defoe, Jules Verne, Rudyard Kipling . . . Our early education about the world came from books like *King Solomon's Mines, The Jungle Book, The Thirty-Nine Steps, Around the World in Eighty Days* and *The Swiss Family Robinson*. As we grew older, we moved on to American pulp fiction such as James Hadley Chase. Mills and Boon romances were a speciality because we could compete with each other on the number of days it took to finish reading 120 pages. In high school we discovered D. H. Lawrence, Charles Dickens and Thomas Hardy. I recall a dog-eared copy of *Lady Chatterley's*

Lover being concealed in the granary, as my sisters and I worked our way through its forbidden pages. At night we held quizzes on the classics while sitting around a paraffin lamp near the fire.

As the years went by, one by one we children left the village and pursued careers. But my father died and my mother stayed on, continuing the same duties she had performed for years. Her life appeared to be static. Yet every one of her children who had dreamed of a life beyond the village had had their chance; the achievements of my parents seemed quite remarkable in that respect.

At dawn, I could hear my mother busy in the yard, gathering firewood and water so that the household might have a cup of tea and a plate of porridge before everyone began their chores. I could also hear her domestic helper sweeping the compound free of dust.

Adam and I rose quickly to enjoy the sunrise bursting over the hills across the river, framing the last big *msasa* tree that remained. I couldn't recall the village ever looking so beautiful, despite the ravages of drought and deforestation. Perhaps as a child I had taken it all for granted. I silently thanked my father for firing us children with the ambition to see the world, because to return to the village after a long absence was a chance to see my childhood again.

Uncle Chakwanda arrived after breakfast with his half-tube of epoxy cement and my husband suddenly remembered the mess we were in regarding the car. For the next hour, Uncle Chakwanda daubed the gaping hole in the sump with the cement while Adam looked on, shaking his head. My uncle good-naturedly ignored his comments: 'Thanks, but you really are wasting your time, you know.' 'You have to have an aluminium arc welder to fix something like that on a BMW and all you've got is a tube of goo and a bit of spit.' 'You've got to be joking. We're never going to get home like this.'

While this was going on, I was sitting on a goatskin mat helping my mother and two of the village women to shell groundnuts. I had known these women for a long time; they had not changed much, except that they seemed to be poorer. When they saw me, they only asked my mother which of the girls I was. 'The one delivered by Mai Hilda and Mai Keti.' The women nodded; they remembered the day I was born. I had an identity in the village – I could not pretend to be anyone else among these people.

In Zimbabwe, people generally speak Shona or Ndebele and, in the case of urban people, fluent English. My mother and her friends were talking in Shona, which was spoken by everyone in the village.

'She was an easy delivery,' said Amai.

'Which year was that?'

'The year her grandfather took a fifth wife.'

'The epileptic girl from across the Save River?'

'Yes, she bore him five children and then left him for one of the church elders.'

'He was too old to perform.'

'True, but he never gave up. He married his eighth wife six months before he died.'

'She came here and asked me if she could be inherited by my husband as his second wife,' my mother replied.

'Yes, I remember that,' said one of the women. 'You told her that your husband was going to marry a second wife. A year later, you brought your niece to be your husband's new wife.'

'That's right.'

Adam came in to announce that, much to his amazement, the BMW had been fixed. Uncle Chakwanda had produced a battered old tin of motor oil, syphoned from the grinding mill, which was apparently still the only other piece of machinery in the area. Nobody would have their maize ground today, but at least we would get home.

It was a question of faith, living in the village, having a patient attitude and believing that things would work out in the end.

When we picked up our bags to leave, we noticed that a chicken had laid an egg on our pillow. Amai and her friends began to ululate: the egg was a sign that meant Sekai was pregnant. A few weeks later, the doctor confirmed that I was indeed expecting a baby. The chickens are never wrong.

FRED D'AGUIAR

'Home'

Fred D'Aguiar (b. 1960) was born in London, and spent his childhood in Guyana, returning to England in 1972. He trained as a psychiatric nurse but later studied at the University of Kent at Canterbury. He has written several plays and two novels, and published several collections of verse, including Mama Dot *(1985),* Airy Hall *(1989) and* British Subjects *(1993) — from which this poem is taken. D'Aguiar is currently based in Florida.*

These days whenever I stay away too long,
anything I happen to clap eyes on,
(that red telephone box) somehow makes me
miss here more than anything I can name.

My heart performs a jazzy drum solo
when the crow's feet on the 747
scrape down at Heathrow. H.M. Customs . . .
I resign to the usual inquisition,

telling me with Surrey loam caked
on the tongue, home is always elsewhere.
I take it like an English middleweight
with a questionable chin, knowing

my passport photo's too open-faced,
haircut wrong (an afro) for the decade;
the stamp, British Citizen not bold enough
for my liking and too much for theirs.

The cockney cab driver begins chirpily
but can't or won't steer clear of race,
so rounds on Asians. I lock eyes with him
in the rearview when I say I lived with one.

Fred D'Aguiar, *British Subjects* (Newcastle: Bloodaxe, 1993), pp. 14–15. Reprinted by permission of the publisher.

He settles at the wheel grudgingly,
in a huffed silence. Cha! Drive man!
I have legal tender burning in my pocket
to move on, like a cross in Transylvania.

At my front door, why doesn't the lock
recognise me and budge? I give an extra
twist and fall forward over the threshold
piled with the felicitations of junk mail,

into a cool reception in the hall.
Grey light and close skies I love you.
chokey streets, roundabouts and streetlamps
with tyres chucked round them, I love you.

Police officer, your boots need re-heeling.
Robin Redbreast, special request – a burst
of song so the worm can wind to the surface.
We must all sing for our suppers or else.

Suggestions for Further Reading

For those who wish to pursue more travel writings of the sort represented in this book, some suggestions for further reading are included here. As with the anthology itself, the emphasis is on first-person factual narratives of inter-continental travel, although a few works of a more imaginative nature are included also. The references are to modern editions, where available; full details are to be found in the Bibliography.

The suggestions are listed geographically, according to the place written about, but it may be useful to first mention a number of diasporic narratives whose scope would defy such a categorization. The complex to-ing and fro-ing between the continents one finds in Equiano's *Narrative* (1969) is matched in twentieth-century autobiographies including those of African-American writers such as James Weldon Johnson (1990), Claude McKay (1995), Langston Hughes (1986, 1993) and George S. Schuyler (1966); African political leaders such as Kwame Nkrumah (1957); musicians such as Duke Ellington (1977), Miriam Makeba (1988) and Manu Dibango (1994); and maverick characters such as Ras Prince Monolulu (1950), Hubert Julian (1965) and Ernest Marke (1986). In fiction, which has the freedom to roam across the generations as well as the continents, these trajectories can be even more extensive: see the diasporic novels of Maryse Condé (1994) and Caryl Phillips (1989, 1994).

There are, as yet, few anthologies specifically devoted to travel writings of the Black Atlantic. Some narratives of journeys between Africa and the United States (in both directions) appear in Drachler (1975); accounts of visitors to Britain up to 1890 are included in Dabydeen and Edwards (1991); and very recent writings by African American women travellers – many of them first published in *Essence* – are showcased in *Go Girl!* (Lee 1997). Some Black writers are included in Oscar and Lillian Handlin's *From the Outer World* (1997), which provides a selection of texts by 'dark-skinned or swarthy twentieth-century visitors' to the United States.

But interest in Black travel narratives is certainly growing. The last decade has seen the reissue of Dean's *Umbala* (1989), Hurston's *Tell My Horse* (1990), Dunham's *Island Possessed* (1994), and Wright's *Black Power* (1995a) and *Pagan Spain* (1995b). There have been translations of several books by Bernard Dadié (1986, 1994a, 1994b); selections from *The Travels of William Wells Brown* (Jefferson 1991); and new editions of Mukasa (1904) and Hughes (1934) are in preparation. Contemporary works finding their way to the travel shelves include Harris (1994), Richburg (1997) and McElroy (1997).

General studies of anthropology and other literatures of travel are largely concerned with European writings in the context of colonial and imperial expansion, and have little to say about Black authors; many of their formulations would probably need to be revised if they did. But their analyses of the ways in which encounters with 'other cultures' are represented are of wider application. Pratt (1992) – perhaps the best introductory work – includes a brief discussion of Wright's *Black Power*. Other wide-ranging studies I have found illuminating include Clifford and Marcus (1986), Clifford (1988, 1997), Buzard (1993) and Todorov (1993). The British-based journal *Studies in Travel Writing*, established in 1997, will doubtless become a key forum for future developments.

The claim by James Clifford that 'feminist ethnography . . . has not produced either unconventional forms of writing or a developed reflection on ethnographic textuality as such' (1986: 20–1) came in for much criticism and the most cited counter-example was the African American author Zora Neale Hurston (e.g. hooks 1991: 143; Behar 1993: 318). Studies of her work tend to concentrate on her writings on the Southern USA where she grew up, but there are some analyses of Hurston's writing on Haiti – the subject of Mikell (1982) and Gordon (1990), and – in conjunction with other North American accounts – of Dash (1988) and Pettinger (1997).

Critical studies of works by other authors include Thomas (1984) and Mudimbe-Boyi (1992) on Bernard Dadié; Weiss (1994) on Richard Wright; Moore (1996) on Langston Hughes; and Riesz (1996) on Bakary Diallo. Gikandi (1997) includes sections on Mukasa, Seacole and others. Gruesser (1990) provides some reflections on accounts of travels to Africa by Black authors. There is also a substantial body of work on slave narratives: useful points of departure are Andrews (1986), Davis and Gates (1985) and Gates (1988).

Gruesser (1997) offers a brief survey of African American travel writing. More general studies of the diaspora often include references to travel writing, even if only in passing: see Drake (1975), Shepperson (1976), Robinson (1983), Segal (1995) and, of course, Paul Gilroy (1993, 1996). And there are useful pointers in C. R. Gibbs' *Black Explorers* (1992).

NORTH AMERICA

Two major accounts of visits to the United States by Africans are Bernard Dadié's *One Way* (1994b) and *America, Their America* by John Pepper Clark (1968).

There are memorable portraits of New York by South Africans Nat Nakasa (1995) and Lewis Nkosi (1983); and Eva de Carvalho Chipenda (1996) also recalls her stay there, meeting leaders of the Angolan liberation movement in exile. Jane T. Creider (1986: 142–52) records her 'impressions of Canada' as she arrives in Ontario from Kenya. *I Was a Savage* (1958) by Prince Modupe concludes with the protagonist working his passage from Freetown to New York, where he jumps ship.

Earlier visitors include the South African Sol T. Plaatje, although only part of the typescript describing his visit of 1921–22 survives, published for the first time in his *Selected Writings* (1996: 289–99). The autobiographies of Nnamdi Azikiwe

(1970) and Kwame Nkrumah (1957) both include chapters covering their time as students in the United States in the 1920s and 1930s.

The travel writings of the Colombian Manuel Zapata Olivella have not yet been translated, apart from a short extract in O. and L. Handlin (1997: 253–9). Paule Marshall's novel *Brown Girl, Brownstone* (1982), narrated by the daughter of Barbadian immigrants living in Brooklyn, is a classic of the literature. Other fictional renderings of Caribbean migration to North America include Cliff (1987), Kincaid (1994), Brand (1988) and Philip (1988).

EUROPE

Early slave narratives, such as those represented in this book, usually include descriptions of life in Europe, where their authors eventually settled. Those of the mid-nineenth century, on the other hand, often end at the point where their protagonist reaches safety in Britain; some which go on to describe their time there are Mary Prince (1987), Douglass (1969), Ward (1855) and Jacobs (1988).

The much-travelled W. E. B. Du Bois wrote many articles on Europe for *The Crisis*, several of them collected in Lester (1971: II, 321–58). The magazine also carried pieces on Paris and London by the poet Countee Cullen, (1991: 551–9). The autobiographies of Claude McKay (1995) and Langston Hughes (1986, 1993) record their travels in Europe, including the Soviet Union. Other visitors to Russia and neighbouring republics include Prince (1990), Abakari (1965), Hughes (1934), Murphy (1974), Lorde (1996), Andrea Lee (1984), West (1995) and Brooks (1996a).

Ocansey (1989) and Mukasa (1904) are among the earliest accounts by Africans of Britain. Salim C. Wilson, known as the 'Black Evangelist of the North' for his mission work in England in the early decades of this century, wrote of his first impressions of London in *I Was a Slave* (1960). Several of the East African life-histories included in Perham (1963) describe journeys to Europe made for a variety of reasons. The autobiographies of Joe Appiah (1990) and Kwame Nkrumah (1957) include sections on their stays in England. Bernard Dadié has written books on Paris (1994a) and Rome (1986), while Blaise N'Djehoya and Massaër Diallo offer two very different perspectives on France and the French in *Un regard noir* (1984).

Narratives of African migration to Europe are found in Casely-Hayford (1983), Cole (1988), Guilao (1994) and Oji (1992). The autobiography of Buchi Emecheta (1994c) includes sections on her early years in London, but refers the reader to her fiction (1994a, 1994b) for more detail. Other African novels and short stories in which the protagonist travels to Europe include Sembène (1974, 1987), Kane (1972) and Darko (1995).

James Baldwin (1995) draws out of his account of his experiences in a Swiss village some much-quoted general reflections. Interviews with less well-known 'American Negroes in exile' in five different European countries are included in Dunbar (1968).

In the preface to the UK edition of his autobiography, the Brazilian soccer legend Pele (1977) reminisces on his encounters with Britain and the British over the years.

Travel pieces about Europe were carried by the Barbadian magazine *Bim* in the 1950s and 1960s: see especially Wickham (1957, 1964) and Figueroa (1958). Born in Jamaica but London-raised, Ferdinand Dennis wrote about his 'journey into Afro-Britain' in *Behind the Frontlines* (1988). The classic novels of Caribbean migration to Britain include Lamming (1980) and Selvon (1985); there are also several published collections of oral history, such as those by Lambeth Council (1988), Ethnic Communities Oral History Project (1989) and Western (1992). Of related interest is a fascinating passage in Carew (1994: 27–33) in which the author helps Malcolm X to imagine an alternative past in which his Caribbean mother had not gone to the United States but migrated later – with her children – to England.

Matthew Henson (1989) tells of his voyage to the North Pole with Peary in 1909; while Allen Counter (1991) followed in his footsteps to Greenland and located the son he fathered – whom he then introduced to Henson's descendants in the United States.

Bakary Diallo's *Force-bonté* (1926) is one of the few published memoirs of an African in French military service during World War I, although there are transcripts of oral testimony in the archives: see, for instance, Lunn (1987). There are numerous accounts of African Americans in the Spanish Civil War – including Robeson (1952), Pickens (1992), Hughes (1992), and the letters of Canute Frankson, published for the first time in Nelson and Hendricks (1996).

One of the few book-length accounts to come out of World War II is Walter White's *A Rising Wind* (1971), about his 1944 investigation into the conditions of Black American servicemen in Europe and North Africa. The oral testimony of soldiers is collected in Motley (1975), while a little-known story by Ralph Ellison (1960) draws on his wartime experiences in Wales as a merchant seaman. Ford (1985) recalls his time in Scotland with the British Honduran Forestry Unit. Other first-hand wartime reminiscences may be found in Bousquet and Douglas (1991). The autobiography of Colin Powell (1995) includes a chapter on his three-year stint in West Germany in the late 1950s.

AFRICA

Perhaps the first recorded journey to Africa by a descendant of slaves is the journal of Paul Cuffe, who sailed to Sierra Leone in 1811–12 (Harris 1972). Fifty years later saw the visit of Delany and Campbell: their reports have now been published together in Bell (1969). Johnson (1882) describes his missionary work in Cameroon; better-known is the much-anthologized account of a visit to Egypt by Edmund Blyden (1873).

Dean (1989) tells of his adventures in South Africa at the beginning of this century. In the 1920s, Claude McKay spent some time in Morocco (1995), and Langston Hughes visited several ports on the west coast as a merchant seaman (1986).

Eslanda Goode Robeson's *African Journey* (1945) writes of her three-month trip made before the war, with her son Pauli. In the postwar period there was a veritable explosion of travel accounts by African Americans – including Biggers (1996), Smith (1970), Lacy (1970) and Angelou (1987). Interviews with 'exiles' living in Ghana and Tanzania are included in Dunbar (1968), while Golden (1983) tells of her marriage to a Nigerian and life in Lagos. Alice Walker kept a journal during her time working on the film *Warrior Marks* in Senegal, Gambia and Burkina Faso (Walker and Parmar 1993). Other recent visits are recorded by Gwendolyn Brooks (1996b) and Eddy Harris (1994).

As well as George Schuyler, there have been a number of Black foreign correspondents working in Africa for major US newspapers: see in particular Dash (1973) and Richburg (1995, 1997).

Accounts by Caribbean writers include George Lamming's 'The African Presence' (1984), while more extended stays form the basis for novels by Maryse Condé (1982) and Miriam Warner-Vieyra (1987).

Belmira Nunes Lopes, born in New England of Cape Verdean parents, recounts two visits to Africa in her autobiography: one to Cape Verde, and the other to Angola and Mozambique (Nunes 1982). Of those Africans who have written of returning to the country of their birth after extended periods abroad, two novels are of special interest: Ousmane Sembène (1957) and Buchi Emecheta (1994d).

SOUTH AND CENTRAL AMERICA AND THE CARIBBEAN

African American travel writings on the Caribbean range from the short description of Jamaica by Du Bois (1986a) to Katharine Dunham's major book on Haiti, *Island Possessed* (1994). Zora Neale Hurston (1990) wrote of both countries, while Belmira Lopes Nunes (Nunes 1982) recalls several years' teaching in Puerto Rico in the 1920s.

George S. Schuyler (1948) wrote a series of articles on various South American countries he visited as a reporter for the *Pittsburgh Courier*. June Jordan has written essays on her visits to Nicaragua (1986a) and the Bahamas (1986b). In *I Sought My Brother* (1981) Allen Counter and David Evans condense the experiences of several trips in search of the 'bush people' of Surinam; the result is 'not a typical academic's account of discovering an uncivilized and backward black tribe. We discovered an experience, we discovered friends and family, we discovered ourselves.'

Journeys back 'home' feature strongly in the work of Caribbean writers in the post-war period, most famously perhaps in Aimé Cesaire's epic poem, *Cahier d'un retour au pays natal* (1971). A few take non-fictional form, such as Amryl Johnson's island-hopping *Sequins for a Ragged Hem* (1988) and Jamaica Kincaid's polemic addressed to tourists visiting her native Antigua (1988). But more frequently, they form the basis of novels and short stories: see, for instance, Marshall (1985a, 1985b), Riley (1985, 1992) and Phillips (1995b).

Bibliography

Abakari, Salim B. (1965) 'Safari yangu-yu bara urusi na ya Siberia' [My journey to Russia and Siberia], in Lyndon Harris (ed.), *Swahili Prose Texts: A Selection from the Material Collected by Carl Velten from 1893 to 1896*. London: Oxford University Press, pp. 262–81. [First published 1901]

Anderson, Marian (1957) *My Lord, What a Morning!* London: Cresset Press.

Andrews, William L. (1986) *To Tell a Free Story: The First Century of Afro-American Autobiography, 1760–1865*. Urbana: University of Illinois Press.

Andrews, William L., Frances Foster and Trudier Harris (eds) (1997) *The Oxford Companion to African-American Literature*. Oxford: Oxford University Press.

Angelou, Maya (1987) *All God's Children Need Travelling Shoes*. London: Virago.

Appiah, Joseph (1990) *Joe Appiah: The Autobiography of an African Patriot*. With a foreword by Henry Louis Gates, Jr. New York: Praeger.

Azikiwe, Nnamdi (1970) *My Odyssey: An Autobiography*. London: C. Hurst.

Baldwin, James (1995) 'Stranger in the Village', in *Notes of a Native Son*. Harmondsworth: Penguin, pp. 151–65. [First published 1953]

Bammer, Angelika (ed.) (1994) *Displacements: Cultural Identities in Question*. Bloomington: Indiana University Press.

Barry, Andrew (1996) 'Lines of Communication and Spaces of Rule', in Andrew Barry, Thomas Osborne and Nikolas Rose (eds), *Foucault and Political Reason*. London: UCL Press, pp. 123–41.

Bechet, Sidney (1960) *Treat It Gentle*. London: Cassell.

Behar, Ruth (1993) 'Introduction'. Special Issue on Women Writing Culture. *Critique of Anthropology*, 13 (4), 307–25.

Bell, Howard (ed.) (1969) *Search for a Place: Black Separatism and Africa, 1860*. Ann Arbor: University of Michigan Press.

Bennett, Louise (1966) *Jamaica Labrish*. Kingston: Sangster's.

Benson, Eugene and L. W. Connolly (eds) (1994) *Encyclopedia of Post-Colonial Literatures in English*. 2 vols. London and New York: Routledge.

Bessie, Alvah and Prago, Albert (eds) (1987) *Our Fight: Writings by Veterans of the Abraham Lincoln Brigade, Spain, 1936–1939*. Introduction by Ring Lardner, Jr. New York: Monthly Review Press with the Veterans of the Abraham Lincoln Brigade.

Biggers, John (1996) *Ananse: The Web of Life in Africa*. Austin: University of Texas Press. [First published 1962]

Blackett, Richard J. M. (1983) *Building an Antislavery Wall: Black Americans in the Atlantic Abolitionist Movement, 1830–1860*. Baton Rouge: Louisiana State University Press.

Blakely, Allison (1986) *Russia and the Negro: Blacks in Russian History and Thought*. Washington, DC: Howard University Press.

Blyden, Edward Wilmot (1873) *From West Africa to Palestine*. Freetown: T. J. Sawyer.

Bolden, Tonya (1997) 'In the land up over', in Elaine Lee (ed.), *Go Girl!* Portland, OR: Eighth Mountain Press, pp. 307–12.

Bousquet, Ben and Colin Douglas (1991) *West Indian Women at War: British Racism in World War II*. London: Lawrence and Wishart.

Brand, Dionne (1988) *Sans Souci and Other Stories*. Stratford, ON: Williams-Wallace.

Brennan, Timothy (1997) *At Home in the World: Cosmopolitanism Now*. Cambridge, MA: Harvard University Press.

Bridglal, Sindamani (1990) 'She Lives Between Back Home and Home', in Rhonda Cobham and Merle Collins (eds), *Watchers and Seekers: Creative Writing by Black Women in Britain*. Cambridge: Cambridge University Press, p. 88.

Brooks, Gwendolyn (1972) 'African Fragment', in *Report from Part One*. Detroit: Broadside Press, pp. 87–130.

Brooks, Gwendolyn (1996a) 'Black Woman in Russia', in *Report from Part Two*. Chicago: Third World Press, pp. 53–75.

Brooks, Gwendolyn (1996b) 'In Ghana', in *Report from Part Two*. Chicago: Third World Press, pp. 44–52.

Brown, John (1855) *Slave Life in Georgia: A Narrative of the Life, Sufferings, and Escape of John Brown, a Fugitive Slave, now in England*, edited by L. A. Chamerovzow. London.

Brown, W. Wells (1852) *Three Years in Europe; or, Places I Have Seen and People I Have Met*. London: Charles Gilpin. Abridged reprint in *The Travels of William Wells Brown*, edited by Paul Jefferson (1991). Edinburgh: Edinburgh University Press, pp. 71–235.

Busby, Margaret (ed.) (1992) *Daughters of Africa: An International Anthology of Words and Writings by Women of African Descent from the Ancient Egyptian to the Present Day*. London: Jonathan Cape.

Buzard, James (1993) *The Beaten Track: European Tourism, Literature and the Ways to 'Culture', 1800–1918*. Oxford: Clarendon Press.

Carew, Jan (1994) *Ghosts in Our Blood: With Malcolm X in Africa, England and the Caribbean*. Chicago: Lawrence Hill.

Casely-Hayford, Adelaide (1983) 'My Life and Times', in *Mother and Daughter: Memoirs and Poems by Adelaide and Gladys Casely-Hayford*, edited by Lucilda Hunter. Freetown: Sierra Leone University Press, pp. 1–60.

Cesaire, Aimé (1971) *Cahier d'un retour au pays natal / Return to My Native Land*. French text with parallel English translation by Emile Snyder. Paris: Presence Africaine. [First published 1939]

Chambers, Iain and Lidia Curti (eds) (1995) *The Post-Colonial Question: Common Skies, Divided Horizons*. London: Routledge.

Chipenda, Eva de Carvalho (1996) *The Visitor: An African Woman's Story of Travel and Discovery*. Geneva: WCC Publications.

Clark, J. P. (1968) *America, Their America*. London: Heinemann.

Clarke, Julian (1992) 'National Exclusions', in Alrick Cambridge and Stephan Feuchtwang (eds), *Where You Belong: Government and Black Culture*. Aldershot: Avebury, pp. 14–32.

Cliff, Michelle (1987) *No Telephone to Heaven*. New York: Vintage International.

Clifford, James (1986) 'Introduction: Partial Truths', in James Clifford and George E. Marcus (eds), *The Poetics and Politics of Ethnography*. Berkeley: University of California Press, pp. 2–26.

Clifford, James (1988) *The Predicament of Culture: Twentieth-Century Ethnography, Literature and Art*. Cambridge, MA: Harvard University Press.

Clifford, James (1997) *Routes: Travel and Translation in the Twentieth Century*. Cambridge, MA: Harvard University Press.

Clifford, James and George E. Marcus (eds) (1986) *Writing Culture: The Poetics and Politics of Ethnography*. Berkeley: University of California Press.

Cole, Robert Wellesley (1988) *An Innocent in Britain: Or the Missing Link*. London: Campbell Matthews.

Collum, Danny Duncan (ed.) (1992) *'This Ain't Ethiopia, But It'll Do': African Americans in the Spanish Civil War*. New York: G. K. Hall.

Condé, Maryse (1982) *Hérémakhonon*. Translated by Richard Philcox. Washington, DC: Three Continents Press. [First published 1976]

Condé, Maryse (1994) *Tree of Life*. Translated by Victoria Reiter. London: Women's Press. [First published 1987]

Cooper, Wayne and Robert Reinders (1967) 'Claude McKay in England, 1920'. *Race*, 9 (1) (July), 67–84.

Counter, S. Allen (1991) *North Pole Legacy: Black, White, and Eskimo*. Amherst: University of Massachusetts Press.

Counter, S. Allen and David L. Evans (1981) *I Sought My Brother: An Afro-American Reunion*. Cambridge, MA: MIT Press.

Creider, Jane Tapsubei (1986) *Two Lives: My Spirit and I*. London: Women's Press.

Cugoano, Ottobah (1787) *Thoughts and Sentiments on the Evil and Wicked Traffic of the Slavery and Commerce of the Human Species . . .* London.

Cullen, Countee (1991) *My Soul's High Song: The Collected Works of Countee Cullen*, edited by Gerald Early. New York: Doubleday.

Dabydeen, David (1994) *Turner: New and Selected Poems*. London: Jonathan Cape.

Dabydeen, David and Paul Edwards (eds) (1991) *Black Writers in Britain, 1760–1890*. Edinburgh: Edinburgh University Press.

Dadié, Bernard Binlin (1986) *The City Where No One Dies*. Translated by Janis A. Mayes. Washington, DC: Three Continents Press. [First published 1968]

Dadié, Bernard Binlin (1994a) *An African in Paris*. Translated by Karen C. Hatch. Chicago: University of Illinois Press. [First published 1959]

Dadié, Bernard Binlin (1994b) *One Way: Bernard Dadié Observes America*. Translated by Jo Patterson. Chicago: University of Illinois Press. [First published 1964]

Danticat, Edwige (1995a) *Breath, Eyes, Memory*. London: Abacus.

Danticat, Edwige (1995b) *Krik? Krak!* New York: Soho Press.

Darko, Amma (1995) *Beyond the Horizon*. Oxford: Heinemann.

Dash, J. Michael (1988) *Haiti and the United States: National Stereotypes and the Literary Imagination*. London: Macmillan.

Dash, Leon (1973) 'The War in Angola'. *Washington Post*, 23–26 December.

Davis, Charles T. and Henry Louis Gates, Jr (eds) (1985) *The Slave's Narrative*. New York: Oxford University Press.

Davis, Thadious M. (1981) 'Double Take at Relais de L'Espadon', in Erlene Stetson (ed.), *Black Sister: Poetry by Black American. Women, 1746–1980*. Bloomington: Indiana University Press, pp. 277–8.

Dean, Captain Harry (1989) *Umbala: The Adventures of a Negro Sea Captain in Africa and on the Seven Seas in His Attempts to Found an Ethiopian Empire*. Written with the assistance of Sterling North. New introduction by George Shepperson. London: Pluto Press. [First published 1929]

Dennis, Ferdinand (1988) *Behind the Frontlines: Journey into Afro-Britain*. London: Victor Gollancz.

Diallo, Bakary (1926) *Force-bonté*, 5th edn. Paris: F. Rieder. [First published 1921]

Dibango, Manu, with Danielle Rouard (1994) *Three Kilos of Coffee*. Translated by Beth G. Raps. Chicago: University of Chicago Press. [First published 1989]

Dodgson, Elyse (1984) *Motherland: West Indian Women to Britain in the 1950s*. London: Heinemann.

Douglass, Frederick (1969) *My Bondage and My Freedom*. With a new introduction by Philip S. Foner. New York: Dover Publications. [First published 1855]

Drachler, Jacob (ed.) (1975) *Black Homeland/Black Diaspora: Cross-Currents of the African Relationship*, Port Washington, NY: Kennikat Press.

Drake, St Clair (1975) 'The Black Diaspora in Pan-African Perspective'. *Black Scholar*, (September), pp. 2–14.

Du Bois, W. E. B. (1971a) 'The Fields of Battles', in *The Seventh Son: The Thought and Writings of W. E. B. Du Bois*, edited by Julius Lester, vol. 2. New York: Random House, pp. 327–9. [First published 1919]

Du Bois, W. E. B. (1971b) 'Africa' In *The Seventh Son: The Thought and Writings of W. E. B. Du Bois*, edited by Julius Lester, vol. 2. New York: Random House, pp. 340–8. [First published 1924]

Du Bois, W. E. B. (1985) 'Harvard in Berlin', in *Against Racism: Unpublished Essays, Papers, Addresses, 1887–1961*, edited by Herbert Aptheker. Amherst: University of Massachusetts Press, pp. 29–33. [Originally written in 1892]

Du Bois, W. E. B. (1986a) 'An Amazing Island', in *Writings*, edited by Nathan Huggins. New York: Library of America, pp. 1167–8. [First published 1915]

Du Bois, W. E. B. (1986b) *The Dusk of Dawn: An Essay toward an Autobiography of a Race Concept*, in *Writings*, edited by Nathan Huggins. New York: Library of America. [First published 1940]

Dunbar, Ernest (1968) *The Black Expatriates: A Study of American Negroes in Exile*. London: Gollancz.

Dunham, Katherine (1994) *Island Possessed*. Chicago: University of Chicago Press. [First published 1969]

Echenberg, Myron J. (1991) *Colonial Conscripts: The Tirailleurs Sénégalais in French West Africa, 1857–1960*. London: Currey.

Ellington, Edward Kennedy (1977) *Music Is My Mistress*. London: Quartet. [First published 1973]

Ellison, Ralph (1960) 'In a Strange Country', in *I Have Seen War*, edited by Dorothy Sterling. New York: Hill and Wang, pp. 103–10.

Emecheta, Buchi (1994a) *Second-Class Citizen*. Oxford: Heinemann. [First published 1974]

Emecheta, Buchi (1994b) *In the Ditch*. Oxford: Heinemann. [First published 1979]

Emecheta, Buchi (1994c) *Head above Water*. Oxford: Heinemann. [First published 1986]

Emecheta, Buchi (1994d) *Kehinde*. Oxford: Heinemann.

Equiano, Olaudah (1969) *The Interesting Narrative of the Life of Olaudah Equiano or Gustavus Vassa, the African. Written by Himself*, edited with an introduction by Paul Edwards. London: Dawsons of Pall Mall. [First published 1789]

Ethnic Communities Oral History Project (1989) *The Motherland Calls: African–Caribbean Experiences*. London: Ethnic Communities Oral History Project.

Fabre, Michel (1991) *From Harlem to Paris: Black American Writers in France, 1840–1980*. Urbana: University of Illinois Press.

Figueroa, John (1958) 'This Travelling'. *Bim*, 7 (26), January–June, 85–9.

Ford, Amos A. (1985) *Telling the Truth: The Life and Times of the British Honduran Forestry Unit in Scotland (1941–44)*. London: Karia Press.

Fryer, Peter (1984) *Staying Power: The History of Black People in Britain*. London: Pluto.

Gates, Henry Louis, Jr (1988) 'The Trope of the Talking Book', in *The Signifying Monkey: A Theory of Afro-American Literary Criticism*. New York: Oxford University Press, pp. 127–69.

Geiss, Imanuel (1974) *The Pan-African Movement*. London: Methuen. [First published 1968]

George, Rosemary Marangoly (1996) *The Politics of Home: Postcolonial Relocations and Twentieth-Century Fiction*. Cambridge: Cambridge University Press.

Gibbs, C. R. (1992) *Black Explorers*. Silver Spring, MD: Three Dimensional Publishing.

Gikandi, Simon (1997) *Maps of Englishness: Writing Identity in the Culture of Colonialism*. New York: Columbia University Press.

Gilroy, Beryl (1989) *Boy-Sandwich*. Oxford: Heinemann.

Gilroy, Paul (1993) *The Black Atlantic: Modernity and Double Consciousness*. London: Verso.

Gilroy, Paul (1996) 'Route Work: The Black Atlantic and the Politics of Exile', in Iain Chambers and Lidia Curti (eds), *The Post-Colonial Question: Common Skies, Divided Horizons*. London: Routledge, pp. 17–29.

Golden, Marita (1983) *Migrations of the Heart*. New York: Ballantine.

Gordon, Deborah (1990) 'The Politics of Ethnographic Authority: Race and Writing in the Ethnography of Margaret Mead and Zora Neale Hurston', in Marc Manganaro (ed.), *Modernist Anthropology: From Fieldwork to Text*. Princeton: Princeton University Press, pp. 146–62.

Gronniosaw, Ukawsaw (1770) *A Narrative of the Most Remarkable Particulars of the Life of James Albert Ukawsaw Gronniosaw, An African Prince*. Bath.

Gruesser, John C. (1990) 'Afro-American Travel Literature and Africanist Discourse'. *Black American Literature Forum*, 24 (1) (Spring), 5–20.

Gruesser, John C. (1997) 'Travel Writing', in W. L. Andrews *et al.* (eds), *The Oxford Companion to*

African–American Literature. Oxford: Oxford University Press, pp. 735–6.

Guilao, Game (1994) *France, terre d'accueil, terre de rejet: l'impossible intégration*. Paris: L'Harmattan.

Guillén, Nicolás (1975) *Prosa de Prisa, 1929–72*. 3 vols. Havana: Editorial Arte y Literatura.

Handlin, Oscar and Lillian Handlin (eds) (1997) *From the Outer World*. Cambridge, MA: Harvard University Press.

Harris, Eddy (1994) *Native Stranger*. Harmondsworth: Penguin.

Harris, Joseph E. (1994) *African-American Reactions to War in Ethiopia, 1936–1941*. Baton Rouge: Louisiana State University Press.

Harris, Sheldon H. (ed.) (1972) *Paul Cuffe: Black America and the African Return*. New York: Simon and Schuster.

Henson, Matthew (1989) *A Black Explorer at the North Pole*. Lincoln: University of Nebraska Press. [First published 1912]

Hinds, Donald (1966) *Journey to an Illusion: The West Indian in Britain*. London: Heinemann.

Hirst, Paul and Graeme Thompson (1996) 'Globalization, Governance and the Nation State', in *Globalization in Question*. Cambridge: Polity, pp. 170–94.

hooks, bell (1991) *Yearning: Race, Gender, and Cultural Politics*. London: Turnaround.

Hughes, Langston (1934) *A Negro Looks at Soviet Central Asia*. New edition in preparation by David Chioni Moore.

Hughes, Langston (1986) *The Big Sea*. London: Pluto Press. [First published 1940]

Hughes, Langston (1992) 'Negroes in Spain', in Danny Duncan Collum (ed.), *'This Ain't Ethiopia, But It'll Do': African Americans in the Spanish Civil War*. New York: G. K. Hall, pp. 103–5.

Hughes, Langston (1993) *I Wonder as I Wander: An Autobiographical Journey*. Introduction by Arnold Rampersad. New York: Hill and Wang. [First published 1956]

Hunton, Addie W. and Kathryn Johnson (1997) *Two Colored Women with the American Expeditionary Forces*. New York: G. K. Hall. [First published 1920]

Hurston, Zora Neale (1990) *Tell My Horse: Voodoo and Life in Haiti and Jamaica*. New York: Harper and Row. [First published 1938]

Jacobs, Harriet (1988) *Incidents in the Life of a Slave Girl*. New York: Oxford University Press. [First published 1861]

James, C. L. R. (1932) 'London: First Impressions'. *Port of Spain Gazette*, 21 and 22 June, 27 July, 4, 11 and 28 August.

James, C. L. R. (1996) *Special Delivery: The Letters of C. L. R. James to Constance Webb, 1939–48*, edited and with an introduction by Anna Grimshaw. Oxford: Blackwell.

Jefferson, Paul (ed.) (1991) *The Travels of William Wells Brown*. Edinburgh: Edinburgh University Press.

Johnson, Amryl (1988) *Sequins for a Ragged Hem*. London: Virago.

Johnson, Charles (1991) *Middle Passage*. London: Picador.

Johnson, James Weldon (1990) *Along This Way*. Harmondsworth: Penguin. [First published 1933]

Johnson, Thomas Lewis (1882) *Twenty-Eight Years a Slave*. London: Yates Alexander and Shepheard.

Jordan, June (1986a) 'Nicaragua: Why I Had to Go There', in *On Call: Political Essays*. London: Pluto Press, pp. 65–75. [First published 1984]

Jordan, June (1986b) 'Report from the Bahamas', in *On Call: Political Essays*. London: Pluto Press, pp. 39–49. [First published 1982]

Julian, Col. Hubert (1965) *Black Eagle*. London: Adventurer's Club.

Kane, Cheikh Hamidou (1972) *Ambiguous Adventure*. Translated by Katherine Woods. Oxford: Heinemann. [First published 1961]

Kaplan, Caren (1996) *Questions of Travel: Postmodern Discourses of Displacement*. Durham, NC: Duke University Press, 1996.

Kelley, Robin G. (1992) 'This Ain't Ethiopia, But It'll Do', in Danny Duncan Collum (ed.), *'This Ain't Ethiopia, But It'll Do': African Americans in the Spanish Civil War*. New York: G. K. Hall, pp. 5–57.

Killingray, David (1986) 'All the King's Men? Blacks in the British Army in the First World War, 1914–1918', in Rainer Lotz and Ian Pegg (eds), *Under the Imperial Carpet: Essays in Black History, 1780–1950*, Crawley: Rabbit Press, pp. 164–81.

Killingray, David and Willie Henderson (1998) 'Bata Kindai Amgoza Ibn LoBagola and the Making of *An African Savage's Own Story*', in Bernth Lindfors (ed.), *Blacks on Stage*. Bloomington: Indiana University Press, forthcoming.

Kincaid, Jamaica (1988) *A Small Place*. Harmondsworth: Penguin.

Kincaid, Jamaica (1994) *Lucy*. London: Picador.

King, Russell, John Connell and Paul White (eds) (1995) *Writing across Worlds: Literature and Migration*. London: Routledge.

Kpomassie, Tété-Michel (1983) *An African in Greenland*. Translated by James Kirkup. London: Secker and Warburg. [First published 1981]

Kristeva, Julia (1991) *Strangers to Ourselves*. Translated by Léon Roudiez. New York: Columbia University Press. [First published 1988]

Lacy, Leslie (1970) *The Rise and Fall of a Proper Negro: An Autobiography*. New York: Macmillan.

Lambeth Council (1988) *Forty Winters On: Memoires of Britain's Post-War Caribbean Immigrants*. London: Lambeth Council.

Lambo, Roger (1994) 'Achtung! The Black Prince: West Africans in the Royal Air Force, 1939–46', in David Killingray (ed.), *Africans in Britain*. London: Frank Cass, pp. 145–63.

Lamming, George (1980) *The Emigrants*. London: Allison and Busby. [First published 1954]

Lamming, George (1984) 'The African Presence', in *The Pleasures of Exile*. London: Allison and Busby, pp. 160–210. [First published 1960]

Langley, J. A. (1973) *Pan-Africanism and Nationalism in West Africa 1900–1945*. Oxford: Clarendon Press.

Laye, Camara (1959) *The African Child*. Translated by James Kirkup. London: Collins. [First published 1954]

Lazard, Dorothy (1997) 'Finding Myself in the World', in Elaine Lee (ed.), *Go Girl!* Portland, OR: Eighth Mountain Press, pp. 221–5.

Lee, Andrea (1984) *Russian Journal*. New York: Vintage. [First published 1979]

Lee, Elaine (ed.) (1997) *Go Girl! The Black Woman's Book of Travel and Adventure*. Portland, OR: Eighth Mountain Press.

Lester, Julius (ed.) (1971) *The Seventh Son: The Thought and Writings of W. E. B. Du Bois*. 2 vols. New York: Random House.

Lévi-Strauss, Claude (1976) *Tristes Tropiques*. Translated by John and Doreen Weightman. Harmondsworth: Penguin. [First published 1955]

Lipsitz, George (1997) '"Frantic to Join . . . the Japanese Army": The Asia Pacific War in the Lives of African American Soldiers and Civilians', in Lisa Lowe and David Lloyd (eds), *The Politics of Culture in the Shadow of Capital*. Durham, NC: Duke University Press, pp. 324–53.

LoBagola, Bata Kindai Amgoza Ibn (1930) *LoBagola: An African Savage's Own Story*. New York: Knopf.

Longmore, Zenga (1989) *Tap-Taps to Trinidad: A Caribbean Journey*. London: Hodder and Stoughton.

Lorde, Audre (1996) 'Notes from a Trip to Russia', in *The Audre Lorde Compendium: Essays, Speeches, Journals*. London: Pandora, pp. 75–94. [First published 1976]

Lunn, Joe Harris (1987) 'Kande Kamara Speaks: An Oral History of the West African Experience in France, 1914–18', in Melvin A. Page (ed.), *Africa and the First World War*. London: Macmillan, pp. 28–53.

Luthuli, Albert (1962) *Let My People Go: An Autobiography*. London: Collins.

McElroy, Colleen J. (1997) *A Long Way from St Louie: Travel Memoirs*. Minneapolis, MN: Coffee House Press.

McKay, Claude (1995) *A Long Way from Home*. London: Pluto Press. [First published 1937]

Makeba, Miriam (1988) *Makeba: My Story*. London: Bloomsbury.

Marke, Ernest (1986) *In Troubled Waters: Memoirs of My Seventy Years in England*. London: Karia Press.

Marshall, Paule (1982) *Brown Girl, Brownstones*. London: Virago. [First published 1959]

Marshall, Paule (1985a) 'Barbados', in *Merle and Other Stories*. London: Virago, pp. 49–67. [First published 1961]

Marshall, Paule (1985b) 'To Da-duh, in Memoriam', in *Merle and Other Stories*. London: Virago, pp. 93–106. [First published 1967]

Merriman-Labor, A. B. C. (1909) *Britons Through Negro Spectacles; or, A Negro on Britons. With a Description of London*. London.

Mikell, Gwendolyn (1982) 'When Horses Talk: Reflections on Zora Neale Hurston's Haitian Anthropology'. *Phylon*, 43 (3) (September), 218–30.

Mills, Sara (1991) *Discourses of Difference: An Analysis of Women's Travel Writing and Colonialism*. London: Routledge.

Modupe, Prince (1958) *I Was a Savage*. Foreword by Elspeth Huxley. London: Museum Press. [First published 1957]

Monolulu, Ras Prince (1950) *I Gotta Horse*. As told to Sidney H. White. London: Hurst and Blackett.

Moore, David Chioni (1996) 'Local Color, Global "Color": Langston Hughes, the Black Atlantic, and Soviet Central Asia, 1932'. *Research in African Literatures*, 27 (4) (Winter), 49–70.

Moore, Samuel (1854) *Biography of Mahommah G. Baquaqua, A Native of Zoogoo, in the Interior of Africa . . . Written and Revised from His Own Words*. Detroit: Geo E. Pomeroy.

Morris, Mary (ed.) (1994) *The Virago Book of Women Travellers*. London: Virago.

Motley, Mary P. (1975) *The Invisible Soldier: The Experience of the Black Soldier, World War II*. Detroit: Wayne State University Press.

Mudimbe-Boyi, Elizabeth (1992) 'Travel, Representation, and Difference; or, How Can One Be a Parisian?' Translated by Mildred Mortimer. *Research in African Literatures*, 23 (3) (Autumn), 25–39.

Mukasa, Ham (1904) *Uganda's Katakiro in England: being the official account of his visit to the Coronation of His Majesty of King Edward VII . . .* London: Hutchinson. [New edition by Simon Gikandi, forthcoming from Manchester University Press, 1998]

Mulzac, Captain Hugh (1963) *A Star to Steer By*. As told to Louis Burnham and Noval Welch. New York: International Publishers.

Murphy, George (1974) *A Journey to the Soviet Union*. Moscow: Novosti Press.

N'Djehoya, Blaise and Massaër Diallo (1984) *Un Regard noir*. Paris: Autrement.

Nakasa, Nat (1995) *The World of Nat Nakasa: Selected Writings of the Late Nat Nakasa*, edited by Essop Patel, 2nd edn. Johannesburg: Ravan Press.

Nayo, Lydia A. (1997) 'A Sharecropper's Daughter Goes to Paris', in Elaine Lee (ed.), *Go Girl!* Portland, OR: Eighth Mountain Press, pp. 231–4.

Nelson, Cary and Jefferson Hendricks (eds) (1996) *Madrid 1937: Letters of the Abraham Lincoln Brigade from the Spanish Civil War*. London: Routledge.

Nkosi, Lewis (1983) *Home and Exile and Other Selections*. New edn. London: Longman.

Nkrumah, Kwame (1957) *The Autobiography of Kwame Nkrumah*. Edinburgh: Thomas Nelson.

Nortje, Arthur (1973) *Dead Roots*. London: Heinemann.

Nunes, Maria Luisa (1982) *A Portuguese Colonial in America, Belmira Nunes Lopes: The Autobiography of a Cape Verdean American*. Pittsburgh: Latin American Review Press.

Nzenza-Shand, Sekai (1997) *Songs to an African Sunset: A Zimbabwean Story*. Hawthorn, Victoria: Lonely Planet.

Ocansey, John E. (1989) *An African Trading or, The trials of William Narh Ocansey of Addah, West Coast of Africa, River Volta*. Accra: Ghana Academy of Arts and Sciences. [First published 1881]

Oji, Apollos O. (1992) *Longing for Home*. New York: Vantage Press.

Oyono, Ferdinand (1989) *Road to Europe*. Translated by Richard Bjornson. Washington, DC: Three Continents Press. [First published 1960]

Pelé (1977) *My Life and the Beautiful Game: The Autobiography of Pelé*. With Robert L. Fish. London: New English Library.

Perham, Margery (1963) *Ten Africans*. London: Faber and Faber. [First published 1936]

Pettinger, Alasdair (1994) 'Ships at a Distance'. *New Formations*, 23 (Summer), 115–21.

Pettinger, Alasdair (1997) '"Talking Patriots": Americans, Haiti, and the "Negro Problem"'. *Studies in Travel Writing*, I, 141–69.

Pettinger, Alasdair (1998) Review of Paul Gilroy, *The Black Atlantic* (1993). *Research in African Literatures*, 29(4), 142–7.

Phillip, Marlene Nourbese (1988) *Harriet's Daughter*. Oxford: Heinemann.

Phillips, Caryl (1987) *The European Tribe*. London: Faber and Faber.

Phillips, Caryl (1989) *Higher Ground*. London: Viking.

Phillips, Caryl (1992) *Cambridge*. London: Picador.

Phillips, Caryl (1994) *Crossing the River*. London: Picador.

Phillips, Caryl (1995a) *The Final Passage*. London: Picador. [First published 1984]

Phillips, Caryl (1995b) *A State of Independence*. London: Picador. [First published 1986]

Phillips, Caryl (ed.) (1997) *Extravagant Strangers: A Literature of Belonging*. London: Faber and Faber.

Pickens, William (1992) 'What I Saw in Spain', in Danny Duncan Collum (ed.), *'This Ain't Ethiopia, But It'll Do': African Americans in the Spanish Civil War*. New York: G. K. Hall, pp. III–18.

Plaatje, Sol T. (1996) *Sol Plaatje: Selected Writing*, edited by Brian Willan. Johannesburg: Witwatersrand University Press.

Potkay, Adam and Sandra Burr (eds) (1995) *Black Atlantic Writers of the Eighteenth Century: Living the New Exodus in England and the Americas*. Basingstoke: Macmillan.

Powell, Colin L. (1995) *A Soldier's Way: My American Journey*. With Joseph E. Persico. London: Hutchinson.

Pratt, Mary Louise (1992) *Imperial Eyes: Travel Writing and Transculturation*. London: Routledge.

Prince, Mary (1987) *The History of Mary Prince, A West Indian Slave*. London: Pandora. [First published 1831]

Prince, Nancy (1990) *A Black Woman's Odyssey through Russia and Jamaica: The Narrative of the Life and Travels of Mrs Nancy Prince*.

Introduction by Ronald G. Walters. Princeton: Markus Wiener. [First published 1850]

Richburg, Keith (1995) 'Continental Divide'. *Washington Post Magazine*, 26 March, pp. 17–33.

Richburg, Keith (1997) *Out of America: A Black Man Confronts Africa*. New York: New Republic/Basic Books.

Riesz, János (1996) 'The Tirailleur Sénégalais Who Did Not Want to Be a "Grand Enfant": Bakary Diallo's *Force Bonté* (1926) Reconsidered'. *Research in African Literatures*, 27 (4) (Winter), 157–79.

Riley, Joan (1985) *The Unbelonging*. London: Women's Press.

Riley, Joan (1992) *A Kindness to the Children*. London: Women's Press.

Robeson, Eslanda Goode (1952) 'Journey to Spain', in Alvah Bessie (ed.), *The Heart of Spain: Anthology of Fiction, Non-Fiction and Poetry*. New York: Veterans of the Abraham Lincoln Brigade, pp. 245–8.

Robeson, Eslanda Goode (1945) *African Journey*. New York: John Day.

Robeson, Paul (1998) *Here I Stand*. With a preface by Lloyd L. Brown and a new introduction by Sterling Stuckey. Boston: Beacon Press/London: Cassell. [First published 1958]

Robinson, Cedric (1983) *Black Marxism: The Making of the Black Radical Tradition*. London: Zed.

Robinson, Cedric J. (1992) 'Black Intellectuals at the British Core', in Jagdish S. Gundara and Ian Duffield (eds), *Essays on the History of Blacks in Britain: From Roman Times to the Present Day*. Aldershot: Avebury, pp. 173–201.

Robinson, Jane (1991) *Wayward Women: A Guide to Women Travellers*. Oxford: Oxford University Press.

Robinson, Jane (ed.) (1995) *Unsuitable for Ladies: An Anthology of Women Travellers*. Oxford: Oxford University Press.

Salkey, Andrew (1971) *Havana Journal*. Harmondsworth: Penguin.

Salkey, Andrew (1972) *Georgetown Journal: A Caribbean Writer's Journey from London via Port of Spain to Georgetown, Guyana, 1970*. London: New Beacon Books.

Salkey, Andrew (1992) *Anancy, Traveller*. London: Bogle L'Ouverture.

Sandiford, Keith A. (1988) *Measuring the Moment: Strategies of Protest in Eighteenth-Century Afro-English Writing*. Selingsgrove: Susquehanna University Press.

Sardinha, Carl Dennis (1976) *The Poetry of Nicolás Guillén: An Introduction*. London: New Beacon Books.

Schuyler, George S. (1937) 'Monrovia Mooches On', *Globe*, July, pp. 10–16.

Schuyler, George S. (1948) 'Racial Democracy in Latin America'. *Pittsburgh Courier*, 17 July to 4 September.

Schuyler, George S. (1966) *Black and Conservative: The Autobiography of George S. Schuyler*. New Rochelle, NY: Arlington House.

Schuyler, Philippa Duke (1960) *Adventures in Black and White*. New York: Robert Speller.

Seacole, Mary (1984) *Wonderful Adventures of Mrs. Seacole in Many Lands*, edited by Ziggi Alexander and Audrey Dewjee. Bristol: Falling Wall Press. [First published 1857]

Segal, Ronald (1995) *The Black Diaspora*. London: Faber and Faber.

Selvon, Sam (1985) *Lonely Londoners*. London: Longman. [First published 1956]

Sembène, Ousmane (1957) *O Pays, mon beau peuple!* Paris: Presses Pocket.

Sembène, Ousmane (1974) 'Letter from France', in *Tribal Scars and Other Stories*. Translated by Len Ortzen. London: Heinemann. [First published 1962]

Sembène, Ousmane (1987) *Black Docker*. Translated by Ros Schwarz. London: Heinemann. [First published 1956]

Sharpe, Jenny (1993) *Allegories of Empire: The Figure of the Woman in the Colonial Text*. Minneapolis: University of Minnesota Press.

Shepperson, George (1976) 'Introduction', in Martin L. Kilson and Robert Rotberg (eds), *The African Diaspora: Interpretive Essays*. Cambridge, MA: Harvard University Press, pp. 1–10.

Sherwood, Marika (1985) *Many Struggles: West-Indian Workers and Service Personnel in Britain 1939–45*. London: Karia Press.

Smith, Graham (1987) *When Jim Crow Met John Bull: Black American Soldiers in World War II Britain*. London: I. B. Tauris.

Smith, William Gardner (1970) *Return to Black America*. Englewood Cliffs, NJ: Prentice-Hall.

Talalay, Kathryn (1996) *Composition in Black and White: The Life of Philippa Schuyler*. Oxford: Oxford University Press.

Terrell, Mary Church (1976) 'Mary Church Terrell's Letters from Europe to Her Father', edited by M. Sammy Miller. *Negro History Bulletin*, 38 (September), 615–18. [Originally written in 1888–90]

Terrell, Mary Church (1996) *A Colored Woman in a White World*. New York: G. K. Hall. [First published 1940]

Thomas, Marion A. (1984) 'Graham Greene Travels in Africa and Dadié Travels in Europe'. *African Literature Today*, 14, 1–11.

Todorov, Tzvetan (1993) *On Human Diversity: Nationalism, Racism and Exoticism in French Thought*. Translated by Catherine Porter. Cambridge, MA: Harvard University Press.

Walker, Alice and Pratibha Parmar (1993) *Warrior Marks: Female Genital Mutilation and the Sexual Blinding of Women*. London: Jonathan Cape.

Walmsley, Anne (1992) *The Caribbean Artists Movement, 1966–1972*. London: New Beacon Books.

Walsh, Alison (ed.) (1991) *Nothing Ventured: Disabled People Travel the World*. Bromley: Harrap Columbus.

Ward, Samuel Ringgold (1855) *An Autobiography of a Fugitive Negro: His Anti-Slavery Labours in the United States, Canada and England*. London: John Snow.

Ware, Vron (1992) *Beyond the Pale: White Women, Racism and History*. London: Verso.

Warner-Vieyra, Miriam (1987) *Juletane*. Translated by Betty Wilson. Oxford: Heinemann. [First published 1982]

Washington, Booker T. (1912) *The Man Farthest Down: A Record of Observation and Study in Europe*. Garden City, NY: Doubleday, Page.

Weiss, Lynn (1994) '*Para Usted*: Richard Wright's *Pagan Spain*', in Werner Sollors and Maria Diedrich (eds), *The Black Columbiad: Defining Moments in African American Literature and Culture*. Cambridge, MA: Harvard University Press, pp. 212–25.

Wells, Ida B. (1970) *Crusade for Justice: The Autobiography of Ida B. Wells*, edited by Alfreda M. Duster. Chicago: University of Chicago Press.

West, Dorothy (1995) 'An Adventure in Moscow', in *The Richer, the Poorer: Stories, Sketches and Reminiscences*. New York: Doubleday, pp. 220–4. [First published 1985]

Western, John (1992) *A Passage to England: Barbadian Londoners Speak of Home*. London: UCL Press.

White, Walter (1971) *A Rising Wind*. Westport, CT: Negro Universities Press. [First published 1945]

Wickham, John (1957) 'Dutch Excursion'. *Bim*, 7 (25) (July–December), 17–24.

Wickham, John (1962) 'Notes from New York'. *Bim*, 9 (34) (January–June), 135–40.

Wickham, John (1964) 'Letter from Geneva'. *Bim*, 10 (39) (July–December), 192–200.

Wilson, Salim C. [Hatashil Masha Kathish] (1960) *I Was a Slave*. London: Stanley Paul. [First published 1939]

Wolfe, George C. (1987) *The Colored Museum*. London: Methuen.

Woodhull, Winifred (1993) *Transfigurations of the Maghreb: Feminism, Decolonization, and Literatures*. Minneapolis: University of Minnesota Press.

Woolf, Virginia (1977) *Three Guineas*. Harmondsworth: Penguin. [First published 1937]

Woolnough, Kristina (1991) 'Is Travel Writing Just One Long Holiday?' *Scotland on Sunday*, 18 August.

Wright, Richard (1995a) *Black Power*. New York: Harper Perennial. [First published 1954]

Wright, Richard (1995b) *Pagan Spain*. New York: Harper Perennial. [First published 1957]

Yates, James (1989) *Mississippi to Madrid: A Memoir of a Black American in the Abraham Lincoln Brigade*. Seattle: Open Hand Publications.

Index

Page numbers of major references are printed in **bold**.